ARRESTED VOICES

RESURRECTING THE DISAPPEARED WRITERS
OF THE SOVIET REGIME

Vitaly Shentalinsky

Translated by JOHN CROWFOOT
Introduction by ROBERT CONQUEST

MARTIN KESSLER BOOKS
THE FREE PRESS
New York   London   Toronto   Sydney   Singapore

THE FREE PRESS
A Division of Simon & Schuster Inc.
1230 Avenue of the Americas
New York, NY 10020

Manufactured in the United States of America

10 9 8 7 6 5 4 3 2 1

Library of Congress Cataloging-in-Publication Data

Shentalinskiĭ, Vitaliĭ
     [Parole ressuscitée. English]
     Arrested voices: resurrecting the disappeared writers of the
Soviet regime / Vitaly Shentalinsky; translated by John Crowfoot;
introduction by Robert Conquest.
          p.   cm.
     Published in Great Britain under title: The KGB's literary
archive.
     Includes index.
     ISBN 0–684–82776–X
     1. Authors, Russian—20th century—Biography. 2. Dissenters—
Soviet Union—Biography. 3. Political persecution—Soviet Union.
4. Soviet Union—History. 5. Politics and literature—Soviet Union.
I. Title.
PG2991.4.S4813   1996
891.709'0042—dc20
     [B]   96–3154
                                                   CIP

ISBN 0–684–82776–X

First published in France as *La Parole Ressuscitée.*
Published in Great Britain as *The KGB's Literary Archive.*

ACKNOWLEDGEMENTS
Lines from "For the resounding valor of millennia to come…" by Osip Mandelstam,
translated by Bernard Meares, in Yevtushenko, Hayward and Todd (eds.), *Twentieth-
Century Russian Poetry*, published by Doubleday, New York, and Fourth Estate, London.
Copyright © Bantam, Doubleday, Dell, 1993.
Reprinted by permission.

CONTENTS

INTRODUCTION
BY ROBERT CONQUEST

This rich and revealing book deploys the circumstances and results of the author's long and difficult campaign to find and publish secret police files of the Stalin period which dealt with literature and with writers.

Generally speaking, the way the Communist regime not merely terrorized, but literally decimated the population of the former USSR is well known. At the same time, we all have a general understanding of the stultifying mental and psychological effects of the Stalinist system. Even so, for most this book will convey yet a further shock and revelation, showing just how the creative minds of Russia were crushed, or corrupted, how meanly as well as how murderously the regime treated the true bearers of the nation's culture.

A century ago Anton Chekhov looking at the already dogmatic revolutionary editors of his time, predicted a future when under the banner of learning Russia, ruled by "toads and crocodiles", would experience in the literary field "narrow-mindedness, enormous pretensions, excessive self-importance, a total absence of any literary conscientiousness ... [and] an atmosphere so stifling that every healthy person will be nauseated".

Shentalinsky's own early experiences well illustrate the "stifling" miasma of semi-literate conformism which continued even when mass terror had long died down. So do his often thwarted though finally successful efforts to obtain his sensitive materials. So, even more, does his account of the malign and petty intrigues for place, power and prestige waged by the survivors of the old and talentless Communist lumpen-intelligentsia.

The author makes no claim to be comprehensive. As he points out, some 1500 writers perished; among them men and women of talent and reputation comparable to those covered here. What he has done is, rather, to present a collection of studies of the fates of a range of striking figures. The historian of the arts and humanities will find here what actually happened to amongst others, Isaak Babel, Boris Pilnyak, Pavel Florensky, Osip Mandelstam, from the highest ranks of culture and literature.

Among the strangest sounding characteristics of the story, from the Western point of view, is that even when they were rehabilitated on the criminal charges for which they had died, false death dates were given. These emerged because when rehabilitation started, it was impossible to reconcile the true execution dates with the fact that relatives had been informed that the sentence was to "10 years without the right of correspondence": so random dates of death at supposed "places of imprisonment" were given on the rehabilitation certificates. That is, even when truths began to come out, they were for years only part-truths. Even in the current edition of the *Encyclopedia Britannica,* Pavel Florensky's death is given as taking place "in exile in Siberia" on 15 December 1943, when in fact he was shot in Solovki in 1937; while Babel is listed dying "in a prison camp in Siberia" on 17 March 1941, when in fact he was shot in Moscow on 27 January 1940. As to their works, in many cases these remained wholly or partly unrehabilitated until the past decade.

Again, anyone not familiar with the Communist period will be horrified by, for example, the way it is here taken for granted that wives and children should be shot or imprisoned for their husband's alleged crimes. And by the combination of a niggling attention to the forms of interrogative records with the frightful tortures behind them, usually unrecorded, but preserved by chance in (for example) the letter of the great producer Vsevolod Meyerhold to Molotov.

Few of Russia's creative minds welcomed the Bolshevik Revolution. An important number of them went abroad. More, hoping for the best, stayed on. From the point of view of physical survival, and of the chance to pursue their vocations, the former made the wiser choice. To give a single illustration: in *The Penguin Book of Russian Verse* which came out in 1962, a check on dates showed that the average age of death since the Revolution of those who had meanwhile lived in exile was 72; of those who remained in or returned to the USSR it was 45.

Shentalinsky covers the period's effects not only on the victims and on cultural persecutors like the dreadful Pavlenko, but also, for example, on the ambiguous figure of Maxim Gorky, who was bamboozled and bribed by Stalin into giving a spurious humanist glow to his rule. In spite of his pre-World War I connections with the Bolsheviks, Gorky had publicly objected to some of the acts of Lenin's regime, and in the late 1920s he had retired to Italy. (That there was no problem with this in Fascist Italy is a strange thought today, when political barriers have long been far more extreme.)

Shentalinsky shows how this supposedly sceptical, supposedly humane, spirit was actually taken to the White Sea Canal penal camps, given the opportunity to speak to prisoners who praised their redemption through labour, and had tears brought to his eyes by the new, humane, socialist penal policies of the Soviet government. And the book he sponsored jointly with Soviet writers and labour camp officials (themselves shot later) was widely published in the West too, as yet one more proof of the superiority of Soviet approaches to crime, as to all other social problems.

The Soviet conception of literary creativity, based on some vague, nonsensical remarks of Gorky's about Socialist Realism, did not provide a successful formula.

It was interpreted as a method which showed not mere actuality, but the historically "typical" phenomena: thus a slum dwelling in a capitalist society even if rare, was typical, while a block of modern flats in a socialist society, even if rare, was in its turn typical. This proposition was actually given the status of dogma at the Nineteenth Party Congress in 1952.

One central fact which this book makes clear is that the Stalinist – and post-Stalinist – attempt to produce talented but servile literature under this rubric was an abject failure. A caste of official writers, deploying Socialist Realism, were indeed widely published, took on positions and privileges, and are to be seen in this book infesting the cultural organisations. There was only one problem: with few exceptions they couldn't write.

Sooner or later they all faded into well-deserved obscurity when it came to any real acceptance: to the degree that even the bureaucracy – even Stalin himself – seem to have seen that something was wrong with the whole conception. Meanwhile, the great writers who perished did so, whatever their political or other views, because in practice they rejected the idea of a controlled literature, of a superiority of the Party over the unprogrammable individual sources of creativity.

Lytton Strachey writes of "the medieval futility, the narrow-minded cynicism" of the Ancien Régime in France; and these two points apply, though in more extreme form, to Russia in the decades before 1991. The structure of state and society was indeed, as scholars like Emmanuel Todd have pointed out, "feudal"; and the combination of philistinism and petty meanness prevailing in the conduct of its paragons equally comparable.

Yet many reassuring things are to be found in this book. It shows that while narrow apparatchiks still abound, not only the true critical or creative intelligentsia, but all other men of good will and good understanding, left or right, see that the vast falsifications and indefensible massacres of the Soviet regime cannot be concealed or palliated.

Some of the more interesting pages are on the author's campaign within the Lubyanka after his long struggle to get a governmental and institutional approval for a search for confiscated literary material, and for documentation on its writers' fates. Even the more literate and far-seeing "security" apparatchiks themselves understood that it would now be useless, and indeed disgraceful, to conceal the actions of their "Stalinist" predecessors. A crucial point is reached in the author's discussions with General Anatoly Krayushkin, head of the secret police ministry archives. Krayushkin has meanwhile analyzed, and refuted, secret police figures on the Terror produced in the 1960s (and accepted as "documentation" by Western pseudo-scholars); and he has been one of the editors of the lately published full text of the secret 1952 trial of the Jewish Anti-Fascist Committee, in which some of the accused denounced the tortures inflicted on them, and quoted vicious anti-Semitic abuse from their interrogators.

Some of the documents Shentalinsky obtained from the secret police files are reports of informers. Babel, who told Ilya Ehrenburg (as the latter tells us in his memoirs) "today a man only talks freely with his wife – at night, with the blankets pulled over his head", in fact spoke with dangerous freedom in what he took to be trustworthy circles. His and Florensky's comments on the regime in agents' reports found in these files are in fact extremely frank and perspicuous. It took many in the West half a century to reach the same conclusions.

We are perhaps inclined to regard the Soviet experience as a now obsolete and even forgettable historical phenomenon. It was indeed a monstrous anomaly, and can be seen in that light. But the full facts are still emerging. And they need to be remembered in all their moral, psychological, and physical horror if we are to learn the lesson they present. For those in Russia, this remains a memory to be faced before they can really go forward into a tolerable future. Nor can the present condition of that long-suffering country be understood until the stark realities of the past, with its still persisting distortions of thought and feeling, are fully abreacted.

It was contemptible as well as terrible. Shentalinsky's cool, ironic tone is that of the traditional Russian humanism which two generations of unprecedented terror and fraud were unable to eradicate. The book is a splendid and devastating counterattack in the interests of truth, justice and the independence of the human mind.

PREFACE

"What's your interest, then?" people asked, when I began to agitate for the stolen words of Soviet writers to be saved and returned to the nation: "Were you in the camps?"

No, I was never arrested. I was not a dissident. They never shut me up in prison or psychiatric hospital, sent me to the camps or expelled me from the country, though I had my own thoroughly negative experiences with the all-pervasive KGB. It would be an over-simplification, anyway, to think of people in the Soviet Union before perestroika as being divided between the ruling Party bureaucrats, a handful of heroic champions of democracy and the rest – a submissive, servile, and easily controlled herd. Things were more complicated than that.

The Communist ideology was not something external, and imposed by force, but lodged itself deep in our minds and thoughts. The Soviet way of life came to seem natural to us and indestructible. There were those who did not accept it. But they lived double lives, compromising with society and thereby trying to preserve their own rights and independence. A few openly rebelled and paid dearly for it. The main battlefield lay within, in the conscience and understanding of each individual.

I can remember very clearly the day that history burst into my life for the first time, although I felt rather than understood the importance of what had happened.

It was 6 March 1953. I was 13 and in the 7th class at school. We lived in a remote, tiny village in the Tatar republic where my father was chairman of the collective farm. Ours was the only radio in the whole village (it worked on batteries, of course, since there was no electricity there yet). One morning father called me and I found him standing, listening to the radio: pale, unusually serious and, most terrible of all, with tears in his eyes. Instead of the usual cheerful marches, I suddenly noticed, the radio was playing quiet, sad music.

"Run round to all the Communists, Vitya, and tell them Stalin has died."

I still did not understand anything myself but the tears started flowing, in response to my father's. I raced about the village, seized with the feeling that something irreversible had happened. The familiar settled world had been destroyed. I ran from house to house (there were only a few Communists in the village and I knew them all), scaring chickens and dogs, hammering on the door as hard as I could and yelling: "Stalin's died! Stalin's died!"

It was as though the world had ended. Distorted faces, exclamations of distress, and tears, tears . . .

Childhood ended three years later. I passed the school-leaving exams and said goodbye to my friends. But 1956 was also the year of the Twentieth Party Congress and Khrushchev's Secret Speech.* Stalin died a second time.

Still, politics hardly interested me then. My great dream was to become a sailor. So I went to Leningrad and began studying at the Arctic Naval College. After graduating I worked for a time as radio operator at the meteorological station on Wrangel Island. Alaska and the American coast were a hand's reach away and, at the same time, we were so cut off that they might have been on another planet. We regularly listened to the "Voice of America" but if American or Canadian airplane pilots or sailors called up our frequency, as happened more than once, we followed instructions and did not reply.

A few years later I moved to Magadan, on the northern shores of the Pacific Ocean. I had begun writing and soon my first book appeared. I was living in the capital of Kolyma but even the slightest allusion to the camps that formerly filled the area was forbidden. Brezhnev was beginning to crack down on dissent and one trial followed another: Sinyavsky and Daniel, Galanskov and Ginzburg, Bukovsky ... However, in thousands of typed copies and sometimes in microfiche, samizdat, uncensored literature, spread across the country. Eventually, the campaign against dissidence reached our distant region.

Like my friends I also read works in samizdat. By then I was working for local television, in charge of literary and dramatic programmes, and studying by correspondence course at the journalism faculty of Moscow University. Soon they started to put pressure on me – why these references to Pasternak, Tsvetaeva or Velemir Khlebnikov? Why not Gorky, Mayakovsky and Sholokhov? (There were also objections to my beard.) I was demoted. Fed up, I decided to fall back on my old profession. Some naval friends had already offered a place on a research vessel, sailing to the Fiji Islands, no less. The boat would not be putting into any foreign ports, but even so my last employers refused me the character reference necessary for such a trip. My childhood dream remained unfulfilled.

By the early 1970s I was living in Moscow. I found a job in the publications department of a research institute and continued to write. And there I remained for the next 10 years. I could read any amount of samizdat in Moscow. The most widely-read of all these underground publications was *The Chronicle of Current Events*.** I also sometimes saw copies of it and, like others, I retyped it and passed it on.

*

* Khrushchev's speech denouncing Stalin was read out at the Congress and then at closed meetings of Party members. The text only became widely accessible in the USSR after perestroika began.
** Samizdat periodical documenting human rights violations and underground publications in the USSR, which appeared regularly from 1968 to 1982.

2

Looking back I can see that my life, and that of all whose work bordered on the ideological, was constantly guided and restricted by red warning signs. These were no longer the draconian prohibitions of Stalin's time – "One step to the right or left is considered an attempt to escape," the escort guards in the Gulag used to menace. "We shall shoot without warning!" However, they were still very tangible.

When wolves are hunted, they are driven from behind and ahead of them red markers, which they dare not cross, guide them inexorably to their doom. Well, one day the red markers were gone, the hunters ran away, and suddenly we found ourselves free and alone in the wild forest of our own history.

"How can you go the Lubyanka?" friends ask me. "How can you have anything to do with the KGB?"

But I do not go there to see the KGB. There, at the Lubyanka, is hidden the truth about the life and death of our best writers. There their manuscripts still lie. I went to find out about those hundreds who were imprisoned and executed and the many other authors who, though not arrested, were persecuted and robbed of their works or the chance to speak all their lives.

CHAPTER 1

FOR PERMANENT RETENTION

Writers have always occupied a special position in Russia. For lack of democratic institutions, the Russian writer has never just been an artist, but a spokesman for the truth and a public conscience as well. Alexander Herzen called Russian literature the "second government", the true authority in society. This book is an authentic and documented account of what happened to writers and their works in the Soviet period.

How did I get involved? A pile of notebooks lie in front of me, scraps that I jotted down, hurriedly, with no thought for style or polish: there was no time then to keep a regular and detailed record, events were moving too fast.

It all started at the very end of 1987. I had just finished my latest collection of verse, *The Green Religion* and was wondering what to do next. For the first time in 70 years our future had become quite unpredictable. Perestroika was in full flood. The Kremlin orators triumphantly proclaimed glasnost and democracy. The people had been granted their freedom but, naturally, only under the continued tutelage of the Communist Party. Few proved ready to take up the challenge of democracy.

One day, early in January 1988, I dropped by the Writers Club.* There I bumped into my old acquaintance, Valentin Ustinov, who headed the Moscow branch of the Writers Union.** "Haven't seen you for ages!" he exclaimed, slapping me on the back: "Where have you been? It's not the time to sit quietly at home. The Moscow writers are going to hold a general meeting any day now. Without an agenda, without a presidium – for the first time a free and open discussion. We're going to talk about our future. Come along with your suggestions!"

I walked pensively along the frosty Moscow streets: did I really not have any ideas to suggest?

Of course, I had. But not for their meetings or for bureaucrats who had always been hostile to artistic freedom. I belonged to the Writers Union but my membership was a pure formality and restricted to the Writers Club itself, with its café, concerts and film shows. The policies of the Union were decided by a bureaucratic elite closely linked to the Kremlin† and the KGB;†† they

---

* From 1932 to 1991 two handsome nineteenth-century buildings in the centre of Moscow accommodated the administration of the USSR Writers Union and a Club for its members.
** The USSR Writers Union was established on Stalin's orders in 1932 to exercise the same monopoly in literature as the Communist Party wielded in ruling the country. See "The Literary – Political Context", p 287.
† Short-hand for the Communist Party's Politburo, the ultimate authority in the Soviet system.
†† The Committee for State Security, as the secret police was known after 1954.

were the watchdogs of the authorities and proponents of the Party ideology.

That January day, however, I hesitated.

What did we need now, more than anything else? I asked myself as I walked home through the gusts of fine snowy dust. Our history had been stolen from us, and what we knew was grotesquely distorted. Yet without the past, there could be no future. Now we must shake off this amnesia. The same was true of literature. In the war the Soviet regime had waged against society the writer belonged to one of the most repressed professions. How many authors had been shot or had perished in the camps and prisons?

Writers, however, keep a quite special reckoning with time. A writer's life does not end when he dies but continues for as long as he is read. In that sense, many of the Soviet literary figures alive today are already dead men, much more so than other deceased writers. If it was not possible to resurrect the writer-victims of communism, then they might be enabled to speak again. At this moment, perhaps, their manuscripts lay imprisoned in a special KGB repository or were concealed from the attentions of state security in a private family archive.

The case files of those arrested are stamped with the words: "Highly confidential" and "To be kept indefinitely". The time had come to cross out the first. And the best way to ensure that the second remained true, and that their memory and their works were preserved forever, was to gain public access to these documents and publish them. Only then would they never be forgotten.

This was not the work for one individual, though. It would need more to take on the Lubyanka.*

When I got home, I drafted the following appeal:

To the general meeting of the Moscow branch of the Writers Union
To the *Moskovsky literator* newspaper

Dear colleagues!
About two thousand writers were arrested in the years after 1917 and roughly one and a half thousand of them did not survive, meeting their deaths in the camps and prisons. These figures are not complete, of course. For the time being, it is impossible to verify them. As Akhamatova said: "I would like to recall them all, name by name, but the list has been taken, there's nowhere to find out." The circumstances and dates of their deaths have either been concealed or falsified; there are large gaps in their official biographies; and the information cited in encyclopedias and textbooks is incorrect.

*The Soviet secret police changed its title eight times (Cheka (1917–23), GPU (1922–3), OGPU (1923–34), NKVD (1934–43), NKGB (1943–6), MGB (1946–53), MVD (1953–4) and KGB from 1954) but for all except the first months of its existence its headquarters were located on Lubyanka Square in Moscow.

Most important of all: when writers were arrested their manuscripts and archives were usually confiscated and ended up in secret repositories. There is hope that some of these papers have survived. Let us try to rescue them! Let us unlock the black box. Only now with democracy and glasnost has this opportunity appeared – if we may believe in a real spring and not just another "thaw".* Let us find out if manuscripts burn!** If we cannot resurrect the dead, we can and must make up for this plundering of the nation's cultural heritage.

I suggest that a special commission be set up by the Writers Union to perform this sacred duty. The commission's members must be elected democratically, with a free discussion of candidates and an open vote.

5 January 1988

Having delivered this text to the newspaper, I called in at the cafe in the Writers Club to try out the idea on my fellow-writers.

A. Listen, old man: this is madness. They'll never let anyone into their archives. All their network of agents are listed there . . . They'd rather blow themselves up together with the files than let someone else read them. All this perestroika is just a bluff, it's a trap.

B. Excellent idea! I'm with you. I can just imagine what riches are to be found there. We must draw the maximum public attention, involve the press . . .

C. Listen carefully. Don't tell anyone. You must go about this very cautiously. Let me give you the telephone number of a high-ranking official in the Central Committee.† Ring him and get his advice. Only don't give me away: don't tell him where you got his number.

D. Don't you have anything better to do? What do you think the Writers Union is? It's a branch of the KGB. Every second member here is an informer . . . Go on writing your verse! Anyway, they burnt all the manuscripts long ago. There's nothing left.

A short while later the newspaper informed me that they would not publish my appeal. It had been vetoed by the Party Committee at the Writers Union, they explained. It was premature, not a "sound move".

I went to talk to them. I found out where the Party Committee had its office: just opposite the restaurant, as it turned out. The secretary of the Party Committee, Zhukov, the author of several novels about collective-farm life, was there.

"My appeal is with you, is it?"

*Common metaphor for the incomplete post-Stalin liberalization under Khrushchev in the late 1950s.

**Reference to *The Master and Margarita*. See chapter 3.

†The officials of the Communist Party's Central Committee monitored and supervised the activities of all other organizations in the Soviet Union.

Listless and irritable, Zhukov gazed at me curiously.

"Ye-es. Take a seat," he replied in a tired voice.

He took out the text, read it through, and sighed.

"Well, now ... The idea is good but they won't understand. They'll treat it as a challenge. Of course, we shall discuss it, but at a plenary session of the publications board, not at a general meeting."

I was amazed. "Why there? This is not just a publishing matter. It's wider than that. It concerns the rehabilitation of many hundreds of writers, the rescuing of their manuscripts and the unlocking of secret archives. It's a question of historical truth and justice ..."

"Do you not trust the plenary session?"

"No, I don't. This commission must be set up by all of us, openly, working together, and not by a small group of administrators. What kind of democracy and glasnost is that?"

"Calm down," advised Zhukov. "I'm not against the idea, I support it. It's just that we must go about things in a different way. And if you do speak at the general meeting, what then? So much hot air. I know what I'm talking about ... If you're still set against the plenary session, we must give it some thought," he concluded.

"How long will you need?"

He shrugged his shoulders.

After this Zhukov began avoiding me. He would point at the ceiling, higher authority must decide! Finally, he gave me a telephone number to ring. What's it got to do with us? they asked, surprised. We are the commission set up by the Censorship Board (Glavlit) to declassify already published literature.* We don't deal with manuscripts ...

"I really can't spend hour after hour discussing this!" Zhukov was the one to lose his patience this time.

"Please tell me where the problem is: who is against it?" I asked.

"No one, everyone is for."

"If the Party Committee won't get involved then I shall act on my own ..."

"Most alarming! What do you think you can achieve without a decision from the authorities?!" Zhukov almost yelled at me.

Then after a pause: "Would you like me to ring up the person at the Central Committee who supervises the Writers Union right now?"

"I would."

"Shentalinsky has come to see me yet again, and this time he's on the warpath ... What should we tell him?"

He turned the receiver towards me: "Vitaly Alexandrovich," said a dispas-

*Until 1 August 1990 all texts intended for publication in the USSR had to be submitted for preliminary censorship by Glavlit. Many works (and their authors) were also subsequently banned and withdrawn from libraries and bookshops.

sionate voice, "your appeal has been passed to one of the secretaries of the Central Committee, a member of the Politburo. At the moment he is abroad. We shall ring you up ourselves."

At home I flipped through the newspapers. As I thought, he must be referring to Alexander Yakovlev, the "architect of perestroika".

A week later they rang me up.

"Your suggestion has been considered. It's a good idea. Please give us a list of repressed writers. A short one, to begin with."

I would only learn of the next steps Alexander Yakovlev took much later, from a confidential dossier about our commission opened in the Procurator General's Office:*

> To Comrade V.I. Andreev
> Head of department for monitoring
> legality in state security bodies
>
> Please examine, jointly with the USSR KGB, the request of A.N. Yakovlev concerning the return of the manuscripts of individuals repressed during the years of the Cult of Personality** and inform me of the results,
>
> A. Sukharev
> USSR Procurator General   25 July 1988

I was invited to come in for a talk with Yury Verchenko, the organization secretary of the Writers Union. For the first time I entered the house on Vorovsky Street described in Tolstoy's *War and Peace* as the Moscow home of the Rostov family. It now accommodated the offices of the "Ministry of Literature".

It was no secret that Verchenko controlled all that went on in the USSR Writers Union. There was also talk that he was a KGB colonel as well, but only the Lubyanka could confirm that. At any rate, writers always tried to see him rather than Vladimir Karpov, the Union's first secretary. It was harder to make an appointment with Karpov and often he was not there, either writing novels about the war or attending government meetings.

Large and pale, Verchenko looked unwell. A chain-smoker, he occasionally chewed a pill instead of lighting the next cigarette.

"It's a good idea. But why did you only appeal to the Moscow branch of the Writers Union? The whole country, every republic, suffered in the repressions, my dear fellow. It must be an All-Union commission!"

---

*In the Soviet (and post-Soviet) legal system the procuracy not only acts as public prosecutor but investigates and monitors the application of the laws by a wide variety of bodies.

**Euphemism referring to Stalin's dictatorship that conveniently avoided mention of his semi-prohibited name.

I agreed.

The writer and poet Bulat Okudzhava was one of the first to support the idea of such a commission. A small group gathered in his comfortable, hospitable Moscow flat to discuss what to do. Among them were the poet Anatoly Zhigulin, sent to Kolyma* as a teenager after the war, and Oleg Volkov, almost the oldest living Russian writer, who had spent 27 years of his long life in the camps. We rang up other writers and secured their support: Kamil Ikramov and Yury Davydov, who had both also spent time in the Gulag, and the literary specialist and journalist Yury Karyakin who, if he had never been behind bars, had frequently clashed with the authorities. An initiative group of sorts was taking shape. All were agreed that this was a most important undertaking. There was only one doubt. Would it be possible to gain access to the secret archives at the Lubyanka? Could there be any kind of dialogue between writers and those who, until now, had kept them under surveillance and harassed them?

We discussed another problem. How were convinced democrats, opposed to the official policies of the Writers Union, to work together with those who ran it? The latter were still orthodox Communist bureaucrats. Yet nothing could be done without them.

"Let the 'ungodly' also do something good, for a change," advised my friend, the poet Vladimir Leonovich. "Give them a chance to show themselves in a good light."

The next step was to get in contact with writers in other Russian cities, in Siberia, and in the other Soviet republics. This also went well and soon we were joined by Viktor Astafiev in Krasnoyarsk, Gevork Emin in Armenia, and Chobua Amirejibi in Abkhazia.

I went back to see Verchenko. To my surprise he was amenable and made no objection to the membership of our commission. He did try, it is true, to insinuate several outspoken traditionalists and "patriots", like Yury Bondarev, and introduce a number of "sacred cows" whom he proposed more for show than any practical help they had to offer. Their presence would only have hindered us and I successfully resisted his candidates.

While we sat talking he had several visitors, some of whom he drew into our conversation. The Kazakh poet Olzhas Suleimeinov and the writer Timur Pulatov from Uzbekistan both agreed to help. The tall thin limping figure of Sergey Mikhalkov came in.

Famous as the author of children's verse, and of the words of the Soviet national anthem, Mikhalkov was chairman of the Russian Federation branch of the Writers Union. He had survived comfortably, without any periods of disgrace or privation, under all the Kremlin leaders from Stalin to Chernenko.

"Seryozha," said Verchenko, "you ought to be on this commission."

---

*Vast inaccessible region in north-east Siberia, containing the most terrible camps of the Gulag.

"I c-c-can't," stuttered Mikhalkov, "I'm a sick man, and can barely keep on my legs ... And I've got f-f-far too much else to do."

"Damn your eyes!" Verchenko croaked cheerfully. "When it comes to denouncing other writers, you're the first to join in. Now you're asked to help them, and you're sick ..."

"Damn your eyes!" Mikhalkov jerked upright, and retorted in the same bantering tone. "You just tot up how many I've helped and how many I've harmed, and then you can speak ..."

Two literary generals sharing a friendly joke.

"I'm sure Sergey Vladimirovich will help us anyway," I intervened, "there's no necessity for him to formally become a member of the commission. You will help us, won't you? It's such a worthwhile cause."

"I'll help, I'll help," growled Mikhalkov. "What else can I do?"

The door flung wide and in marched the large, broad-shouldered figure of Vladimir Karpov, first secretary of the USSR Writers Union.

Karpov was something of a "legend". During the war he worked in intelligence and was made a Hero of the Soviet Union. Later he was imprisoned twice, once for a "political" misdemeanour, once for a straightforward criminal offence. Today he was a successful member of the Soviet elite, in charge of the Ministry of Literature. "I am a bureaucrat of the Gorbachev era!" he would declare.

"Volodya, what good timing!" greeted Verchenko. Once he had briefly explained to Karpov what we were discussing, he suddenly, and to my astonishment, added: "You ought to chair this commission, Volodya."

"Oh no," Karpov objected, "That will just start the writers gossiping again. Karpov's put himself in charge of yet another commission. I'm doing far too much already."

"But this isn't just any commission," Verchenko continued to persuade him. "You're a former zek* yourself. And you know perfectly well that to get something like this off the ground, you must have someone in the government and the Central Committee. We won't get anywhere without you!" Turning to me Verchenko winked knowingly. Karpov gave his consent.

We did not entirely manage to avoid the "patriot" wing of the literary world. The chief editor of the conservative monthly *Nash sovremennik*, Stanislav Kunyaev, sent a peremptory message from the hospital bed where he then lay, demanding to be included in the commission. We naïvely agreed.

Later he would seriously hamper our work by waging a public campaign against Alexander Yakovlev, our most powerful intercessor. Kunyaev alleged that Yakovlev was a traitor, serving the cause of American imperialism and international Zionism, and he defamed other members of the commission such as Anatoly Zhigulin. For the time being, however, all was going well.

---

*A now common adaptation of the official abbreviation z/k from *zaklyuchyonnyi*, prisoner.

In early December an announcement appeared in the newspapers:

Decision of the Secretariat of
the USSR Writers Union

To be returned to the nation

... The secretariat of the USSR Writers Union has established a commission for the literary heritage of repressed and deceased writers (chairman, Vladimir Karpov, vice-chairmen, Anatoly Zhigulin and Vitaly Shentalinsky) ...

The commission will concentrate on the search for manuscripts, documents, letters and memoirs, their professional analysis and publication, and the popularizing of the work of repressed writers in the mass media ... The necessary measures must be taken to commemorate each writer and restore an objective assessment of their life and work. The necessary materials must be compiled for their posthumous rehabilitation.

The secretariat of the USSR Writers Union is appealing to Soviet people and to the public abroad to send manuscripts, letters, memoirs, documents, photographs and all that is linked to the life and work of unjustly repressed writers to the following address ...

Almost a year had passed. The idea had now acquired legal status within the Soviet Union. I could not have imagined then that in only a few short years the USSR itself would disappear and, with it, the Writers Union. The idea, however, would survive.

A new year, 1989, was just beginning. The storm of political passions in the country was growing. But on New Year's Eve we drank our champagne and toasted one another hopefully. We had lived to see things change and whatever happened next it could not be worse than before.

The Anti-troika

Once my original appeal had reached the Central Committee and evoked a response I sent on the short list they requested. It contained 13 names: Isaac Babel, Artyom Vesyoly (Kochkurov), Alexander Voronsky, Nikolay Gumilyov, Ivan Kataev, Nikolay Kluyev, Mikhail Koltsov, Osip Mandelstam, Boris Pilnyak, Ivan Pribludny, Dmitry Svyatopolk-Mirsky, Pavel Florensky and Alexander Chayanov.

While we were setting up our commission the Central Committee also went to work, behind the scenes. In January Yakovlev received the following letter from the Procurator General's Office (I would only learn of its contents later, when I read the dossier which that office kept on our commission):

Confidential
To Secretary of the CPSU Central Committee
Comrade Alexander Yakovlev

Dear Alexander Nikolaevich,
Discharging your commission to make enquiries about the manuscripts
and letters of a number of writers repressed in the 1930s and to make
them available for literary use, the USSR Procurator General's Office
together with the USSR KGB have made enquiries and studied the
relevant archival materials.

Examination has shown that the writers indicated in the list submitted were indeed illegally sentenced in the 1930s. According to the
available documents, the correspondence of Mikhail Koltsov
(Friedland) with the writer Ilya Ehrenburg, and other materials that
were confiscated during the former's arrest, were sent for permanent
storage in the Institute of World Literature on 21 January 1965.

No manuscripts were confiscated during the arrests of Alexander
Voronsky and Yakov Ovcharenko (Ivan Pribludny).

As concerns the personal notes, manuscripts and letters confiscated
from Isaac Babel, N.I. Kochkurov (Artyom Vesyoly), Ivan Kataev,
Dmitry Svyatopolk-Mirsky, Alexander Chayanov and Boris Pilnyak
(Vogau), during their arrest, it has not proved possible, after thorough
investigation and additional verification by the USSR KGB, to establish
their subsequent fate.

USSR Procurator General
A.Ya. Sukharev

The Procurator General's assistant Laptev rang me up. "We have finished our
work," he said. "Unfortunately, we could not find any manuscripts . . ."

The Procurator General's Office and the Lubyanka had apparently decided
they could do without our help. They had finished the job, in order not to begin
it. There was no reason to trust them: all they had ever done, up to now, was to
deceive us. I did not doubt for one moment that this was simply an excuse, and
that they wanted to rid themselves of the tiresome writers as quickly as possible.
Neither was I convinced that the manuscripts had completely vanished. They
might, quite likely, have remained in the investigation files as material evidence
of the "crimes" of their authors.

I tackled Karpov: "They're bluffing. We must look at the files ourselves.
Otherwise people will say that your commission is just a way of keeping the
archives closed rather than opening them up. They'd be right, too."

After grumbling for a while that he could not spare the time, Karpov ordered up his black limousine and off we went to the Procurator General's office.

At the well-known building on Pushkin Street we were met politely and invited into Andreev's office. It was his responsibility to ensure that the KGB kept to the law in its activities. We were offered tea but as soon as we raised the subject we'd come to discuss, he and his assistants expressed a certain bemusement: "But the work has already been finished . . ."

Once again I presented my arguments.

Andreev cast me an amused and disbelieving look and turned to Karpov: "I don't understand, Vladimir Vasilievich . . . If your writers are in search of new subjects then we can supply any number of ideas. For instance, we recently tracked down a fascist mass murderer who served under the Germans and shot our partisans. He was living in Brazil. What a story that would make! Or there's some sensational new material about Captain Marinescu, the heroic submarine commander – I think you wrote something about him once, didn't you, Vladimir Vasilievich? What a man!"

They began to discuss the famous Soviet war hero. They talked for some time and Andreev began glancing at his wristwatch.

"Could we return to the subject of our visit?" I intervened. "When can we begin work?"

There was an awkward pause. Then Andreev asked, looking to one side, "How do you imagine going about it?"

"I think we should set up a working group and include someone from the Procurator's Office, someone from the KGB and someone from our commission. Then we'll begin to study the files of the repressed writers, one by one. Everything that's of historical or literary value should be published. That's what artistic rehabilitation means. If the individual has still not been legally rehabilitated, then that's a job for you . . ."

"What did you say?" asked Andreev. "A group of three people? You want to set up a new 'troika'?"*

"An 'anti-troika', let's say!" I parried. "People were tried and shot under Stalin on the orders of the 'troika' without any investigation or trial. We shall be doing just the opposite, restoring truth and justice . . ."

The mood became quite jolly.

"There's another difference," Karpov added, "as well as the procurator and the representative of the Cheka, there always used to be a Party official to make up the threesome. In this case, the writer replaces the Party . . ."

"Quite right too!" I could feel that things were now going our way.

"And who do you propose should represent the writers in this working group?" Andreev continued.

*Extra-judicial commissions that tried and sentenced the overwhelming majority of "political" offenders under Stalin.

14

"Let Shentalinsky do it," Karpov, laughing, pointed at me. "Every initiative must be punished."

"Prepare an official letter and we shall consider the matter," concluded Andreev.

Karpov stayed behind in Andreev's office for quite a while. All the way back to Vorovsky Street he teased me about my new responsibility. When we arrived, however, he promised: "Well, I'll also do my bit. I'll have a talk to some influential people . . . We can't leave you to battle on your own now, can we?"

It was not long before some interesting visitors came to see our commission.

Perhaps it was our trip to the Procurator's Office, or Alexander Yakovlev again lending his support. Or perhaps it was the influence of another member of the Politburo, the then KGB chief Victor Chebrikov,* that prompted their appearance (Karpov, so he confidentially informed me, had met Chebrikov at a government dacha or sanatorium somewhere and mentioned the subject to him). For whatever reason, two dapper, confident and and cheerful KGB officers turned up at the Writers Union: General Strunin, head of the KGB press bureau, and Colonel Krayushkin from their Archives department.

Karpov received them in his spacious office, decorated with portraits of the founders of Socialist Realism, carpets from the Central Asian republics depicting their national poets, outsize presents and other dated Soviet kitsch. During the inevitable opening pleasantries our host listed all the captains of literature who had sat behind the same table: Gorky, Fadeev, Fedin . . . "But you don't know whose office this was during Lenin's lifetime, do you?" he enquired. "The Father of the Nation, no less." At one time the People's Commissariat of Nationalities was housed here, and it was then headed by Joseph Stalin.

Finally we got down to business.

"Anatoly Krayushkin is just the man you need," said Strunin. "He will take on this work. You should consider yourselves fortunate."

"We have already had a search through our own archives," began Krayushkin. "Certain things we found then have been handed on to Main Archives Administration. You may also take a look at these materials." He paused significantly. "For example, we found the diary of Mikhail Bulgakov, an essay by Andrey Bely, and notes by the historian Tarle and the actor Oleg Dal** . . . " He modestly fell silent.

No one spoke for a moment.

Neither Bulgakov or Bely had ever been arrested, let alone imprisoned. How, we asked, had their papers ended up at the Lubyanka?

"That kind of thing happened . . . there were various ways. Let's not go into

---

*When Yury Andropov succeeded Brezhnev as leader of the Party in 1982, he was replaced as head of the KGB by Fedorchuk who, in 1985, was himself succeeded by Chebrikov.

**Oleg Dal was a popular stage and film actor of the 1970s. Yevgeny Viktorovich Tarle (1875–1955) was an historian, and author of works on the Napoleonic period; his biography of Napoleon was amongst Stalin's favourite reading.

detail . . . The important thing is, they've survived."

We agreed. Of course, we would read these materials and publish them. But what about our list of repressed writers?

"That's a bit more difficult," Krayushkin responded. "The investigation files are classified 'Confidential' and 'Highly Confidential'. We do not have the right to show them to private individuals. That's the law!"

But we were not private individuals, I remonstrated, we were an official public commission. What should we do now?

"In your case, nothing. We've got to think again. We'll find a way. First we'll see for ourselves what's left in the files: it was a long while ago, and the staff have changed several times since that terrible period. I have your list in front of me. Whom shall we start with? In alphabetical order, Babel? No objections? Then write down my telephone number . . ."

Illegal activities

At last, it seemed, things were really moving. We had received a photocopy of an extremely interesting diary kept by Mikhail Bulgakov and were preparing it for publication. Gradually, however, the euphoria that followed our meeting with the KGB men evaporated.

I frequently rang up Krayushkin.

"Ring me back in a month's time . . ."

"We're examining the file. You must understand, it takes time and we have a lot of other work to do."

"Please, stop trying to rush us . . ."

"Krayushkin is away on business . . ."

"Krayushkin is on leave . . ."

The months passed. The commission went to work. After the announcement of its creation, we were inundated by a flood of letters, bulky packages, and telephone calls. People sent us verse, prose, memoirs, documents, photographs and drawings through the post or brought them in themselves. They travelled up from other towns and cities in order to hand us things that, under the constant threat of searches and arrest, they had written or kept concealed for years and decades. They were themselves the authors, or had been entrusted by others to keep their works; certain papers had survived quite by chance. We encountered some famous names and others that were barely familiar or quite unknown. One elderly man brought us his prison diary from Siberia: he did not trust the post, so he came to Moscow by train, spent the night at the station since he had nowhere to stay, and appeared the next morning at our commission.

"Take them and print them!" he said, as he handed over the notebooks. "Now I really believe the time has come . . ."

There was also a response from those who justified the repressions or had actually participated in them. During the first Thaw, under Khrushchev, Anna Akhmatova commented: "The prisoners are returning and two Russias are looking one another in the eye: those who sent people to the camps and those who were imprisoned there." Now these two Russias were again confronting one another and this time, perhaps, were even less inclined to seek reconciliation.

"You have no right to investigate these matters," anonymous callers told us. "You'll regret it."

Certain writers were also hostile. Their anxiety was quite understandable. If the Lubyanka archives were opened they would be revealed as fertile authors in a different genre: their denunciations would acquire, for the first time, a mass readership. Yet more numerous were those members of the Writers Union who were unreformed and incorrigible Stalinists and simply prevented by their convictions from accepting our initiatives.

In January and March we held open meetings of our commission which were attended by people from all over the Soviet Union. The discussions were passionate and stormy. It turned out that there were enthusiasts everywhere, from the Baltic to the Pacific Ocean, who had lovingly collected and preserved testimony about this most tragic period in the history of Russian literature.

As our archive grew by leaps and bounds, and demanded an outlet to the public as a whole, I realized that we would have to completely rewrite the history of this period. We only knew the tip of that iceberg termed Soviet literature.

Meanwhile, the third member of our anti-troika had also set to work. Alexander Valuisky, from the Procurator's Office, announced that the writer and agronomist Chayanov and the poet Osip Mandelstam had been rehabilitated. Furthermore, he was independently tracking down the materials in his office concerning the fate of Babel.

Nothing had changed at the KGB, however. Perhaps, they were vetting me thoroughly before they allowed me into their archives. If so, they were taking their time. More probably, the rapid shifts in the political situation were to blame. The advance towards democracy had halted, the conservatives were fighting back and Gorbachev was wavering to and fro between the different factions, trying to maintain equilibrium and unite the irreconcilable. Each shift on the political barometer affected our cause.

Once, driven to exasperation during a conversation with Krayushkin, I burst out: "Anatoly Afanasievich, we are simply asking you to hand back what does not belong to you, things that your predecessors stole from the nation."

"You know, if you are going to start talking to us like that," he replied with equal passion, "then how can we consider working together?" and slammed down the receiver.

I felt like someone who has made his way into a labyrinth and suddenly realizes that he no longer knows the way back or how to move forward.

At this time the new KGB chairman Kryuchkov began saying a lot in his numerous press interviews about glasnost. I drafted a letter to him from the Writers Union, stating that representatives of the KGB for inexplicable reasons were not responding to the requests and demands of writers and did not, apparently, want to cooperate with us. The commission was a professional and competent body and could guarantee that any archival materials that passed through its hands and were then made public would not be distorted or used provocatively. We could see no convincing arguments, I wrote, for holding up a matter of such literary and public importance any longer.

Karpov refused to sign the letter. It would be interpreted as undue pressure. No, he suggested, it was better to give them a call.

"Ring them up now!"

After numerous excuses, he nevertheless dialled a number on the special telephone that linked his office directly to the highest state officials, including the KGB. Kryuchkov's deputy Pirozhkov answered the phone. They talked, but Karpov's manner was so wheedling and pitiful that I realized nothing would come of it.

That summer I made a journey up to the White Sea with Volodya Leonovich. We sailed out to Solovki, the islands on which the first Soviet concentration camp was set up in 1922. There we decided we must publish a protest against the sabotaging of our efforts. Why not announce that the KGB were blocking our work?

"For goodness sake, don't do that!" warned Yury Karyakin when I asked his advice. "You won't frighten the Lubyanka with such an attack, only alarm them and spoil everything. Carry on as before: keep up the pressure . . . I can also weigh in as USSR People's Deputy and raise the matter at the Congress."*

He was, of course, quite right. The Lubyanka, like a giant clam, had begun to open. One careless move, however, and it would shut tight again, and you might lose an arm as well when it did so.

Soon after this conversation (it was already August), Krayushkin himself called me: "Come in to see us. We have the materials ready."

The Lubyanka is a formidable fortified complex in the centre of Moscow. Several massive multi-storey blocks, old and new, shod with granite pediments, are linked together by corridors that pass above and below ground. From Lubyanka Square, a wide road sweeps down to the Bolshoi Theatre and the Metropol hotel, and on to the Kremlin, the Manege and the old University building. Until August 1991 the square was dominated by a statue of "Iron Felix", the founder of the Cheka, Dzerzhinsky. Before the 1917 October Revolution the

*In spring 1989 the first multi-candidate elections in the Soviet Union for more than 70 years were held to the USSR Congress of People's Deputies.

building fronting the square belonged to the Russia Insurance Company. Since then it has been the permanent headquarters of an organization whose name has changed several times, but whose function has always remained the same: the Cheka, GPU, OGPU, NKVD, NKGB, MGB, MVD, KGB . . .

Like the majority of my contemporaries, I had until then only looked at this hydra from the outside. I tried not to pay it any attention but still it exerted an hypnotic influence. Each citizen of our vast country knew that the Lubyanka was watching him. At any moment, it could take charge of his life and then there was no power that could defend him.

I walked through three sets of enormous doors from the hot noisy square into a cool and spacious hall. The corporals carefully checked my pass and thoroughly studied my passport.* We climbed the broad staircase dominated by a white bust of Yury Andropov. The corridor had a high ceiling and was so long and wide that one could easily ride down it on a bicycle or even a horse. It was quiet, and seemed deserted. Nothing appeared to have changed here for many years. Probably it had looked just the same under Stalin . . .

We entered a small office on the second floor. White curtains concealed the view. On the table lay a bulging yellowish file.

Krayushkin smiled: "You're the first writer, it seems, who has come here of his own free will."

I smiled back. The same thought had just occurred to me.

He handed me a photograph and several typed pages.

"This is the photo from Babel's investigation file and these provide the essence of the case against him."

I skimmed through the pages. A meagre precis from the file's contents, they contained what were, for the most part, widely known facts and biographical details.

"But couldn't I have a look at the file itself? At least for a few hours?"

"No."

"Why, is it a state secret?"

"No, there are no major secrets here. Or in most such files. There are certain purely internal matters, though, concerning our work, that our superiors consider need not be made public."

"What exactly?"

"Well, the number of the investigation file, for example, the names of the investigators, the reports of our agents . . . All kinds of things."

"Why ever do you need to conceal that now?"

"You see this classification?" Krayushkin started to become agitated. "It says 'Highly confidential'! Let the Supreme Soviet or the government alter the rules and untie our hands. Are you suggesting that we should break the law? Are you

*Universal and obligatory identity document for use only within the USSR.

inciting us to commit a crime?'"

"But then I can't say I've laid my hands on Babel's file!"

He smiled again and held out the file: "Now you can . . ."

I had rather more success at the Procurator General's Office. Valuisky had tracked down Supervisory file No 3904-39 on Isaac Babel. His office compiled such dossiers on all who were convicted. Before he would allow me to see the file (it also bore the stamp CONFIDENTIAL) Valuisky asked: "Did they let you look, at the Lubyanka?"

"Yes," I replied, though not at the files themselves.

"And you saw Babel's file?"

"Yes, I saw it," I was able to reply, with a quite clear conscience.

I became immersed in the procurator's dossier. It proved far more interesting than the skimpy pages I had been given at the KGB. Here, for the first time, I saw copies of several documents from "investigation file No 419 on Isaac Babel" and, most interesting of all, appeals in Babel's own hand that he wrote to the Procurator's Office just before his death.

Soon these materials were published in the popular *Ogonyok** weekly as the first in a new series called "To be kept indefinitely". In my preface I supplied everything: the file number, the names of the writer's brutal interrogators and the denunciations and reports of the secret police's anonymous agents and informers.

I anxiously awaited the reaction of the Lubyanka. It was not long in coming.

"Where did you get that material?" demanded Krayushkin gloomily, "at the procurator's office? The people in our press relations group want to talk to you. Then come to my room and see me."

There were several unfamiliar people sitting in Strunin's office.

"We are not against opening our archives," one of them said, "but let's reach some agreement. There are certain things that have nothing to do with literature but concern our sphere of activities. You have begun to examine the files. There you will come across reports by our agents: there is no point in publishing them, and if you must cite them then simply say, 'It came to the attention of the NKVD'. The source doesn't matter. What do you need the informers for?"

A phrase came into my head: "The nation should know who its informers are." But I did not repeat this familiar demand.

"Why are you so worried about them?" I asked. "It all happened half a century ago, it's already history. You want censorship and half-truths, again?"

"Now, now, why talk in those terms? . . . But we shall not surrender Pavlik Morozov,** my dear Vitaly Alexandrovich."

*(Lit. Little Flame): a magazine which publishes popular fiction and non-fiction and became prominent during the late 1980s as an outlet for perestroika material.
**A Young Pioneer who denounced his father for defending kulaks during collectivization in the early 1930s. See chapter 8.

"Pavlik Morozov is no longer a hero these days."

"No one has yet abolished the class struggle!"

"But they have, that's just the point," I replied. "It's Gorbachev's greatest achievement. He has declared that universal human values take priority over class loyalties! It seems not everyone has noticed that . . ."

There was a silence. Suddenly there was nothing more to say.

"Nevertheless, we are relying on you to behave with tact and restraint," they said as we parted. "Why don't you show us what you are writing?"

"What for? Once it is published then I shall with pleasure present you with a copy."

They had swallowed my publication, and resigned themselves to its existence but decided that, for appearances sake, they should make some effort to keep me under control.

The laws were out of date and reasonable people at the KGB understood that. As men and women who gave and obeyed orders, they could not ignore the law. If someone else did, however, they felt they could rest easy.

The Babel file again lay on the table in Krayushkin's office. This time, at last, I was allowed to open it.

CHAPTER 2

"I BEG YOU TO HEAR ME"

THE FILE ON ISAAC BABEL

Arrest

16 May 1939. It is early morning and Moscow is still fast asleep. The only sounds are the peaceful chirruping of the birds and the caretaker's broom sweeping the courtyard.

At 5 am the iron gates of the Lubyanka swing open and a car departs. It has not far to go: up to the Boulevard, and then to No 4, Nikolo-Vorobinsky Street. Several soldiers get out and calmly find the flat they need. They knock. A sleepy young woman comes to the door.

"Is the master at home?"

"No, he's at the dacha. Why?"

"We need to search the loft: we're looking for someone."

Two of the soldiers climb up into the loft; the others stand about, waiting.

"Get dressed. We'll go and fetch your husband. He knows where the man we're searching for is . . ."

The car races out of Moscow for half an hour along the Minsk Highway, and turns off towards Peredelkino, the writers' colony.

The soldiers enter the dacha. Its owner is still asleep in his room. His wife knocks at the bedroom door and as soon as he appears the visitors hurl themselves at him: "Hands up!" they order, as they rapidly search him for weapons, "You're under arrest!"

Perhaps that is how Isaac Babel would have described such an episode, had he been allowed to finish the book he was writing about the Cheka.* Instead, that May morning he himself became a helpless prisoner of the NKVD,** arrested on the orders of Lavrenty Beria.

While the dacha was searched, Babel and his wife Nina sat silently together holding hands. They watched as papers were piled up and tied into bundles. Nine folders full of his manuscripts, notebooks and letters would be sent with the writer to prison.

"They didn't let me finish it," said Babel. Then he whispered quietly to his wife: "Let André know," meaning his friend the French writer André Malraux.

*The Extraordinary Commission for Combatting Counter-Revolution, Speculation, Sabotage and misuses of authority (the first Soviet secret police) was set up in 1917 by Felix Dzerzhinsky.
**From 1934 onwards the entire People's Commissariat of Internal Affairs or NKVD was taken over by "state security".

As they drove back into Moscow Babel tried to joke with his captors: "You don't get much sleep, do you?" And in a low voice, to his wife: "Please see that our girl grows up happy."

The doors of the Lubyanka swallowed up the car. For the next 15 years, until 1954, nothing certain would be known about the fate of Babel.

They drove his wife home and searched the flat in Moscow, seizing a further 15 folders of manuscripts, 18 notebooks and pads, 517 letters, postcards and telegrams, and 245 various loose sheets of paper ... They even tore pages out of books with dedicatory inscriptions to Babel.

By that time Babel himself was being searched. His passport and the keys to the flat and the dacha were confiscated. So even were certain necessary trifles: toothpaste, shaving cream, braces and garters, a soap-case, a bath sponge and, it is recorded in the receipt stitched into his case-file, "the thong from an old pair of sandals".

The arrested man was left no opportunity to take his own life. The procedure had been minutely thought out and planned. By stripping the individual of each last item that still linked him to everyday life and to his family they rendered him insignificant and helpless. What was an unshaven and unwashed man, in ill-fitting laceless shoes and falling trousers, against the might of the all-powerful state?

They photographed Babel, took his fingerprints and gave him the standard form to fill in. Was this the last photograph that would ever be taken? It was difficult not to ask oneself at this point. The finger-printing hinted, they consider you a criminal. The form demanded that the arrested man wrote down everything about himself, so that his life could be examined and assessed, and anything suspicious uncovered.

> Born, 1894, in Odessa. Writer. Not a Party member. Jewish. Last place of work, USSR Children's Films Studio, State Publishing House. Higher education received at Kiev Commercial Institute ...
>
> Family: father, a commercial trader, died 1924; mother, Fenya Aronovna Babel, 75, a housewife, lives in Belgium; wife, Antonina Nikolaevna Pirozhkova, 30, engineer with the Metro Construction and Design Institute; children, a daughter Lidiya aged 2 years, a daughter Natalya (from first marriage) aged 10 years (lives in France); sister, Maria Shaposhnikova, 42, lives in Belgium.

All the formalities completed, the arrested man was led away to a cell in the Inner Prison, a six-storey yellow building with small barred windows that stands concealed within the Lubyanka's inner courtyard. There, the necessary testimony would be beaten out of him.

The first record of interrogation is dated 29–31 May. Perhaps Babel had already been interrogated before that. If so, no records have been preserved in the file: until now he had not given the investigators what they needed.

Interrogation

On 29 May Babel was taken from his cell to the investigator's office.* For three days and nights NKVD interrogators Schwartzmann and Kuleshov would not release him until they had the confession they wanted. It was no easy task. However, they were experienced and took it in turns so as to get some rest in between.

> Record of the cross-questioning of prisoner
> Babel, 29–31 May 1939.
> *Q.* You have been arrested for treacherous anti-Soviet activities. Do you acknowledge your guilt?
> *A.* No, I do not.
> *Q.* How can you reconcile that declaration of innocence with the fact of your arrest?
> *A.* I consider my arrest the result of a fateful coincidence and of my own inability to write. During the last few years I have not published a single major work and this might be considered sabotage and an unwillingness to write under Soviet conditions.
> *Q.* You wish to say that you have been arrested as a writer? Does that not strike you as an excessively naïve explanation for your arrest?
> *A.* You are right, of course. Authors are not arrested because they can no longer write.
> *Q.* So what is the real reason for your arrest?
> *A.* I often went abroad and have been friendly with leading Trotskyists . . .
> *Q.* Please explain why you, a Soviet writer, found yourself attracted to enemies of the country you were representing abroad. You will have to confess your criminal, treacherous activities . . .

At this point the interrogator began to quote from testimony given by the writer Boris Pilnyak and by Stetsky, who had headed the cultural and propaganda section of the Central Committee. (By then both had already been shot.) Babel was described as a Trotskyist, but only in passing, without any specific detail. No proof whatever was provided.

"Do not wait until we force you! Begin your confession."

We can only speculate as to how the interrogation actually proceeded. What we have before us is the record fabricated by the two interrogators and the only indication of Babel's involvement is his signature at the end of each page. The

*The official title of Babel's tormentors.

farcical opening in which the person under investigation was asked to prove his own guilt and explain why he had been arrested is astounding. Yet this was one of the innovations of Soviet jurisprudence.

The only crime Babel was ready to confess was an inability to write. In fact, this was not the case. He may have published little, but, as the quantity of confiscated manuscripts shows, he was writing a great deal. He was no opponent of the Soviet system but he served his own talent rather than the authorities. Babel's real crime was his artistic independence. The interrogator denied that he had been arrested for being a writer, but that, in fact, was exactly the case. Yet there was no such offence in the Criminal Code, so some other charge had to be made.

We know how the NKVD interrogators got what they wanted. Apart from the threats and beatings, there were more subtle forms of torture, for instance, the promise to take vengeance on other members of the family. If one method did not work, then another would almost certainly prove effective. Babel himself had direct experience of the cruelty of the Cheka. For five months in 1918 he had served as a translator for the Cheka in Petrograd; he had seen his fill of interrogations and executions and collected a vast amount of material documenting the atrocities of the Revolution. His keen writer's interest in such matters remained with him all his life, and he laced his stories liberally with tears and bloodshed. It was Babel, after all, who said that the world had consumed the Communist International "sprinkled with gunpowder and seasoned with the best blood". Now he would have to supply some of the blood himself.

No matter how thick and impenetrable the prison walls, no matter how hard the NKVD tried to conceal what went on in their "investigators" offices, some echo has reached us in the outside world. The case file on the theatrical director Vsevolod Meyerhold still contains the letter he wrote from prison to Molotov, the head of the Soviet government. It is a chillingly detailed account of how "truthful confessions" were obtained:

> ... The investigators began to use force on me, a sick, 65-year-old man. I was made to lie face down and then beaten on the soles of my feet and my spine with a rubber strap. They sat me on a chair and beat my feet from above, with considerable force .... For the next few days, when those parts of my legs were covered with extensive internal haemorrhaging, they again beat the red-blue-and-yellow bruises with the strap and the pain was so intense that it felt as if boiling hot water was being poured on these sensitive areas. I howled and wept from the pain. They beat my back with the same rubber strap and punched my face, swinging their fists from a great height ...
>
> When they added the "psychological attack", as it's called, the physical and mental pain aroused such an appalling terror in me that I was

left quite naked and defenceless. My nerve endings, it turned out, were very close to the surface of my body and the skin proved as sensitive and soft as a child's. The intolerable physical and emotional pain caused my eyes to weep unending streams of tears. Lying face down on the floor, I discovered that I could wriggle, twist and squeal like a dog when its master whips it. One time my body was shaking so uncontrollably that the guard escorting me back from such an interrogation asked: "Have you got malaria?" When I lay down on the cot and fell asleep, after 18 hours of interrogation, in order to go back in an hour's time for more, I was woken up by my own groaning and because I was jerking about like a patient in the last stages of typhoid fever.

Fright arouses terror, and terror forces us to find some means of self-defence.

"Death, oh most certainly, death is easier than this!" the interrogated person says to himself. I began to incriminate myself in the hope that this, at least, would lead quickly to the scaffold . . .

Meyerhold was arrested at the same time as Babel and taken to the very same interrogators. The name Schwartzmann, for instance, is to be found at the end of both Meyerhold and Babel's case files. There can be no doubt that the methods of "active investigation", the veiled and respectable term used in public, were also practised on Babel, though, naturally, this is not indicated in the record of his interrogation. Otherwise, it is difficult to explain why he first resolutely refused to admit his guilt and then, unexpectedly, and without any visible cause, "confessed". The transformation of the writer Babel into an "enemy of the people" had begun.

In fact, he had already considered, several times before, what would happen if he was arrested. Once, at Gorky's dacha, he asked the then secret police chief Yagoda: "Genrikh Grigorievich, how should a person behave if he finds himself in your hands?" "Deny everything," replied the master of the Lubyanka. "No matter what accusations we might make, he should keep saying 'No' to everything. Deny everything and then we are powerless . . ."

So Babel had been expecting it to happen. Nevertheless, he still proved unprepared. "I no longer see any sense in denying that my guilt before the Soviet state is grave indeed," he suddenly announced. "I am ready to make a full confession."

Babel was true to his word. In addition to the dialogue with his two investigators he also wrote out his own testimony in the form of notes. Even there we can easily trace a harsh and alien will behind these jottings. Questions have been written on the pages by the interrogators themselves. It may be Babel's handwriting but they are not his own thoughts. Comparing the two texts we find, in a number of cases, that not only the contents but several phrases or entire sentences are identical. These notes served as a rough draft from which the carefully edited, final version of the official record was produced. The interrogators excluded those parts where Babel denied his guilt. They removed all that might serve as an alibi and reinforce his reputation as a Soviet writer, for instance, his friendship with both Gorky and Mayakovsky – in fact, they excluded everything positive in his biography. In its place they exaggerated and inflated each piece of compromising material. Those important observations and generalizations which raised his comments above the primitive and preconceived level his interrogators required were also left out. The original records of his interrogations, for good reason, were not included in the file: it only contains typed copies and does not indicate the time at which each interrogation session began or ended. In 1954 when the Procurator's Office rehabilitated Babel these were noted as serious procedural infringements.

Beria himself described the depositions drawn up by Schwartzmann and Rodos (both involved in Babel's interrogation) as "real works of art"– or so they would declare, when they themselves were eventually put on trial. A truer indication of the interrogators' abilities is suggested by their level of education. Lev Schwartzmann left school at the age of 14, while Boris Rodos only stayed at school until he was 11: "I'm an uneducated man," he would unashamedly acknowledge in his application for a pardon. Yet after the war Rodos delivered lectures to students at the college of the Ministry of Internal Affairs and was author of study aids on "preparing arrested persons in the cells for investigation". In 1956 the judges asked Rodos what a certain Babel, whose case he had investigated, did for a living.

"I was told he was a writer."

"Have you read a single one of his stories?"

"What for?"

It is hard to imagine the "torments of creativity" that Babel endured in the NKVD investigator's office. Urged on, probably, by a promise that he would be freed, he created for himself an extraordinary new fictitious identity and provided an imaginary account of the pernicious influence of the Trotskyists. He spoke of his own fatal effect on others and turned himself inside out, revealing the most intimate and private facts of his life. It did not come easily. First he drew up a plan. Then he made numerous drafts, crossing out and restoring, returning several times to express the same idea in a different form . . .

Though he was forced to lie, we still occasionally detect a confiding sincerity and flashes of profound thought in what he wrote. Enigmatic incomplete phrases are scattered in these notes: "To get one's ideas across . . . A kind and cheerful man, against cruelty . . . I realized that my subject . . . was the story of the life of one 'good' man during the Revolution . . ."

The historian Boris Souvarine, looking back over his meetings with Babel in Paris, recollected the following conversation:

> "So you think there are valuable literary works in your country that cannot be published because of political conditions?"
>
> "Yes," replied Babel. "They're in the GPU."*
>
> "How do you mean?"
>
> "Whenever an educated person is arrested and finds himself in a prison cell, he is given a pencil and a piece of paper. 'Write!' they tell him."

It was happening now. For three days and nights Babel would write and talk. The testimony he gave, in his own hand and officially recorded in his interrogation, forms a kind of memoir. Separating the obvious lies from the truth, we find that Babel tells us much of interest about his time and himself. In what follows we shall trace the course of his interrogation in both the official record and the notes he himself made. Parallel documents, they complement and supplement one another, and only by reading them together do we gain a more or less complete picture.

> My first stories were published in 1916 in *Letopis*, the monthly journal edited by Maxim Gorky. The Revolution and Civil-War years interrupted my literary activities. I started to publish again in 1922 when excerpts from my reminiscences of service with the First Cavalry Army began to be printed in Odessa and Kiev newspapers. These excerpts would later make up the book entitled *Red Cavalry*. In 1923 I took the stories to Moscow and gave a few of them to Mayakovsky and *LEF* but began to publish all I was writing in Voronsky's *Krasnaya nov** ...*"

Only at this point does the official deposition take up Babel's biography:

> *Babel.* My first work, *Red Cavalry*, appeared in 1923, most of the stories being printed in the journal *Krasnaya Nov*. The then chief editor, the noted Trotskyist Alexander Voronsky, displayed a great interest in me. He wrote several enthusiastic reviews of my work and introduced me to the writers who had gathered around him: ... Vsevolod Ivanov, Boris Pilnyak, Lidiya Seifullina, Sergey Yesenin, Sergey Klychkov and Vasily Kazin. Somewhile later, Leonid Leonov joined the Voronsky group and, after he had written his epic poem "The Lay of Opanas", so did Eduard Bagritsky –

---

*State Political Administration, title of secret police from 1922 until 1923.
*(Lit. Red Virgin Soil): a major literary monthly of the 1920s where the Fellow-Travellers in particular were published. See chapter 7.

Interrogator. Do not try to conceal the anti-Soviet thrust and purpose of your meetings and ties with Voronsky behind such literary talk. All such attempts will be unsuccessful!

Babel. From the very beginning Voronsky would tell me and the other writers that we were the salt of the Russian earth. He tried to convince us that writers should only mingle with the masses in order to replenish their store of observations. When they wrote, though, they should disregard the masses and the Party since, in Voronsky's view, it was for the Party to learn from the writers and not vice versa . . .

One day in 1924 Voronsky invited me to visit him at home, telling me beforehand that Bagritsky would be reciting "The Lay of Opanas" which he had only just completed. Apart from myself, Voronsky invited the writers Leonov and Ivanov, and Karl Radek. That evening we had arrived and were drinking tea when Voronsky warned us that he had also invited Trotsky to attend the reading. Soon Trotsky, accompanied by Radek, appeared. After listening to the poem, Trotsky spoke approvingly of Bagritsky's new work and began to ask each of us in turn about our biographies and our plans as writers. He then spoke at length about how we must become better acquainted with the latest French literature.

Radek, I remember, made an attempt to introduce politics into the conversation. "Two hundred thousand copies of this poem should be printed and distributed but our dear Central Committee is most unlikely to do that." Trotsky looked severely at Radek and the talk returned to literary matters. Trotsky began to ask if we knew foreign languages and were keeping up with the latest in Western writing. He could not imagine Soviet writers being able to develop further without it, he said . . . I never met Trotsky again . . .

Interrogator. Recall in full the conversations that took place among the named writers.

Babel. In 1928 I was at Voronsky's flat with Pilnyak, Ivanov, Seifullina and Leonov, and the Trotskyists Lashevich and Zorin.* Voronsky's dismissal from *Krasnaya nov*, it was said, would be an irreparable loss for Soviet literature, and those who opposed him were unable, through ignorance or lack of authority, to unite the best representatives of Soviet literature as he had successfully done. I remember the embittered attacks Lashevich made on the Central Committee for, supposedly, its wrong management of literature; Ivanov's non-committal silence; Seifullina's frank and vocal indignation; and the unease of Pilnyak. It was then that plans were made to publish the Pereval collections and the *Krug*

*High-ranking Communist officials, S.S. Zorin (Gombarg) was arrested and shot in 1937, while M.M. Lashevich died in August 1928.

almanach, both to be edited by Voronsky, in competition with *Krasnaya nov* under its new editors. We all promised to work for these new publications.

Literary conversations at Voronsky's flat inevitably turned to politics, and an analogy was drawn between his fate and the removal of Trotskyists from leading positions in the government which would do the country untold damage . . .

Voronsky was dismissed as editor of *Krasnaya nov* and exiled to Lipetsk for his Trotskyism. He became ill there, and I went to see him, staying for several days . . . I remember Voronsky then telling me how, the night before he was due to leave Moscow, Ordzonikidze* had rung him up and asked him to come to the Kremlin. They spent several happy hours together, recalling their time in exile** and the years before the Revolution. When they were already saying goodbye, Ordzonikidze told Voronsky: "Let's embrace, even if we are political enemies. One of my kidneys is not working and, perhaps, we'll never meet again . . ."

The most interesting parts of the official deposition are these passages where Babel speaks for himself, and is not just providing the answers the interrogators want. Soon, however, he is interrupted and their exchanges return to the pre-determined pattern.

Undoubtedly constant contact with Trotskyists had a fatal effect on my writing. For a long while it concealed from me the true visage of our Soviet land, and was the cause of the spiritual and literary crisis that I suffered for many years. The assertions of the Trotskyists that the proletariat had no need for a state or, in any case, that the building of such a state was of no interest for literature: their claims that all the undertakings of the Soviet state were temporary, relative and unstable in nature: their prophesy of the imminent and inevitable catastrophe could not help but imbue me with a lack of confidence in what was going on around me, and infect me with nihilism and a sense of my own exclusiveness . . .

The interrogator demanded specific examples. Babel began to denigrate his own work:

Red Cavalry was only an excuse for me to express my appalling mood and had nothing to do with what was happening in the Soviet Union. Hence the emphasis on all the cruelty and absurdities of the Civil War, the artificial introduction of an erotic element and the depiction of only

*Member of Stalin's Politburo. See "Biographical Notes".
**Here and elsewhere "exile" refers to banishment to distant parts of the Soviet Union (or the old Russian Empire), or a ban on living in specified urban centres.

the most outrageous and sensational episodes. Hence the complete failure to describe the role of the Party in pulling together the then still insufficiently proletarian-minded Cossacks to form regular forces and constitute the impressive unit of the Red Army that the First Cavalry army became.

As far as my *Odessa Stories* are concerned, they indubitably reflect the same desire to retreat from Soviet reality and set against the daily tasks of construction the colourful, semi-mythical world of Odessa's gangsters. Their romantic depiction was an unconscious appeal to young Soviet people to imitate them . . .

Babel was requested to do the same for Voronsky and his circle, painting their difficulties as writers as the bitter fruit of Trotskyism:

Voronsky's basic idea was that the writer should create freely and intuitively, giving the most vivid reflection in his books of his own unrestrained individuality . . .

This fundamental condition for any artistic endeavour was treated by the interrogator as a deadly sin, and the cause of the various writers' misfortunes:

There followed a series of unsuccessful and lifeless works by Vsevolod Ivanov, including the novella *Brigadier Sinitsyna*. In a fit of despair, Ivanov burnt one book on which he had been working for a long time. I learnt of Ivanov's decadent attitudes in recent years from Kataev who said he was, as always, wavering to and fro in search of literary and political stability and dissatisfied with his lot . . . In numerous conversations, Seifullina complained to me that she found it increasingly difficult to write because of her uncertain and despairing view of the world. In recent years Seifullina's inner discord with contemporary reality has led her to entirely abandon literary work and activities and take heavily to drink . . .

In his own notes, Babel gave a detailed analysis of the metamorphosis he and his fellow-writers experienced:

When Voronsky was exiled we became the strongholds of his influence on the younger generation of writers, and attracted those who were dissatisfied with Party policies towards the arts. Siberian "pro-peasant" writers formed a group around Seifullina and Pravdukhin, adventurers and other dubious figures were drawn to Pilnyak, while my reputation for literary "independence" and as a "fighter for quality" attracted those who were inclined towards formalism. What attitudes did I encourage in them? A disregard for the organizational forms of writers' associations (the Union of Soviet Writers,* etc), the idea that Soviet literature was in decline, and a critical attitude to such Party measures as the struggle with formalism and the approval of things that were useful but of limited artistic value . . .

What did we talk about over a cup of tea? We told each other penitent tales about the old departed Russia in which, alongside the bad, there had been much that was good. Sentimentally, we recalled the onion domes of the monasteries and the idyll of small provincial towns. Even the Tsarist prisons were depicted in positive, sometimes moving, terms and the jailers and secret policemen of the day appeared in these stories to be slightly odd, not at all bad kinds of people. The Revolution was condemned for the mortal sin of "under-estimating" so-called good men, like the Pyatakovs, Lasheviches and Serebryakovs . . . **

Here I should add some words about myself. It would be untrue and self-disparaging to claim that Voronsky was to blame for all my short-comings. He had a limited influence on me: I thought him a mediocre critic and as a politician, too impressionistic. However, I wholeheart-edly adopted his division of revolutionaries into "bad and good people" and it would be the cause of all my woes, both personal and literary. One of Voronsky's basic commandments was that we should remain faithful to ourselves, our style and our subject matter. All might change around us, he considered, but the writer grew only within himself, enriching his soul; this inner process could go on independently of outside influences. I wanted to continue working while maintaining such strange ideas. That was why all my attempts to cope with a real Soviet subject ended in failure.

I wanted to describe the Zvenigorod business that Yevdokimov† told me about (the capture in the Ukraine of Zavgorodny and the other gangsters). Nothing came of the attempt because I only presented the human relations between these criminals and ordinary Soviet people, not their political dimension.

I wanted to write a book about collectivization but that majestic process, in my thinking, became torn up into petty and unconnected fragments.

I wanted to write about Kabardia [in the North Caucasus] but stopped halfway because I was unable to separate the life of that small

*The formal title of the Writers Union, established in 1932.
**G.L. Pyatakov and L.P. Serebryakov were revolutionaries and leading figures in the Party; they were accused of anti-Soviet activities in 1937 and shot. (Lashevich, see footnote on p 29.)
†Evidently E.G. Yevdokimov, a major NKVD official until his arrest in the late 1930s.

Soviet republic from the feudal methods Kalmykov used to rule it.

I wanted to write about the new Soviet family (taking the story of the Korobovs as my starting point) but here again I was a hostage to my deadening objectivity and personal pettiness . . .

Ten burdensome years were expended on these efforts and only recently have I at last found respite – I realized that my subject, about which so many want to hear, is that of self-denunciation; it is the fictional, pitiless and truthful story of the life of one "good" person in the Revolution. And, for the first time, this subject came easily to me. I did not finish it, but it took a different form and has become the record of a judicial investigation . . .

Babel was building up a picture of the prodigal and repentant writer. Yet behind the appropriate phraseology of this confessional genre, he offers us a glimpse of the real reasons for his inability to write. The list of his failures is eloquent: the uniform of the Soviet writer, cut to suit the tenets of Socialist Realism, bursts at the seams when measured against his talent.

He would never be able to write "as required", he realized now, "like all the others". He had recognized his true hero, the "good person" who had made the Revolution and then fallen its victim, destroying the world in the name of high ideals only to be buried by its ruins. This was the fate of his friends and, now, of Babel himself. That was why the last form of self-expression he was permitted were the depositions of his interrogation, the rough drafts of a tragedy of the Revolution that no one had yet written.

In 1927 and 1932 I visited Paris and was ecstatically greeted by the Menshevik and Kadet* wings of the Russian emigration. They listened enraptured to my tales of the Soviet Union while I naïvely supposed I was painting a positive picture. When I ask myself now why I felt so free and uninhibited in their company, I can see that there was, in essence, no difference between them and the spirit that dominated Voronsky's circle. My internal emigration had occurred before I ever travelled abroad and it continued after I came back. The nature of my conversations and attitudes did not change.

I was acquainted with many writers, workers in the film industry and other cultured people. My authority among them was high, and they valued my sense of style and gifts as a story-teller. All my life I was both slave and master of this reputation. Philistine discussions of politics, literary gossip, and denigration of Soviet art all blended together in these

*Kadet refers to the Constitutional Democrat Party; Menshevik to the more moderate wing of Marxist Social Democracy. Political rivals excluded by the Bolshevik coup in October 1917.

conversations. Outwardly this was the witty and inconsequential chatter of "interesting people", occasionally punctuated by expressions of distress at various shortcomings. In fact, these conversations echoed serious thoughts and feelings.

One subject was constant. Over a period of years I continually attacked the idea that writers be organized into a union, asserting that extreme decentralization was required in such matters, and that the means used to direct and manage writers should be infinitely more flexible and less apparent. I would resort to witticism and suggest that "rotten liberalism" be introduced in literary affairs; I joked that 70 per cent of the writers living in Moscow should be exiled and resettled all over the Soviet Union, nearer to the things they had to describe. I sharply criticized almost all the measures being taken by the Writers Union and protested against the building of housing, settlements and rest-homes for writers, as the beginnings of an anti-professional trend. I refused any posts or voluntary work in the Union and made fun of it. I should add, though, that I never concealed my ideas on this score, just as I never concealed my opinions on other more serious matters.

When I met my personal friends – Eisenstein, Utyosov, Mikhoels and Kataev – we would discuss the trials, the arrests and literary policies. When we talked about the trials, I remember, we said that if the principle of judicial contest [between prosecution and defence] were to be introduced, this would only be to the good, and would make what happened in the courtroom more convincing . . .

I cannot now recall every comment made during these conversations (I only saw some of these friends every one or two years) but I remember that there was no disagreement. We all thought the same, and I felt I was moving in the right company . . .

During the formal interrogation Babel added:

I used to tell my friends that it was not the individuals so much as the generations that were changing in the country . . . the best and most gifted political and military figures were being arrested, and I complained that Soviet literature had become colourless and had no future. It was, so to speak, a product of its day and a consequence of the contemporary situation. At the same time, I would say that I myself had reached a dead end and could find no way out again . . .

Each time Babel began to express important generalizations he hesitated; his thoughts lost momentum and were again forced back into their straitjacket. In his notes, for instance, he began to write about the biographies of "good people" but as soon as he had made reference to the "immense and tragic nature" of his time, it was as though his hand was taken over by another. As if hearing the inevitable question of the interrogator, demanding to know, "Of what tragedy are you speaking?" he continued:

> I suggested that the basic misfortune of these people was that they had not understood the role and importance of Stalin. They had not appreciated in time, that only Stalin had the qualities needed to become leader of the Party and the country. I remember a conversation about Lenin's Testament* (with Eisenstein, I believe) during which it was said that the choice of the Leader for such people as Voronsky was an emotional question and one of private opinions, and that by the very nature of his character, his lyrical inconsistency, Voronsky could not attain a mature and rounded political view.

In this ambiguous passage we can detect a quite different meaning to the propagandist, pro-Stalin views of his contemporaries. Babel was talking of the anti-Stalinist tragedy of "good people" who had not yet perceived the true, murderous nature of Stalin and were doomed because Stalin, and no one else, was fitted to be the ruler of the first socialist country in the world.

When he analyzed his past as a writer, Babel divided it into two periods. During the first he was influenced by the "nationalist principles" of Alexander Voronsky; during the second, by the "Westernizing tendencies" of Ilya Ehrenburg, another old friend.

Many continue to express amazement that Ehrenburg remained untouched when his friends were arrested and shot, one after another. In his own memoirs he also struck an amazed pose and exclaimed, by way of explanation: "Accident! The throw of the dice!" The answer is too facile. According to Babel, Ehrenburg liked to call himself the "Cultural Ambassador of the Soviet Union". The mission he conscientiously performed suited Stalin all too well: just look, it is possible to almost be a Formalist** and citizen of Europe in the USSR – what repression of culture are you complaining about? Had Ehrenburg once overstepped the limits he would have quickly been brought back in line. He was a clever performer, however, and survived to outlive all his friends.

In his notes Babel described Ehrenburg's influence on Soviet writers:

> During his trips to Moscow Ehrenburg stirred up envy of "daring" Western literature (Hemingway, Caldwell, Céline) and of the unlimited

*In 1923 a semi-paralyzed Lenin dictated a letter to the Central Committee, his "Testament", which, in particular, recommended that Stalin be removed as the Party's General Secretary.
**Here Formalism is being used as a catch-all term for artists who did not conform to the canons of Socialist Realism, officially imposed since 1934.

choice of subject accessible to Western writers. For many years he served as a capable and clever propagandist of the most extreme trends in Western literature, battling for their translation into Russian, and contrasting the refined technique and formal richness of Western art with "Russian amateurishness". I repeated exactly the same views and found not only agreement but the clear sympathy of the most varied people: Olesha, Sobolev, Gerasimova, Bergelson, Fink, Boris Levin, Fedin, the film directors Eisenstein, Alexandrov, Raytmann, Solntseva, the Vakhtangov Theatre actors Goryunov and Kuza and P. Markov who headed the literary department at the Moscow Art Theatre.

We shared a negative and often contemptuous attitude to that which seemed to be approved in Soviet literature (with the exception of Sholokhov and [Alexey] Tolstoy) and, on the contrary, inflated the significance of those who were not taking an active part in literary life – Mandelstam, Zabolotsky and Prishvin. It was common ground for us to proclaim the genius of the slighted Shostakovich and to sympathize with Meyerhold. These conversations, of course, were never as clear-cut as that. They contained a mixture of positive and negative views, disbelief went hand in hand with optimism, and the same emotion might be expressed in quite different words. The sources of this literary dissatisfaction, however, were one and the same ... I can recall my last conversation with Fadeev, a few months ago. We talked about the tasks facing Soviet literature and about particular writers. I found a greater will to victory in Fadeev than among others and a passionate determination to put things right. Yet from our conversation I retained the impression that he made the same assessment of the situation as we did, and that we obviously shared the same tastes and aspirations ...

Interrogator. The investigators are not interested in your anti-Soviet conversations so much as your directly hostile activities. Tell the truth, what Trotskyist tasks were you given to carry out?

Having thoroughly examined Babel's attitudes in Russia, the interrogator shifted attention to his trips abroad. Babel remembered that in 1927, during his first visit to Paris, he met the White emigre writers Remizov and Osorgin, the poetess Marina Tsvetaeva, Vadim Andreev, the son of the writer Leonid Andreev, and a group of young poets who came to the flat at 15 rue Villa-Chauvelet where he was staying. Babel could not recall having done anything wrong. He had told his visitors what was going on in the USSR and taken some manuscripts from the younger writers to be published there, but without success. He had petitioned for Vadim Andreev to be allowed to return to Moscow and bought a manuscript work from Remizov (this was immediately entered in the deposition as "provision of material aid" to a White emigre). It was then that he first got to know Ilya Ehrenburg, who soon became his friend, and through him made the acquaintance of the French writers Chamson, Vaillant-Couturier, Moussinac and Nizan.

During his second trip to Paris in 1932–3 Babel not only saw writers who were politically neutral but also those who opposed the Soviet system. The director Alexey Granovsky introduced Babel to the Menshevik Boris Nikolaevsky, who had written a book about Azef, the famous Tsarist agent provocateur. Granovsky wanted to make a film about Azef and had invited both to work on it, Babel to write the screenplay and Nikolaevsky to act as consultant. The interrogator could find nothing seditious here. He merely noted the information that Nikolaevsky had managed to transfer the valuable Karl Marx archive from Berlin to France and that Babel had told his new acquaintance about his journeys through the Ukrainian countryside, vividly depicting "many fearful scenes there and disorganization on a massive scale". This new friendship did not last long. Babel asked Dovgalevsky, the Soviet ambassador in Paris, whether he should work with Nikolaevsky or not. When the former described Nikolaevsky as a dangerous enemy, Babel did not risk a further meeting. Admirable caution!

Neither did Babel's account of his meeting with another opponent of the Soviet regime, Boris Souvarine, yield anything for his interrogators. They became acquainted at the studio of the artist Annenkov. Naturally, they discussed the Soviet Union, the young generation there, and literature; they recalled, with compassion, the internal exile of such Leninist revolutionaries as Radek and Rakovsky and talked about the leading figures in the Comintern. Babel gave Souvarine several Soviet books and, on his return to Moscow, sent him two collections of Lenin's works . . .

Babel made a most unconvincing spy. The interrogator began to display his impatience and tried to secure the needed answer:

> You met widely with foreigners among whom there were many agents of intelligence services. Did none of them ever try to recruit you? . . . We warn you that the slightest attempt to conceal any detail of your hostile activities will be immediately exposed.

It is not hard to guess what lay behind such threats because each time they were made Babel began to provide the most extraordinary confessions:

> In 1933, during my second visit to Paris, I was recruited by the writer André Malraux to spy for France . . .

Babel the Spy

After such a success the interrogator could take a break, ring home, and have a bite to eat. Perhaps he also gave his prisoner something to eat and drink, allow-ing him to recover a little, and remember all the details of his life in Paris. Then he pressed on with the interrogation:

> *Interrogator.* Now tell me where and when you became a spy.
>
> *Babel.* It was in 1933 ... Ehrenburg acquainted me with Malraux, of whom he thought very highly and introduced to me as one of the brilliant representatives of young radical France. During our frequent meetings, Ehrenburg would tell me that the leaders of the most varied ruling groups in France listened to what Malraux had to say, and that his influence would grow as the years passed. This indeed proved true ... I'm referring to Malraux's rapidly growing popularity in and beyond France itself ... Malraux had a high opinion of my work as a writer and Ehrenburg, for his part, advised me to encourage Malraux's support in every possible way. It was essential, Ehrenburg persuaded me, to gain a firm footing on French soil and he considered Malraux the best guarantee of that.
>
> *Interrogator.* It's not clear what you needed a firm footing on French soil for? Did you not have such a firm footing on Soviet soil?
>
> *Babel.* Almost all my family live abroad. My mother and sister live in Brussels and my ten-year-old daughter and first wife live in Paris. So I intended, sooner or later, to settle in France, and I talked about this with Malraux ... He said that at any moment he would be ready to provide the necessary help and, in particular, promised to organize the translation of my works into French.
>
> Malraux went on to say that he had wide contacts in French ruling circles and named among his closest friends Daladier, Blum and Herriot. ... During one of my last meetings with Malraux he already began to talk in more practical terms, declaring that an association made up of those who, like us, thought and felt the same would be important and valuable for the cause of peace and culture.
>
> *Interrogator.* What did Malraux mean when he referred to the "cause of peace and culture"?
>
> *Babel.* Malraux had in mind my espionage work for France ...

It is difficult to say who is speaking at this point. Is it Babel, who has already mastered the "rules of the game" and can now do no more than play up to his interrogator, giving the simplest human relations quite the opposite meaning? Or did the interrogator himself write this reply into the deposition, and then force Babel to sign the bottom of the page? In either case, the falsification is quite evident. The facts that Babel goes on to provide themselves rebut his "confession":

Malraux informed me that he intended to write a big book about the USSR but did not have access to the sources that a writer living permanently in the Soviet Union could provide. Malraux promised to visit the USSR often and suggested in future, when he himself was absent, that we could keep in contact through our common friend Ilya Ehrenburg. *Interrogator.* Clarify the nature of the espionage material that Malraux was interested to receive.

Socialist morality, family life and sport interested him, Babel recalled: so did artistic freedom, the fate of several writers and leading political figures, and, since his French friend was a former airforce pilot, the state of Soviet aviation. Babel himself informed Malraux that the Soviet Union was creating a powerful air force, training up new pilots, building aerodromes, and possessed magnificent aircraft designers like Mikulin and Tupolev. Special importance in the preparations for the coming war was being given to parachute-jumping as a sport and to physical exercise . . .

Information of this kind was available in any Soviet newspaper.

In 1934 Malraux visited Moscow as a guest of the Congress of Soviet Writers* but only briefly saw Babel there. A year later they met again, this time in Paris at the anti-fascist congress "in Defence of Peace and Culture".

It was during the unbearably hot summer of June 1935 that Bertrand Russell, André Gide, Henri Barbusse, Lion Feuchtwanger, Aldous Huxley, Karel Capek, Virginia Woolf and J.B. Priestley and many others gathered in the vast hall of the Mutualité. The Soviet delegation, the largest of all, was headed by a prominent Party figure, Shcherbakov, and the Party journalist, Mikhail Koltsov. Its members were chosen for their loyalty to the Soviet system and they were in belligerent mood, making thunderous ideological pronouncements, challenging their opponents and whipping up the enthusiasm of the audience. Their success can be seen from the warm applause that greeted André Gide when he declared: "For us now the USSR presents a spectacle of incomparable importance and great hope. Only there are there real readers . . ."

Other opinions were voiced, it is true. The Italian anti-fascist Salvemini attempted to bring the audience to its senses: "Is the bitter cold of Siberian villages to which the ideological opponents of the regime are exiled any better than German concentration camps? Is not Trotsky as much an emigre as Heinrich Mann?"

This speech, however, was drowned by indignant cries, and clearly did not match the general mood.

*First and, under Stalin, only congress of the new Writers Union at which the doctrine of Socialist Realism was affirmed.

Two figures stood out incongruously in the Soviet delegation: Babel and Pasternak. Babel now testified in detail about his heretical stance:

> At first I was not included in the Soviet delegation to the Congress and, as I learned later, had been co-opted, together with Pasternak, at the insistence of Malraux. Pasternak and I were given an extremely warm welcome.
>
> *Interrogator.* We are not interested in the warmth of the welcome you received, but in the nature of your treacherous ties with Malraux. Describe them.
>
> *Babel.* Malraux considered that the Soviet delegation had not prepared properly: our speeches were not interesting and only reflected the official point of view. And indeed, certain of these speeches, for instance that of Vsevolod Ivanov, which had been drafted and agreed with the leaders of the Soviet delegation, contained many tactless and unwise remarks. For instance, he said that each writer in the Soviet Union was assured of a definite amount of living space, a kitchen and even a bathroom. Speeches of this kind made a rather comic impression and did not offer any political or artistic analysis of Soviet literature ... It was undoubtedly also a mistake that Kirshon, the most repugnant figure in the Soviet delegation, was allowed to take the stage at the most important moments of the Congress. For instance, it was he who was entrusted to speak in rebuttal of the quite strong Trotskyist wing of the congress, led by the Frenchwoman Magdeleine Paz, when he had no literary or political authority in the eyes of the other delegates ... Together with Ehrenburg, I formed the opposition to the leadership of the Soviet delegation ...

In the notes that he himself wrote, Babel gave a brief sketch of that delegation: "... Not translated abroad, excessive numbers of non-Russian writers, no authoritative figures ... Bickering: Koltsov taking his own line, persuading Shcherbakov, opposed by Ehrenburg, intervention of French writers. My speeches and that of Pasternak delivered in French, of no interest to others ... "

The interrogator demanded that Babel give a very detailed account of Ehrenburg in his notes:

> Ehrenburg maintained constant contact with Malraux and they spoke with one voice over the International Association of Writers.* They visited Spain together and translated each other's works. He passed every kind of information about life in the USSR to Malraux and warned me that I should not converse with anyone or trust anyone other than

*Henri Barbusse set up the International Association of Revolutionary Writers and Artists in 1932.

Malraux. He was extremely sparing with his words, and difficult to make friends with. He always considered it of extreme importance to keep Malraux well-disposed towards the Soviet Union and protested sharply if Soviet representatives did not pay Malraux sufficient attention ...

Furthermore, Soviet writers when they arrived in Paris always visited Ehrenburg first of all. Acquainting them with the city, he would "instruct" them as he thought best. All the writers who visited Paris were subjected to the same treatment: Ilf and Petrov, Kataev, Lidin, Pasternak, Olga Forsh, Nikolay Tikhonov ... Perhaps only Alexey Tolstoy, who had his own circle of acquaintances there, did not rely on Ehrenburg. During the 1935 Congress Tolstoy met with White emigres and was friendly with Maria Budberg.* She went to great lengths to introduce Tolstoy to influential English circles ...

The gruelling, three-day interrogation continued. Babel's interrogators cross-examined him relentlessly about his next meetings with Malraux, in Moscow and then in the Crimea in spring 1936, to which they had travelled together to visit Gorky.

I passed Malraux information about conditions in the collective farms, based on my personal impressions on visits to the villages of the Ukraine. He wanted to know if the Ukraine had recovered from the famine and difficulties of the first years of collectivization ... He also wanted to find out what had happened to the Ukrainian kulaks who had been exiled to the Urals and Siberia. I gave Malraux detailed information about all the questions he raised and gloomily sketched the negative sides of life in the collective farms ...

At the end of 1936 Malraux and Babel exchanged letters. They discussed the campaign against the "Formalists" which had started in the USSR and, in particular, against Shostakovich, the poets Pasternak and Tikhonov and the writers Shklovsky and Olesha. In their next letters they mentioned the death of Gorky, the state of literature, and the trials of Zinoviev and Kamenev, Pyatakov and Radek.** In Babel's opinion the trials "convinced the workers but were arousing incomprehension and a negative reaction among parts of the intelligentsia". Malraux suggested that Babel write a series of articles about collectivization for the *Nouvelle Revue Française*.

Again the interrogator returned to the figure of Ehrenburg who, in his view, must have served as contact between Babel and Malraux.

---

*Effectively Gorky's last wife and, simultaneously, mistress of H.G. Wells. See chapter 12.
**Gorky died on 18 June 1936. Kamenev and Zinoviev were tried in August and immediately executed; Pyatakov and Radek were tried in January 1937.

In 1936 Ehrenburg expressed alarm, following the trials of the Zinovievite-Trotskyists, that his patron Bukharin was now in danger.* He also asked me about the new people in charge of the Party, and Yezhov in particular ... I told Ehrenburg all that I knew about Yezhov, a man with whom I was personally acquainted ...

It was at this point that the name of Yezhov, Stalin's "Iron Commissar" and until 1938 the man in charge of the Great Purges, first appeared in Babel's testimony. Babel not only knew Yezhov personally: fate decreed that their lives were inextricably bound together.

I told Ehrenburg all that I knew about Yezhov ... and then I sketched the state of affairs within the Party, as I understood them. The most important aspect, I considered, was that the time for discussion and educated, analytical individuals had passed. The Party, just like the country as a whole, I told Ehrenburg, was being put on a war footing. Not only new methods and new people were needed now, but a new type of literature: one that presented simple political messages and offered unthinking entertainment ...

During his last visit to Moscow in summer 1938 Ehrenburg was very upset that his own position in the Soviet Union had been undermined. He was extremely scared he might not be given an exit visa, and this reduced him to such a state that he refused to leave his apartment. Our conversation constantly returned to two subjects. First, the arrests. In Ehrenburg's view, the continual wave of arrests forced all Soviet citizens to break off any relations with foreigners. Second, we discussed the civil war in Spain ...

Babel provided additional information about this last meeting in his own notes. When the arrests came up in conversation, he expressed "his usual idea that there should be a freer atmosphere in the court" and Ehrenburg agreed with him. Babel also let his friend know about the clouds that were gathering over the Yezhov family. A close family friend Simeon Uritsky had been arrested and Yezhov's wife,** an editor at the *SSSR v stroike*† journal where Babel also worked, was in a tense and nervous state: there was gossip at work that her husband had taken to drink and that they were no longer on good terms ...

About the other, Spanish, theme Babel wrote:

I told him that the war would end in defeat ... He, I remember, said that for all the muddle, incompetence and often treachery, the front in Spain

*Bukharin was tried in March 1938 and immediately executed.
**Yezhov's wife Yevgenia was married first to Alexander Gladun, then to Khayutin, and is variously referred to as Khayutina-Gladun, Khayutina-Yezhova, Gladun-Yezhova and Yezhova.
†(Lit. USSR in Construction).

was the only place where one could breathe freely. Since it would come to an end sooner or later, all that remained was to flee to the Soviet Union (which did not suit him), where force and a new discipline were the only way forward (and so much the worse for us). He indicated that now he was most interested by the new cadres in the Party, the Soviets and the economy, people who had grown up entirely during the Soviet period, and by the problem of replacing those cadres which had proved unsatisfactory ...

It is difficult to say how frank Babel was about Yezhov in his conversations with Ehrenburg. But when, towards the end of this first interrogation, his tormentors began to probe the secrets of his private life Babel was forced to tell them the whole story. This linked him directly to Yezhov's wife and his interrogators stubbornly pursued the subject, determined to give it a criminal and political slant.

> *Interrogator.* The investigators are aware of your intimate ties and spying connections with the English intelligence agent Yevgenia Khayutina-Yezhova. Do not try to hide the facts from us. Give us a truthful account of your relations with Yezhova.
>
> *Babel.* I first became acquainted with Yevgenia Yezhova in 1927 in Berlin, where I stopped on my way to Paris. She was then married to a certain Gladun and worked as a typist at the Soviet commercial mission in Germany. The very first day there I visited the commercial mission and met Ionov, whom I had known before in Moscow. He invited me to his flat that evening and it was there that I got to know Gladun. As I recall she greeted me with the words: "You don't know me but I know you well. I saw you once at a New Year's celebration in a Moscow restaurant."
>
> We drank a good deal and then I invited Gladun to drive around the city in a taxi. She agreed enthusiastically. In the taxi I persuaded her to come back to the hotel with me. There, in those furnished rooms, we became intimate and maintained our contacts until I left Berlin ...

Babel was abroad for the first time. The wine and the taxi-ride went to his head, and beside him sat a woman who gave herself readily, but who would in time prove fatal to all her three husbands and to her new lover.

> At the end of 1928 Gladun was already living in Moscow and had begun working as a typist at the *Krestyanskaya gazeta** edited by Simeon Uritsky. When I returned to Moscow we resumed our intimate relations, visiting a room that Gladun kept for the purpose in Kuskovo outside Moscow ...

* (Lit. Peasant Paper): Central Committee publication, 1929–39.

His interrogators were dissatisfied. They had forced from him the details of his private life for the sole purpose of uncovering his activities as a spy. But in return they received a quite categorical reply:

I know nothing about any Gladun-Yezhova's spying connections ... In political terms, Gladun was then a typical little "featherhead",* who parroted others' words and spouted all the usual Trotskyist terminology ... In the latter part of 1929 we ceased to meet and I lost touch with her. Some time later I learnt that she had married a leading official in the People's Commissariat of Agriculture called Yezhov, and had moved into a flat with him on Strastnoi Boulevard ...

I made the acquaintance of Yezhov either in 1932 or 1933 when he was already the deputy head of the Central Committee's personnel department. I avoided visiting him too often since I detected a hostile attitude on his part. It seemed to me that he was aware of my ties with his wife and that it would strike him as suspicious if I was too frequent a visitor. I saw him only five or six times in my life, the last being at his dacha in summer 1936 when I brought my friend the actor Leonid Utyosov to visit. When we met we never discussed politics. The same was true of his wife who, as her husband's career advanced, outwardly adopted the manners of an ultra-Soviet woman.

Interrogator. For what purpose did Yezhova encourage you to work for the *SSSR v stroike?*

Babel. It was indeed Yezhova who invited me to work for the journal, of which she was effectively the chief editor. With occasional intervals, I worked there from 1936 until the day of my arrest. I most often met Yezhova in her official capacity as editor and from summer 1936 onwards, she never again invited me to her home ... All I recall is that once I handed her a letter from the widow of the poet Bagritsky, appealing to her to intercede for Vladimir Narbut, her arrested brother-in-law. Yezhova refused, however, claiming that her husband did not discuss his work with her ... That is all I can tell you about my relations with the Yezhov family.

The interrogation was coming to an end. All were tired. The interrogators did make one more attempt, it is true, to establish that Babel had enjoyed criminal ties with Trotsky himself and with his son Lev Sedov. Yet when he denied it, they decided that was enough. They would not leave him in peace, though, they promised, until he had disclosed all his "hostile secrets".

*An allusion to the story by Chekhov, "Dushechka", whose heroine, several times married, each time adopted the views of her very different husbands.

The interrogators had not succeeded thus far in establishing any evidence or proof of Babel's activities as a spy or saboteur, and there was, of course, none to be obtained. They did have a confession, however, and could report back to their superiors. The following letter has been preserved in the correspondence files of the NKVD:

> Highly confidential
> 7 June 1939
> To Central Committee, Comrade Zhdanov
>
> I hereby enclose the deposition of the cross-examination of prisoner Isaac Babel, former member of the Union of Soviet Writers, dated 29-31 May 1939, concerning his work as an anti-Soviet spy.
> The investigation is continuing.
> USSR People's Commissar of Internal Affairs,
> Beria

It was Zhdanov who was in charge of literature at the Central Committee and was now keeping a special eye on the Babel case. Meanwhile, his fellow writers had also been petitioning:

> USSR Union of Soviet Writers
> USSR Litfond*
> 8 June 1939
> Confidential
> To USSR People's Commissar of Internal Affairs, Comrade L.P. Beria
>
> On 22 May this year the NKVD sealed a dacha belonging to the Litfond of the USSR Union of Soviet Writers which was temporarily at the disposal of the writer Babel, now under arrest by the NKVD ... The board of the Litfond of the USSR Union of Soviet Writers requests you, Comrade Beria, to issue an instruction transferring the said dacha to the Litfond to be further used for its original purpose, by offering it to members of the Writers Union for their work and recreation.
> Chairman of the board of the USSR Litfond,
> K. Fedin
> Director of the Litfond,
> Oskin

To the letter has been added the resolution "To be transferred" and the signature Lavrenty Beria.

*The Litfond or Literary Foundation was originally established in 1859 by Turgenev, Chernyshevsky and others to aid writers. Closed after the Revolution, it was restored in 1934 as part of the new monopolist Writers Union.

Less than a month had passed since Babel was arrested. The investigation had barely begun, his guilt was not proved and the trial was still far away: yet the writers were already trying to get their hands on his dacha and had given him up for dead.

A Terrorist Trotskyist

On 10 June Babel was again called for interrogation. This time his interrogators Kuleshov and Serikov cross-examined him about his ties with military leaders who had already been arrested and shot. For the most part these were former commanders of the Red Cossack corps (Primakov, Schmidt, Ziuka, Kuzmichev – the "Trotskyist cavalrymen", as the investigators called them) and commanders of certain other units (Okhotnikov, Dreitser and Putna). By this time Babel had already prepared his own notes which served as a basis for the interrogation.

First he drew up a plan:

> Describe the Red Cossack corps. Decorated with numerous awards, they never regarded me as a political figure. I was famous then, they eagerly made my acquaintance. When did I learn about the trials; they took pity on me and encouraged me to write. They said I was being passed over . . . I was a trump card in their anti-Soviet environment . . . They gave me many themes. Military subjects – their stories – a living chronicle – a halo of heroism . . .

Then Babel developed the set theme in more detail in his notes:

> What linked us together? First of all, their ecstatic and unconditional admiration for my cavalry stories (I am not boasting, simply trying to recreate a true picture of the time). They knew these stories almost by heart and passionately sang their praises on all appropriate and inappropriate occasions. I could not help enjoying this or becoming friendly with these people. I was attracted also by the glory that attached to them as heroes of the Civil War; at first sight, their striking characters and their easygoing and noisy comradeship won me over . . .
>
> I was then considered to be something of a "war writer" and I moved mainly in military circles. They told me all about their private lives and I followed them with interest, considering that the trajectory of their exceptional biographies offered invaluable material for a writer. I knew of their Trotskyist views in 1924-27 but not one of them murmured a word about the crimes they were planning . . .
>
> Always on the look out for "interesting people" and not finding them

close to hand, we were attracted to their demonstrative bravery, reck-
lessness and uninhibited comradeship and struck by the levity with
which they treated things we were accustomed to regard with respect.
In this way the path along which a Soviet writer should advance (I am
speaking of myself now) was obscured, my sense of the future distorted,
and the inner and artistic crisis that has led me to my downfall began to
develop...

All Babel's acquaintances and friends were undeniably suspicious figures. Yet
where was the evidence of his counter-revolutionary activities? Marking time,
the interrogators again returned to literature and the arts and demanded testimony about the organization that Babel supposedly founded and headed.

> *Babel.* I shall begin with the film director Eisenstein. Throughout 1937
> I worked with him on the production of *Bezhin Meadow*... Eisenstein
> considered that the organizers of the Soviet film industry were prevent-
> ing gifted individuals from revealing their talents to the full... His artistic
> failures enabled me to conduct anti-Soviet conversations with him, in
> which I argued that there was no place for the gifted in the USSR and that
> the policies of the Party towards the arts prevented creative innovative
> work, artistic independence and the demonstration of genuine skill...
>
> Just as frequently, I met with Solomon Mikhoels, the head of the
> Jewish State Theatre. With reason, he considered himself an outstand-
> ing actor and was constantly dissatisfied that the Soviet repertoire gave
> him no chance to demonstrate the extent of his talents. He was extremely
> disapproving of the plays of Soviet dramatists, which he contrasted with
> the repertoire of old and classic plays...

Then Babel talked of the writer Yury Olesha:

> I have known Olesha ever since I lived in Odessa during the first years
> after the October Revolution. Then, when we both became writers, we also
> became personal friends, sharing the same literary tastes and views...
> *Interrogator.* The investigators are not interested in literary tastes but in
> Olesha's anti-Soviet attitudes.
> *Babel.* I was coming to that. Olesha's acute disappointment with his fate
> as a writer, and the collapse of his lengthy attempts to create something
> new, reduced him to a state of despair. Today he is, perhaps, the most
> striking representative of the bohemian section of disorientated and
> desperate writers... His tireless outbursts in taverns were a form of live
> agitation against the literary policy whereby writers such as Olesha
> could barely make a living and were forced to kick up the kind of fuss
> that he did. One such public row succeeded another and in this respect

47

he was following in Yesenin's footsteps. He used to publicly attack particular representatives of Soviet literature, yelling: "You have stolen my money! You are using my money, stealing my success, and taking away my readers. I demand only one thing – that I be allowed the right to despair!"

That was his favourite theory. He made of his struggle for the "right to despair" a literary banner which, one might say, enjoyed no little success in attracting both writers and people working in films . . .

If Olesha, in an effort to preserve his human dignity, asserted his right to despair, then Babel insisted on his right to be silent. At the first Congress of Soviet Writers in 1934 he joked eloquently: "My respect for the reader is so great that I keep quiet and do not speak. I have been acknowledged as a great master in the art of silence . . ."

After describing each member of his "anti-Soviet group", Babel turned to its "subversive" activities:

We either ignored the outstanding works of Soviet literature or were dismissive of them, instead praising lone individuals who had not played an active part in the country's literary life . . . When talking with young authors I praised the White emigre writers Bunin and Khodasevich and was sharply critical of the main contingent of Soviet literature. Sympathetically I conveyed the state of tormenting crisis in which the former supporters of Voronsky now found themselves, and appealed for "objectivity" . . .

We interpreted Mayakovsky's suicide as the poet's conclusion that it was impossible to work under Soviet conditions. We declared that the articles opposing Shostakovich were a campaign against a genius. We attributed Eisenstein's artistic failures to the hostile efforts of Soviet officials responsible for the film industry.

We made every attempt to get in contact with the educated West . . .

It was not enough to make Babel a French spy: he had to be linked to the Austrian intelligence service as well. To do so, it was sufficient that he knew Bruno Steiner, the representative of an Austrian firm in Moscow, and had for a time shared his Moscow flat. Once again there was no proof of espionage and it remained unclear exactly what information Babel could have transmitted to Steiner. Furthermore, in his own written testimony Babel completely rejected all such suspicions. The investigation had reached an impasse and wavered to and fro, searching for any kind of incriminating evidence. Falling back once more on the link with Yezhov's wife, the interrogators again proposed the most improbable fabrication.

Babel was forced to sign testimony that his former mistress had confided in him the plans to assassinate Stalin and Klim Voroshilov, the People's Commissar for Defence, that she had been making with the head of the Komsomol, Kosarev. Dozens of people were supposedly involved. The plotters intended to kill the two leaders in the Caucasus or in Yezhov's apartment in the Kremlin or, if that failed, at a dacha outside Moscow . . . Yevgenia Yezhova had requested Babel to act as no less than recruiting agent for those who would perpetrate this wicked act. He immediately listed the young writers and journalists he knew as the potential villains in this drama. Moreover, he supposedly also knew of the terrorist conspiracy being hatched by Yezhov himself.

Babel, it seems, was no longer resisting but agreed to everything that the interrogators demanded. Perhaps he nursed the secret hope that the more absurd the story became, the more obvious his innocence would appear.

Having thoroughly confused their charge and themselves lost track of their argument, the interrogators broke off the cross-examination.

The leader of the anti-Soviet writers' organization was left, waiting in his cell. Meanwhile, the interrogators were busily at work. A certain Rayzman of the Security Administration's 2nd department requested those excerpts from the testimony of Babel and Mikhail Koltsov (also now under arrest) that referred to the writers Ehrenburg and Olesha. The senior interrogator, Schwartzmann, gave his permission: "Comrade Serikov, provide the necessary quotations . . ."

No one had yet been charged but new victims were already being selected. Babel's arrest, evidently, was just an opening manoeuvre. Beria and his associates had decided to invent an "anti-Soviet organization" among writers in order to destroy the most independent and gifted of them, extracting the evidence from the writers themselves during interrogation. Let them incriminate one another!

The investigators scraped together whatever they could find in the depths of the Lubyanka by way of compromising material about Babel. They uncovered his note to Noah Bliskovetsky who had sought the famous writer's opinion about his work:

Dear Noah Markovich,
I liked the chapter. It reads easily and simply (that means, it's been well thought through) and the first pages start with considerable zest. If you have written any more, please do send it. You must type it up and then I can add notes in the margins about particular phrases. I have the impression that it could make a good book and that you must continue. Write to me.
30 November 1934, Yours,
Isaac Babel

This was also sewn into the investigation file as evidence, although it is hard to detect anything criminal in its words.

On 19 June Babel was allowed to read the decree defining the pre-trial restrictions imposed on him and the charges that would be brought. From this document he learned that there was already "sufficient testimony to convict him" under four different sections of Article 58 (Counter-revolutionary crimes) – as a member of a Trotskyist organization, for having worked as a spy, and for having prepared a terrorist act against the leaders of the Party and the government ...

One more example illustrates how the case against Babel was put together. On 21 June the writer prepared the next portion of notes and four days later the interrogators renewed their efforts to find out something more about the "criminal" ties between Babel and Malraux. Again we can trace how the interrogator took what Babel had written and reworked his words.

> *Babel.* As a result of the Paris Congress, Malraux had the idea of setting up a monthly journal which would promote the counter-revolutionary ideas of André Gide under the cover of "artistic" independence.
> *Interrogator.* What practical steps did Malraux take towards setting up such a journal?
> *Babel.* Nothing came of it, in fact, since Malraux went off to Spain in 1936 and I never saw him again. That is all that I wish to tell you.
> *Interrogator.* That is far from all. What role was this journal supposed to play in your spying activities?
> *Babel.* I know nothing about that.

From Babel's own notes we learn that one of the editors of the proposed journal was to have been Gorky. When the interrogators drew up the record of their cross-examination, however, they removed his highly respectable name from the "black list" of participants. For the same reason, probably, the interrogators made no use of Babel's account of how the idea of the journal began to be put into practice, although this is the most interesting part of the story:

> Malraux came to see Gorky about the idea in spring 1936. He tried to obscure its anti-Soviet essence with grandiose plans for the [International] Association [of Writers] to publish a new encyclopaedia of culture, and with provocative talk about the decline in literary standards and the purely humanitarian aims of the new publications. Outstanding Western writers were indeed successfully involved in the journal idea. When Feuchtwanger was in Moscow he told me of his intention to publish a series of articles about the Soviet Union in the journal, and said that a number of other pieces had been submitted by Dreiser (about American censorship), Rafael Alberti (about young

Spanish writers) and by certain French authors. I also sent Malraux a story that had been blocked by the Soviet censors, and articles about Soviet films and the new working-class family in the USSR (based on material about the Korobovs). My review of Soviet film-making was negative. I was sharply critical of the artistic methods of Soviet directors and characterized the screenplays (with the exception of *Chapaev** and *We Are from Kronstadt***) as being colourless and schematic. The tone and contents of this article agreed with the basic assessment that Soviet art was in decline. I do not know what happened to these articles, which I sent via Roland Malraux. The civil war in Spain prevented André Malraux from carrying out his plan to publish such a journal and I lost touch with him in 1939 . . .

In the notes Babel then continued his confession:

What did I say to writers and film-makers when they asked me for advice? I told them about the "theory of sincerity" and of the necessity for working to deepen their artistic individuality, no matter whether society needed it or not. "A book is the world seen through an individual", and the less restrained and more complete that personal revelation, no matter what the nature of the writer, the greater the artistic merits of his works. Neither moral nor public considerations should stand in the way of this revelation of the individual and his style. If you are fundamentally flawed, then perfect this flaw in yourself and raise it to the level of art. The opposition of society and your readers should push you towards a still more stubborn defence of your positions, but not towards a change in your basic methods of work . . .

We hardly find any theoretical reflections about art and the role of the writer in Babel's books. He thought in images, like a poet. How much more important, then, is this enforced exposition of his artistic credo for which the interrogators could find no use at all. Perhaps he committed it to paper because he sensed there would be no other chance. Perhaps there was even a secret calculation that one day, suddenly, his notes might be read by another reader, and not just his interrogators. Yet this was no essay about his works, he remembered. The tone changes:

Giving formal approval to Soviet subject matter, in practice I sowed doubts. I alarmed writers and artists, who yearned to depict living reality, chilling their enthusiasm with outwardly convincing arguments about the standardization of their art and its use by the state. The reader would

*A film by Sergey and Georgy Vasiliev, 1934.
**A film by Yefim Dzigan, 1936.

be obliged to accept them, I said, but inwardly feel repulsed ... These "theories" led to painful contradictions, the collapse of personal and artistic values, and created an atmosphere of dissatisfaction and discontent.

Babel went on to describe his closest friends.

In conversations with Eisenstein in 1936 and 1937, the main theme was the need to find a subject that would emphasize, rather than dilute, his negative qualities, i.e. Eisenstein's tendency towards mysticism, trick effects and naked formalism. Stubbornly, we continued to work on the flawed *Bezhin Meadow*, with considerable expense of time and money, a film in which the death of the Pioneer Pavlik Morozov took on the nature of a religious, mystical performance of Catholic extravagance.

My talks with Mikhoels, who was trying by every means fair and foul to get my excluded play *Sunset* back in the repertoire, were of the same kind. So were those with Goriunov, one of the managers of the Vakhtangov Theatre, who wanted my play *Maria*, banned by the State Repertory Committee, to be allowed again. Their efforts to get my plays back on the stage went hand in hand with our propaganda against the current Soviet repertoire and its supporters, and against the new policies of the Moscow Art Theatre. Its productions of such plays as *Enemies, Earth* and *Dostigaev and Others** were, we declared, inevitable and predictable failures. The attention devoted to the best theatre in the country had created a hothouse atmosphere, we said, and this was dulling the brilliance and innovation that formerly distinguished its work ... Our love for the People was artificial and theoretical and our concern for their future, simply an aesthetic category. We had no roots among the People, hence the despair and nihilism that we disseminated.

One of the missionaries of such despair was my fellow Odessan Olesha, whom I have known for 20 years. He deported himself as the living embodiment of the damage inflicted on "art" by the Soviet system. A gifted man, he attracted young writers and actors who bore grudges, or were cheap sceptics and high-living failures, with his passionate denunciations of this harmful influence. His film *A Severe Young Man* cost the Kiev film studios several million roubles to make and then turned out to be an indescribable lampoon of the Komsomol. It was never released and the costs had to be written off. His other film *The Bog Soldiers* received a frosty, almost hostile, reception from the public which only made him more embittered. Nothing came of his attempts,

Enemies (1935-6 season) and *Dostigaev and Others* (1938-9 season) were plays by Gorky; *Earth* (1937-8 season) was written by Nikolay Virta.

over many years, to write a play (widely advertised before he had ever written it). This inevitable and predictable series of failures placed him in the ranks of complaining, embittered and resentful people ... Quite naturally, neither I nor Olesha nor Eisenstein were operating in a vacuum in 1936-7 and we felt the mute but, to us, clear sympathy of a great many other artists and writers: Valeria Gerasimova, Shklovsky, Pasternak, Boris Levin, Sobolev and many others. This sympathy exacted a heavy toll since the flaw of inner confusion and impotence could also be felt in their work ...

Babel was incriminating his friends. Yet we should not be quick to condemn or pardon him from our safe distance. Interrogation by the NKVD reduced individuals to a point where they were no longer responsible for their words. Emotional torture, added to the physical torments they suffered, drove them to a mental disorder verging on insanity. In his letter to Molotov, Meyerhold described this condition:

> ... There was one other terrible circumstance that contributed to my collapse, and total loss of control over myself.... Immediately after my arrest I was cast into the deepest depression by the obsessive thought, "This is what I deserve!" The government thought, so I began to convince myself, that the sentence I had received ... was not sufficient ... for my sins ... and that I must undergo yet another punishment, that which the NKVD was carrying out now. "This is what I deserve!" I repeated to myself and I split into two individuals. The first started searching for the "crimes" of the second, and when they could not be found, he began to invent them. The interrogator proved an effective and experienced assistant and, working closely together, we began our composition. When my fantasy started running out, the interrogators took over ... they prepared and revised the depositions (some were rewritten three or four times) ...
>
> I still could not think at all clearly because a Damoclean sword dangled over me: constantly the interrogator repeated, threateningly, "If you won't write (invent, in other words?!) then we shall beat you again, leaving your head and your right arm untouched but reducing the rest to a hacked, bleeding and shapeless body." And I signed everything ...

False testimony against themselves and against others was torn from individuals reduced to the final stages of suffering. There were cases when the person being interrogated averted violence, aware that he could not withstand it. One inmate of the Lubyanka, a BBC correspondent, announced: "I shall say everything you want. As an Englishman I cannot permit myself to be beaten about the face."

In all of Babel's testimony, which was distorted for the ulterior purposes of the interrogators, he never provides one instance of criminal activity by his friends. Yet even this degree of incrimination would torment him unbearably until his last hour.

At the end of his own notes, Babel again talked of himself in remarks that balance between truthfulness and his false role as penitent:

> The gaze of many was fixed on me. After a lengthy silence people expected major, brilliant and life-affirming works and my silence became a trump card for anti-Soviet-minded literary circles. Over the last years, I had only published a few short stories ("Di Grasso", "The Kiss", "The Court" and "Stupak"). These were of insignificant content, infinitely removed from the interests of socialist construction and they irritated and disheartened the reading masses. I should add that I was also preparing major works at this time (the drafts have been found among my papers) but they were not proceeding smoothly and I was painfully aware of their insincerity. I sensed the contradiction between my unchanged and abstractly "humanistic" viewpoint and the works about the New Man that the Soviet reading audience was waiting for, books that in artistic form explained the present and pointed forward into the future.
>
> Gorky's words were confirmed: he had often spoken to me about the dead end that awaited me. He made a great effort to bring me back to Soviet literature and during our conversations he demonstrated a warm-hearted consideration and passionate concern for Soviet art. It was a great cause of distress for him to realize that I, one of his pupils, disregarded his wise, cautioning voice and deceived the (perhaps exaggerated) hopes that were placed on me. The voice was heeded, but late – among my papers may be found the draft I had begun to make of a comedy and of tales about myself that were an attempt at merciless self-denunciation, a desperate and belated attempt to make good the harm I had done to Soviet art. A feeling of duty and a sense of public service never guided my literary work. Writers and artists who came into contact with me felt the fatal influence of this emasculated and sterile view of the world. The harm my activities caused cannot be quantitatively assessed, but it was great. One of the soldiers on the literary front who enjoyed the support and attention of the Soviet reader when he began his work, and who had been guided by Gorky, the greatest writer of our era, I deserted my post and opened the front of Soviet literature to decadent and defeatist emotions . . .

Denunciations

At the Lubyanka they were not concerned about legal niceties. "Show me a man, and I'll show you the law to fix him!" One and a half months after Babel's arrest procurator Raginsky finally signed and approved the arrest warrant. First they seized an individual, in other words, then they put together some justification for removing him from society.

The investigators had worked their way through a mound of case files that contained some mention, however slight, of Babel. This, probably, explains the delay in producing the warrant. If his name occurred, after all, he must be an accomplice.

As long ago as 1934 Babel's acquaintance Dmitry Gaevsky (condemned to be shot as a "Trotskyist terrorist") had testified:

> Since Stalin and the Central Committee were the soul and organizing force behind the Five Year Plan, consistency obliged us to concentrate our fire on those targets, using the resources at our disposal. Since it was impossible to make a frontal attack we prepared the way by a quiet, cowardly undermining manoeuvre, using anecdotes, slanders, rumours and gossip . . . We had first to render the opponent pathetic in order to finish him off more easily later. The leaders invented this underhand weapon . . . and its role was, from day to day, to spread these creations . . . out to the provinces and deep inside the Party. There were several work-shops where this weapon was prepared. Okhotnikov, Schmidt, Dreitser and Babel were responsible for this activity . . .

We shall never know what Gaevsky actually said. The semi-literate parody of the interrogator is quite apparent here. Gaevsky's testimony was so absurd and comic that it made no further appearance during Babel's investigation. It was quoted in the arrest warrant, however.

Alexander Gladun, former director of the Kharkov machine-tool building works, provided the following testimony (he had also been condemned to be shot as a "Trotskyist terrorist"):

> I first saw Babel in our apartment at 20 Tverskoi Boulevard; he was invited home by my former wife Yevgenia Khayutina. He was especially indignant about Party policy towards literature: "They print any kind of rubbish," he declared, "but they won't print me, Babel" . . .

The testimony of another "Trotskyist terrorist", Simeon Uritsky, was also quoted. (The former director of the All-Union Book Chamber,* Uritsky had also

---

*Organization compiling bibliographical information on all books and articles published in the Soviet Union.

been condemned to be shot.) In this case the interrogator unashamedly manipulated the material: Uritsky had only been interrogated on 22 May but now his testimony was being cited in support of Babel's arrest a week earlier:

> In 1928 and 1929 I went to parties given by Gladun (his wife Yevgenia had been my mistress since 1924) and there, apart from Gladun and Yezhov, I often met the writer Babel who took part in our anti-Soviet conversations.
>
> Later, in 1935, I learned from Yevgenia that she had been Babel's mistress as well. Once, when she was tidying up her room in my presence, she came across some letters from Babel. She treasured these letters, she told me. Later she said that Yezhov had rummaged through her wardrobe searching for letters from Babel, which he knew existed, but did not find them. I have told you about this incident because these letters are undoubtedly of interest.
>
> I was often there when they met: in her flat in Kiselny Street (when Babel was sometimes accompanied by the actor Utyosov), at Zina Glikina's salon, or in the offices of the *SSSR v stroike*. During these meetings I became convinced that Babel held Trotskyist views. I asked him why he did not write. He replied that an author must be sincere in what he writes but that his sincere views could not be printed, because they were not in tune with the Party line. He felt, he would say, that he must publish at least something, and that his silence was becoming a clear anti-Soviet statement . . .

In the original record of Uritsky's interrogation Babel's remark is actually expressed in different words: ". . . his silence was becoming dangerously eloquent . . ." The interrogator had edited the text to suit his purpose.

> *Uritsky*. I recall one meeting at Zina Glikina's salon, soon after the trial of the military.* Babel was in a very bad mood. I asked him why and Yevgenia answered for him: "There are people very close to Babel among the condemned." As I walked her back to the Kremlin,** we talked about Babel. Yevgenia said that he was very close to a great many Ukrainian Trotskyists in the army, that their friendship was firm and political, and that each arrest of a leading military figure predetermined the necessity for Babel's own arrest. Only his European fame could save him . . .

*On 11 June 1937 the press announced that numerous leading military figures (including Marshal Tukhachevsky, Generals Yakir, Uborevich and Primakov) had been arrested. The following day their execution after a closed trial was reported.
**Yezhov and his wife then had an apartment in the Kremlin.

Again the interrogator has altered the text. Uritsky spoke of the "possibility", not the "necessity", of Babel's arrest. Such apparently petty details demonstrate the methods of the Lubyanka. The discrepancies between many dates and facts in the testimonies of various people did not disturb them at all, everything was grist to their mill.

Yet where was the proof? At this point, "information from agents" makes its appearance in the file.

> Information from agents over the period from 1934 to 1939 confirms the counter-revolutionary Trotskyist activities of Babel. A source reported that . . .

"Information from agents" were denunciations and the "sources" were secret agents or informers. Their identities remain firmly concealed in other top secret safes. Babel had been under surveillance since 1934, and not so much by the full-time agents of the NKVD as by a great variety of people, including his fellow-writers. For reasons of envy, loyalty to the regime or obligation to the security forces they informed on him.

Ironically, thanks to their efforts, we can now learn some of Babel's thoughts of the time that he could not then publish or even trust to paper.

In February 1938 "a source reported":

> Babel began to talk about Yezhov. He had seen how things stood in the Yezhov family, he said, and that one close friend of the family after another was being arrested. Babel knew that he was in line as well, and so if he talked about this then it would only be to his friends. He let Kataev and some others know something about his friendship with Yezhov.
>
> Babel said that he was very worried: German specialists (the advisers Pepelman and Steiner) had lived with him and were "close friends". Now he was afraid that he had told them too much in 1936 before they left the USSR. "I have a feeling that the Germans will send someone to recruit me . . ."

In November 1938 the "source reported" on Babel's reaction to the trial of the "Right-Trotskyist Bloc". Babel nourished no illusions.

> It was a monstrous trial. It was monstrous in the narrow-minded way it trivializes every issue. Bukharin evidently tried to raise the trial to a theoretical level but was not permitted. They quite deliberately selected disgraceful criminals, Tsarist secret policemen and spies like Sharangovich (I was told awful things about the way he behaved in Belorussia – excluding people from the Party, organizing provocations etc.) to set alongside Bukharin, Rykov, Rakovsky and Rozengolts.

Rakovsky was actually a landowner's son, it's true, but he gave all his money to the revolution. They will die in the conviction that the political tendency they represent has perished, and with it the Communist Revolution. Trotsky convinced them, after all, that Stalin's victory meant the end of the Revolution . . .

The Soviet system only survives thanks to ideology. Without it all would have been over 10 years ago. It was ideology that enabled them to carry out the sentence on Kamenev and Zinoviev. People are becoming as accustomed to the arrests as to the weather. The subservience with which the Party and members of the intelligentsia accept the idea of imprisonment is horrifying. All this is typical of a state regime.

Just before Babel's arrest the "source" reports:

In February 1939 Babel said: "The present leadership of the Party know perfectly well what people like Rakovsky, Sokolnikov, Radek, Koltsov and so on, represent. They just won't say so in public. They are marked with the stamp of great talent, and stand head and shoulders above the mediocrities of the present leadership. Yet once the latter have the slightest access to power, they become merciless: arrest! execute! . . .

Yet what was the immediate pretext for Babel's arrest in May 1939? Not one of those quoted so far, including the informers, had testified that the writer had committed serious crimes, such as espionage. All they had noted were his critical remarks about the regime. There was one man, however, who had made such accusations and was now somewhere nearby, in a similar cell at the Lubyanka.

In Babel's investigation file there is an excerpt from the deposition of Nikolay Yezhov on 11 May 1939. Five days before Babel's arrest, the former head of the Secret Police had the following dialogue with his interrogator (the same Kobulov who signed Babel's arrest warrant):

Q. It is not entirely clear why Yevgenia Yezhova's friendliness with these people struck you as suspicious.
A. I found it suspicious because I knew that Babel, for instance, had written hardly anything during the last few years and spent all his time in dubious Trotskyist company. Furthermore, he was closely linked to a number of French writers who could in no way be considered sympathetic to the Soviet Union. Not to mention the fact that Babel emphatically declined to bring his wife, who has lived for years in Paris, back to the USSR but preferred to travel there to see her . . .

Yezhova was particularly friendly towards Babel . . . I suspect, though only on the basis of my personal observations, that my wife and Babel were also involved together as spies . . .

With one blow, Yezhov took revenge both on his wife and her former lover. The blow was carefully judged, and he knew what would follow. Rather than admit his jealousy, he found it easier to call his rival a spy.

Q. What evidence do you have for such an assertion?
A. I heard from my wife herself that she had known Babel since approximately 1925. She always assured me that she had never been intimate with Babel. Their ties were limited to her wish to keep in touch with a talented and original writer. Babel visited us several times at home, at her invitation, and I, naturally, met him as well.

I observed that in his dealings with my wife Babel was demanding and rude and I could see that my wife was simply afraid of him. I realized that the explanation lay in something more serious than my wife's literary interests. I excluded the possibility that they were having an affair because Babel would hardly be as rude to my wife when he knew the position I occupied.

When I asked my wife several times if she also had the same relations with Babel as with Koltsov, she either kept silent or weakly denied it. I always supposed that she replied in this non-committal way simply to conceal from me her spying connections with Babel. Evidently she did not wish to let me know all the numerous channels through which she maintained her contacts . . .

Babel was given this document to read, and signed a chit in the file that he had done so. In this way he learned the immediate cause of his arrest. In the charge sheet the slanderous denunciation by Yezhov would take pride of place: "unmasked by the testimony of N.I. Yezhov, an arrested member of the conspiracy . . ."

In October 1938 Yevgenia Yezhova entered a sanatorium near Moscow, diagnosed as suffering from a mild manic-depressive disorder, "asthenic-depressive condition (perhaps cyclothymia?)". The country's best doctors treated her but in a month she was dead. The autopsy describes her as "a woman of 34, medium height, well-developed physique . . ." and entered the cause of death as an overdose of luminal. Possibly it was a case of suicide. However, the sentence on Yezhov alleged he had "organized a number of murders of those he wished removed, including his wife . . ."

On 7 December 1938 Yezhov was dismissed. Beria replaced him as People's Commissar of Internal Affairs and four months later, after Stalin's usual cat and mouse game, Yezhov was himself imprisoned on 10 April 1939. Yet even then he continued his bloody career, dragging down his wife's first husband, Khayutin, and, finally, the writer Isaac Babel . . .

A typical Bolshevik of the Stalin era, the diminutive "Iron Commissar" or, as Trotsky called him, Marshal of the Secret Police, would request before he was shot: "Please let Stalin know that I shall die with his name on my lips."

What was it that drew Babel to the Yezhov family, like a moth towards a candle? Above all else, it was his professional interest as a writer. He had worked for a long time on a book about the Cheka, gathering material, talking to leading Chekists, eagerly listening to their stories, and jotting down remarks in his notebook. There were even rumours that a few copies of his "novel about the Cheka" had been printed for Stalin and members of the Politburo but not met with approval. Most probably this is a legend but it does not lack some basis in fact.

In his memoirs, Ilya Ehrenburg wrote that his friend understood the danger of these contacts but wanted, as he himself put it, to "unravel a mystery". Once Babel told Ehrenburg: "It's not a question of Yezhov. Of course, Yezhov is very active, but that's not the explanation . . ."

We even have some indication of what Babel thought and said in his cell at the Lubyanka. An archivist of the Federal Counter-Intelligence Service* came across some curious documents, when examining the cases of Babel's cell mates.

In July and August 1939 Babel was held in cell 89 of the Lubyanka's Inner Prison. Lev Belsky, a former deputy head of the NKVD (shot in 1940), shared his cell. Talking of "false testimony", Belsky stated:

> Such testimonies are the luck of the draw. The writer Babel was in the cell with me, and we were both being interrogated at the same time. I called myself a German-Japanese spy while Babel was accused of spying for Daladier. When the German-Soviet alliance was concluded, Babel downheartedly remarked that he was now quite certain to be shot and congratulated me on having probably escaped a similar fate . . .

A Return to the Truth

For two months the investigation proceeded no further. Perhaps Serikov, Kuleshov and Schwartzmann had earned a well-deserved vacation. Or, perhaps, their superiors were dissatisfied and had taken them off the case. Whatever the truth, on 11 September Babel's case was unexpectedly transferred to a fresh trio of investigators: Akopov, Kochnov and Rodos.

That same day, probably at the instigation of the interrogators, Babel wrote a penitent letter to Beria himself:

*Russian successor to the KGB.

To the USSR People's Commissar for Internal Affairs

The Revolution made it possible for me to write, and opened the way to happy and useful labour. My inherent individualism, my false literary views, and the influence of Trotskyists, among whom I found myself at the very beginning of my literary career, all forced me to leave this path. Each year my writing became less useful and more hostile to the Soviet reader. Yet I considered that I was right, not the reader. Because of this fatal gulf the very inspiration of my art began to dry up. I tried to escape the bondage of a blind and self-satisfied narrow-mindedness but these attempts proved feeble and pathetic. Salvation came to me in prison. Over the months I have spent in prison I have understood and reconsidered my views more, perhaps, than in my entire previous life. With horrifying clarity the mistakes and crimes of my life rose before me, the decay and foulness of the circles I moved in, which, for the most part, were Trotskyist. With my entire being I sensed that these people were not only enemies of the Soviet people and traitors but also promoted a view of the world that in every respect contradicted simplicity, clarity, happiness and physical and mental health, and was opposed to all that goes to make up true poetry. This view of the world found expression in cheap scepticism, the parading of professional disbelief, a fastidious exhaustion and decadence from the very first years of the revolution, a swaggering bravado and a promiscuous private life, in which the filthiest depravation was elevated into a principle. In my solitude I could see the Soviet land with new eyes as she is in reality, indescribably beautiful. How much more tormenting, then, was the vision of the abominations of my past life . . .

Citizen People's Commissar. During my interrogation, possessed solely by the desire to purge myself and repent, I have recounted my crimes, without any pity for myself. I also want to settle accounts for that other side of my existence, my literary work, which went on, hidden from the outside world, painfully and with interruptions, but unceasingly. I am appealing to you, Citizen People's Commissar, let me put the manuscripts confiscated from me in order. They contain the draft of an essay on collectivization and the collective farms of the Ukraine, materials for a book about Gorky, the drafts of several dozen stories, a half-finished play, and a completed film scenario. These manuscripts are the result of eight years work and I had intended to have a part of them ready for publication this year. I also appeal to you to let me at least draw up the plan for a book where in fictional form I would tell the story, in many ways quite typical, of what led to my fall and my crimes against the socialist motherland. That fatal path now stands before me in tormenting and pitiless clarity. With pain I sense how the inspiration and strength of my youth are returning to me. I burn with the desire to work, to repent and to condemn a life wrongly and criminally wasted.

By this point Babel probably no longer believed that he would survive. Any of the charges under which he stood accused carried the death penalty. This was a last feverish effort to return to his writing, in the hope that before the end he would be able to put his manuscripts, "eight years' work", in order. The attempt failed. How like he was in this to another prisoner of Stalin, Father Pavel Florensky, who, when he learned that the OGPU had seized his manuscripts, cried in despair: "A lifetime's work has perished . . . this is worse than death itself . . ."

Another month passed. On 10 October the new investigators summoned Babel to his last interrogation.

Suddenly and unexpectedly the prisoner rejected part of his previous testimony. Babel was preparing to meet his end. This time we do not have a typed copy of the deposition in front of us but the original, hand-written record of Lieutenant Akopov:

> Q. Accused Babel, do you have anything to add to your previous testimony?
> A. I can add nothing, since I have said everything about my counter-revolutionary activities and work as a spy. However, I would like the investigators to note that when I was giving my preliminary testimony I committed a crime, even while in prison.
> Q. What crime?
> A. I slandered certain people and gave false testimony about my terrorist activities.
> Q. Are you trying to create difficulties for the investigators?
> A. No, that was not my intention since I am nothing as far as the NKVD is concerned. I lied to the investigators by reason of my own faint-heartedness.
> Q. Tell us whom you slandered and when you were lying.
> A. The testimony I gave about my counter-revolutionary ties with Yezhov's wife (Gladun-Khayutina) was false. It is untrue that I carried out terrorist activities under the direction of Yezhov. I also know nothing about the anti-Soviet activities of those surrounding Yevgenia Yezhova. I fabricated my testimony about S.M. Eisenstein and S.M. Mikhoels. I confirm that I spied for the French and the Austrian intelligence services. However, I must add that the information I passed to foreign intelligence services did not contain anything concerning defence matters . . .

Evidently, Babel's tactic was to gradually negate the achievements of the interrogators, first defending others and then himself. As long as he was in the hands of the NKVD he could do nothing. But ahead lay the trial and then he would tell the whole truth and deny all charges. Yet his fate was already sealed. It no longer made any difference what he said or did.

Immediately after this interrogation Akopov drew up another document, confirming that the investigation had been completed.

All the formalities were observed. A Dr Kuzmich came to Babel's cell to examine him and noted that the prisoner had chronic bronchitis. In all other respects, we must presume, he was fit.

In only three days the charge sheet was ready: "The preliminary investigation having been completed, investigation file No 419 is now to be handed over to the USSR Procurator General's Office to be transferred to the jurisdiction of the court." There follows a string of signatures: investigator Akopov, senior investigator Kochnov, the head of the investigation department Sergienko and his deputy Rodos. To them was added the name of Military procurator Postnikov who approved the document. Babel's attempt to withdraw part of his testimony had been totally ignored.

Still, for some reason, they were in no hurry to hand the case over to the court and held it back for another month, waiting for special instructions.

On 5 November "prisoner I.E. Babel, former member of the Union of Soviet Writers", as he signed himself, wrote an appeal to the USSR Procurator General on a small scrap of paper.

> I understand from certain words of the investigator, that my case is now being examined by the USSR Procurator General's Office. I wish to make a statement that concerns the essence of the case and is of the greatest importance. I beg you to give me a hearing.

The next day Captain Mironov, the prison director, forwarded Babel's appeal.

Just before the Revolution Day holiday (on 7 November), Babel's widow Antonina Pirozhkova recalls, a young NKVD man came to the flat in Nikolo-Vorobinsky Street and asked her to give him trousers, socks and handkerchiefs for Babel.

> How fortunate that I had managed to move Babel's trousers from his room to mine during the search. The socks and handkerchiefs were in my wardrobe. I sprinkled my perfumes on the handkerchiefs and gave all these items to my visitor. I so wanted to send Babel some greeting from home – a familiar scent, at least.
>
> When we talked over this visit with my mother, we concluded that it was a good sign, a change for the better, it seemed to us.

For Babel that scent was perhaps the last message he received from home.

Верх. Прокурору СССР—

от арестованного И. Бабеля,
бывш. члена Союза Советских
писателей.

Со слов следователя мне стало известно,
что дело мое находится на рассмотрении
Прокуратуры СССР. Желая сделать
заявления, касающиеся существа
дела и имеющие чрезвычайно
важное значение — прошу меня
выслушать.

И. Бабель

5. XI. 39.

Верховному прокурору СССР—
от арестованного И. Бабеля, бывш.
члена Союза Советских писателей

В дополнение к заявлению моему
от 5/XI 39 вторично обращаюсь с прось-
бой вызвать меня для допроса. В по-
казаниях моих содержатся непра-
вильные и вымышленные утверж-
дения, приписывающие антисо-
ветскую деятельность людям —
честно и самоотверженно рабо-
тающим для блага СССР. Мысль
о том что слова мои не только
не помогают следствию, но
могут принести моей родине
прямой вред — доставляет
мне невыразимые страдания
Я считаю первым своим долгом
снять со своей совести ужасное
это пятно.

И. Бабель.

21. XI. 39.

Two of Babel's appeals to the USSR Procurator General from the Lubyanka's Inner Prison (5 and
21 November 1939), in which he attempted to save those he had denounced by retracting his
statement. See pp 63 and 66.

Председателю Военной Коллегии
Верх. Суда СССР

от арестованного И. Бабеля, бывш.
члена Союза Советских писателей.

5/XI, 21/XI – 39 года и 2/I 40 года я писал в
Прокуратуру СССР о том, что имею сдел...
крайне важные заявления, по суш...
моего дела и о том, что меня в пока-
заниях оклеветал ряд не в чем непо-
-винных людей. Ходатайствую о раз-
-...бе по поводу этих заявлени...
был до разбора дела выслушать
Прокурором Верховного Суда.
Ходатайствую также о разреше...
мне пригласить защитника: о
вызове в качестве свидетелей – А.
Воронского, писателя И. Эренбурга,
писательницы Сейфуллиной, реж
-сера С. Эйзенштейна, актера С. Михоэ...
и секретаря редакции „СССР на стро...
Г. Островской.
Прошу также дать мне возможность
ознакомиться с делом, так как я
читал его больше четырех месяцев
тому назад, ...
... и память моя многих ничего не
удержала.

И . Бабель

25.I.40.

"Babel told me that it did no good to sign the depositions," Grents wrote in a statement for his interrogator, "and repeatedly told me in conversation that I was a fool to do so. I would do better to renounce the testimony I had given during the investigation. Under the constant pressure of such conversations, I was influenced by Babel to renounce my own testimony. I greatly regret that I behaved incorrectly and herewith confirm my original testimony."

Without waiting for a reply from the Procurator's Office, Babel wrote a second appeal in an equally shaky hand on another scrap of paper:

> Further to my appeal of 5 November 1939, I am addressing you a second time with the request to be summoned for cross-examination. There are incorrect and fictitious assertions in my testimony attributing anti-Soviet activities to persons who are working honestly for the good of the USSR and without any thought for themselves. The idea that my words might not only fail to help the investigators but be of direct harm to my motherland is causing me indescribable suffering. I consider it my first duty to remove this terrible stain from my conscience.

Babel retained no hope for himself but was tormented by the fate of others. Meanwhile the investigators yet again held back the case, this time until 2 January 1940. The Military procurator was in a hurry to proceed: "The case has been completed, and it must be handed over to the court . . . There are no grounds for any further extension." Someone decided otherwise. Perhaps they still needed Babel to justify further arrests, or to stage yet another show trial.

In December they no longer accepted money for Babel from his wife at the Lubyanka. He was in Butyrki prison. From there he sent his third appeal to the Procurator's Office:

> At the NKVD Inner Prison I wrote two appeals to the USSR Procurator General's Office, on 5 and 21 November 1939, stating that I had incriminated innocent people in my testimony. I do not know what has happened to these appeals. The idea that my testimony may not only not aid in ascertaining the truth but mislead the investigators causes me constant torment. Apart from what I said in the deposition of 10 October, I also attributed anti-Soviet actions and tendencies to the writer I. Ehrenburg, to G. Konovalov, M. Feierovich, L. Tumerman and O. Brodskaya and to a group of journalists (E. Kriger, E. Bermont and T. Tess). This is all lies, with no basis in fact. I know these people to be honest and loyal Soviet citizens. This slander was prompted by my own

66

faint-hearted behaviour during the cross-examination.

This note is covered with official stamps and resolutions and many words and phrases are underlined in red and green pencil.

On 22 January another note was added to the charge sheet by the procurator: "Send the case to be heard by the Military Tribunal . . ."*

The end was in sight.

Sentence

Babel fought to the end. On 25 January, the day before the court was to meet, he received the indictment and immediately wrote an appeal to the chairman of the Military Tribunal. These were the last words Babel wrote:

> On 5 and 21 November 1939, and on 2 January 1940, I wrote to the USSR Procurator General's Office that I had an extremely important statement to make concerning my case and that I had slandered a number of quite innocent people in my depositions. I request that the procurator of the Supreme Court consider these appeals before the case is heard.
>
> I also request be allowed to invite a defence attorney, and to summon as witnesses A. Voronsky,** the writers I. Ehrenburg and Seifullina, the film director Eisenstein, the actor Mikhoels and R. Ostrovskaya, secretary of the *SSSR v stroike* editorial board.
>
> I also ask permission to see the case file since I read it more than four months ago, in a hurry and late at night, and I can barely remember any of it now.

The court sat the next day, 26 January 1940. Evidently, the hearing took place in Beria's office in Butyrki prison itself, according to the unspoken procedure. The head of the Secret Police had an office in all the city's prisons but since he "worked" mainly at night, they were free to be used by the judges during the daytime.

The Military Tribunal was chaired by Vasily Ulrich. Small, bald, with a tiny moustache on his square impassive features, he and his two assistants, Kandybin and Dmitriev, were highly experienced in hearing such cases. They were dealt with rapidly, each taking no more than 20 minutes.

Babel was brought in. The "identity of the accused was established".

Ulrich. Have you received the indictment?
Babel. Yes, I have received and read it. I understand the charges.

---

*The Military Tribunal of the Supreme Court was empowered to try cases of treason, espionage, terror and sabotage.
**Babel did not know that Alexander Voronsky had already been shot, three years before in 1937.

67

Ulrich announced the composition of the bench.

> *Ulrich.* Do you object to any of the judges?
> *Babel.* No . . . But I would ask you to let me read the case file, to invite a defence lawyer and to summon witnesses, those whom I indicated in my statement . . .

The judges conferred and then declared the petition had been declined as lacking sufficient justification.

> *Ulrich.* Do you admit your guilt?

At last Babel could tell the whole truth. He would have no other chance:

> I do not consider myself guilty. All the testimony I gave during the investigation is false. I did meet at one time with Trotskyists but there was no more to it than that . . .

The judges looked through the case file and quoted Babel's remarks about political repressions.

> *Babel.* I disavow that testimony.
> *Ulrich.* You did not have criminal connections with Voronsky?
> *Babel.* Voronsky was exiled in 1930 and I have not seen him since 1928 . . .
> *Ulrich.* What about Yakir?*
> *Babel.* I only saw Yakir once, and we talked for 15 minutes. I wanted to write something about his division.
> *Ulrich.* And your foreign ties, do you also deny them?
> *Babel.* I visited Gorky in Sorrento and I stayed with my mother in Brussels; she lives there with my sister who left the Soviet Union in 1926 . . .

The judges again quoted from his depositions in the case file, this time about his meetings with Souvarine.

> *Babel.* I did meet Souvarine but knew nothing about his hostility towards the Soviet Union.
> *Ulrich.* And you knew nothing about Malraux either?
> *Babel.* I was friendly with Malraux but he did not recruit me as a spy, we talked about literature and about the Soviet Union . . .
> *Ulrich.* But you yourself testified that you worked as a spy with Malraux.
> *Babel.* That's not true. The Communist Vaillant-Couturier introduced me to Malraux. Malraux is a friend of the Soviet Union and was very helpful with translations into French. What could I tell him about our aviation? Only what I knew from reading *Pravda*, and he did not ask

*Army general executed in June 1937. See footnote on p 56.

about anything else. I categorically deny that I was linked with French intelligence. Or with the Austrian intelligence service. Bruno Steiner and I were simply neighbours at the hotel and then, for a time, shared a flat ...

The judges moved on to the charge of terrorism.

Ulrich. Did you have any ties with Yezhov?
Babel. I never had any conversations about terror with Yezhov.
Ulrich. You testified under investigation that the assassination of Comrade Stalin was being prepared in the Caucasus.
Babel. I heard talk of that kind in the Writers Union ...
Ulrich. Then what about the preparations of the Kosarev-Yezhova band to kill Stalin and Voroshilov?
Babel. That is also an invention. I used to meet Yezhova because she was editor of the *SSSR v stroike* journal and I was working there.

The judges again quoted from Babel's previous testimony, and again he denied it:

Babel. I visited Yezhova's flat and met with friends at her home but there were no anti-Soviet conversations there.
Ulrich. Do you wish to add anything to the present record?
Babel. No, I have nothing to add.

The examination of the case was over. The accused was allowed a last word.

In 1916, when I had written my first story I took it to Gorky ... Then I participated in the Civil War. In 1921 I began writing again. Recently I have been very occupied with a work of which I completed the first draft by the end of 1938. I am totally innocent, I have not been a spy and I have never committed any acts against the Soviet Union. In my testimony during the investigation I libelled myself. I have only one request, that I be allowed to complete my last work ...

The judges withdrew and returned immediately. Ulrich pronounced the verdict that had been decided long before:

In the name of the Union of Soviet Socialist Republics ... the Military Tribunal of the Supreme Court ... has examined the case ... and established that Isaac Babel ... was a member of an anti-Soviet Trotskyist group ... an agent of the French and Austrian intelligence services ... linked to the wife of the enemy of the people Yezhov ... and was drawn into a conspiratorial terrorist organization. ... Having found Babel guilty, the Tribunal sentences him to the highest penalty, to be shot ...

The verdict is final and to be put into effect without delay . . .

Today we know the exact date and even the hour when Babel died: 1.30 am on 27 January 1940. Babel's name was first in a list of 16 to be executed. His remains were cremated the same day.

"We have no information where he is buried," they told me at the Lubyanka when I had finished reading Babel's file.

Stalin's mass murderers carefully concealed the burial places of their victims. In the decades that followed these common graves disappeared under trees, houses and factories, and were covered with asphalt and concrete. Yet with time even this secret became known.

There were a great many executions in early 1940. Among those shot then were Babel (27 January), Koltsov and Meyerhold (2 February) and Yezhov (4 February). The Lubyanka eventually disclosed, after a search through its labyrinthine archives, that the bodies were taken away from the prisons at night to the crematorium at the former Donskoi Monastery in central Moscow. The ashes were then tipped into a pit at the cemetery there. The remains of the executioners and their victims mingled together in a common grave, and among them, in all probability, lie those of both Babel and Yezhov.

When the pit was filled to overflowing it was levelled and for many years a modest stone explained that this was "Common grave No. 1" which contained "unclaimed ashes, 1930 to 1942 inclusive". The stone remains there to this day but now it backs on to a monument, formally inaugurated in August 1991, which bears the inscription: "Here lie buried the remains of the innocent tortured and executed victims of the political repressions. May they never be forgotten!"

It was autumn when I went there. The leaves were falling and a few old women stood talking in low voices by the monument. I wandered off among the graves, and pulled up with a shock, 20 paces away. One of the tombstones read "Khayutina, Yevgenia Solomonovna, 1904-1938". Even in death she was here, next to Babel and Yezhov.

Babel's study in his Moscow flat, where his family continued to live, remained sealed. Two years after his arrest new occupants moved into the study, an NKVD investigator and his wife. Yet even when sharing her life with such neighbours, his widow continued waiting hopefully, sending off enquiries about him to various bodies. "He is alive, well and being held in the camps," they would reply. In 1947 she was officially informed "He will be released in 1948 . . ." Her spirits picked up and she re-decorated the flat. He did not return but rumours continued to report that Babel had been seen by others, in Kolyma or in the Krasnoyarsk Territory.

Fourteen years passed. Stalin died and the "Thaw" began. The relations of those who had been arrested started searching for their loved ones. Antonina

Pirozhkova also submitted an official request for information.

On 18 December 1954 the Military Tribunal reached a decision:

> At his trial Babel did not recognize his guilt and declared that during the preliminary investigation he had been forced to slander himself and other persons ... A number of people mentioned in Babel's testimony, and supposedly accomplices in his criminal activities, were never arrested and no action was taken against them (they include Ehrenburg, Kataev, Leonov, Ivanov, Seifullina and others). The case against Komsomol leader Kosarev was closed for lack of a corpus delicti ... An examination has been made of the files on Uritsky and Gladun. Their testimony was included in Babel's case file as documentary evidence of his guilt but it has been established that they subsequently renounced their testimony as a fabrication."*
>
> The Procurator General's Office has also established that the former NKVD employees Rodos and Schwartzmann, who took part in investigating the Babel case, are now under arrest for falsifying investigation files.
>
> Having examined the materials in the case file, and being in agreement with the decision of the procurator, the Military Tribunal of the USSR Supreme Court has ruled that: "The sentence on I.E. Babel be quashed in the light of newly discovered circumstances and his case be closed."

Yet even then falsehood continued to pursue the writer. On the back of the final page of the procurator's verdict of rehabilitation the facts are unambiguously stated: "The sentence on I.E. Babel was executed on 27 January 1940." Yet one and a half months later the Military Tribunal would instruct the Main Military Procurator's Office, the KGB and the Ministry of Internal Affairs to "inform Pirozhkova that Babel has been rehabilitated and that he died while serving his sentence in the camps on ... " and in the blank space a firm hand has added a date in ink: "17 March 1941."

A month later, in March 1955, the widow received the official reply. "Babel died, while serving his sentence, on 17 March 1941," she was informed, and this time the date had been typed. For decades this would be the date given in all the textbooks and encyclopedias.

And the manuscripts, all 27 folders? On the day of Babel's arrest they were packed up into seven parcels, each closed with a wax seal, and a certain Kutyrev, a junior lieutenant in the NKVD, following somebody's orders, removed them as documentary evidence from the file. From then on all trace of them disappeared.

*"... my testimony was given under physical pressure from the investigator," Gladun stated during his trial.

CHAPTER 3

UNDER THE HEEL

THE FILE ON MIKHAIL BULGAKOV:
A STORY IN SIX ACTS, WITH EPILOGUE

Act I: The Search

"Quite right, quite right!" shouted Korovyov, "you confirm my suspicions. He was watching the flat. [...] so was the man in the ground entrance! And the one standing in the passage into the courtyard!"

"And do you think they'll come and arrest you?" asked Margarita.

"Most certainly they will, my charming queen, most certainly!" Korovyov replied. "Something tells me they will come. Not immediately, of course, but in their own good time: they will most certainly come..."

The scene is from the *Master and Margarita*. On 7 May 1926 they came for the writer himself. Not to arrest him, for the time being, but only to conduct a search. Bulgakov's wife remembered the OGPU* man's surname, Slavkin. He was accompanied by an assistant in a pince-nez and their landlord had been brought along as a witness.

They did not find Bulgakov at home and would not begin without him. For a while they sat there silently. Then the landlord told the joke about the Jew standing on Lubyanka Square who was asked if he knew where the State Insurance company's offices were. Since their premises were now occupied by the OGPU the Jew punned: "I don't know where Gosstrakh is now, [State-Insure or, as it also sounds to Russian ears, State-Fear] but Gosuzhas [State-Horror] is over there."

He laughed at his own joke. They fell silent again until the master of the house appeared. Once Bulgakov had arrived, his visitors went straight to work, upturning the armchairs and probing them with strange long needles. "Well, Lyuba my dear, if your armchairs start shooting back, I shall not be responsible," said Bulgakov.

They did not arrest the writer but they confiscated his manuscripts, including a very outspoken diary that he had called "Under the Heel". The secret police had been keeping Bulgakov under surveillance for a long time and he was aware of it. In turn, he had been keeping his eye on them. In the confiscated diary there is the following passage:

*The OGPU or United Main Political Administration was the title used by the secret police from 1923 to 1934.

Night of 2–3 January 1925

An amusing incident. I did not have any money for the tram so I decided
... to walk. I set off along the embankment. There was a half moon in
the mist. For some reason, the Moskva was not frozen in the middle and
ravens were sitting on the ice and snow near the banks. Lights shone
across the river, in Zamoskvoreche. I was walking past the Kremlin. I
had drawn level with the corner tower, when I looked up, halted and
began to gaze up at the Kremlin; I had just thought to myself, "How long,
Lord, how long . . ?" when a grey figure carrying a briefcase loomed out
of the mist behind me and looked at me. Then he hooked on to me. I let
the figure overtake me and for a quarter of an hour we walked together.
He spat over the parapet, and so did I. I managed to shake him off near
the plinth of the Alexander* monument . . .

After the search the "grey figure" attached himself still more firmly to
Bulgakov. They had decided to give the writer a fright and let him know that
he was henceforth under special observation. Whatever he did or wrote they
were watching him. And they now had some compromising material, the
confiscated diary.

What was so seditious about this notebook that it had to be seized? Rumours
circulated among contemporaries that the members of the Politburo themselves
took it in turns to read the contents. Perhaps they were alarmed that Bulgakov
could see through all this "fusty, Soviet, servile riff raff" (a phrase from one of the
entries) and read the "dog's hearts" of the new leaders; they feared, perhaps, that
he would use his talent to reveal them to others as well.

There can be no doubt that Bulgakov was deeply offended by this intrusion
and by the surveillance of his life and work. Moreover, he had no intention of
knuckling under.

On 24 June he sent Rykov, the chairman of the Council of People's
Commissars (the Soviet government), the following complaint:

> On 7 May 1926 representatives of OGPU conducted a search of my flat
> (Search Warrant 2287, Case No. 45). They seized the following manu-
> scripts, as noted in the deposition, which are of great personal value to
> me: two copies of the novella *The Heart of a Dog*, and "My Diary" (three
> notebooks).
>
> I most earnestly request that they be returned.

Bulgakov would be twice called in to talk to the investigator and cross-
questioned but the manuscripts were not handed back. Again and again, over a

---

*Before the Revolution a statue of Tsar Alexander III had stood in front of the Christ the Saviour
Cathedral. Now only the plinth remained.

period of several years, he demanded their return, making his appeals through Gorky and his first wife Yekaterina Peshkova, who headed the Political Red Cross.* The results were negative. The consequences, however, were quite tangible. An application to make a two-month journey abroad was turned down.

Act II: The Diary

In his insistent demands that the diaries be handed back, Bulgakov admitted that these manuscripts contained something of "great value", reflecting his "mood over the past years".

He had, in fact, written the diary for himself alone and did not conceal anything there. It contained his instant reaction to events, themes for his fictional works, and an attempt at self-analysis. Like the doctor he once was, taking the pulse of a patient, Bulgakov followed the condition of his country and gave a correct and pitiless diagnosis. A young writer who had not yet published a single book, he already had a clear idea of his own talent, the extent to which he was rejected by the present order, and the threat that hung over him.

> *2 September 1923*
> For all my depression and nostalgia for the past, I sometimes feel explosions of confidence and power, even in this ridiculous temporary privation, inhabiting a vile room in a vile house. Even now I can feel how my thoughts take flight and am sure that I am incomparably stronger as a writer than all the others I know.
>
> It is very hard to be a writer now. It's difficult for someone with my views to be printed or to make a living . . .

> *26 October*
> My intuitions about other people have never let me down. Those gathering around *Nakanune*** are a quite exceptional bunch of swine, and I can only congratulate myself on having got involved with them. I shall have a hard time of it later, when I need to restore my good reputation. Yet with a clear conscience I can admit one thing to myself. It was iron necessity that forced me to publish in their newspaper. If it had not been for *Nakanune*, neither my "Notes on the Cuff" nor much else in which I was able to write honestly and truly would have appeared. I would have had to be exceptionally heroic not to print anything for four years, and

*The Political Red Cross was set up in 1918 to help those imprisoned or exiled for political reasons. It closed in 1937.
**(Lit. On the Eve): a pro-Soviet and Moscow-financed emigre newspaper published in Berlin 1922–4.

to hold my tongue in the hopes that in future I would again be allowed to speak. Regrettably, I am not such a hero.

6 November
Now I must study. The voice that unsettles me today must be prophetic. I can be nothing but a writer.

A year passed. By then Bulgakov was keeping his distance from most other Soviet writers. Any contact with them met resistance and drove him back to the one place where he was free, in his writing.

26 December 1924
I have just come back from spending the evening with Angarsky, an editor with Nedra publishers.* There was the kind of talk you hear everywhere now: about censorship, attacks on it, discussions of "artistic truth" and "falsehood" ... I could not help intervening several times and saying that it is hard to work nowadays, and I attacked the censors and made other remarks that I should not have been making at all.

Lyashko, a Proletarian writer, who feels (instinct) an insurmountable antipathy towards me, barely concealed his irritation: "I do not understand what 'truth' comrade Bulgakov is talking about? Why do we need to depict everything?"

And when I began to say that the present epoch was a swinish period he said with hatred: "You're talking nonsense ..."

I had no time to reply to this amicable remark because at that moment we rose from the table. There's no escaping the boors.

Night, 28 December
... This evening I read my story "The Fatal Eggs" at Nikitina's flat.** On my way there, I felt a puerile desire to dazzle and to show off. Returning, my emotions were mixed. Is it a satire? or a provocative gesture? or, perhaps, it's a serious work? If so, it's half-baked. In any case, of the thirty people there not only were there no writers, but none of them has the slightest idea about Russian literature.

I'm afraid that I might be hauled off to a "place not so far from here" for all these heroic feats.

Bulgakov's lack of money and his domestic difficulties are a constant theme in the diary. He made fun of them, and transformed them into elegant comment: "For as long as I am without a proper flat, I am not a person but only half a person";

---

*Nedra publishers were based in Moscow and issued Bulgakov's *Diaboliad* and "The Fatal Eggs".
**Eudoxia Nikitina, a literary critic, each Saturday hosted a salon at her flat.

"Question: How can my wife's summer coat be turned into a fur coat?" For the time being, his inherent joie de vivre kept him afloat:

Night, 28 December 1924
 "My wife is a great help in distracting me from my thoughts.* Recently I have noticed that when she walks, she swings her hips. It is frightfully silly considering what other worries I have, but, it seems, I really am in love with her. One thought interests me, though. Could she have become so comfortably settled with any other man . . . or only with me?"

A few days later the same theme recurs:

 How awful! I am falling more and more in love with my wife. It's so unfair. For ten years I did not think of myself . . . All women were the same to me. Now I can even be reduced to mild jealousy. She is somehow attractive and sweet. She's plump as well. I did not read the papers today.

The OGPU investigators who got their hands on this diary probably did not give more than a cursory glance at these entries. Purple passages and self-analysis! They had almost certainly read nothing else he had written and were looking for quite different information. What were his political views? Whose side was he on?

Bulgakov provided abundant evidence of this kind as well. He thought a great deal about politics, almost every day, and confided his ideas to his diary:

30 September 1923
 Politics, they go on and on about the same foul and unnatural politics . . . They're fighting the Communists in Bulgaria. Wrangel's soldiers are taking part,** defending the government. I have no doubts whatsoever that these second-class Slav states are as barbarous as Russia and offer a superb breeding-ground for communism. Our newspapers are blowing up the events out of all proportion but, who knows, perhaps the world really is splitting into two halves, communism and fascism.
 What will happen, nobody knows.

Or perhaps not. In another entry for the same year Bulgakov presciently suggested, long before World War Two, that: "It is possible that the world really is on the verge of a universal struggle between communism and fascism."

There are many comments about Communist Party leaders.

 Today the papers carried a bulletin about Trotsky's health. It begins "On

*Lyubov Belozerskaya, Bulgakov's second wife, whom he had met earlier that year.
**Baron Wrangel and some of his troops had found refuge in monarchist Bulgaria after the Civil War ended.

5 November last year L.D. Trotsky was ill" and ends with the words "Vacation for no less than two months and complete discharge from all responsibilities". Comment on this historic bulletin is superfluous.

On 8 January 1924 Trotsky was given the push. God alone knows what will happen to Russia. May He come to her aid!

The next entry is about Lenin:

Syomka has just informed me (5.30 pm) that Lenin has died . . .

A simple statement of fact, none of the tears and vows required in public. When he turned to Kalinin, in the same year, the irony is evident:

Yesterday it was announced that Kalinin's carriage had been struck by lightning (he was in the provinces somewhere). The coachman was killed. Kalinin was quite unharmed.

He writes about every aspect of life in the Soviet republic. Our Soviet citizen goes to work.

22 October 1923
There was a wonderfully grotesque incident at work today. The "initiative group of non-Party members" at *Gudok** suggested a meeting to discuss aid for the German proletariat. When N. opened the meeting the Communist R. appeared and nervously made an ominous announcement: it was an "unheard-of thing for the non-Party members to call their own meetings," he said, and demanded that the meeting be closed and a general meeting called. At this N. turned pale but replied that the Party cell had already given its permission.

It was all straightforward after that. The non-Party members voted as one for the Party officials to invite all their members, and flattering words were spoken. The Party members turned up and responded by agreeing to donate twice as much (two days wages, not the one to be paid by the non-Party members), thereby delivering a resounding slap in the face to the non-Party donkeys.

After paying his tribute to the German proletariat, the Soviet office-worker leaves to go home:

12 September 1924
Something new: in the last few days completely naked people (men and women) have appeared in Moscow with sashes across their shoulder

---

*(Lit. Train Whistle): Bulgakov first worked in the letters section and then wrote sketches for the Railway Workers Union weekly publication.

reading DOWN WITH SHAME. They squeezed on to the trams. The trams stopped and the public expressed its indignation . . .

Night, 20-21 December 1924

Moscow is filthy and yet there are more and more lights. Two phenomena, strangely, live side by side: life is getting back to normal and, at the same time, is rotting alive, it's gangrenous. In the centre of Moscow, starting from Lubyanka Square, the Water and Canal company has begun test drilling for an underground train network. That is life. The Underground will not be built, however, because there is no money for it. That is the gangrene.

A scheme for road transport is being devised. That is life. There is no public transport, however, because there are not enough trams. It's ludicrous: there are only 8 motorized buses for the whole of Moscow.

Flats, families, scholars, work, comfort and practical conveniences are all in a state of living decay. Nothing is moving at all. All has been devoured by the hellish maw of Soviet red tape. Every step a Soviet citizen takes, every movement he makes, is a form of torture, that uses up hours, days and sometimes months.

The shops are open. That's a sign of life. But they don't stay in business. That's gangrene.

It's the same for everything.

The literature being published is abominable.

Snapshots of Moscow life in the 1920s. A few days later there is the following entry:

A very hard frost. This morning the plumber unfroze the pipes. This evening, though, as soon as I had come home the electricity went off, everywhere.

The Soviet citizen has arrived home. This might have been his last refuge but it too is a socialist dormitory, a communal flat.

5 January 1925

"How is this all going to end?" a friend asked me today.

Such questions are repeated automatically, dumbly, hopelessly and indifferently and on every possible occasion. In his flat at this very moment the Communists in the room across the corridor are getting drunk. There's a sharp unpleasant smell in the corridor. One of the Party members, my friend informs me, has drunk himself to a swinish oblivion. My friend was invited to join in and he can't refuse. He enters their room with a polite and obsequious smile. They're always inviting him in. He comes to me to get away and then all he does is curse them. This will certainly all end, one way or another. Of that, I am sure.

Bulgakov's contemporary falls asleep as the drinking goes on all around. He should have considered himself lucky. Because the knock at the door was quite as much a part of daily reality as the plumber and the communal kitchen.

15 April 1924
There have been numerous arrests in Moscow of people with "good surnames". Again they're exiling people . . .

21 July 1924
I[lf] and Y[ury] O[lesha] have arrived from Samara. There are two trams working in the city. One says REVOLUTION SQUARE-PRISON, the other SOVIET SQUARE-PRISON. Or something like that. All roads lead to Rome, in other words!

On the evening of 5 January 1925 he looked through issues of the atheist magazine *Bezbozhnik* (The Godless). In amazement, he commented:

It is not just the blasphemy, although that is, of course, unprecedented . . . The gist of it is that Jesus Christ, no less, was a good-for-nothing and a fraud . . . I have these claims before me in writing. It's not hard to guess whose work this is. Such a crime is quite priceless . . .

And after all these incontrovertibly "counter-revolutionary" statements the author still had the nerve to go on protesting:

Please forward my complaint and return my diaries.

Act III: Manuscripts Don't Burn

Three years passed. Bulgakov had survived the poverty, homelessness and anonymity of his first years in Moscow when he kept his diary. The thunderous success of his plays and early prose had briefly won him fame and praise, just at the time, in fact, that he was deprived of his ill-fated diary. Thereafter he was afflicted by growing persecution and public rejection.

On 24 August he wrote to his brother Nikolay who had just moved to Paris:

I must tell you, dear brother, my position is an unhappy one. My destruction as a writer was completed in 1929. I have made one last effort and have submitted an application to the USSR government, asking to be permitted to travel abroad with my wife for any length of time they allow . . . If my application is rejected then we can consider the game is over, put away the pack, and snuff out the candles . . . I am not being faint-hearted, brother, when I tell you that my death is merely a question of time ...

He wrote the same to Maxim Gorky:

> Why force a writer whose works cannot exist in the USSR to stay in the country? To ensure that his death is inevitable?
> All my plays are banned;
> not one line I have written is being published anywhere;
> I have no work ready to sell, and do not receive a single kopeck in royalties;
> not a single institution or individual replies to my appeals and complaints:
> in a word, everything that I have written over the last ten years in the Soviet Union has been destroyed. All that now remains is to destroy me as well. I beg them to make a humane decision, and let me go!

It was at this very moment, when the writer had been reduced to a state of despair, that the authorities made a concession. At long last, they returned his manuscripts. And what did Bulgakov do with the long-awaited diary?

> Breaking my fingernails I pulled the thick notebooks apart, setting them upright between the logs and ruffling the pages with the poker. ... At times, the ash became too much for me and began to smother the flames but I battled with it ... Familiar words flickered before my eyes, and though the yellow inexorably crept up the pages even then the words could still be read. They only disappeared when the paper turned black and I furiously finished them off with the poker ...

Just like the Master burning his great, unrecognized novel, so Bulgakov destroyed the diary which had been a captive of the Lubyanka for the last three years. It was an eloquent gesture. His private confessional had been desecrated by the "grey figure's" filthy hands and he did not want to preserve such obviously compromising material. He would never keep a diary again.

He had reached a turning point in his life. He could see no place for himself in Russia and could only trust to fate, leaving it to the government to take the crucial decision.

Until his death in 1940, however, a mystical fear for his manuscripts pursued him. His widow Yelena Sergeevna* recalled that just before he died Bulgakov suffered from the delusion that his manuscripts were being taken from him. "Is there someone there?" he asked uneasily.

*Bulgakov's third wife Yelena Shilovskaya whom he married in 1932.

Once he made me get out of bed and then, leaning on my arm, he walked through all the rooms, barefoot and in his dressing gown, to make sure that the manuscript of the *"Master"* was still there. Then he lay back high up against the pillow and placed his right hand on his hip like a knight.

"Let me have a look." Woland stretched out his hand, the palm upwards.

"I'm afraid I can't do that," the Master answered, "I burned it in the stove."

"I beg your pardon, but I don't believe that," answered Woland. "It can't be true. Manuscripts don't burn."

In this case, the famous phrase proved true. The writer destroyed his diary and yet we can still read it today For, though the manuscript did in fact burn, the text survived in the Lubyanka's devilish maw. The secret police made a show of returning the diary but with foresight they first photographed it and then had a typist make a copy of it. They hid it well, just in case. It was found by the archivists of the Lubyanka and handed over to our commission, the role of Woland being played this time by Anatoly Krayushkin.

This was not the end of the Bulgakov file, however. While I was working on the diary and, with the help of experts, overcoming the problems in the text and in the careless copying of an unskilled typist ("torn out", "page torn out of the original" it notes) Krayushkin gave me yet another dossier. The secret police had preserved these compromising diaries not from any curiosity but in order to keep the writer under their thumbs for the rest of his life. In addition, they had kept a separate secret file on Bulgakov.

Act IV: The Letter

The slender file bears the classification "Highly Confidential" and, along the top, an intimidating string of letters: Cheka – GPU – OGPU – NKVD – NKGB – MGB – MVD – KGB.

File from the Secret section of the OGPU
Letter sent to the USSR government by the dramatist M. Bulgakov (author of the play *Days of the Turbins*) requesting that he be shielded from unfounded critical attacks in the press and helped to find a job. Opened, April 1930. Closed, April 1930. For permanent retention.

The folder contains three documents. The first is a formerly unknown note which Bulgakov himself wrote by hand:

2. IV 1930 г

В Коллегию Объединенного
Государственного Политического
Управления

Прошу не отказать направить
на рассмотрение Правительства
СССР мое письмо от 28. III 1930 г,
прилагаемое при этом.

[подпись]

Москва, Б. Пироговская 35-а, кв. 6
телеф. 2-03-27

Михаил Афанасьевич
Булгаков

Bulgakov's handwritten note to the OGPU of 2 April 1930. See p 83.

2 April 1930
To the collegium of the United State Political Administration [OGPU]
Please do not obstruct the submission of my letter of 28 March 1930
(herewith enclosed) for the consideration of the USSR government.
Mikhail Bulgakov

Once he had sent the letter Bulgakov tried to imagine what would happen next, and to guess what the reaction of the authorities would be. Sometimes he fantasized and acted out his own characteristically sarcastic fictional version.

Some of his improvised tales were committed to memory by his widow Yelena Sergeevna.

LET'S IMAGINE THAT ...

Mikhail Afanasievich, at the end of his tether, has written a letter to Stalin. *Here I am, writing these plays*, it goes, *but no one stages them or prints them anywhere* ... Signed: *Yours, Trampazlin.*
Stalin receives the letter and reads it.

STALIN. What's this here? Tram-pa-zlin ... Doesn't make any sense. (*Presses a button on the table.*) Send me Yagoda.

YAGODA *comes in and salutes Stalin.*

STALIN. Listen here, Yagoda, what does this mean? Look, here's a letter. Some writer has sent it and the signature is "Yours, Tram-pa-zlin." Who is he?

YAGODA. I've no idea.

STALIN. What did you say? Do you dare to give me such an answer?! You're supposed to see through a brick wall! Half an hour to give me the answer!

YAGODA. Yes, your majesty.

Leaves, and returns in half an hour.

YAGODA. Your majesty, it's Bulgakov.

STALIN. Bulgakov? What's going on here? Why is my writer sending me such a letter? Send for him immediately!

YAGODA. I obey, your majesty. (*Leaves.*)

From the materials in the secret dossier we can reconstruct what probably happened in reality.

The second document is the famous letter Bulgakov sent to the government, typed and with his own signature. The contents are well known and were circulated widely in samizdat before being published finally in the late 1980s. For that publication, however, a copy preserved in the Russian State (formerly Lenin) Library was used. No one knew whether Bulgakov sent this specific text or another, and whether it was addressed just to Stalin or to other members of the government. At last I held the original in my hands and, sixty years after it was written, all doubts were resolved.

Then no one yet knew about this desperate and provocative challenge apart from the author and Yelena Shilovskaya who typed it and would, in two years time become his third wife. At this critical moment in his life as a writer his private life also entered a crisis and, just as the "secret friend" Margarita entered the life of the Master, so Yelena Shilovskaya came with her Underwood typewriter to his flat on Pirogovskaya Street. Unlike her literary reflection, however, Yelena Sergeevna did not then desert Bulgakov but stayed and supported him in all his trials.

One of the first to read the letter took his time, marking those lines that struck him as important. We shall not reproduce the entire text here but only those sections where Genrikh Yagoda, the head of the OGPU, underlined entire sentences and paragraphs with his thick pencil. (Bulgakov added emphasis by printing in capitals: the two styles have been preserved here.)

28 March 1930

TO THE USSR GOVERNMENT

After all my works were banned, many citizens who know me as a writer could be heard all offering the same advice:

Write a "communist play" (I enclose quotations in inverted commas) and also send a repentant letter to the USSR government, recanting the views I had formerly expressed in my literary works, and giving assurances that henceforth I would work as a fellow-travelling writer who was devoted to the idea of communism.

The purpose: to save myself from persecution, poverty and, ultimately, inevitable death.

I did not heed this advice. [...]

The desire ripened within me to put an end to my sufferings as a writer and forced me to appeal in a frank letter to the USSR government. [...]

My purpose is far more serious.

I can prove with the documentary evidence I possess that the entire press of the USSR, and all other institutions entrusted with supervising the theatrical repertoire, have been asserting WITH EXCEPTIONAL VIRULENCE all the years that I have been writing that the works of

Mikhail Bulgakov cannot exist in the USSR.

I wish to state that the Soviet press is QUITE RIGHT.

For me the starting point of this letter is provided by my lampoon, *The Crimson Island*. [. . .] I shall not take it on myself to judge how witty my work is. I will admit, however, that a menacing shadow looms throughout the play. And this is the shadow of the Main Repertory Committee. It has been rearing up those helots, eulogists and cowed "lackeys". It has killed artistic thought. It has wrecked Soviet play-writing and will end by destroying it altogether. [. . .]

When the German papers write that *The Crimson Island* is the "first call in the USSR for freedom of the press" they are telling the truth. I admit this. It is my duty as a writer to battle against censorship, no matter what form it takes and under what regime, as it is my obligation to issue appeals for freedom of the press. I am a passionate supporter of such freedom and suppose that if any writer imagined he could prove that he did not need such freedom he would be like a fish publicly asserting that he could live without water. [. . .]

ANY SATIRIST IN THE USSR MUST QUESTION THE SOVIET SYSTEM.

Am I conceivable in the USSR?

[. . .]

I ask you to take into consideration, that for me being unable to write is the same as burying me alive.

I AM REQUESTING THE USSR GOVERNMENT TO ORDER ME TO LEAVE THE COUNTRY IN THE SHORTEST POSSIBLE TIME, ACCOMPANIED BY MY WIFE LYUBOV YEVGENIEVA BULGAKOVA.

I am appealing to the humanity of the Soviet authorities and request that I, a writer who cannot be of use in his own fatherland, may magnanimously be set at liberty.

If, nevertheless, that which I have written proves unconvincing and I am doomed to a lifetime's silence in the USSR, then I request the Soviet government to give me a job [. . .]

I am offering the USSR the services of a thoroughly honest specialist, an actor and director who, without a shadow of sabotage*, undertakes to conscientiously stage any play, beginning with Shakespeare and ending with contemporary works [. . .]

If this also is impossible then I request the Soviet government to act

*An allusion to the campaign against "bourgeois" specialists. In May 1928, 53 engineers and technicians at the Shakty mines in the Donbass region were publicly tried and sent to prison for "sabotage" and "economic counter-revolution".

ПРАВИТЕЛЬСТВУ С.С.С.Р.

[рукописные пометки]

Михаила Афанасьевича Булгакова
|Москва, Б.Пироговская, 35-а, к.6|

Я обращаюсь к Правительству СССР со следующим письмом:

I.

После того, как все мои произведения были запрещены, среди многих граждан, которым я известен как писатель, стали раздаваться голоса, подающие мне один и тот же совет:

Сочинить "коммунистическую пьесу" |в кавычках я привожу цитаты|, а, кроме того, обратиться к Правительству СССР с покаянным письмом, содержащим в себе отказ от прежних моих взглядов, высказанных мною в литературных произведениях, и уверения в том, что отныне я буду работать, как преданный идее коммунизма писатель-попутчик.

Цель: спастись от гонений, нищеты и неизбежной гибели в финале.

Этого совета я не послушался. Навряд ли мне удалось бы предстать перед Правительством СССР в выгодном свете, написав лживое письмо, представляющее собой неопрятный и к тому же наивный политический курбет. Попыток же сочинить коммунистическую пьесу я даже не производил, зная заведомо, что такая пьеса у меня не выйдет.

Созревшее во мне желание прекратить мои писательские мучения заставляет меня обратиться к Правительству СССР с письмом правдивым.

2.

Произведя анализ моих альбомов вырезок, я обнаружил в прессе СССР за десять лет моей литературной работы 301 отзыв обо мне. Из них: похвальных было - 3, враждебно-ругательных - 298.

Последние 298 представляют собой зеркальное отражение моей писательской жизни.

Героя моей пьесы "Дни Турбиных" Алексея Турбина печатно в стихах называли "СУКИНЫМ СЫНОМ", а автора пьесы рекомендовали, как "одержимого СОБАЧЬЕЙ СТАРОСТЬЮ". Обо мне писали, как о "литературном УБОРЩИКЕ", подбирающем объедки после того, как "НАБЛЕВАЛА дюжина гостей".

86

Я предлагаю СССР совершенно честного, без всякой тени вредительства, специалиста режиссера и актера, который берется добросовевестно ставить любую пьесу, начиная с шекспировских пьес и вплоть до пьес сегодняшнего дня.

Я прошу о назначении меня лаборантом режиссером в I-й Художественный Театр - в лучшую школу, возглавляемую мастерами К.С. Станиславским и В.И.Немировичем-Данченко.

Если меня не назначат режиссером, я прошусь на штатную должность статиста. Если и статистом нельзя - я прошусь на должность рабочего сцены.

Если же и это невозможно, я прошу Советское Правительство поступить со мной, как оно найдет нужным, но как нибудь поступить, потому что у меня, драматурга, написавшего 5 пьес, известного в СССР и заграницей, налицо, В ДАННЫЙ МОМЕНТ, - нищета, улица и гибель.

Москва, 28 марта 1930 года.

First and last pages of Bulgakov's famous letter of 28 March 1930 to the USSR government, showing passages marked by OGPU chief Yagoda. (The complete text may be found in English in J.A.E. Curtis, Manuscripts Don't Burn, Harvill, 1992, pp 103–10.)

towards me as it sees fit but to take some action, because AT THE PRESENT MOMENT I, a dramatist and author of five plays known in the USSR and abroad, am confronted by poverty, homelessness and imminent death.

The letter was quite clearly prompted by the public hounding of Bulgakov, which was the equivalent of his civic "execution" as a writer. The only person who could resolve this dramatic impasse was Stalin. Bulgakov had no choice but to enter into a dialogue with the Leader.

Yet Bulgakov was not just defending himself but the right of an author to freedom of expression and to life. The reaction to this public challenge would likewise have a wider resonance.

The author had reason to expect an answer. Everyone knew that Stalin paid particular attention to Bulgakov, considering him perhaps the most gifted and important dramatist in the USSR. As is confirmed by the Moscow Art Theatre's records, Stalin came to see *Days of the Turbins* no less than 15 times.

The challenge had been issued. What would be the response?

Act V: The Decision

Bulgakov's version.

LET'S IMAGINE THAT . . .

Brrm! Brrm! A motorcycle pulls into the Kremlin. Misha enters the hall and there sit Stalin, Molotov, Voroshilov, Kaganovich, Mikoyan and Yagoda.

Misha halts at the door, and bows deeply.

STALIN. What's this? Why barefoot?

BULGAKOV (*sadly throwing up his hands*). Well, truth to tell . . . I have no boots . . .

STALIN. What's this? My writer has no boots? Disgraceful! Yagoda, off with your boots, give them to him.

YAGODA *takes off his boots and with revulsion passes them to Misha. Misha tries to pull them on, but it's no good. . .*

BULGAKOV. They don't fit.

STALIN. Whatever kind of feet have you got, Yagoda?

Finally MOLOTOV's *boots fit* BULGAKOV's *feet.*

STALIN. There we are! Good. Now tell me, what's your problem? Why did you write me such a letter?

In fact, Bulgakov's fate was decided six weeks after he wrote the letter. Any of the passages noted by Yagoda would have been enough to send him to the Lubyanka. Something quite different happened. Heavily underlining the writer's name, Yagoda added the following resolution to the top of Bulgakov's letter: "Give him the opportunity to work where he wants, G. Ya., 12/IV."

Of course, the head of the OGPU could not take such a decision on his own. The letter had been addressed to the government and Yagoda knew of the Leader's special attitude to Bulgakov. The very style of the resolution is reminiscent of Stalin.

The challenge was taken up and the reply, in spite of Bulgakov's amazing boldness, was positive. Why such a conciliatory gesture was made becomes clear from the third document in the secret dossier.

It is a report to the OGPU entitled "The Letter of M.A. Bulgakov". It is undated and the author remains unknown. Judging by the text, however, it was written by someone close to literary and theatrical circles. We can only guess whether this opinion was freely volunteered or commissioned by the OGPU. It seems clear that the author was not personally close to Bulgakov because he used the services of others.

The Letter of M.A. Bulgakov

There is a great deal of talk in literary and intelligentsia circles about Bulgakov's letter.

People are saying the following.

When Bulgakov's position became intolerable (exactly why will be explained below) he wrote three letters with the same contents, in a fit of despair, to I.V. Stalin, F. Kon (in Glaviskusstvo*) and the OGPU.

In these letters Bulgakov wrote, with characteristic venom and sarcasm, that he had worked in the Soviet press for a number of years, that he had several plays [to his credit] and about 400 newspaper reviews, of which 398 were unfavourable** to the point of persecution, and calling for little short of his physical extermination. This persecution had made of him a leper: not only theatres began to avoid him but also editors and even representatives of those organizations where he wished to find a job. A quite intolerable position had been created, not

---

*The Arts department at the People's Commissariat of Enlightenment.
**In his letter Bulgakov mentioned a total of 301 references to his work over 10 years, only three of which were favourable.

only psychologically but also in a purely material sense, bordering on poverty. Bulgakov asked that either he and his family be allowed to go abroad or he be given the chance to work.

When Felix Kon received this letter he wrote a resolution: "In view of the unacceptable tone of this letter, it will not be considered . . ."

Here we shall interrupt the OGPU informer's report for a moment.

Act VI: The Phone Call

Bulgakov's version.

LET'S IMAGINE THAT . . .

STALIN. . . . So tell me what the problem is? Why did you write me such a letter?

BULGAKOV. Well, you see . . . I write play after play, but what's the point? For instance, at this moment a play of mine is sitting at the Moscow Art Theatre. They won't put it on, they won't pay any money . . .

STALIN. Is that so! Just one moment. Wait a minute. (*Makes a telephone call.*)
Is that the Art Theatre, yes? Stalin speaking. Get me Stanislavsky. (*Pause.*) What? Dead? When? Just now? (*To Misha*) You see, he died when they told him. (*Misha sighs heavily.*)
Just one moment. Wait a minute. Don't sigh. (*Makes another telephone call.*) Is that the Art Theatre, yes? Stalin speaking. Get me Nemirovich-Danchenko. (*Pause.*) What? Dead?! Also dead? When? (*To Misha*) You see, he also died just now when they told him.
Never mind, just a minute. (*Makes another telephone call.*) Then get somebody else! Who's that? Yegorov? Listen here, Comrade Yegorov, there's a play lying around in the theatre (*winks at Misha*) by the writer Bulgakov. What's that? You also think it's a good play? And you would like to stage it? When were you thinking . . . (*covers the mouthpiece with his hand and asks Misha:* When do you want?*)

BULGAKOV. Lord, if they could only put it on in even three years time!

STALIN. Tsk tsk! (*To* YEGOROV) I don't like interfering in theatrical affairs but it seems to me that you might put it on (*winks at Misha*) . . . in three months time . . . What? In three weeks time? Well, that's not bad. And how much are you thinking of paying for it? (*covers the mouthpiece with his hand and asks Misha*: How much do you want?)

BULGAKOV. Mmmh . . . let's say . . . well, no less than 500 roubles!

STALIN. Ai-ai-ai! (*To* YEGOROV) Of course, I'm not a specialist in financial matters but it seems to me that you ought to pay 50,000 roubles for a play like that. What? 60,000? Well, go on then, pay him that! (*To Misha*) There you are, and you were saying . . .

As we know, despite the "unacceptable tone" of Bulgakov's letter, Stalin and Yagoda did give it their consideration and on 12 April they permitted the writer to live and work.

Only two days later another writer, Mayakovsky, would commit suicide.

The unnamed OGPU informer continues the story:

Several days passed and then the phone rang in Bulgakov's flat.
"Are you Comrade Bulgakov?"
"Yes."
"Comrade Stalin will now speak to you."
Bulgakov was quite convinced that this was a hoax but he waited all the same. Two to three minutes later he heard a voice over the telephone: "I apologize, Comrade Bulgakov, that I could not reply quickly to your letter but I was very busy. I was very interested by your letter. I would like to have a talk with you. I don't know when it will be possible since, as I said, I am extremely occupied but I shall let you know when I can see you. In any case, we shall try to do something for you."
As soon as the conversation had ended Bulgakov rang up the Kremlin and said that he had just had a call from someone who said he was Stalin. They replied that it had indeed been Comrade Stalin. Bulgakov was quite amazed.
Some time afterwards, almost the same day, Bulgakov received an invitation asking if he could find the time to visit Glaviskusstvo. F. Kon met Bulgakov with every consideration, offering him a chair etc.
"What's the problem? Whatever are you up to, M.A.? What on earth could be the matter? What do you want?"
"I would like you to let me travel abroad."
"Come now, come now, M.A., there can be no question of that, we value you so highly," etc.
"In that case, then at least give me the opportunity to write, to work, to do something."
"But what do you want, what can you do?"
"Anything at all! I could work in an office, be a notary, a theatre director, I could . . ."
"In which theatre would you like to be a director?"

"To be quite honest, I consider the Moscow Art Theatre the best and closest to me personally. That's a place I'd work with pleasure."

"All right. We'll give it some thought."

With that, the conversation with F. Kon came to an end.

Soon Bulgakov was invited to come to the Moscow Art Theatre where a contract had already been drawn up for him as a director . . .

This report was very cunningly put together. It is full of respect for Bulgakov and, at the same time, of unconcealed admiration for Stalin. None of those whose words are quoted are identified by name. If someone had wanted to play down the serious nature of Bulgakov's duel with the authorities they would have presented the story in this light, transforming it into a convenient legend of the wise ruler and his malicious servants rather than consider the contents of the letter.

It has a value, however, as one more version of the historic encounter between the Master and the Leader. The account of the telephone conversation is accurate and is confirmed by the testimony of Yelena Sergeevna and Lyubov Yevgenievna who were both standing next to Bulgakov when he picked up the phone. The only thing missing is Bulgakov's request to let him go abroad: that would have rather spoiled the radiant picture.

The document proves how cunningly and carefully Stalin operated. He calculated each move and every gesture was aimed at confirming the myth that he was a magnanimous and wise ruler and, moreover, a patron of the arts. The report continues:

The whole story, everyone says, resembles an attractive legend, and to many seems simply incredible.

It is important to note down the conversations that are now going on about Stalin in literary and intelligentsia circles.

One has the impression that the dam has burst and now all have seen Comrade Stalin's true face.

There was, after all, it seemed, no name around which more venomous opinions seemed to cluster – a fanatic who was leading the country to disaster, who was considered to blame for all our misfortunes etc, a bloodthirsty creature, crouching behind the Kremlin walls.

Now people say: "Stalin really is an outstanding man and, just imagine, he's simple and accessible."

One of the actors from the Vakhtangov Theatre: "Stalin has been to see *Zoya's Apartment** a couple of times. He said with an accent: "It's a good play. I can't understand why they first permit it and then

---

*Bulgakov's play was finished in late 1925 and had its premiere in 1926. It was withdrawn from the repertoire in March 1929.

ban it. A good play. I can't see anything wrong with it."

People recall a meeting with him when he was still either Commissar for Nationalities or in charge of the Workers and Peasants Inspectorate: he was very simple, without any arrogance and talked to everyone as an equal. There was never any haughtiness.

Most important of all, they say that Stalin has nothing to do with the chaos. He was following the right policies but is surrounded by swine. It was they who hounded Bulgakov, one of the most gifted Soviet writers. Various literary good-for-nothings made their career by persecuting Bulgakov and now Stalin has slapped them down.

It should be said, that the popularity of Stalin has developed a simply extraordinary form. He is spoken of with warmth and affection, and the legendary story of Bulgakov's letter is being retold in various forms.

Epilogue

Bulgakov's version.

LET'S IMAGINE THAT . . .

After this Stalin finds he simply cannot live without Misha, they are always together. But one day Misha comes up and says:

BULGAKOV. I must go to Kiev for about three weeks.

STALIN. What kind of a friend are you? What shall I do?

But Misha goes all the same. STALIN, *all on his own, longs to see him.*

STALIN. Misha, Misha! My Misha's gone. I'm so bored, what shall I do? Go and see a play, perhaps?

A parody, of course, for reality was much less idyllic. In fact, the duel continued.

It is hard to say who won, if either. Stalin managed to deceive his contemporaries: Bulgakov was allowed to live and write his best work, *The Master and Margarita*.

After the conversation with Stalin Bulgakov was taken on as an assistant director at the Moscow Art Theatre, the *Days of the Turbins* was revived, and he could earn his living again. But none of his other plays was put on and only after his death, and after Stalin had also quitted the stage, did he begin to be published once more.

Bulgakov was not himself arrested. He spent his whole life, however, waiting for the knock at the door, "under the heel" of the regime. In this respect his fate was like that of many other writers to whom the authorities applied various "preventive measures": if not arrest, then a ban on publication or travel abroad, deprivation of work and the means of survival. The psychological deformation that resulted hastened the end.

Bulgakov did not consider himself a hero but it required considerable courage to remain a writer in such circumstances. In the verse she wrote in memory of him, Anna Akhmatova spoke of his "magnificent disdain". The victory in the duel, finally belonged to the Master. But he did not live long enough to celebrate it.

CHAPTER 4

AT THE LUBYANKA

The Heirs of Iron Felix

"They didn't send the files from Leningrad for you again," Boris Olegovich tells me, "there was no wrapping paper left, they say."

When I need a photocopy the Xerox is broken; if it's dark in the room, there's a shortage of light bulbs and supplies won't issue any more. Now there's nothing to wrap up parcels in. It's difficult to tell when they're being serious.

"Well then, while they're looking for paper in Leningrad, let's get on with something different, shall we?" I suggest.

"You're disturbing me!" Ivan Sergeevich intervenes. "Find somewhere else to work." I decide not to react to provocation.

"Boris Olegovich, where can I work?"

"You know how difficult it is here," he sighs. "I can't think where to put you . . ."

Another morning's work at the Lubyanka begins. I'm in the archives department on the second floor. I don't know the ranks of the two KGB men there because I've never seen them in uniform. They certainly demonstrate their different characters.

Boris Olegovich is slight and agile, and always very occupied. He says little but is polite, looks you directly in the eye, and talks in an undertone. A very neat and fastidiously tidy man, he only does what he is told: "My superiors will have to decide that," he says in difficult cases, "I'm only a small cog here."

Sitting opposite him is a very different personality. Ivan Sergeevich is massive, a large belly spilling over his trousers, and he is noisy, harsh and categorical. Negligent in everything he does, as if it is below his dignity, he is never in a hurry. "Some more dust for you to breathe," and he tosses the files onto the table.

This morning, watching as his colleague takes some files out of the safe for me, the irrepressible Ivan Sergeevich again butted in: "That's right, give them all the files, and then they'll get royalties for publishing our agents' names!"

This time my patience snapped.

"How dare you!" I yelled. "As long as people like you still work here, nothing will change. And everyone will continue to hate the Lubyanka!"

Ivan Sergeevich turned purple and left the room without a word, slamming the door behind him.

Later in the endless Lubyanka corridor Boris Olegovich tried to calm me down: "Don't mind him, he gets so worked up recently . . ."

95

"The wounded animal is more dangerous," I replied. Why did I ever begin, I think to myself.

Today, as it turns out, they had found me a good place to sit.

The window looks out into a courtyard, which is filled with containers and boxes. A deep wellshaft surrounded by tall walls completely masks the sky. Solitary snowflakes twirl down. It must have got colder outside. In here it's stuffy and the air is stale.

This is a standard office in the Lubyanka. A writing table, and nearby, another with several telephones. Some have a crest on them. A cupboard, clothes hanger and, in the corner, a large metal safe. There is also one exotic touch: a drooping lemon bush on the marble windowsill (my archivists have an aquarium full of fish in their room).

"Don't touch anything," I was warned.

It is silent apart from the ticking of a clock. Where is the usual inhabitant of this room – dismissed or promoted for his behaviour during the recent August putsch?* Sick or away on business?'

On the wall, there is a large street map of Moscow and the following framed text:

> The work of a Chekist is hard and thankless in personal terms, and very responsible and important for the state ... The Chekist can only be a warrior in the cause of the proletariat when he feels the support of the Party for every step he takes ...

A quotation from Dzerzhinsky. And now the poor devils have neither support nor even the Party. They no longer have a master.

Well, Felix Edmundovich, I think gazing at the photograph of Dzerzhinsky on the wall, can you help me travel back to that different era, contained in the file that awaits me on the table? The record of the things that you and your heirs, the men with "passionate hearts, cool heads and clean hands", have been doing in the name of the Revolution for the last 70 years?

Going down to the canteen in the middle of the day I suddenly find myself alone in the lift with Ivan Sergeevich. We do not look at each other and I realize that I am not angry with the man.

Perhaps he doesn't hate me either, only the misfortune that has befallen him. What did he and his colleagues feel when their idol Dzerzhinsky was toppled from his pedestal in August 1991 and the memorial plaque to Yury Andropov was daubed with a swastika? When the furious crowd threatened to storm the building?

*The attempted putsch of August 1991.

The canteen at the Lubyanka is abominable. The old fairy tales that they over-feed their staff, and charge them almost nothing, are not true. Poor quality and high prices. The serving women are also scowling and unfriendly. Still, when you remember that this used to be a part of the Inner Prison, life begins to look a little better.

I like reading all the signs and notices at the Lubyanka. Simple curiosity not espionage is my motivation but occasionally I still get the feeling I'm spying. For instance, when I read on a poster of the Dzerzhinsky Club, 12 Greater Lubyanka Street, the instruction "Only to be displayed in State Security buildings".

It is offering:

- A Discotheque,
- A talk by Dr Shatalova "The reason for living and believing in miracles"
- Family Evening "Give the women flowers!"
- Meeting of the Dzerzhinsky literary club's poetry section [!!]
- Excursion to Dostoevsky museum: the art of Roerich
- Guest comedians . . .

What do they have to laugh about, I wonder, that we should not be allowed to hear?

However, the most interesting notice was the one I read today as I was leaving the canteen. Inside the door there was a fading paper:

Dear guests!
Over the last month the following items have been removed from our service area: 70 children's plates, 117 dessert plates, 173 plates, 40 stainless steel forks, 40 aluminium forks, 21 stainless steel knives, and 170 glasses.
Total value, 3057 roubles.
  Spare a thought for the staff. We have to pay for lost cutlery and plates from our own pockets. Please return all plates and cutlery to the canteen.
The canteen staff

There is a notice on the other side of the door as well.

Results of raid.
  A raid to collect plates has been carried out in offices on the first and second floors of building No 2. We want to thank the staff who helped us.
  As a result the following items have been returned to the canteen: 28 aluminium forks, 12 teaspoons, 3 knives and 43 plates.

I was so intrigued I copied the text into my notebook. The notice was not marked "confidential" so I hoped I was not leaking some secret information. The very next day, however, it was announced on television that a great many KGB generals and officers were being dismissed for the basest offences: they had illegally taken possession of dachas, flats, cars and had even stolen consignments of televisions and refrigerators. The plates, forks and glasses in the Lubyanka canteen ceased to appear so strange.

General Krayushkin

We were sitting in General Krayushkin's office (yes, he had now been promoted), after the latest session of our "anti-troika", drinking strong tea with tasty rolls.

"You're an excellent secret service man, you know," I said.

"Why?"

"We have met countless times but I still know almost nothing about you."

After that Krayushkin would talk a little about himself. I don't know if they continued to maintain a file on me at the Lubyanka but, looking through my notebooks, I find that I built up my own dossier on Krayushkin.

A tall, red-cheeked man with a simple villager's face and a strong handshake, born in the provincial central Russian city of Kaluga at the end of the war, he at first struck me as the ideal obedient officer. The longer we worked together, however, opening up the archives, the less simple he seemed. I found him an attractive person and wondered why he had ended up in an organization that all decent people avoided like the plague.

"It isn't as clear-cut as that," he replied. "You'll be surprised but I always dreamed of being an actor. I used to perform at school concerts and belonged to the drama and dance clubs. I even applied to drama college after school and got a place there . . ."

"So what happened?"

"I went back to see my parents and there were my call-up papers for the army. Not the usual service, though. I was allocated to the special regiment guarding the Kremlin. I consider myself lucky that I was one of the very few to be selected as sentries outside Lenin's Mausoleum and inside, by the sarcophagus . . ."

I was fascinated.

"I always used to wonder, what are those lads thinking about as they stand there? Is it hard work?"

"I stood a total of 500 hours there . . . Of course, there is a psychological pressure, and a sense of responsibility. You know that everyone is watching you. And when you march you want to present a handsome spectacle."

"But why, after that, the KGB and not the stage?"

"While I was serving at the Kremlin someone from the special section attached to our regiment suggested that I work for the security service. I have other plans, actually, I replied. I know, he said, but our work is rather similar to what you hoped to do. Think about it . . . And, gradually, after a great deal of thought, I decided. If you go in for something artistic you must be very sure of your talent not to end up playing minor supporting roles. I did not have that confidence . . ."

"No regrets?"

"The way things turned out I managed to develop my abilities to a great extent in the security service. It also demands intellect and improvisation, after all. Any person plays his role in life, doesn't he? If you've decided to do something then you must devote yourself wholly to it. Only then do you uncover your own abilities . . ."

Krayushkin went to the KGB college, and graduated as a legal specialist with knowledge of foreign languages. He worked in counter-intelligence, at defence plants in Novorossiisk and Chelyabinsk. In 1976 they moved him to Moscow where he began to work in the archives, first at the depository outside the city and then in the central archive. Then he was a senior lieutenant. He advanced from deputy head of the archive until today he wears a general's stars and heads the entire Registration and Archive Section of the Security Ministry.

"Are you a Communist?"

"I was, of course. In the Committee you actually were not allowed not to join the Party," he replied. "After the August putsch, though, as you know, the President issued a decision that the security services should be depoliticized. I was totally behind this decision: we must guard the interests of the legitimate authorities."

"But you were a Communist for many years. When did your views begin to change – not just overnight with the putsch?"

"Of course, views change slowly but in fact it was most of all in the last few years.

"I went from school to the army, and moreover into a special regiment, and from there to the KGB college. Then I immediately joined an organization which led a life quite isolated from society. We had our own special tasks and lived at arm's length from everyone else: I did not have to see and feel how ordinary people, or, say, the intelligentsia lived."

"And the putsch . . . ?"

"It caught me quite unawares! I was driving to work and heard about it over the radio . . . All that week we sat on tenterhooks at the Lubyanka. We watched out of the window as they pulled down the statue of Dzerzhinsky, and threatened to storm the building. We were ready for anything. But I was quite clear in my mind that our superiors had gone against the people's wishes and the course of history."

"But things didn't go smoothly for you with the new management: I was told that you submitted your resignation?"

"I did, because I felt that they suspected me and did not trust me. I couldn't work in such conditions. But they did not accept my resignation and even entrusted me with a more important post. All these years when political debates and struggles were going on, we had a quite specific job to do, working in the archives. I was one of the first to begin the present rehabilitation."

This was indeed true. I discovered that long before perestroika began Krayushkin had quietly been filling a separate card index with materials about writers, actors and artists who had been arrested or shot.

"When I was still a child I heard a lot of talk from my parents and relations about how the nation had drowned in blood and sorrow in the 1930s and 1940s. It sunk in very deeply. So when the time came I was well prepared for the work." Krayushkin's father was an agronomist and his mother, an accountant; they brought up the young Anatoly in the Urals.

"When things seemed to be disintegrating totally in the service and we didn't know what would happen tomorrow, I repeatedly told my staff: you're doing a worthy job and no one can doubt its necessity. Therefore get on with your work and don't become distracted!"

I never could have imagined that I would enter the Lubyanka and work there, reading and re-reading these historical documents.

Then the doors of the KGB began to open. I saw its present inhabitants. Varied individuals, also caught up in this historical change, men and women, who must obey orders. The heirs of Iron Felix did not come from another planet. They are members of the same nation, and will follow where it leads.

CHAPTER 5

A RUSSIAN LEONARDO DA VINCI:

THE FILES ON PAVEL FLORENSKY

Before me lay a bulging file. I opened it and was confronted by face after face – young, old, men and women – several pages of photographs pasted into the record of the investigation. At once I realized that these people were doomed. In one way or another they had all been destroyed. I shut the file. Then, steeling myself, opened it once more.

There was a list of 80 names. Theologians, priests, monks, scholars, crafts-men, traders, nurses and peasants had been arrested as accomplices by the OGPU and accused of a single "crime", their faith. It was the only thing of which they were indisputably "guilty", since all the other accusations were falsified and invented. An abyss had yawned to swallow them up. As I worked my way through the search and arrest warrants, depositions, official notes and receipts I tried to glimpse what had really happened to them.

Among the names was that of Pavel Florensky. Today he is often referred to as the Russian Leonardo da Vinci. His main theological work, *The Pillar and Ground of the Truth*, was published in 1914 and became a major event for the "silver age" of Russian thought and literature; it brought its author fame when still a young man. "In Father Pavel both love of learning and of the church, both Athens and Jerusalem, have met," wrote another religious thinker, his friend Sergey Bulgakov. Florensky was, at one and the same time, a mathematician, physicist, inventor and engineer, who combined research with a vast range of practical work. He lectured and he worked for scientific journals, institutions, and experimental laboratories. He also wrote poems, and studies of history, language and art.

He himself considered that his main calling was as a priest and pastor. A living bridge between the Orthodox Church and the intelligentsia, in many ways Pavel Florensky defined the spiritual atmosphere of the day.

As a scholar and scientist his interests were both wide-ranging and profound. He studied the biosphere and what he termed the pneumatosphere, "that special part of matter which is drawn into the orbit ... of the spirit". He studied time and space, the theory of relativity, aspects of language and popular culture, the orga-nization of museums, Greek symbols, electrical engineering, the properties of different materials and geology. A random sample of his publications is astound-ing in itself: "At the Watershed of Thought" (on art), "Dielectrics", "The Number as Form", "Philosophy of the Cult", "The Early Russian Names for Precious Stones", "Filling Compounds for Cable Sleeves".

Yet it is not the sheer quantity of his writings that is important. In every sphere he was an innovator, a pioneer of new trends and currents in both science and culture. It is our misfortune that the great majority of these works were not published while he was alive. He was too far ahead of his time. Only today can we see him as he really was.

In the files on his two arrests, however, Florensky is an obscurantist, a criminal and a menace to society who was kept constantly under close observation and persecuted up until his death.

The last period of his life was until recently the most mysterious. It was hidden away from us in secret archives and shrouded in conjecture and legend. We did not even know exactly when he died, or where and how. Then the current occupants of the Lubyanka were forced to pull the three massive files on his two arrests out of their fire-proof safes. The veil of mystery surrounding the last 10 years of his life was finally lifted.

"People of the Past"

In spring 1928 the OGPU began to build up its case against the "counter-revolutionary centre" at the Trinity-St Sergey monastery* in the town of Sergiev Possad, some 70 km north east of Moscow.

All Pavel Florensky's life was linked to the monastery. He studied and then taught at the Spiritual Academy there. He was consecrated a priest and served in one of its churches. With his large happy family he lived in a wooden house near the monastery, constantly engaged in study and research. He could think of no better place to be: "In the future I imagine this monastery becoming a Russian Athens, a living museum of Russia, which bubbles over with study and creativity, a place where institutions and individuals, in peaceful cooperation and benevolent competition, together strive to create a full and balanced culture, to bring a new Hellas into being ..."

These ideals were now brutally attacked and destroyed. The newspapers and magazines published one exposé after another. On 12 May a certain A. Lyass wrote in the *Rabochaya gazeta* (Workers' Newspaper):

> All kinds of "people of the past" – but mainly Grand Dukes, ladies-in-waiting, priests and monks – have built themselves a hive at the so-called Trinity-St Sergey monastery. If formerly the Grand Dukes protected the priests, now the priests are protecting the Grand Dukes ...
> Soon after the October Revolution the monasteries, those vipers' nests

---

*Founded in the mid-fourteenth century by St Sergey of Radonezh, confessor of Dmitry Donskoi, Prince of Moscow. From the outset the monastery was associated with Russia's revival after its liberation from the Mongol-Tatar yoke; by the early twentieth century the town of Sergiev attracted many tens of thousands of pilgrims each year.

of parasites and scroungers, were disbanded. The monks, however, decided otherwise and have adapted to present circumstances. This can no longer be tolerated. This hive of Black Hundreds must be destroyed. The relevant bodies must pay particular attention to the town of Sergiev ...

On 17 May, M. Am-ly, the special correspondent of *Rabochaya Moskva*,* joined in:

The ancient walls of the former Trinity-St Sergey monastery are mute witnesses of a grey-haired antiquity. How much they could tell the world about the shocking things that took place here! The revolutionary storm hardly touched the centuries-old walls of this former citadel of depravity. A sign merely appeared on the west side of the feudal wall: THE SERGIEV STATE MUSEUM. Concealed behind this saving label, the most stubborn "authorities" have settled in here, like two-legged rats who scuttle away with valuable old items, conceal a mass of filth and emit a filthy stench ...

The anonymous author then turned to particular individuals and came to Pavel Florensky:

Certain "learned" authorities are publishing religious books for mass distribution under the label of a state research institution. In most cases these are simply collections of "holy" icons, crucifixes and other such rubbish ... Here is one of those texts. You may find it on page 17 of the extensive "scholarly" work by two research associates of the museum, P.A. Florensky and Yu.A. Olsufiev.** It was issued by one of the state publishing houses in 1927 under the title *Ambrose Troitsky, a Fifteenth-century Engraver*. The authors, for example, explain: "Of the nine dark pictures (engravings appended to the book, M.A.) eight definitely refer to events in the life of Jesus Christ, while the ninth depicts the beheading of John [the Baptist]."
You have to be very crafty and insolent fellows to present such nonsense to Soviet readers under the title of a "scholarly book" in the tenth year of the revolution. Every Young Pioneer† knows that the legend that Christ existed is nothing more than a priestly fraud.
At last! Following the outcry in the press about what is going on in Sergiev a commission has just arrived from the Main Research Administration and sealed the archives ...

*(Lit. Working Moscow.)
**An historian and art specialist, who died in a Soviet labour camp in 1939.
†Communist youth organization for schoolchildren aged between 10 and 14.

All the above-quoted excerpts come from the investigation file where they were incorporated straight from the newspapers and magazines. The press was thus used as both informer and provocateur. Public opinion had been prepared.

A week later the OGPU carried out an extensive raid on the monastery and the surrounding area. A large group of priests and lay members of the church were arrested and brought to Butyrki prison in Moscow. The operation was intended to strike at two targets. The first was the Orthodox Church which had already been fundamentally weakened. The second was the remnants of the Russian gentry, including prominent members of the aristocracy: they had gathered around the monastery for protection and it, like churches in the past, offered them a last refuge.

They came to arrest Florensky early on the morning of 21 May 1928. The warrant was signed by Genrikh Yagoda himself, the head of the OGPU. It was the commissar in charge of operations, Zhilin, who arrested Florensky and searched his house. He did not, thank God, then examine the author's manuscripts. A semi-literate low-ranking officer, Zhilin would hardly have made any sense of them. He instead saw sedition in a Red Cross badge and a photograph of the last tsar, both of which he confiscated as incriminating material. The successful "removal" of Florensky was communicated to headquarters in Moscow at 10 am.

When he arrived at the Lubyanka Florensky was given the usual form to fill in: Florensky, Pavel Alexandrovich, 46 years old, of gentry family, son of an engineer, born in the town of Yevlakh in Azerbaijan, graduated from Moscow University and the Spiritual Academy; wife, three sons and two daughters; scientific researcher; head of the material studies department at the Institute of Electrical Engineering, an editor of the *Technical Encyclopedia*, and former professor of the Spiritual Academy.

Had he ever been in court before? "Yes, for preaching a sermon in 1906 against the execution of Lieutenant Schmidt," wrote Florensky in a rapid scribble of minute letters that is now difficult to decipher. The Schmidt affair had been the only occasion on which Florensky permitted himself to make a remotely political statement: Pyotr Schmidt, a revolutionary, led the uprising against the tsar in Sebastopol during the 1905 revolution, was tried, and shot on 6 March 1906. Now, if ever, was the moment to turn this incident to his own advantage. Florensky would not do so, however. He did not want his action to be misinterpreted, even for his own good. The sermon had been a purely moral act, undertaken in defence of an individual and not of a political doctrine.

In fact, he had never made any secret of his attitude towards politics. A year before his arrest he wrote in his autobiography:

I have almost nothing to say about political issues. My own inclinations, occupations and interests, and my understanding of history have always led me to shun politics. Historical events, I am convinced, unfold according to laws of social dynamics that have still to be discovered and they certainly do not proceed in the way their participants intend. Moreover, I consider it harmful for society when scholars and scientists, whose vocation it is to be dispassionate experts, become involved in politics. I have never in my life belonged to any political party whatsoever.

This autobiography was no private composition but was submitted to an official Soviet institution. Florensky now continued to defend such views at the Lubyanka.

While filling in the form he also explained the origins of the "incriminating material". The Red Cross badge had been given to him "after I helped carry the wounded from the front [during World War I]. The photograph of the reception with the Tsar was handed to me, with several other photographs, after the death of one priest."

No formal charge was presented to the arrested man.

On 25 May the one and only interrrogation took place. Florensky himself wrote down the answers.

The photograph of the Tsar was produced and shown to him.

Q. Why do you keep this? What does it mean?
A. I keep the photograph of Nicholas II in memory of Bishop Antony [Florensov].*
Q. What is your attitude to the tsar?
A. I am well-disposed towards him, and I feel pity for someone whose intentions were better than those of other men but who had the tragic destiny of becoming a ruler.
Q. And your attitude to the Soviet authorities?
A. I am well-disposed towards the Soviet authorities and am engaged in research of a secret nature for a [Soviet] military institution. I took up the work voluntarily and myself suggested this field of investigation. I regard the Soviet authorities as the only real force capable of improving the conditions of the masses. I do not agree with certain measures taken by the Soviet authorities but am unconditionally opposed to any [outside] intervention, whether military or economic.
Q. With whom have you discussed your disagreements with the Soviet authorities?

*Florensky's confessor whom the writers Blok, Bely and Merezhkovsky, among others, came to visit at the Donskoi monastery in Moscow.

A. I have not had any conversations with anybody about those measures with which I am not in agreement . . .

The others arrested in the same case were also interrogated then. Most likewise declared their loyalty to the present authorities or, at most, asserted apolitical views ("any authority is God-given", "the Soviet authorities leave me alone and I do not interfere with them"). Some were fatalistic in the attitude. "I have never spoken out against the Soviet authorities anywhere," stated Sophia Tuchkova, daughter of Count Tatishchev and a medical nurse, "since I consider that such an upheaval [as the Revolution] in our lives arose naturally in the course of history. I have also never spoken about the desecration of churches on the part of the Soviet authorities. I consider this a natural occurrence in history although to begin with it was hard for me as a religious person to bear."

Only Larin, the higumenos (father superior) of the Monastery of the Paraclete, firmly declared: "As long as I am alive I shall never refuse to serve the church!" Alexandra Mamontova, an artist and daughter of the industrialist and art patron Savva Mamontov, also showed her character: "I am not a supporter of the Soviet authorities because of the persecution of religion and restrictions imposed on believers. I prefer not to say who my visitors are . . ." (Abramtsevo, the country estate where Mamontov gathered artists and writers about him, is located not far from the monastery in Sergiev.)

Florensky had long been on friendly terms with Alexandra Mamontova. At the height of the Revolution in 1917 he had sent her a prophetic letter:

> Naturally, all that is going on around us causes great distress. I hope and believe, however, that once this nihilism has exhausted itself and proved its worthlessness, everyone will have had enough of it. It will become hated and then, once all this vileness has come to nothing, our hearts and minds will turn again to the Russian Idea – not lethargically and circumspectly, as before, but with renewed desire . . . I am sure that the worst still lies ahead: the crisis has not yet passed. But I believe that the crisis will purify the Russian atmosphere . . .

There was, it may be added, one tsarist police officer among this very mixed catch. Former Lieutenant-Colonel Mikhail Banin had earlier "recruited and run informers, and arrested revolutionaries". A note added to the file stated that in the Soviet period he "was registered as an OGPU informer for the Sergiev district". Banin was now asked to "aid the OGPU, but he turned the offer down". This evidently explains his heavy sentence: 10 years in the Far Northern camp of Solovki in the White Sea.

The case was quickly dealt with. On 29 May the charge sheet had already been drawn up:

From information obtained by its agents, the Secret Section of the OGPU learned that, as anti-Soviet forces were becoming more active, the following citizens, who were all "people of the past" (Grand Dukes and Duchesses, Counts etc) had begun to present a certain threat to the Soviet system, ie in respect to the measures the authorities are taking in a whole number of fields. The information at the disposal of the OGPU from its agents began to find confirmation in press reports.

Investigator Polyansky suggested that formalities be dispensed with and the case be handed over to the Secret Section's troika. This meant either a camp sentence or even the death penalty. His superiors were more circumspect. Such extreme measures might provoke undesirable reactions and alarm ordinary people, they decided. Exile would be sufficient: in this way we shall punish them and, at the same time, appear humane.

On 8 June all those detained were sentenced to be exiled. Florensky figured as No 25 in the record of the sitting of the OGPU collegium's Special Board:

> To be released from detention and deprived of the right to reside in Moscow, Leningrad, Kharkov, Kiev, Odessa, Rostov-on-Don and the following provinces and districts, and obliged to remain in a fixed place of residence for three years.

On 14 July, after saying farewell to friends and family, Florensky set out for Nizhny Novgorod, the town where he had chosen to live and would be "under the supervision of the Nizhny Novgorod OGPU". (More than 50 years later Andrey Sakharov would be exiled to the same city, by then renamed Gorky.)

An additional note clarified the deportation procedure: "The departure of each of the convicted persons must be organized so that they do not wander freely round the city but are escorted directly to their train by [OGPU] employees."

Fortunately, Florensky's exile only lasted for a few months. The pre-revolutionary compassion for victims of political persecution still had not entirely disappeared. Gorky's former wife, Yekaterina Peshkova, who headed the "Political Red Cross", managed to secure the annulment of his exile. A new decree of the Special Board followed: "To be released before the end of sentence and permitted residence anywhere in the USSR."

Florensky returned home and the Secret Police left him in peace for a few years more.

"May it...die with me"

"From exile I have returned to 'hard labour'," commented Florensky, once back in Moscow.

To all appearances his life resumed as before, an intensive existence, entirely filled with work and study. It was as if he had never been at the Lubyanka or sent into exile. Florensky resumed his experiments and studies, he wrote and gave lectures, and he served both in the church and at the Institute of Electrical Engineering.

His unusual figure, however, drew ever-increasing attention and comment. Even in appearance, he stood out. Everywhere he went he wore the cassock and tall cylindrical *kamilavka* or headgear of an Orthodox priest, his eyes lowered, head bent, engrossed in reflection. At best, he seemed an incurable crank. Obviously, he was "not one of us" . . .

"Who is that?" Trotsky once asked in amazement, when he spotted Florensky's white cassock. Trotsky, a man of little modesty concerning his own intellectual abilities, then headed, among his many other posts, Glavelektro, the Main Electrical Administration. On one of his tours of inspection, Trotsky again noticed the white cassock in the basement laboratory.

"That's Professor Florensky," he was told.

"Yes, yes, I know . . ."

Trotsky approached Florensky and magnanimously invited him to participate in a forthcoming congress of engineers.

"Only you'll have to wear something else, of course."

"I have not renounced my vows as a priest," replied Florensky, "and cannot dress in any other way."

"You can't? Well then, come like that."

When Florensky mounted the stage an incredulous whisper ran through the audience: a priest is going to address us! Though the report he gave was brilliant and earned its applause, still those who heard it were more amazed by its author. Just imagine: a priest and at the same time a professor, an incorrigible idealist and yet with such knowledge of the exact sciences. The times did not favour such strange birds, however.

It was his fellow scientists who began the campaign against him. The harassment started after the publication of Florensky's book on *The Imaginary in Geometry* where he gave his own interpretation of the Theory of Relativity, and the appearance of his article "The Mathematical Applications of Physics". (The latter contains a description of the electrical integrator, the prototype of modern analogue computers.) The critics did not refute his scientific views. They preferred to portray him as an incorrigible enemy. Everything was then interpreted in terms of class, and often scientific disputes did not lead to the truth but to imprisonment.

His next arrest, therefore, on 26 February 1933, did not surprise him.

"A priest-professor, and an extreme right-wing monarchist in his political views," was the description provided in the official note on his arrest.

This time the Secret Police were better prepared. During their search of the flat he had been provided in Moscow by the institute they confiscated books, manuscripts and even family heirlooms and mementos of his mother's Caucasian forebears. The record of the search described the sabre, knives and broadsword as "offensive weapons".

The head of the Moscow Region OGPU's secret political section, Shupeiko, was in charge of the case. "The guilt of this member of the counter-revolutionary 'Party for the Rebirth of Russia'", he wrote of Florensky, "has been established by the testimony of Professor Gidulyanov ..."

Florensky first heard of this political party, and Professor Gidulyanov, at the Lubyanka. Only a few days would pass, however, before an extraordinary document appeared: Florensky's own testimony.

At this point the pages in the file appear, at first sight, to be blood-stained. They were damp and the red ink Florensky was using ran. He laboured long at this composition. First he drew up a three-page rough draft, then an expanded version five pages long, and finally an appendix that gave the organizational plan of the "counter-revolutionary" party:

> Fully aware of my crimes against the Soviet system and the [Communist] Party, I wish to express in this document my profound repentance for my criminal membership of the nationalist-fascist centre ...

Another document, sewn into the file, casts light on this unexpected transformation. It indicates how Florensky found himself caught up in an investigation where the lives of other prisoners hung in the balance. Faced with the choice, he quite consciously agreed to shoulder the sin of falsehood and self-incrimination.

The letter from law professor Gidulyanov had been sent from Kazakhstan. Gidulyanov was arrested before any of the others named in the case, processed on the "conveyer" of round-the-clock interrogation, and then exiled to Central Asia for 10 years. He was now writing to the procurator's office, he explained, in the hope that he might open the eyes of the Soviet legal system to the arbitrary behaviour and insubordination of the OGPU, and also undo at least a little of the damage he had caused to a great many innocent people, among them Pavel Florensky.

In his complaint-cum-confession, Gidulyanov gives a detailed description of the entire investigation. To be more exact, he describes how the case was itself fabricated during the course of an interrogation that employed every well-known method: intimidation, force, threats of execution or of reprisals against other members of the family, bribery and the use of provocateurs. In the end Gidulyanov had been forced to cooperate, to acknowledge his own "guilt" and incriminate others.

Each truthful statement he made, Gidulyanov writes, and every request to check the veracity of what he was saying, "met with derision and all kinds of abuse of my person". His truthful testimonies "were ripped apart, crumpled up and thrown in my face".

My interrogator, a young man called Shupeiko, himself formulated my counter-revolutionary convictions in such crude terms that, had I been a free man, I would have been appalled. He made me sign these depositions, saying that people were not punished [in the USSR] for their convictions and that if I did not sign his text he would sign for me instead . . .

For as long as it was a question of violence against myself and such stupidities I stood my ground. So then they tried a different tack. They began to treat me with exceptional kindness and gentleness and transferred me to a cell where I was better fed. Shupeiko told me that I was a victim, that I did not know what the OGPU could be like, and that I should believe no one but him alone – for he was my judge, investigator, prosecutor and defence counsel. I was in no danger and would be released and allowed to continue my university work as before. I just needed to disarm, and place myself wholly in the hands and at the mercy of the OGPU. To prove that I had really disarmed, however, I must admit to being a member of a counter-revolutionary organization. Moreover, the worse the crimes I took on myself, the more sincere my confession and the more frank my repentance would be considered.

I was put in a cell with a certain agronomist called Kolechits, who justified the theory of self-disarmament. Kolechits aided me to correct my depositions, showing me what I should change, and he explained to me what he called the "Aesopian language of the OGPU". All of this meant that what they needed from me, when they said self-disarmament, was not the truth but something that had the appearance of the truth.

As a specialist in the history of judicial procedures I could discern in all of this a peculiar form of trial by confession. In the early Middle Ages this was termed the *purgato vulgaris* and later, the *purgato canonica* . . . The suspect, in the medieval trial by confession, we should explain, was not considered innocent even when there was no evidence against him. He himself had to prove his innocence by performing acts that would re-establish his good reputation. Soviet justice, which claimed itself to be the most advanced in the world, had reverted to the level of feudal times.

Having lulled myself with these academic parallels, and being quite unversed in the use of such tactics and of all kinds of provocation on the part of the investigative bodies, I believed their reassurances about [the need for] disarmament. In order to please the OGPU I began to "make efforts" and the more they demanded proof of my repentance, the more deeply I incriminated myself . . .

Shupeiko would work on me in the following way. I would be brought to him and he would prompt me and ask leading questions so as to point me in the desired direction. Then I would "regurgitate" for him. In this way appeared the "literary composition" (Shupeiko's own expression) that I set down on paper as if it were the "honest" truth, and which I then signed: "Written in my own hand and in accordance with the truth". As time passed Shupeiko became so frank about his methods that I wrote everything he wanted at his dictation, all the time considering this to be disarmament. As a reward I was promised my liberty . . .

I placed myself completely in the hands of the OGPU secret-political section and allowed myself to become the director and play the leading tragic role in the trial of some nationalists who, the OGPU decided, were to be transformed into nationalist-fascists. To disarm myself I declared that I was the organizer of the Committee of a nationalist organization that, after several revisions by the OGPU, was christened the "nationalist centre". Moreover, I was instructed who the other members of this mythical committee were: my colleagues Chaplygin, Luzin* and Florensky who were already being held by the OGPU.

Of those mentioned I had never met Professor Florensky and saw him for the first time when we were formally confronted in the OGPU. That was why they forced me to make his acquaintance there . . .

Gidulyanov proved a real find for the OGPU. He named dozens of members of the intelligentsia: all those he could remember, and all those his interrogators suggested, were drawn into the case. The same investigator then introduced Gidulyanov's formulations, word for word, into the testimony of the other prisoners. One after another, a series of self-incriminatory statements systematically linked all the supposed accomplices together in a single "criminal" plot:

As a sign of my greater penitence, I had to take the leading role myself. I, supposedly, was in communication with Florensky in Zagorsk [Sergiev], and through him entered into contact with Chaplygin and Luzin. That was how the mythical committee arose! Chaplygin was chairman, I was the secretary, Florensky the ideologist, and Luzin was in charge of our foreign ties.

*Academician Chaplygin (1869–1942) was a specialist in mechanics and director of the hydrodynamics institute in Moscow; Academician Luzin (1883–1950) was a mathematician and professor at Moscow University.

I cobbled together the platform of the nationalist party myself with the kind assistance of Radzivilovsky, the head of the secret-political department, who wrote out my "extensive testimony" himself. The party would begin its operations after the capture of Moscow and the military occupation of Russia by the Germans. Furthermore, the principle of "Soviets without Communists",* under the patronage of a capitalist system, was made the basis of this platform.

As a result of this fantastic "extensive testimony" Radzivilovsky promised me my freedom and that I would return to my academic activities ...

Gidulyanov's fantasy became particularly extravagant when he reached Florensky:

The ideologist of this nationalism in the spirit of a medieval Russian "orthodoxy, statehood and national character" was the outstanding philosopher and theologian Professor Florensky, who was on the right wing of our Central Committee ... According to our plan, Florensky was, on the one hand, to be the spiritual leader of our "Union" and, on the other, the organizer and head of a religious hierarchy of troikas among the priests of Moscow's 600 churches and in the periphery and, where they still survived, among the monks ...

Several of the others arrested also provided the testimonies the investigators needed. A case had been put together, a crown of thorns prepared. Now Florensky faced a severe moral ordeal – an encounter with this scared, exhausted, humiliated and hopelessly compromised man. The investigators brought him face to face with Gidulyanov: "At the meeting Radzivilovsky organized for me, I persuaded Professor Florensky to follow our example and sincerely admit his guilt, since he was hindering our release by his stubbornness."

It was at this moment that Pavel Florensky decided to change his behaviour.

Florensky understood what I was saying. When Shupeiko demanded that I tell him the surname of the German electrical engineer with whom I had supposedly visited Florensky, I understood that the latter had also begun to incriminate himself. I christened this German "Ludwig Stein" and made him a Jesuit who, supposedly, had been sent to Russia by the Pope in order to meet me and conclude an Act of Union [between our churches] ...

All of Florensky's life had prepared him for this decision. When the release of several people from the hell of the Lubyanka and his own self-humiliation were weighed on the scales of his conscience he could only choose the latter. He

*The slogan of the mutinous sailors in the 1921 Kronstadt Uprising.

preferred to sacrifice himself for the sake of others. Florensky once wrote:

> In the past there have been righteous men with a particularly acute awareness of the evil and sin that floods the world who did not consider themselves to be free of this corruption. Deeply grieving, they bore within them a feeling of responsibility for the sins of the world as well as their own shortcomings.

Now he too became just such a righteous man.

All through early March, day after day, Florensky was summoned for interrogation, given pen and paper and forced to repeat Gidulyanov's account. The language and literary style, not to mention the ideas, betray the alien authorship. His interrogators, Shupeiko and Rogozhin, would then write "Deposition" at the top of each page: they did not even bother to observe formalities and write out the testimony themselves in the form of question and answer.

Nevertheless, Florensky himself can still occassionally be heard through this nonsense, involuntarily voicing thoughts dear to his heart. For example:

> Public education should not be centralized or unified. As far as possible, secondary schools and institutes of higher education should be relocated outside large cities, and many different types of educational institution should be set up ... Special attention must be devoted to creating reading matter for the broad masses – textbooks and handbooks, popularizations of technical knowledge and other such literature, the writing of which should be entrusted to the most outstanding minds in the country ...

Then, at the end of his testimony, Florensky was unable to keep up the pretence any longer and effectively negated what he had written hitherto:

> The tactical measures of the nationalist-fascist centre were extremely poorly elaborated, and this was the weakest point. The reason was the participation of scholars and scientists who had never been politicians nor taken part in underground or "above"-ground activities ...

Having sketched out the organizational plan that was forced on him, he immediately added that it had "actually not been put into action" and that he "had no idea" whether the people indicated there had "actually been involved"!

There follows a quite extraordinary confession. "I, Professor Pavel Alexandrovich Florensky, a specialist in electrical engineering, in my political horizons am a medieval, approximately fourteenth-century, romantic ..." A most peculiar fascist and enemy of the Soviet regime.

As they relentlessly processed their prisoner at the Lubyanka, the secret police did not leave his apartment unattended. They poked around everywhere there in search of seditious materials. Finally, his wife Anna Mikhailovna, tiring of these visits, asked them: "What are you looking for? Manuscripts?" and opened wide the doors of a cupboard in which shelf after shelf was neatly piled with files containing her husband's research.

At this her visitors faltered. Clearly they would not be able to find their way through this scholarly labyrinth. "Nothing was confiscated during the search," they wrote in their report, "since no copies of *The Pillar and Ground of the Truth*, or other books on mysticism or pornography, were found . . ."

The scholar's flat, however, astonished the OGPU operatives. The record barely conceals their amazement and envy:

> Florensky lives in a large flat of 5–6 big rooms and has a separate study in which his enormous library is concentrated, in bookcases that reach up to the ceiling (in the study and in the next room). He also has a number of collections of old coins, metals and other minerals . . .

This vivid description provoked a swift reaction. Their superiors issued an order for the removal of the library and it was taken away. Or, to put it bluntly, it was stolen and the apartment wrecked. This time the OGPU men came when the family were out, cut the lock from the entrance door, and broke into Florensky's son's room and took some of his belongings. They even took the plates and saucepans from the kitchen. Then they made an inventory of the items in the two already officially sealed rooms in order to confiscate them, and they forbade the house manager to show this inventory to Florensky's wife. The raiding party was headed by Comrade Shupeiko, Florensky's interrogator.

Was there no one in Moscow to intercede for Florensky? One courageous man did speak out: Ludwig Martens, chief editor of the *Technical Encyclopedia* and an old revolutionary. His letter to Mironov, the head of the OGPU economic administration, is in the file:

> During the Wreckers' Trial* I made an appeal to you to consider the case of Professor P.A. Florensky, who has [again] been held in detention by the OGPU since February this year. Professor Florensky is one of the most important Soviet scientists and what happens to him will be of great significance for Soviet science as a whole, and for a great many of our research institutes. Being convinced that his arrest is the result of a misunderstanding, I am appealing to you yet again to personally look into this case.
> With Communist greetings,
> Ludwig Martens

This appeal drew no reaction.

*See footnote on p 85.

On 30 June 1933 the head of the secret-political section Radzivilovsky confirmed the charge sheet. This was a vast "opus", 30 pages in length:

> The Moscow Region OGPU has uncovered and destroyed a counter-revolutionary nationalist-fascist organization calling itself the "Party for the Rebirth of Russia". The organization was headed by ... Professors Florensky and Gidulyanov, and Academicians Chaplygin and Luzin. It in fact grew out of the surviving remnants of the monarchist organization "People's Union for the Rebirth of Russia" which was crushed by the OGPU in 1930 ... It had established links with the White Guard emigres and organized a confidential meeting with Hitler ...

The case was sent to the Special troika of the Moscow Region OGPU. A month later Florensky was convicted under Article 58:10 – 11 (anti-Soviet propaganda and participation in a counter-revolutionary organization) to 10 years in corrective labour camps. What kind of court this was is described in Gidulyanov's letter:

> Before meeting with the procurator, Shupeiko drilled me in how to behave and what I should say. He advised me, moreover, not to bother with formalities in dealing with the procurator's office since my fate depended not on the procurator but on the OGPU – two members of the troika were from the OGPU* and one from the procurator's office.
>
> When, in those conditions, I was informed that I had been sentenced to 10 years' exile in Kazakhstan ... the announcement was totally and staggeringly unexpected ... It was only then that I understood the abyss into which, under the banner of self-disarmament, my trusting, inexperienced nature and my lack of civic courage had led me.
>
> When they announced the terms of my exile, the leaders of the OGPU could not help knowing that all my testimony was fabrication. They understood perfectly well that all these depositions were a "literary composition" – a stage-managed performance and, moreover, not a very clever one since it would collapse like a house of cards if tested ...

The case did indeed collapse. But only a quarter of a century later. When those convicted were rehabilitated in 1958 the decision of the court noted:

> There are no materials in the file that could serve as a justification for the arrest of Florensky (and other persons tried in the same case). Witnesses were not cross-examined, and those who carried out the investigation have been found guilty of falsification. Florensky (and other persons) were unjustly convicted without proof of their guilt.

*The third member of the troika was formally a representative of the Party but often belonged to the OGPU Party committee.

Let us finish reading Gidulyanov's epistle to the procurator's office, though:

I regarded my exile as a well-deserved retribution for my spineless and stupid behaviour in [the hands of] the OGPU ... I fear revenge on the part of OGPU agents. They threatened to send my wife to Solovki if I made a complaint about the confiscation of my library. Hence my fear that the same fate may befall me ...

The present letter is a private confession and I ask you to respect the confidence of the confessional. I have not made any copies or drafts of it, although the OGPU did not make me sign an agreement of confidentiality nor ask for my word that I would keep all that happened there a secret. Nevertheless, I do not want everything that happened to me within the walls of the Moscow OGPU [organization] to be made public. May it remain a secret and die with me.

I ask your forgiveness for my frankness. I remain your obedient servant,
Professor P. Gidulyanov
Dixi et animam levavi
(I spoke and my spirit was eased)

"May it ... die with me." The professor was mistaken about that. The Procurator's Office immediately passed his letter to the OGPU where it was sewn into the file. Gidulyanov had earned himself a lighter sentence than the others by his efforts to help his investigators. He did not save himself, though. The letter which "eased his spirit" sentenced him a second time: once again he was arrested and this time, shot.

In August, after almost half a year in prison, Florensky was sent to the Soviet Far East. He was transported in a railway waggon with criminals and so arrived without any possessions, starving and tormented, at the mockingly-titled "Free" corrective labour camp. There yet another terrible shock awaited him. His wife wrote to tell him that his library had been confiscated. In one of his letters from the camps he would write:

All my life has been devoted to philosophical reflection and scientific research. I never took the time for a vacation or for amusements and pleasures. Not only all my time and efforts but the greater part of my small earnings went on this service to mankind (spent buying books etc). My library was not simply a collection of books but a selection made according to already thought-out and well-defined subjects. One could say that my works were already half-written but preserved in the form of summaries of books to which only I knew the key ... The work of my

116

entire life has now been lost . . . The destruction of the results of my life's work is much worse, for me, than my own death . . .

At the age of 52 Florensky had to begin his life over, in the camps. The one thing that no one could take from him, his belief in God, helped him find the strength to start again.

Even there he managed to renew his scientific activities and when the camp authorities decided to make use of such an expert and transferred him to the experimental research station in the town of Skovorodino on the Amur river he resumed work with his characteristic energy and vision. Soon he had mastered a totally unfamiliar field, studying the permafrost and establishing its economic uses. He organized and carried out a series of original experiments, planned a book, and sent articles to the Academy of Sciences in Leningrad. In Skovorodino he wrote a long lyric poem entitled "The Oro", began to prepare a dictionary of the language of this small local Siberian ethnic group, and taught the other prisoners Latin.

Meanwhile an implacable destiny prepared a new blow. Unexpectedly Florensky was placed in solitary confinement and then rapidly transferred, under special convoy, to another camp. What caused this sudden change in his fate – whether a new denunciation or a specific order – the Lubyanka archives do not say. All we learn is that exactly a year after he had been sent to the Far East he was travelling back in the opposite direction, across Siberia and the Urals to the White Sea, to Solovki.

Solovki

Florensky came ashore here in October 1934, after a terrible journey during which he was again robbed. He wrote to his wife, "I was hungry and cold and became very weak and emaciated."

Fifty years later I made the journey to Solovki, to the old island monastery in the White Sea where the Gulag began. With me I took the published collection of the letters he wrote when he was imprisoned here. I walked along the same paths and examined the monks' cells where he had lived in captivity. Nothing, however, could disperse the mist of speculation and legend that surrounded the last chapter in his life. It was not until I opened his Lubyanka dossier and there found the third and final investigation file on Pavel Florensky that it become possible to complete the story and provide an account of the last years, months and days of his life.

Only in his first letter from the new camp can a note of hopelessness be detected. Thereafter, his letters were again filled with a reviving force and determination. Florensky was looking for ways to occupy himself and here he found a new problem to deal with, the extraction of iodine and agar-agar from seaweed.

With mounting enthusiasm he became involved in this work, devising the technology, and constructing the apparatus. As a result Solovki acquired its own factory and industrial enterprise, the Iodine enterprise (and Florensky made a dozen patented discoveries and inventions in the process!). During the war this iodine would save thousands of soldiers' lives. Florensky himself, though, would then no longer be alive.

As his letters home testify, Florensky was once again interested in everything – scientific inventions, recollections of childhood, philosophical reflections, observations of the Northern Lights and local birds, and comments on books he had read. Although he was rarely allowed to send letters, and then only through the censor, Florensky found words for each member of his family, his wife, mother and children.

This was the visible part of his life. There was another, however, concealed side to his existence that was recorded in the surveillance records and documents of the camp security office. The third investigation file on Pavel Florensky consists, for the most part, of one type of document, marked "Highly confidential", and containing agents' reports or, to put it plainly, informers' denunciations. He was, it seems, closely watched in Solovki and each of his movements was reported to the administration. All these reports are marked with the abbreviation ASE, Anti-Soviet Element, and it is recorded, with meticulous care, when they were delivered and "registered" at the secret political section, 3rd unit of the 8th Solovki division of the White Sea–Baltic Canal.*

The zeal of the informers today enables us to learn something more about the last months of Florensky's life. We hear his voice and share the thoughts that he could not express in his letters.

On 10 September 1935 Florensky became involved in a conversation, in the "Smith's block" where he was living, with two other prisoners. The informer (code-name "Khopanin" in the report) was present and noted down every word:

> *Bryantsev.* I heard over the radio that in Austria they're handing out nine to eighteen months hard labour for crimes against the state. Here they'd certainly "top" you for the same.
>
> *Florensky.* You're right, in the Soviet Union they punish people for no reason at all. They kept demanding at the Lubyanka that I name the people with whom I supposedly held counter-revolutionary conversations. After I had stubbornly refused to cooperate the interrogator said: "Of course, we know that you do not belong to any organization and have not been carrying out any political agitation! But if something does

*The canal built to link the Baltic and the White Sea, praised for its "re-education through labour" of tens of thousands of peasants, intellectuals and ordinary criminals in a collective work involving many noted writers, was completed in May 1933. See chapter 12.

happen our enemies could place their hopes on you, and no one can tell whether you would refuse if they suggested that you spoke out against the Soviet system . . ."

That's why they give people such long terms of imprisonment. It's a policy of prevention. "We can't behave like the tsarist government," the interrogator told me, "and punish people for an already committed crime. Our job is to anticipate. Do they expect us to wait until someone has committed a crime and only then punish them? No, that's no good. We must nip it in the bud, that's more reliable!"

Litvinov. If that's their policy then the whole of the Soviet Union will soon be in the camps.

Bryantsev. It's not much better in the Party itself at the moment. The Party members are also being harassed.

Florensky. That's true. A great many noted Old Bolsheviks are now imprisoned in the political isolators.

Bryantsev. I'm following what's going on in Germany. In essence, Hitler's policies are very similar to the policies of the USSR.

Florensky. You're right, and although the policies are very crude it must be admitted they are effective . . .

Three days later "Khopanin" brought his masters a report about another conversation in the "Smith's" block:

Florensky. The most frightening thing is that once we return from the camps our entire life will have been crushed and corrupted. And if something goes wrong, we shall be the first to be imprisoned again.

Litvinov. When I was being interrogated there was a man in my cell who was given three years for getting drunk and shooting at a portrait of Kalinin.

Florensky. Do they really value Kalinin that highly?*

A note has been added to this denunciation: "These characters are being kept under observation". A further resolution reads: "Pay particular attention to these prisoners. They are working in the Srilobolotory [sic]," ie in the Scientific Research Institute laboratory.

Surrounded by such semi-educated guardians, it is hardly surprising that Florensky, for all his humility and tolerance, at times could not conceal his pain and bitter disappointment. He wrote to his wife:

My life's work has been destroyed, and if humanity, for whom I surrendered my private life, considers it possible to utterly destroy that which was created for its own good, then so much the worse for humanity . . . I

---

*Mikhail Kalinin was formally head of state, but was known to exercise little influence.

know enough of history and the way in which thought has evolved historically, to foresee a time when people will begin to search for separate fragments of the destroyed work. Yet this does not cheer me at all, but, rather, is dispiriting: how hateful is human stupidity, which has existed from the beginning of history and seems determined to continue until the end . . .

Another informer, "Yevgeniev", reported remarks Florensky made during a conversation on 15 January 1936 about the possibility of early release from the camps:

> Personally I would not expect any good to come of it. It's more peaceful here in the camps and, at least, you don't sit waiting to be arrested each night. That's how people are living out there now, after all: as soon as night falls, they wait for visitors to come and invite them to the Lubyanka . . .

On 26 December "Yevgeniev" reported Florensky's remarks about the famous chemist Ipatiev* who had not returned to Russia from abroad (there is no indication, incidentally, that his watchers knew whom he was talking about):

> I neither condemn nor approve Ipatiev's action. Each man is master of his own fate. He weighed things up and decided that for him the right thing was to stay, and he remained. There can be no talk of treason here. He did not betray anyone but simply decided that it is better to live beyond the reach of our camps . . .

Florensky himself, knowing the danger he faced, had the opportunity to emigrate after the Revolution, as did many of his friends. Did he regret now that he had not done so?

His friend, Father Sergey Bulgakov, gave some thought to this:

> It was no simple question of chance that he did not emigrate then. Of course, a brilliant scientific life and, probably, world fame would have awaited him there. But the latter meant little to him, it seems. Of course, he knew what might happen to him and could not help knowing when the fate of his own country spoke so mercilessly of this [. . .] We could say that life offered him a choice between Paris and Solovki. He chose his native land, even though it meant Solovki, because he wanted to share the fate of his nation to the end. Father Pavel was organically incapable of becoming an emigre, and did not wish to become one, in the sense of

*Vladimir Ipatiev (1867–1957), a member of the Russian Academy of Sciences, decided not to return to Soviet Russia in 1927 from a study tour abroad.

being separated, voluntarily or against his will, from his motherland. He and his destiny are the pride and glory of Russia although they are, at the same time, one of its greatest crimes.

There is a final undated report. Florensky and another prisoner were going to the library, talking loudly and gesticulating. Agent "Comrade" followed them, listening attentively. They were discussing the coming war. Florensky remarked:

> The supposition of that well-known strategist and Party ideologist Trotsky that war will soon begin, is being confirmed. It's a law: wars periodically break out every 15–20 years . . .

This brief and apparently harmless report had far-reaching consequences. It formed the basis for a special "Note on P.A. Florensky": "Is carrying on counter-revolutionary agitation in the camp, and praising the enemy of the people Trotsky." Furthermore, it was signed not by the camp security office but by Senior Major Apeter of State Security, head of the Solovki prison.

This document, sewn into the file at the very beginning, incontrovertibly proves that the report by "Comrade" gave the pretext for giving the prisoner an additional sentence. It is not difficult to establish when this happened. In June – July 1937 the camp was reorganized. The iodine factory was closed, the camp was converted into a prison and new camp bosses from the NKVD replaced those there before. There were mass executions and some of the prisoners were hurriedly loaded onto barges and despatched to an unknown destination, also, it was said, to be shot.

A letter dated 4 June is already full of tragic premonitions:

> Everything and everyone has gone. For the last few days I have been appointed as night watchman, guarding our output in the former iodine factory. The bitter cold in the deserted factory, the bare walls and the howling wind that bursts through the broken glass of the windows, make it hard to do anything. As you can see, I cannot even write a letter properly with my frozen fingers . . . Life has died away and, more than ever before, we now feel ourselves cut off from the mainland . . . It's already 6 am. The snow is pouring down and a frantic wind spins it round and round. The broken ventilation panes bang to and fro in the empty rooms as the wind bursts through. Alarmed cries of seagulls reach me. With all my being I feel the insignificance of man, his works and all his strivings . . .

With that, Father Pavel's links with home were broken. What followed were legends.

"How did he die?" I asked Florensky's grandsons. "What do you know about his last days?"

We were sitting, talking quietly, in one of the halls of the Spiritual Academy at the Trinity-St Sergey monastery. Higumenos Andronik teaches at the Academy while his cousin Pavel Florensky is a geology professor. Following two of their grandfather's different vocations and interests, they were united by their devotion to his memory and efforts to publish his works and make them more widely known. Pavel Florensky replied: "We were told officially that he died in 1943, but we have never believed that. There exist at least a dozen different versions of his death: shot in Kolyma during the war (that's what Solzhenitsyn wrote), killed accidentally in the Moscow Region by a falling log, shot in Vorkuta,* shot after being released from Siberian camps, murdered by criminal inmates, drowned on the barge when the Solovki camp was closed down, or died of hunger on Solovki. Then there is the legend that he worked for years in an NKVD *sharashka***, helping to make the Soviet atom bomb ..."

"That's going too far!" I exclaimed in amazement.

"I'm not so sure. My grandmother, Anna Mikhailovna, once said to me: 'It's a good thing Pavel did not survive this long.' I was staggered. Why, I asked her. 'Because he'd be making atom bombs now ...' And it's true that he foretold and foresaw a great deal. In a letter to my father from Solovki, for instance, he described methods for studying different ores (father was also a geologist) and recently I have been using the very same methods to study rock samples from the Moon. In his letters grandfather also gave an analysis of 'heavy water'. Well, we now know what that is, one of the components for making atom bombs. So grandmother had some grounds for her apprehensions ..."

Andronik quietly and gently joined in: "People have told us, and sent us letters, describing how Father Pavel converted many people in Solovki to Christianity. He always kept a rusk or crust of bread to help the hungry. When his coffin was carried out of the hospital, according to one legend, all the prisoners, even the most brutal criminals, knelt down and took off their hats. Even if it's a legend, it's most revealing ..."

When we met the Lubyanka archives were still inaccessible.

A narrow strip of paper, folded in two. On one side is typed "Florensky, Pavel Alexandrovich"; on the other, "To be shot, Florensky Pavel Alexandrovich" and a tick marked with a thick red pencil.

This is an extract from the minutes of a sitting of the NKVD Leningrad Branch's Special Troika. The date is 25 November 1937 and the signature,

*A major centre of camps in the Far North.
**A research institute or plant controlled by the secret police and employing both free and imprisoned specialists.

Lieutenant Sorokin. In the execution list of the troika which was sent from Leningrad to Solovki Father Pavel was number 190.

The very last document in the Solovki investigation file was enclosed in a special yellow envelope and closed with a round seal:

> The death sentence passed on Florensky Pavel Alexandrovich by the Leningrad Region NKVD Troika was executed on 8 December 1937.

> Commandant of the Leningrad Region NKVD,
> Senior Lieutenant K. Polikarpov.

At last we know exactly when and where Florensky died.

In one of his letters from Solovki, Florensky wrote:

> The universe is so organized that only at the price of suffering and persecution can the world be given anything. The more selfless the gift, the harsher the persecution and the more severe the suffering. That is the law of life, its fundamental axiom ... Greatness must pay for its gift in blood ...

CHAPTER 6

SEVENTH HEAVEN

THE FILES ON NINA HAGEN-TORN AND GEORGY DEMIDOV

The Word of God

"What time is it?"

"I'm ordered not to say."

The Peter and Paul Fortress in Petersburg. The prisoner was in cell No 5 in the Alexey ravelin. Convicted of being a member of a secret society, planning an uprising against the tsar and preparing his comrades, in plans and words, for the revolt. Punishment: 20 years solitary confinement. Allowed to read only the Bible. For all this time the only living soul at his side was a mouse. The highly dangerous criminal, the Decembrist* Gavriil Batenkov, tamed the mouse with crumbs of bread and caresses.

Buried alive, how could he tap a message to the outside world from this stone coffin?

"What's the time?"

"I'm ordered not to say."

So Batenkov then turned his gaze inwards:

> The man of God exists entirely within. His face is turned to the Light which he can clearly see and his ear to the Word which clearly speaks to him. . . . What people say and think, or events, remain outside. Within, the voice of God.

"A light shines within the human brow!" vowed Batenkov, and he set out on a journey that led upwards since all horizons were closed.

> I had a revelation, the Word of God . . .
>
> In November 1827 I began to experience a strong and pious ecstasy, an unshakeable faith in God; I began to express my thoughts in verse and clearly sensed that this was a higher force acting within my soul . . . I felt myself a Creator, the equal of God, and with God decided to destroy the world and built it anew . . .

This extraordinary experiment lasted 20 years. A record was preserved in a manuscript made up of a stack of loose sheets and a thick notebook covered in a tiny, barely decipherable hand; there is also a pile of letters addressed to Tsar

*The Decembrist uprising took place on 14 December 1825 on the Senate Square in Petersburg.

Nicholas I. Batenkov recorded religious and philosophical investigations, verse, plans for reorganizing the state, mystical revelations . . .

Did the Tsar ever see these letters and writings? We do not know. On a report about Batenkov from the chief of police, however, Nicholas added in his own hand: "Proven to have taken leave of his senses." As someone observed, Nicholas was a man deprived of imagination. For Batenkov it was the only thing that remained.

At one time I contemplated writing a novel about Batenkov. Nothing came of the idea but it was reborn, years later, and unexpectedly, when I started reading contemporary materials.

The Muses of Kolyma

It is a paradox, but for many loss of liberty unleashed their creative and spiritual capacities. Not just the professional writers but thousands who had no links with literature were impelled by arrest and imprisonment to find words for their experience. In the camps, in prison and in exile, words often remained the only, saving draught of liberty.

Towards evening the lock squealed and snapped. The door opened wide. "Exercise!"

We were taken to the lift. It was a long way up. The door opened. A frosty bite to the air. I got out.

The night sky was lit from below by the city lights. A searchlight directed a brilliant beam into the roofless cage. Concrete walls of human height; 6 feet above them, a wire net, and beyond, the nets over other cages. One could walk 20 paces in a circle. Above the cages, reflecting the lights, the sky glimmered and swirled. Starry snowflakes danced in the beam. From far below rose car horns, tram bells and the rumble of the large square. The cages were on the roof, on the seventh floor. I stood still and looked.

The snowy stars whirled. Verses came to me in their rhythm:

Having got up to pray, silent I stand,
Raising my heart like a candle.
If it lights with a radiant flame
Then I shall have the unfathomable answer.

My weary brain throbs at my temples,
The wax falls in white drops.
In my melting heart, faith bursts into life
with an unperishable flame.

Faith in what?

In the fact that, in spite of everything, there is still a sky above us. Fate lent a helping hand – we were taken up onto the roof and not lowered down into the well of the courtyard. Here was an exit from the cage to the dance of the snowflakes, to the black sky above. They will not be able to do anything to me!

Verse becomes a necessity in prison. It harmonizes our conscious-ness in time ... The individual can swim up out of prison, mastering time as he would space. Those who dig down in their minds to the level of rhythm and release themselves into its current will not go mad. The snowflakes in the searchlight also danced to a rhythm, white against the black sky. Mastering rhythm is liberation ... They will not be able to do anything ... The door of the cage snapped: "Exercise over!"

The cell was in the Inner Prison at the Lubyanka. The author of these reminiscences, Nina Hagen-Torn.

As I read through the dozens of manuscripts brought to our commission I was particularly interested in any that referred to Kolyma. This was not just because I had lived there for several years, visited numerous sites of the former camps and become friendly with many one-time zeks. (I had also written more than once about that other Kolyma, but then no one would publish such articles.) The commission quite simply received more about Kolyma than any other part of Stalin's Gulag and these proved to be the most interesting and valuable manu-scripts of their kind. "Kolyma forms an entire continent within the Gulag Archipelago, and deserves to be described separately ..." commented Solzhenitsyn. "Why was so much written about it, while memoirs about the other camps almost do not exist? Perhaps because the most gifted prisoners were all taken there?"

The photograph shows a young girl with a dazzling smile, a direct and trusting gaze, magnificent plaits reaching down to her waist, and delicate hands wrapped around her knees. Someone has written, "Sunshine!" on the snap and that was what she remained throughout her life. Nothing disfigured her soul, broke her spirit or extinguished that smile.

I learned of her fate from her daughter. She phoned the commission, invited me to visit her, and showed me the lovingly preserved books and manuscripts of her mother.

Nina Hagen-Torn was both beautiful and wise. Born with the century in 1900, she was the daughter of a Russified Swede, a professor at the Military Medical Academy in Petersburg. In childhood her reckless daring would fill her family with horror: she rode horses, climbed pine trees on the dunes, and put out to sea alone in a canoe.

At Petersburg University she studied ethnography, wrote verse and was taught by Andrey Bely. She conducted her own research and made expeditions to the Russian North and the Volga region. Between these journeys she inhabited a quite different world, the literary Petrograd (as Petersburg was renamed in 1914) of those years. She recalls the times she met with Andrey Bely:

> Acquaintance with him uncovered levels of consciousness, perhaps of preconsciousness, of which I had not been aware. ... It was a quite different perception of the world: the individual soared above so that he could see into the invisible.

The life that followed would lead twice to prison and the Gulag, in 1937 and then again in 1947, to the camps of Kolyma and Mordovia. There Hagen-Torn would strive not merely to survive but to commit everything to memory and then put it into words.

> The second time round the "meat-grinder" worked more smoothly. There was no longer the sadistic romanticism of 1937 when we could hear people screaming and groaning through the walls. Then we had whispered of beatings and tortures and the investigators spent sleepless nights, extracting fantastic plots from tormented individuals. Now the interrogators had changed. In 1947 I no longer encountered maniacs, sadists and virtuosi but officials who followed ready-made scenarios in their interrogations.
>
> During my first interrogation the major yelled and used obscenities because that was indicated in his script. When, unexpectedly, a middle-aged and well-brought-up woman used the same language in return, he lost his nerve.
>
> Another investigator made me stand against the wall. He demanded that I sign a deposition containing self-incriminating confessions I had not made. I refused. Tired and not knowing what to do, he leaped towards me, furious, brandishing his fists: "I'll beat you senseless! You wretched woman! Sign it!"
>
> I looked him straight in the eye and speaking very distinctly, said: "And I shall bite off your nose!"
>
> He stared intently at me, leapt back and drummed furiously on the desk with his fists out of sheer frustration.
>
> More frequently it was a seated affair. They led me into the office and the investigator, who did not allow one near his table, said: "Sit down. Tell me about your anti-Soviet activities."
>
> "There's nothing to tell."
>
> The investigator would start leafing through some papers, as if he was

studying them. Or he might just read the newspaper. A primitive attempt to play on our nerves, to exploit the anxiety of the prisoner. There was no real thought behind it. According to instructions the prisoner would be getting anxious and so these hours also counted as interrogation. Once I asked: "How much do you get paid for interrogations? Double time, or more?"

"That's none of your business!" he roared. "You're here to answer my questions, not ask your own."

Another time when I was sitting there and he was reading, a second investigator came in and asked: "Well? when are you going for the test?"

"I've still got the Spartan state to do, then I'll go."

I understood that he was preparing for an examination on Ancient Greece.

"The Spartan state?" I asked softly. "Want me to tell you about it?"

He frowned but the newcomer asked with interest: "What do you do?"

"I have a doctorate in history."

"OK! Out with it, then! Tell us what you know. We shall check how ideologically correct your thinking is."

He sat down. Both were clearly overjoyed. I gave them a lesson on the history of Greece and we parted amicably.

"Go back to the cell and have a rest. It'll soon be evening meal," said my investigator.

Back down in the lift, through the corridors, the guard clicking his keys, and I was in my cell. The bowls with a gruel of pearl barley already stood on the table and the women were sitting on the benches.

"Time and space, time and space," I thought to myself, pacing up and down the cell. You could either leave the same as you had entered or, if you could not stand the pressure, go off your head . . . And you would, if you did not learn to travel in your mind, turning image-thoughts almost into reality. Without rhythm this activity would also drive you mad. Rhythm was both guide and helper.

I recalled how, when I was lying on the cot in the Kresti,* I saw Africa:

> *In the caressing light*
> *Of the plane-tree shade*
> *Black children*
> *Knelt down*
> *On pattern-striped mats*

*(Lit. Crosses): the main remand prison in Leningrad, so called from the disposition of its several wings.

Why were those black children, the leaves in the plane-tree shade, and the dried reddish lumps of earth so strangely familiar? Because I had been able to dive deep within myself, and gather and concentrate in that image everything I had ever known about Africa. Then I intensified this image until it began to feel real, and I left the cell . . .

I laughed at my mastery of space. Approaching the women sitting in the corner like hens on a roost, I asked: "Would you like me to recite some verse?"

"Very much!"

I began to recite, alternating my own verse and those of others. Each day they would ask: "Tell us something else!" I would repeat Blok, Pushkin, Nekrasov, Mandelstam, Gumilyov and Tyutchev. Their faces brightened. Like a damp sponge wiping dust from a window, their eyes became clearer. Each was now thinking not just of themselves, but of the shared human condition . . .

By now I was on my third investigator. I couldn't get on with him. I refused to sign the deposition he had drawn up: it was full of monstrous accusations to which I was supposed to confess. He had me transferred to the punishment cell. This cell, or "box" as the warders called it, was a low brick recess without a window. The idea was that anyone held there would rapidly use up all the oxygen and begin to suffocate. There were tiny holes in the iron door at floor level but we were forbidden to sit on the floor in order to suck in the air. The peephole in the door would open and a voice would say: "Get up!"

The prisoner began to gasp. Roughly every half hour the warder glanced through the peephole. When he saw that the prisoner was losing consciousness he opened the door and said: "To the toilet!"

The prisoner leapt up joyfully. While he was walking to the toilet and while he was there, he could breathe. His eyes grew brighter and his mind became clearer. They were not allowed to stifle us completely during investigation so the jailer on duty would monitor this oxygen-deprivation.

One way to escape this dulling of the mind was by becoming immersed in images that led to a clear and intense feeling of space, and then transforming these images into a rhythm.

I tried to go back to my early days in the North. I remembered and restored my memories till they reached an exceptional clarity, sailing down the great, bright North Dvina river. I tried to put these visions into verse:

Wide the translucent sky
Mirrored in that bright stream.

> *Take what you need in life,*
> *Squeeze it tight in your child's small fist.*

Even in the deepest stone-walled box you can teach yourself to hear the lapping water, see its silvery radiance, and cease to notice that you are locked in and that your body cannot reach air or sky. There is a particular joy when you free your will from your captive body and can take control of your mind. It is as if a free wind is blowing through your head and calls across the millennia to all your imprisoned brothers and sisters. And we, captives all, support one another in our sense of liberty. I found within myself a defence not only from the stifling box but from the onslaught of all that would not fit into my way of thinking. This was transformed into an epic poem over five years. I cannot say how far it was a true literary work. However, it is a monument to my inner freedom, a way of making the soul invulnerable.

One of Hagen-Torn's companions in misfortune, K.S. Khlebnikova-Smirnova, recalled a few years after the former's death:

In that fearful life, where people had prison numbers stitched to their garments and had no contact with normal existence, it was a miracle to meet someone who seemed to soar above all the horror of the camps. Meeting Nina was just such a miracle.

I was then in hospital recovering from typhoid. We lay on the board beds, side by side, engrossed in our own sorrows. Almost all had been accused of crimes they did not commit. Nina Hagen-Torn, who was known for her kindness, used to visit us and look after us. She tried not only to ease our physical sufferings but our mental distress also. She read her own verse and the poetry of others, she described her expeditions. For a period of time we would forget our own bitter lot. . . . Nina worked within the compound as a "horse": several women were harnessed to a cart in summer, or a sledge in winter, and dragged barrels of water and of firewood to the canteen or the hospital. The work was hard and the women were not young. Nina did not become downhearted, however. "The horse is a noble animal," she would say. "It's good to be a horse!" There were a great many sick Ukrainian girls in the camp. Nina organized an academy and helped them study Russian literature and history. Later several of them went to study languages at university. Apart from her teaching, Nina wrote a long poem about Lomonosov* while she was there. During a search the jailers confiscated it. "Go on writing and bring it to me for safekeeping," said the camp security officer. "When

*Mikhaylo Lomonosov, early eighteenth-century Russian polymath, son of a fisherman on the White Sea.

130

you're released I'll post it to you . . ." And he kept his word, he sent what she gave him.

Returning to her native Leningrad after release, Hagen-Torn worked for many years in the Ethnographic museum, publishing scholarly articles and monographs. She wrote two volumes of prose, memoirs and a book of verse (Akhmatova and Pasternak recognized her poetic gifts). And she continued to write about the Gulag:

My acquaintances know that I am writing about the camps. "One must show who the country was deprived of!" they repeat. I won't quarrel with that. But I have to show something else. I want to show what happens to the way different people think when they are deprived of the right to do as they like with their own body.

The body became the property of the state, an object at the disposal of an impersonal force. This was not slavery, because that means belonging to a master. Slaves and masters inevitably developed relations: masters were hated or loved, fought against, praised and were asked for mercy. The master was a living person and thus could not be an omnipotent force of nature. The slaves in Ancient Egypt were enslaved by a blind machine. Yet they, for the most part, were in origin foreigners who could dream of their motherland. In the Soviet camps the majority did not come from another country. It was easier for the foreigners there – and they had also been gathered from all the ends of the earth, starting with Germany and ending with Japan and Korea – since they were prisoners of war. But those who had been rounded up in their own country began to feel like cattle being driven off to slaughter.

How well I began to understand and sympathize with animals after I'd been in the camps! Like them, we had been totally helpless in the face of a blind and omnipotent force.

Having been a beast of burden filled me with a great pity for all haltered, fettered and chained creatures. I found out that the expression in the eyes and the behaviour of a creature delivered into the hands of an unlimited power hardly differed, whether they walked on two legs or four. For many years I worked with horses and was a carter. I know how animals resist and how they submit. There is no great difference between a herd of horses, a herd of cows or a herd of people.

This should not make us despise human beings but respect animals . . .

"It is a great shame that your verse cannot be published. Don't get downhearted, though: its time will also come," the poet Ilya Selvinsky wrote to Hagen-Torn. "In this respect, you are not alone. Entire novels and tragedies lie sleeping in their lairs, waiting for spring."

Nina Hagen-Torn did not live to see that spring. She died in 1986.

* * *

The hammer banged reveille on the rail outside the camp HQ, at 5 am as always. Time to get up. The ragged noise was muffled by ice two fingers thick on the windows and soon died away.

These are the opening words of *One Day in the Life of Ivan Denisovich* by Alexander Solzhenitsyn.

For the hero of "Dubar", a story that circled anonymously for years in samizdat, the day began in exactly the same way:

The miserable "tzing" of the piece of rail hanging at the corner of the gate house carried weakly through the log walls of the barrack and the thick layer of ice on its small windows.

The coincidence is hardly accidental. That was how thousands of days began for all the prisoners in the Gulag. However, the second author's story then takes a different turn. The administration has ordered a prisoner to bury a new-born baby that has just died, a "stiff" or *dubar*, as the deceased were termed in the jargon of the Gulag.

Surmounting the disappointment and revulsion that, in anticipation, I already felt towards what I would see, I unrolled the sheet and uncovered the upper part of my dead charge's small body.…

The contrast between my expectations and what I saw was so great that in the first instant I had a feeling that is usually described as not believing one's eyes. When that had passed a more complicated feeling replaced it. I had a sense of guilt towards the dead child and another, long unfamiliar, but infinitely warm, moving and tender sensation.

The tiny little yellowish-pink body seemed dazzlingly clean in the orange rays of the polar sun. And so live and warm that I had to fight the desire to wrap it up against the cold.

The child's head on its plump neck with deep infantile folds was thrown slightly backwards and to one side; the eyes were fast shut. The infant seemed to have fallen asleep and be smiling with its slightly open, toothless mouth. The frost had preserved this tiny statuette of the most delicate tissues in exactly the same pose as at the moment of its unconscious and, evidently, painless end. There was nothing at all of death or suffering about it. [. . .]

Under the calloused armour of harsh indifference built up over many years of the unrelieved and cruel existence as a prisoner there stirred a

132

deeply buried tenderness. This vision from another almost forgotten world stirred within me much that I thought had died long before, discarded, as it were, for lack of use. There was, probably, also an unsatisfied paternal feeling and a vague memory of my own, long discontinued childhood ...

Paradoxically, the tiny corpse made me think of life: that somewhere, even if infinitely far away, such a life went on, and that people freely made and gave birth to children who rewarded their fathers and mothers with such smiles, innocent and therefore still more happy beings ...

I felt like doing something more for the child I was burying. So I knocked the blade off the spade handle with my pick and broke the handle into two uneven halves. Then I pulled out a length of string and fastened the two pieces together. I drove this improvised cross into the burial mound ...

Suddenly I was seized by a feeling of piety, like a Christian believer in church. Thoughts of food, rest and warmth vanished somewhere else. Probably it was that moving state of exalted ecstasy familiar only to truly religious people. Under its influence I unfastened the tags of my camp-issue cloth hat and bared my head. Immediately the frost seized it in red-hot pincers and my ears were painfully burned. Reality had not changed. I put the hat back on, knocked several round drops of ice, large as hailstones, from my coat, picked up my tools and began to go back down the valley. [...]

The frozen drops on the breast of my coat were not tears of grief. Not at all. For all the warmth and tenderness of my feelings towards the buried child, they recalled far more those sensations of spiritual lucidity one feels, for example, when contemplating a great work of art. I did not feel grief but a gentle, pure sadness. And yet another elevated feeling that, probably, was closest of all to a sense of thankfulness. I was thankful to the dead child for reminding me of life and through his death somehow affirming its existence.

A woman had brought her father's manuscripts to our commission from Kharkov in the Ukraine. She did not find us immediately. First, she saw an official in the Writers Union who, as it happened, had also been in Kolyma, before he took up literature, and in the Gulag. However, he had been a zek but was one of those who guarded them. She timidly asked: "You have a commission in the Writers Union for those who were imprisoned."

"We do. What of it?"

"Probably many people come to you. You're already swamped with manuscripts?"

"Yes, an awful lot. Simply piles of them! It's time to shut up shop."

The woman turned round and left. Luckily she did not go straight back to the station but tracked us down and handed over the manuscripts. Among them was the tale "Dubar". That was how the author of this already well-known story was finally revealed.

His name was Georgy Demidov.

Demidov was born in 1908 in a worker's family in Petersburg. He showed a very early interest in science and technology and worked his way up from a factory hand to a senior lecturer at the electro-technical institute in Kharkov. In 1938 he was called in, supposedly, for a check on his passport. This "verification" would continue for the next 18 years. When the interrogator threatened to arrest his wife and six-month old daughter Demidov signed a phony self-incriminating confession but refused outright to name anyone else. He was sentenced to be sent to a corrective labour camp for participating in a Trotskyist counter-revolutionary terrorist organization.

Demidov spent 14 years in Kolyma, 10 of them on gang labour, the hardest work of all. A man of strong character and a lively mind, he survived when so many of his fellow prisoners remained among the melancholy hills of Kolyma. He himself commented:

> Even someone who is quite incapable of observation and comparison cannot fail to grasp the full tragedy of that "Auschwitz without the crematoria", the phrase for which I was given my second sentence in 1946.

Soon after his second term of imprisonment began Demidov's wife received a telegram announcing that her husband had died. Later in a letter to his daughter Demidov explained:

> My poor little girl! I was so terribly far away then, in a vast gloomy land, in prison. I had no hope that I would ever come out again. I was sure I would die there. So I thought I was only slightly anticipating events by giving out that I was dead. I sent that telegram to release you and Mama from my existence which I thought could only do you harm . . . I could not deceive her though.

The KGB would not let him out of their sight after he was released until his death in 1986. In 1980 searches were carried out simultaneously in several cities where people had copies of his manuscripts. His own flat was searched several times and all his writings confiscated. Three novels, three long tales, more than 20 short stories and his favourite last work, an autobiography, were removed. Shortly before this his dacha where all the drafts were kept had burned down, leaving him at 72 without a single one of his works.

Fortunately his daughter was of the same temperament as her father. After stubborn and lengthy petitioning his manuscripts were returned to her after his death. Demidov used to say:

> Writing costs me a great deal. I always make myself ill with it although I'm not yet a wreck, far from it. Everyone asks me, "What's the matter, has something happened?" If I could answer I'd say, "Yes, something has happened, a very short while ago. Less than 30 years ago. And it didn't just happen to me."

* * *

> *Kolyma, Kolyma,*
> *What a wonderful place!*
> *Twelve months of winter,*
> *Summer all the rest.*

These bitter couplets were commonly cited in the camps. Yet Kolyma is indeed a beautiful region. I came of my own free will in a quite different period, and spent seven happy years there. It was there that my son was born and my first book was published.

The other Kolyma was a different matter. The river Kolyma gave its name to the Kolyma Territory and then to a historical phenomenon. For 20 years from 1934 to 1954 several million prisoners were brought here to this, the largest island in the Gulag Archipelago, and held in camps that were scattered over an area several times larger than France, from Indigirka to the Bering straits. Some returned, many did not.

Cut off from the world by expanses of sea and mountain, Kolyma was the ideal place for labour camps. Without a special permit it was impossible to enter or leave the area and here the Gulag had its highest mortality and cruellest conditions.

I remember Butugychag, the Black Rocks as the local Evenk people call it, a gloomy ravine, lost among countless hills and mountains. We arrived in the summer and it took our vehicle a long while to make its way up the valley along the stream beds overgrown with lilac-red willowherb. We passed the ruins of the uranium mine, the shell of the enriching plant with its gaping dark windows and doors, and the collapsed entrances to the mine shafts. We climbed still higher, and the mountain slopes closed in around us, cutting off the sun. It became dark and cold. Then before us lay the camp.

To be more exact, what was left of the camp: massive buildings made of uncut stone with iron grills on the windows, piles of half-rotten shoes and rusty tin cans, and the roads made by thousands of prisoners' feet that were still not overgrown. There was no sign of a human presence. We did not enter the camp immediately, though.

A bear barred our path. Only when we approached him very close did he, with evident unwillingness, retreat.

"He shouldn't have let you in!" said Anatoly Zhigulin, the other vice-chairman of our commission, when I told him about this trip. "It's no place for idle curiosity!" (Zhigulin himself had been a prisoner there.)

We had come to examine the site. Might this be the place to organize a memorial to the victims of Kolyma? Now I think my colleague was perhaps right. It would be wrong to cut roads here and turn such a place into a museum, bring excursions and make solemn speeches. Nature itself, in the shape of that bear, seemed to lay a ban on Butugychag.

* * *

There is yet another category of manuscript that cannot be termed literary works in the straightforward sense. Their force and value lies in their naked authenticity and the eloquence of the facts they relate.

A simple school notebook. Inside it, without any commas and with mistakes in spelling and grammar, was written the following, in large uneven letters:

> Moscow Union of Writers This material needs to be rewritten
>
> Please forgive handwriting and punctuation marks I have catarac[t] and also double stroke two times I have been paralyzed. It is eight years now that I have been paralyzed because of my nervous system. You ask why are your nerves that way I shall tell you as it happened . . .

Ivan Vasilievich Okunev sent us his memoir from Krasnoe village in the Lipetsk Region. In 1938 this 20-year-old was arrested and sent to Kolyma only because his passport was no longer valid.

> They brought us to Kolyma. Instead of shoes they gave us two sleeves from worn-out work coats and one pair of mittens and that was all for two years. We worked at the face in the goldmines and the sleeves quickly tore on the chippings at the face and the padding came out and our bare toes would become frozen. Then in December when work was being allocated the camp boss Kuliev announced that if anyone had a request they should say before they went off to work.
>
> So we two began to ask for sleeves. Another two waved ragged mittens over their head. The four of us were instructed to step out of line and the rest were ordered off to work. We were taken to the punishment cell. Kuliev beat on the rail to summon the firemen. We could hear and see through the gaps in the planking how they ran up with a fire hose. They turned it on and pointed it at us. We ran from one corner to another but they kept it pointed at us. We shouted called for papa and mama cursing

them all we could. And that day it was minus 50 degrees and the chassis of an automobile cracked with the frost.

They sprayed us for half an hour and then the water ran out. Four hours later Kuliev came and began to say that we should go back to the barrack but we had all frozen together and could not move. Then he called over the fireman who came with a small axe and began to cut us apart. I was standing at the back and they cut me free first and dragged me to the door. They yelled off to the barrack quick march! But my padded trousers had frozen stiff and I said I could not. Ill help you! A kick in the back and I flew out of the cell and face down into the path which they had trampled bust my lip two teeth ended up in my mouth and it became salty from the blood.

Two firemen ran up and rolled me with their feet towards the barrack there were about 25 yards to the barrack. But when they rolled I turned into a snowman the snow stuck to my wet clothes and froze. Then they stood me with my back to the barrack and began to knock off the snow with their rifle-butts so hard my bones ached. I fell down. Then they dragged me by my feet into the barrack and behind me rolled up the others. Tears lamentations the curses of the guards. I lay on the lower board beds opposite the stove. In the night I woke up my head hurt stabbing pain in my chest a high temperature.

In the morning the barrack orderly announced time to get up. I began to wake my wet accomplices but two were dead. I was taken to the medical unit. The doctor asked my surname name and patronymic and said we are namesakes. Then he asked where I came from. I said Moscow and he seemed overjoyed and said we are both from the same town. He said he had been chief consultant to the Kremlin. Why did they did imprison you? They accused me of murdering Maxim Gorky.* Thats all I remember but I did not ask his surname.

Over a month he cured me. I had pneumonia. The fourth one of us died in the medical unit and I remained alive. Ivan Vasilievich treated me and I recovered. Then he said he wanted me to remain. He asked was I afraid of dead men? I said Im only afraid of the living. Then Ill give you a job. Two kilometres away from the camp stood the morgue. I had to keep the stove going during the night and unfreeze the corpses and in the morning two doctors came and would [a]natomize them.

So every evening they brought 18 corpses on a horse and I stood six corpses against three of the walls. They leaned frozen against the walls and stood up while they were unfreezing. It was dark inside. The stove

---

*No doctor of this name and patronymic was directly involved in Gorky's treatment. See chapter 12.

was an old fuel barrel the resiny firewood burned hot the sides of the stove were red. I throw on firewood and walked about talking to them who came from where were they married or not? That young lad had probably not even married yet? Youve left a girl behind and probably shes waiting? But mine has got married theres no doubt such pretty girls do not wait around for long. What was yours called? Mine is Tonya Chubarova and Im thinking of her now. A beauty.

I was unfreezing in the morgue until 1945.

But then the war we never knew about ended. Post did not get through but once they hung up a trick box. Many wrote complaints but after the writers were called out and beaten unconscious ...

Not far from our camp there was a hill and a tractor stood on it. They brought [prisoners] in from other mines in trucks covered with canvas they cried farewell they drove past our camp.

There they stood people by the readymade trenches started up the tractor and shot them with a machinegun.

I thought of writing this down so that people know what Kolyma means and I was thinking Ill die and they wont know where those who were killed are buried. There were thousands.

Perhaps one of the writers can rewrite this. Excuse the handwriting I have been paralyzed twice and as I write now my shoulder is trembling. I am crying I remember what Ive lived through. I would call it the Road to Calvary. Rewrite it! Let the young know and most important let them honour the memory. Now I shall die peacefully. I have told almost everything.

After reading this it is easy to say: That's it, that's enough! What else can be said about the prisons and the camps? Yet we must read and write about this experience. The nations of the Soviet Union were subjected, perhaps, to the most terrible experience, the most fearful experiment, in history. If we do not have all the answers why it happened and what was its purpose, one thing, at least, is clear: it must be inscribed for all time on the rolls of history, more indestructibly than the cuneiform of ancient Babylon and Urartu.

For apart from the example of humanity they set us, these witnesses also testify to something else – the power of the word to save. One of them, Nina Hagen-Torn, expressed this in a neat formula:

Those who dig down in their minds to the level of rhythm and release themselves into its current will not go mad ... Verse, like the chanting of the shaman, leads the individual into the expanses of the seventh heaven ...

CHAPTER 7

A BULLET IN PLACE OF A FULL STOP

THE FILE ON BORIS PILNYAK

The World Contracts

Boris Pilnyak was on trial long before his arrest. During the last years of his life the same nightmarish incident began to recur with increasing frequency. He would run into acquaintances somewhere and they would ask in amazement: "Is it you?"

"It's me . . . Who else could it be?"

"But we'd heard that you'd been arrested."

Meanwhile, he was working on a novel. He spent time with his little son and his young wife, he planted fruit trees at his dacha in Peredelkino. Guests would visit and tell him about the latest arrests. The postman brought the newspapers and there he read denunciations of the most recently unmasked "enemies of the people": among them were those who only yesterday had been his friends. The conversations and newspaper reports constantly repeated the same question: "Is it really you? They still haven't arrested you?"

He kept working, every day, no matter what happened, to drive away his fears. His novel was already almost finished. The idea had come to him long ago, to write about the roots of the Russian Revolution and about himself.

To begin with Pilnyak had been very fortunate as a writer. He rapidly won success and then fame. Neither was this a temporary and aberrant celebrity but an acclaim honestly earned through work and talent. In the 1920s he was one of the most widely read and popular Soviet writers, the author of a dozen collections of short stories and of novels translated into many other languages. In 1929 he was elected chairman of the All-Russian Union of Writers.* A brilliant experimenter and modernist, he headed an entire school of writing.

There was, however, another hierarchy in Soviet literature. There he was considered no more than a "Fellow-Traveller", a disdainful term invented by the People's Commissar for Enlightenment Anatoly Lunacharsky. (Trotsky, who had a liking for labels, delighted in applying this term, right and left.) In the literary world the fellow-travellers were those suspect and tainted writers who, though they accepted the Revolution, were neither members of the Party nor of proletarian origin: Yesenin and Babel, Pasternak and Zamyatin, Zoshchenko, Alexey Tolstoy and many others. There were undisputed masters among them

*Founded in 1919 by Osorgin, Berdyaev and others, this small non-political association occupied Herzen House throughout the 1920s. See footnote on p 219.

but none of them was indisputably Soviet. The public significance of a writer was determined not by his gifts but by weighing him on the scales of ideological loyalty. Babel was declared a revolutionary Fellow-Traveller. Vsevolod Ivanov was simply a Fellow-Traveller. And when the term was applied to Pilnyak it was only used in inverted commas: a "Fellow-Traveller".

Perhaps the trouble started then, with those ominous inverted commas. Or else Stalin, who personally kept an eye on all talented individuals, instructed his literary agents to maintain a special watch on Pilnyak.

Whatever the cause, there were good reasons to be attentive. Pilnyak was one of the first to reveal the seamy underside of the Revolution. He saw past the slogans and the marches to the pitiless whirlwind unleashed when a beast "as elemental as a wolf" had been set loose. Stalin was particularly fond of wolves, as it happens: he would doodle sketches of the grey beasts of prey on his papers. In Pilnyak's books the Bolsheviks roamed about in packs. The "leather coats", the "handsome lads in their leather jackets", kept on the move, their goal was "enerjetrical fuctioning" – the writer overheard this expression being used by a communist, who later became a People's Commissar and one of the country's rulers:

> That's what we know, that's what we want, that's how we've fixed things and – finito! And you and the rest can go to the devil! Get that, you sour-sweet lemonade-sipper?!

And at the head of this new species, half-man, half-wolf, Pilnyak, in his *Tale of the Unextinguished Moon*, placed "Number One" or the "Unbending Man". No one could fail to recognize Stalin in this figure.

From the very outset the Party began roping in the Fellow-Travellers like wild horses, and attempted to train them to perform as it wanted. Finally, it stopped using such gentle methods: if they could not be forced to follow the dominant ideology they were not allowed to publish any more.

It was the year of the Great Breakthrough that decided Pilnyak's fate as a writer. In society as a whole 1929 marked the beginning of Stalin's autocracy. In literature it was mirrored by a political campaign, unprecedented in virulence and scale, that came to be known as the "Pilnyak and Zamyatin Affair". The pretext was the publication abroad of works by the two writers: Zamyatin's novel *We*, Pilnyak's short novel *Mahogany*.

In Zamyatin's words, the two authors acquired a demonic status in Soviet literature. They became the targets of a campaign of public harassment organized by the authorities and readily taken up by the press and other writers. When these attacks had reached a peak Zamyatin acted decisively. He appealed directly to Stalin for permission to emigrate and this was granted, the last occasion of its kind.

Pilnyak found himself alone, quite undefended, against a massive and mounting chorus of criticism. The ideological watchdogs vigilantly observed to ensure that no one remained on the sidelines.

Articles from *Literaturnaya gazeta** and *Komsomolskaya pravda*** were added to Pilnyak's file at the Lubyanka as accusing voices that confirmed his guilt. The titles convey the level of criticism: "A Hostile Network of Agents in the Ranks of Soviet Writers", "Boris Pilnyak, Special Correspondent for the White Guard Supporters", "Investigate the Union of Writers", "The Lessons of Pilnyakism" ...

In all this unbridled calumny one review in particular stands out. It is entitled "Our Position":

> I have not read Boris Pilnyak's short novel *The Tale of Mahogany* (is that the right title?) or, for that matter, other tales by him and many other writers.
>
> To me a finished literary work is like a weapon. Even if that weapon were above the class struggle – such a thing does not exist (though, perhaps, Pilnyak thinks of it like that) – handing it over to the White press strengthens the arsenals of our enemies.
>
> At the present time of darkening storm clouds this is the same as treachery at the front.
>
> We must give up subject-less literature-mongering.
>
> We must put an end to the irresponsibility of writers.
>
> Pilnyak's guilt is shared by many. Who? That's a story in itself.
>
> For instance, who handed over a third of the Federation† to the union of Pilnyaks?
>
> Who always defended the Pilnyaks from the tendentiousness of REF?††
>
> Who made this writer feel sure of the right of geniuses to extra-territorial class immunity?

The author of this menacing tirade was none other than Vladimir Mayakovsky.

A disgruntled Gorky complained to Central Committee secretary Andreev:

> Pilnyak has been forgiven for his story about the death of Comrade

*(Lit. Literary Gazette): a weekly paper that would soon become the organ of the new Writers Union.

**(Lit. Komsomol Truth): the daily paper of the Komsomol and as such often more orthodox and virulent than the Party paper *Pravda*.

†The Federation of Soviet Writers' Associations (set up in 1926) embraced RAPP, the All-Russian Union of Writers, the Peasant Writers Union and some other smaller groups.

††REF, the Revolutionary Front of Art, was a short-lived literary grouping founded by Mayakovsky in 1929 after he left LEF (1922–8).

Frunze and yet it is there asserted that the operation was unnecessary and carried out at the insistence of the Central Committee.

Gorky had no need to worry. The "leather coats" had forgotten and forgiven nothing. However, Pilnyak's hour had not yet come.

Zamyatin risked all and won. Pilnyak never plucked up determination to openly defy the regime. He preferred to trim, publicly recanting, putting on a clever show of Soviet enthusiasm and purging his mistakes by writing ideologically correct works. This was a cunning way of restoring good relations with the powers that be, a form of psychological defence that had something in it of the Russian "holy fools" and simpletons who are the heroes of many of his books.

Inwardly Pilnyak had been broken by the 1929 campaign and would not recover. He tried, of course, to restore his former position and get back in step with the times. However, he was not trusted any longer and he could not shed the mask he had been forced to wear.

The determination to know and to see, which he had formerly preached, began to weaken. New themes made their appearance: "Each epoch has its own psychology . . ." he now stated.

In the 1920s he had argued that:

> The more gifted a writer is, the more politically inept he becomes . . .
> The writer is only of value when he exists outside the system . . . I have won the bitter fame of a person who kicks against the pricks.

In the 1930s he would vow his loyalty to the Party and socialism and praise Stalin:

> He is truly a great man, a man of great determination, of great deeds and words.

In the 1920s Pilnyak would assert, "The courts should not and cannot be as strict as the judgement the individual passes on himself" and appeal for compassion. In the 1930s he demanded that the "enemies of the people" be punished even before sentence had been passed and called on people to "destroy each individual who infringes our Constitution."

This was no longer, as before, an alternation between blindness and insight but a brazen cynicism. Mikhail Prishvin, another Fellow-Traveller, remarked after a conversation with Pilnyak:

> I have understood the emptiness of all who declare their loyalty to the Party.

In his books there appeared new heroes, double-dealers and conformists who gave up their private lives to public affairs not for the sake of high ideals but simply to save themselves and then, suffering, started to disintegrate from such a double existence. Pilnyak followed the same path as his heroes.

As he wrote his last novel they closed in on him.

Arrested shortly before Pilnyak, the poet Konstantin Bolshakov recounted during his interrogation how Pilnyak had begun to rush about, sensing that retribution was close at hand:

> They were then slating Pilnyak for his past sins – for helping the Radek family in exile, for his friendship with Voronsky, and the books the latter encouraged him to write. Pilnyak became nervous, went to visit various officials and made penitent speeches at the Writers Union. He confided to me that he would soon have nothing to live on, people wanted to finish him off, and he feared this more than anything. But I could see that he was afraid of something else as well.

Bolshakov's testimony, appended to Pilnyak's file, give us a feeling of the atmosphere of those years. Before people were arrested they were driven to the brink of insanity and suicide by the all-pervading fear and suspicion. This was also a way of reforging the human soul:

> Pilnyak dragged me back to his dacha. When we were alone together I started talking about the trial of the united Trotskyist–Zinovievite centre. Pilnyak said that Trotskyism had nothing to do with it. Anyone could be convicted of Trotskyism now. Anyone who did not think like the leading article in *Pravda* was already a Trotskyist. "You and I are also Trotskyists," he said. Later he returned again to this theme and began to say that all his friends were Trotskyists, not just because they had been in the Opposition but because they refused to conform.
>
> I started to talk about my own inevitable death and said that if war broke out I would have to either seek out death myself or they would shoot me. As a member of the gentry and a former officer they would not trust me. Pilnyak listened gloomily and without saying a single word.
>
> Soon after I began to notice symptoms of the illness which forced me to remain in bed for three months. When I had recovered I hid from people, and from rumours and conversations, but friends would bring the rumours with them and they themselves came round to talk. The arrests scared people and evoked a muted and furious anger. I thought to myself, infuriated, they are taking away the individual's right to doubt.
>
> Pilnyak asserted that they would come and arrest people again, that our arrest was also nearing and did not even conceal the fact that he feared arrest himself and that almost everyone in Peredelkino was afraid of him. Rumours, each more fantastic than the last, were the only thing

that mattered to us and nourished us. I reduced my circle of acquaintances to a minimum. There was some kind of monstrous nightmare in my head. I was afraid to have a drink in case my subconscious might surface when I had become drunk . . .

At this point the interrogator halted Bolshakov: "We have no interest in your emotional state!"

While Pilnyak was finishing off his novel, the NKVD operatives were writing an extensive note about his arrest.

"It is not apparent from the materials in the case file," reads the decision rehabilitating Pilnyak in 1956, "what was the pretext for his arrest." The procurators in charge of the writer's rehabilitation were inattentive – or else they did not want to look too closely.

I found the relevant document in the procurator's office itself, in the supervisory file on his former wife Olga Shcherbinovskaya, an actress with the Maly Theatre. (For some reason it had been removed from Pilnyak's investigation file, and was not at the KGB but in the procurator's office.) Shcherbinovskaya was arrested and sent to the camps, as was his last wife Kira Andronikashvili (also an actress), for the sole reason that she was closely linked to the seditious author.

It became clear from this modestly titled "Note" that many of the accusations made at meetings of the Writers Union and in the offices of various publishers and journals found their way to the investigator's desk. They were transferred directly from the minutes of those gatherings into the depositions in Pilnyak's file.

The following was recorded at a meeting of the editorial board of the monthly *Novy mir* on 1 September 1936, attended by Pilnyak:

> *Ivan Gronsky (chief editor).* You have retorted that you are distancing yourself from the enemies in your works. Which works? The *Tale of the Unextinguished Moon*, perhaps, or the *Mahogany*? These works were written on the direct instructions of the Trotskyists. Whether you consciously or unconsciously directed them against the Revolution is another matter . . .

Let us turn to the note on his arrest:

> Pilnyak's close ties with the Trotskyists found expression in his work. A large number of his writings were pervaded by the spirit of counter-revolutionary Trotskyism (The *Tale of the Unextinguished Moon* or *Mahogany*).

Further on during the same meeting, Gronsky raised the accusation that Pilnyak had been providing the exiled Karl Radek with practical help:

This is a weighty defect in your biography and, since you now call yourself a non-Party Bolshevik, you must remove this defect . . .

Turning back to the arrest note:

When Radek and other Trotskyists were in exile Pilnyak used his own money to help them.

The testimonies exacted from the writers already arrested and in the hands of the NKVD interrogators (Arosev, Guber, Bolshakov, Zarudin) were fully exploited here as well. One refers to Pilnyak's friendship with Trotskyists, another to the anti-Soviet company he kept, a third talks of the writer's terrorist plans and a fourth, of his spying activities. There was even a contribution from Spain. The long arm of the NKVD had managed to capture Andreas Nin, the general secretary of the POUM, the Spanish Trotskyist party, and letters from Pilnyak were found in his archive. These referred to another well-known Trotskyist, the writer Victor Serge, then exiled to Orenburg. And then there were the inevitable informers' reports . . .

"It is essential to arrest him and carry out a search," concluded Captain Zhurbenko, the head of 9th section of State Security's 4th department, who had compiled the Note.

Summer 1937 was over. Pilnyak had almost finished the draft of his novel. All that remained was to write out a clean version and add the final full stop. At that moment "the handsome leather-coated lads" climbed off the pages of his books and came to get him.

Pilnyak's dacha is still there, in the very centre of Peredelkino, next to that of his friend Boris Pasternak. The garden gate between the two was never closed. That day, 28 October, Pasternak came in and congratulated the Pilnyaks: their son was three years old. It was already getting late and dark when a car stopped outside the house.

A large number of strangers in NKVD uniform spilled out of the vehicle. An officer called Veprintsev presented a search warrant and a warrant for the arrest of the writer. Two Caucasian daggers were confiscated, as were a Corona typewriter, correspondence and the manuscript of Pilnyak's latest novel.

The novel disappeared without a trace. In its place there appeared a blue official file, Case No 14488 of the Main Administration for State Security.

"Thou sayest"

NAME: Pilnyak-Vogau Boris Andreevich
PLACE AND DATE OF BIRTH: Mozhaisk, 1894
NATIONALITY: Volga German

MEMBERSHIP OF PARTY: Not a Party member
PROFESSION: Writer of fiction
SOCIAL GROUP: Free professional

They removed his tie and belt. Then the prisoner's case was handed over to investigator David Abramovich Rayzman.

They first met on 2 November, five days after the arrest. Rayzman told his charge what the accusation was: counter-revolution, terror and espionage. That same day Pilnyak wrote a repentant letter to Yezhov:

> I ask myself whether the NKVD was right to arrest me and answer, they were right . . .

His statement was typed and the signature is clear and firm. Pilnyak's strategy was consciously adopted and indubitably suited the investigator otherwise he would not have been given access to a typewriter. He would provide the proof of his guilt and hope thereby to avoid unnecessary torment and suffering.

> All I have left is a brain and that is also beginning to grow dim. I'm talking to someone and suddenly that person vanishes and in his place there sits before me a frightful and bloody state.

The speaker is Ivan Moskva, one of Pilnyak's characters. In his letter to Yezhov, the writer said:

> My life and my actions show that I was a counter-revolutionary, an enemy of the existing order and the existing government. If this arrest will be only a lesson for me, ie, if I remain alive, I shall consider this a wonderful lesson and make use of it so as to live out the rest of my life honestly. Therefore, I want to be quite open to you in describing all my counter-revolutionary activities.
>
> It would be wrong if I acknowledged myself a Trotskyist. I was not. I had dealings with the Trotskyists, just as I had dealings with other counter-revolutionaries – I had dealings with all who shared my counter-revolutionary views . . .
>
> In our conversations during those years I and those who thought like me were agreed that the political situation inside the country was very tense. The oppression of the individual and artistic creativity by the state was creating an atmosphere not of companionship but of alienation and loneliness, and was destroying the concept of socialism . . . I shall provide detailed testimony about the nature and dates of these conversations during the investigation.
>
> Because I do not wish to hide anything I must also mention espionage. Since my first trip to Japan in 1926 I have remained in contact with

Professor Yonekawa, an officer on the General Staff and an intelligence agent. Through him I became a Japanese agent and carried out my espionage activities. Moreover, other Japanese came to visit me, and so did foreigners from other countries. I shall describe all of these things in detail during the investigation.

When some were interrogated they underwent a change of heart, or at least give that impression, and freely libelled themselves. One of the heroines of Pilnyak's novel *The Doubles* had so subordinated her existence to that of society that she even spoke of herself in the third person.

There were other reasons, however, for not resisting. I shall write what they demand and then at least they won't torture me. Those who had invented these Soviet methods of investigation, the most experienced Chekists, often immediately demanded pen and paper when they themselves were arrested and unconditionally confessed to every crime. Sometimes they even wrote out the entire deposition for the investigators, inventing their imaginary dialogue ... If I lie today then maybe I shall survive to tell the truth tomorrow.

More than a month passed before the prisoner was first taken for interrogation. That first cross-examination lasted, however, many hours. Pilnyak was interrogated by two men, Rayzman and his boss, Zhurbenko who was now already a major.

The deposition was written out by the interrogator and the document was the usual and quite conscious mixture of truth and falsehood. All were lying there, for different reasons.

On 11 December 1937 Pilnyak was brought for interrogation. The investigators began to trace his treachery back to the first years of the Revolution and Pilnyak began his forced confession:

> I began to struggle against the Soviet regime during the first years of the Revolution. During the period of War Communism,* at a time of intense class struggle I remained in Kolomna,** writing stories and, in essence, waited to see what was going on in the country: I thought "it's none of my business" and "let's see what the upshot is". For a very long time this was my decisive attitude as a writer and as a human being.
>
> I felt sympathetic towards the "Scythians"† in 1920, then I joined forces with the "Serapion Brotherhood"†† and though I did not formally

---

*A reference to period 1918–21 when, under conditions of Civil War, extreme and utopian Communist ideas were proclaimed and implemented.
**A small medieval town not far from Moscow.
†A literary group from the early days of the Revolution, including Blok, Bely, Yesenin and others.
††A group of young writers in Petrograd, who proclaimed the renewal of literature and the primacy of art over ideology in the early 1920s. See "The Literary–Political Context", p 287.

belong to the group I shared all its literary tendencies and political aspirations. At the head of this group stood Yevgeny Zamyatin... Before this, as far back as 1919, I became a member of the Union of Writers, which brought together writers with the same attitudes as me, ie, people who had hidden away from the Revolution ...

In autumn 1922 a number of writers were invited to Moscow in a telegram from Kamenev. He suggested that we organize a writers' collective, a publishing house and an almanac. No political demands were set before us during the conversation with Kamenev, and we were made independent masters of the publishing house... Some while after, the first meeting to organize our work was held in Kamenev's office. There we were given a free hand to write and print whatever we liked. The main task of our writers' collective was to gather around us all the new writers who had appeared. The effective director of this collective was Voronsky, then editor of *Krasnaya nov*. Our counter-revolutionary aspirations, especially those of Zamyatin and myself, were completely in accord with Voronsky's mood and his literary philosophy. This was to confirm my friendship with him for many years to come ...

If in this passage we place the adjectives "counter-revolutionary", "anti-Soviet" and "Trotskyist" in inverted commas we can see what Pilnyak's co-authors contributed to the text. Further on, Pilnyak testified:

It was then that Voronsky sent me to see Trotsky. I remember that Mayakovsky and Pasternak were also with him at the time ... Trotsky talked to us about internationalism in literature and said that it made no difference to him where he made a Revolution, in Moscow or in Rome. Trotsky did everything to charm us ...

I then considered my teacher in literature Andrey Bely and, as I have already said, my elder comrade Zamyatin to be very close friends. As far back as the period of War Communism the closest of all to me was the poet Pasternak ...

From informers' reports the Lubyanka was very well aware of the friendship between Pilnyak and Pasternak. Certain information obtained from such sources is cited in the Note preceding Pilnyak's arrest:

In 1933 Pilnyak tried to draw B. Pasternak into his group. This growing friendship found outward expression in the anti-Party obituary for Andrey Bely and in the letter to *Literaturnaya gazeta*, jointly signed by Pasternak and Pilnyak, in defence of the Trotskyist Zarudin. It has also been established that they agreed to keep the French writer Victor Margueritte (who had signed the appeal in defence of Trotsky) informed about the oppressed position of Russian writers, so that this information was made known in French writers' circles. In 1936 Pilnyak and Pasternak had several secret meetings with André Gide, who was visiting the USSR, during which they gave him tendentious information about the situation in the Soviet Union. There can be no doubt that Gide used this information in his book against the USSR.

The Lubyanka was also keeping a close watch on Boris Pasternak. They could arrest him at any moment. It is said, however, that when all was ready and Stalin was informed, he dismissed the idea: "Leave that cloud-dweller in peace!"

During his interrogation, Pilnyak gave a detailed account of the story behind his most famous and controversial work, *The Tale of the Unextinguished Moon*. The GPU seized all the copies of the May 1926 issue of *Novy mir* in which it was printed from the printing works; if anyone had already received a copy the GPU sent its operatives who gave them a receipt and confiscated it. Polonsky, the chief editor of *Novy mir*, was severely reprimanded. Pilnyak had dared to unveil the internal Party intrigues and describe how "Number One" ordered his favourite soldier, a Civil-War hero, to have an operation and then ensured that he would not come round after the anaesthetic . . .

> It was Voronsky who gave me the idea of writing this novel. As I wrote I read passages to my comrades of the time and, in particular, to Agranov.* Agranov told me several details of Frunze's illness. Then there was a meeting in my flat to discuss the novel. In attendance were Polonsky, the editor of *Novy mir*, Lashevich whom I had invited as a military expert . . . They all approved of the work but Polonsky considered that a preface was needed, and it was written there and then . . .
>
> The novel was banned, as it happened, when I was in China. On my return I appealed to Skvortsov-Stepanov, chief editor of *Izvestiya*, to decide my fate. He was very considerate towards me and during our conversation said that the story was a talented work. Skvortsov-Stepanov promised his support and organized a meeting with Rykov.** Rykov advised me to write penitent letters, which I did.
>
> Subsequently Radek expressed his sympathy and gave me practical help. I should add that Radek read this novel in manuscript and even participated in its editing . . . Radek was the first who began to speak to me openly and sharply against the leadership of the Party. In our

*Yakov Agranov (1893–1938), then a deputy head of OGPU, was on friendly terms with many writers, notably Mayakovsky. At the same time he was directly implicated in the deaths of Gumilyov and Chayanov. He was shot in August 1938.
**Until 1930 Alexey Rykov was a member of the Politburo and headed the Soviet government as chairman of the Council of People's Commissariats.

conversations Radek claimed that Stalin was departing from Lenin's line while he, Radek, Trotsky and others among their supporters were the true Leninists. Their removal from leading posts was, he asserted, a distortion of the Leninist line and as a consequence, said Radek, a struggle between the Trotskyists and the Stalinites was unavoidable . . .

By this time Radek had been publicly tried and condemned as an enemy of the people and Rykov would soon suffer the same fate. Voronsky, the central figure in the literary world of the 1920s, had also been shot.

When Voronsky began to organize the Pereval group we agreed that I would not officially align myself with them but should take an active part in the group's work. I would attend the meetings of Pereval so as to demonstrate my solidarity with them. My second Trotskyist work dates from this period. In 1928, together with Andrey Platonov, I wrote the essay "Che-Che-O" which was published in *Novy mir*. This ends with the suggestion that the locomotive of socialism will not reach the station of "Socialism" because the brakes of the bureaucracy will make its wheels melt . . .

In the essay itself this is expressed rather differently:

If they set a supervisor over the train-driver then the locomotive of history will burn itself out, dragging along with the brakes on . . .

At the very same time the first, free and non-political All-Russian Union of Writers was disbanded.

There was a feeling in the Union of Writers that it would be a good thing if literature was released from the Party. When we discussed the state of affairs in literature and in the Party at our illegal gatherings we tried to prove, using every means available, the oppressive nature of censorship and suppression of literature by the Party. These statements were concealed behind a policy of political non-alignment, free speech and pure art . . . In defining the nature of the Union of Writers it must be said that there was no Party cell there. In 1929 I was elected chairman of the Union and in that very year it was liquidated as an anti-Soviet organization . . .

It was then that I wrote my most sharply anti-Soviet novel *Mahogany* which was published abroad. This novel proved a watershed for writers: Were they for the Soviet regime or against it?

At the same time as the Union of Writers ceased its activities, the Pereval group began to fall apart. Voronsky was sent into exile. *Mahogany* was being slated and my authority among writers was

The assembled Union of Soviet Writers leaves the Rostov house to join the annual May Day parade past the Soviet leaders on Red Square, 1930s.

From left to right: Voroshilov, Molotov and Stalin, with and without Yezhov, admiring the Moscow–Volga canal built by slave labour. Photographs from before and after December 1938, when Yezhov fell from power as head of the secret police.

Left: Father Pavel Florensky, 1912, shortly before his celebrated work *The Pillar and Foundation of Truth* appeared.

Above: Prisoner Florensky; photograph from his investigation file, 1933.

Above: Georgy Demidov, late 1930s, shortly before his arrest.

Right: Nina Hagen-Torn, 1916, aged 16. Youthful ethnographer and secretary of Volfil, the Free Philosophical Society founded by Andrey Bely and others.

Osip Mandelstam; photograph from
his investigation file, 17 May 1934.

Above right and detail: Osip Mandelstam caught in the foreground of a photograph of a cardinal's funeral, Paris, 1908. The photograph was later issued as a postcard, which Mandelstam happened upon and sent to his mother with the following inscription: "Dear Mother! I send you my physiognomy reproduced by chance on this card. One might say that I turned round on purpose to be able to send you my good wishes."

Congress of RAPP (Russian Association of Proletarian Writers), late 1920s. Victims, informers and executioners. Outlined in the centre (*from left to right*) Kirshon, Averbakh, Fadeev and Stavsky.

Above: Boris Pilnyak at the Lubyanka; photograph from his investigation file, 1937.

Left: The last photograph of Isaac Babel, from his investigation file, 1939.

Vsevolod Meyerhold; photograph from his Lubyanka dossier, 1939.

The last photograph of Nikolay Klyuev, at the Lubyanka; from his investigation file, 1934.

Andrey Platonov in 1922, at the same age as the hero of his *Technical Novel*. This work was unknown until Platonov's investigation file was opened.

Stalin and his last head of secret police, Lavrenty Beria (left).

Mikhail Bulgakov in the mid 1920s, at about the time he was writing his ill-fated "Diary", whose survival we owe to the secret police habit of copying documents that came into their hands.

Maxim Gorky on his visit to the Solovki camps in 1929 with leading OGPU men (including Gleb Boky), whose work ("re-education through labour") aroused Gorky's enthusiasm.

Gorky with his son Maxim, daughter-in-law Nadezhda (Timosha), with whom OGPU chief Genrikh Yagoda was besotted, and grand-daughters Marfa and Darya.

From right to left: Genrikh Yagoda, Maxim Gorky and his secretary, Pyotr Kryuchkov.

The Solovetsky monastery in the White Sea was the first Soviet concentration camp. Here, in 1937, Father Pavel Florensky and many other prisoners were executed.

Prisoners' cemetery in the notorious Kolyma region of the Gulag Archipelago.

undermined. With Voronsky we then decided to set up a new literary organization and created the "1930s" circle. We asserted that literature was oppressed, that the tasks being set before literature could not be fulfilled, that writers were bound hand and foot and were only entitled to write within strict limits, and that literature was being debased. Zarudin, I[van] Kataev and Andrey Platonov were active participants in meetings of the "1930s" circle and Pasternak attended one or two meetings, considering them to be acceptable in spirit. As a literary group the "1930s" circle fell apart in spring 1930 but some of those involved remained on friendly terms and kept in touch until very recently, helping and seeing each other . . .

The Union of Writers was transformed into the Union of Soviet Writers. The overwhelming majority of writers joined the new Union but remained committed to the same principles they had held before re-organization. When Pasternak went to work in the organizational committee of the Writers Union I made all kinds of attacks on him and our relations even became difficult for this reason. As a consequence of my then particularly hostile attitude to the policies of the Party and its leadership, I boycotted the Writers Union and did not therefore speak at the Writers Congress.* The Congress struck me as a hypocritical bureaucratic venture and the addresses given by writers there, lying and double-dealing . . . Over a number of years all my public aspirations as a writer derived from a desire to be "a leader" but nothing came of this. I suffered one failure after another and in the end the majority of writers abandoned me, having understood the anti-Soviet essence of my aspirations . . .

Pilnyak was trying to take all the blame on himself and shield his friends, many of whom were either already arrested or living under the threat of imminent arrest. He could not entirely avoid naming names, however. The interrogators were expert at alienating even friends. At a strategy meeting in the NKVD on 3 February 1935 the same Yakov Agranov, by then deputy People's Commissar for Internal Affairs, would define the methods to be used:

Our tactic for crushing the enemy was to confront all these scoundrels and set them against each other. It was a difficult task. It was essential to turn them against one another because all these traitors were closely bound together.

Pilnyak's ties with foreign writers was a particular theme during his investigation.

*Held in Moscow in 1934, the Congress confirmed the monopoly of the new Union and of the doctrine of Socialist Realism.

He was well known in Europe, America and Japan. Not only were his books read abroad, but he himself travelled widely and became acquainted with many noted literary figures. Among those individuals placed by fate between Russia and Europe and between the Revolution in the East and civilization in the West Victor Serge occupied a unique position. Serge (Kibalchich) served both French literature and the Russian Revolution. Rejected by the latter as a Trotskyist, he was sent back again to Europe and eventually died in Mexico.

In his *Memoirs of a Revolutionary* Serge quotes Pilnyak as having once said:

> There is not a single thinking adult in this country who has not at some time thought that he might be shot . . .

In his depositions during the interrogation Pilnyak gave a detailed account of his friendship with Serge. Their conversations were quite open and frank: they discussed the horrors of collectivization, the terror, and the impossibility of either living or writing when the country was in such a condition . . .

> We concluded that the political situation was extremely bad. An unprecedented oppression of the individual by the state could be felt, there were not even the minimal rights to express an opinion and we were now living under siege. This was not socialism since socialism implied an improvement in relations between people whereas we were being encouraged to behave like savage beasts . . .
>
> As a result of our discussions, Serge and I reached the conclusion that we must let the Western public know what was happening in Russia . . .

Soon such an opportunity arose. Panait Istrati arrived from Paris and was met with great ceremony by the Soviet government as a revolutionary writer from Europe. In origin Rumanian, he wrote in French and was then very popular – Romain Rolland called him the "Balkan Gorky". Istrati travelled all over the country, surrounded by attention from the Party and the secret police who were both intent on seeing yet another book praising the USSR appear in the West.

Victor Serge acquainted Istrati with Pilnyak. To begin with Pilnyak did not want to meet him: there was no point, he thought, in talking to writers who allowed themselves to be so easily led. Serge nevertheless brought Istrati to see the writer.

> *Istrati.* You didn't want to see me? That's exactly why I came. Tell me, why did you not want to see me?
> *Pilnyak.* Because you do not look at our country as you should but only through the eyes of official representatives. You accept too many congratulations and express your thanks too often. You have a false

assessment of the situation here and if you write about it then it will be a
sugary picture and not the truth . . .
Istrati. I would like to know the truth.

So then Pilnyak and Serge began to open Istrati's eyes. As one example of
injustice, they told him about the "Rusakov case". An elderly worker and father
of six, Rusakov had been ejected from his flat in Leningrad as the result of a
provocation. (Rusakov's elder daughter was married to Serge and the younger,
to another Frenchman Pierre Pascal.) This story, as a model of life in the Soviet
Union, so astonished Istrati that he then went to Kalinin, the nominal head of
state, to obtain justice for the family.

Not long afterwards Istrati published a three-volume work in Paris,
written together with Victor Serge and Boris Souvarine. It attracted a great deal
of attention and Istrati was promptly denounced in the Soviet *Literary
Encyclopedia*: "proved to be the most shameless renegade. His works are
crude counter-revolutionary libels." The interrogator demanded of Pilnyak:

> *Interrogator.* So you were the main source for treacherous information
> against the Land of the Soviets?
> *Pilnyak.* Yes, I am guilty before the Soviet people for having tried to
> discredit the Soviet Union in the eyes of the Western intelligentsia by
> passing on this treacherous information through Istrati . . .

Still, even by Soviet standards, the books written by Pilnyak and others were
insufficient grounds to condemn a man.

There appeared in the deposition a note about the gathering of writers at
Voronsky's flat in autumn 1932 when a plan to assassinate Stalin supposedly first
arose:

> Voronsky delivered a speech which in essence said that such a regime
> had been created in the country and in the Party that it was impossible
> to live. If the Party was using terror against the Trotskyists then they must
> respond likewise. Voronsky became so excited that he exclaimed:
> "Stalin must be shot!"

Next Pilnyak recorded various criminal conversations with his writer-friends
Pasternak, Fedin and Vesyoly:

> I have known Pasternak for many years . . . One day someone from the
> Writers Union drove out to get his signature on a letter demanding
> that Tukhachevsky* and co be shot. Pasternak hid so as not to sign this
> letter and said to me: "This is moral torture" and asked straightaway if

*Marshal Tukhachevsky was tried in 1937 and shot immediately.

I would not go round to Eydeman's wife* and express my sympathy.

I was especially close to Fedin. We often talked about the unbearable regime within the Party and the lack of trust with which the individual was surrounded. We regarded this regime as a form of terror . . . To begin with Fedin was indignant with Trotsky: "That monkey who sits abroad and tries to seize power in Russia not asking us whether we want to be under his heel or not" . . . But the incomprehensible and inexplicable arrests turned Fedin against the leaders of the Party, Stalin and Yezhov as the executor of Stalin's will. We agreed that there was only Stalin and the Party did not exist, and that the country was threatened by inevitable catastrophe. Fedin was afraid of war with the Germans: "that 70 million-strong mass of hungry and convinced Nazis will then crush Russia under their iron boots."

Just before his arrest Pilnyak had a similar conversation with Artyom Vesyoly:

"What about you, Artyom? You're a revolutionary Bolshevik and member of the Party. How do you feel in the Party?"

"Like a lone wolf . . ."

"But if you're a real revolutionary and Bolshevik how could you let yourself become a wolf in your own Party?"

"It's a long story. I can't say anything without a bottle of vodka," Artyom replied with irritation and fell silent. "I want to belong to the Party and they tell me, your place is out in the alley . . ."

After another pause, he added pensively:

"I'd even take my revolver and go after . . ."

"Who would you go after?"

"Who do you think? Stalin, of course!"

Artyom Vesyoly was a decisive brave man whose deeds usually matched his words. Pilnyak understood after this conversation that his friend had also been driven to the brink of despair. He was himself, he admits, in a distraught and frenzied state. (Vesyoly was arrested on the same day as Pilnyak, also in Peredelkino. They would be interrogated at almost the same time and even share the same interrogators. Vesyoly also wrote a penitent letter to Yezhov.) These were still only conversations, however, there were no examples of terrorism:

We have information that you were preparing to commit a terrorist act. Confess!

*R.P. Eydeman was a famous Red Army officer, a writer and friend of Pilnyak. He was shot in 1937.

The prisoner confessed to everything they demanded. He and his friends had thought up a plan to kill Yezhov. They would either get into his flat, with the help of women they knew, or simply attack him on the street. The vigilance of the NKVD had forestalled the plan by arresting them all in time.

The interrogator asked Pilnyak exhaustive questions about his foreign acquaintances and in the deposition each of them became a spy, each contact a transfer of orders and simple conversations a cover for handing over secret information. No explanation was provided why Pilnyak should have become a Japanese spy. No mention is made of money or pressure: voluntarily and without any selfish motive he "became an agent among certain sections of the intelligentsia." The enemy agents received information about public life in the USSR, about literature and the groupings within the Writers Union – he even told them the surnames of various writers.

The first interrogation was over. No incriminating facts had been established but this did not worry Pilnyak's investigators: it was merely important to observe the formalities. However, there were some slips somewhere.

The original hand-written deposition is not in the file, although it should be. Instead there is a typed copy signed by Pilnyak. And there is something wrong about the signature. It has been added, as usual, at the bottom of every page and again under some, but not all, of the answers. In places it is so unlike Pilnyak's own signature that we may doubt its authenticity. Only a hand-writing specialist could say whether it was forged or written in a very depressed state.

On 26 March 1938 Pilnyak was taken for his second and last interrogation. Rayzman was tidying up the testimony. Now he was asking about Pilnyak's journey to the USA in 1931. All the investigator could make of what the writer told him was this:

> I could not speak out openly against the USSR and the Party but I turned my visit into a tourist trip, thereby blurring the public significance that friends of the USSR had wanted to give it . . .

The investigation file on Pilnyak is a mixture of truth, falsehood and half-truths. Alongside the sincere distress the writer felt for the state of his country and its people, and his dislike for despotism and censorship, we also find Pilnyak slandering himself and others, and offering fantastic inventions that were either demanded or suggested by his interrogators.

The names of others came up inevitably. They were shifted from one file to another. They were often proposed by the interrogator and then inserted in the prisoner's final deposition. Of many of his statements then Pilnyak could certainly have replied to the interrogator in the words of the Gospel: "Thou sayest."

Even then, the theme of resistance and hatred of Stalinism can be heard here. Pilnyak and his friends were natural enemies of despotism, no matter how hard they tried to reach accommodation with the regime. And sooner or later it would destroy them.

"I have become a different person"

On 20 April Pilnyak received a copy of the charge sheet and learned that his case would come before the Military Tribunal. He was certainly also thoroughly prepared by his investigators and told that he must not recant but keep up the farce till the end.

The trial took place next day. The irreplaceable Ulrich presided, assisted by military jurists Zaryanov and Zhdan*, and by secretary of the court Batner. The sitting lasted from 5.45 to 6 pm.

The chairman announced the case and the articles infringed. The secretary to the court informed the judges that the accused was ready and that no witnesses had been called. The judges assured themselves that the accused was Boris Pilnyak-Vogau and the latter did not submit any petition for a new panel of judges.

Hurriedly the secretary read out the charge sheet with its string of signatures ranging from Rayzman up to the USSR Procurator General, Vyshinsky.

> *Ulrich.* Do you acknowledge your guilt?
> *Pilnyak.* Yes, entirely. I also fully confirm my deposition. During the interrogation I told the whole truth and I have nothing to add.

The judicial investigation was over.

The accused man was allowed a last word.

> I very much want to work. After being held in prison for so long I have become quite a different person and look on life with new eyes. I want to live, to work hard, I want to have paper in front of me on which I could write something of use to Soviet people . . .

The judges withdrew to confer.

The sentence announced on their return was formulated in the same indifferent bureaucratic clichés. Convicted of belonging to "anti-Soviet, Trotskyist, subversive and terrorist organizations", of preparing to assassinate Stalin and Yezhov, and of spying for Japan, Pilnyak was sentenced to the "ultimate penalty". The sentence was "irrevocable and to be carried out immediately".

A small yellowing slip of paper adds:

*Their ranks respectively: army, division and brigade military jurists.

Sentence carried out ... Lieutenant Shevelev, head of 1st special section's 12th department

The post-Stalin volume of the *Literary Encyclopedia* stated that Pilnyak died in 1937, his family were given 1941 as the year of death. Neither is correct. Boris Pilnyak died on 21 April 1938.

The next paper in the file is more recent and refers to the writer's rehabilitation. Pilnyak was arrested without the sanction of the procurator, stated the Military Procurator's Office in 1956. The testimony of Bolshakov, Artyom Vesyoly and Pilnyak himself was refuted by new investigation. There were no grounds for his conviction following an investigation that made use of illegal methods. All charges were therefore withdrawn against him and the case closed for lack of a corpus delicti.

Among those who gave the character references formally required for Pilnyak's rehabilitation was Ivan Gronsky. Now he would admit that Pilnyak was no enemy of the people. He continued to speak, however, of his "more than cautious attitude" to the writer. He "naturally, was obliged to check all those working for the journal, especially those linked to the Trotskyists and, in the first instance, of course, Boris Pilnyak," said Gronsky, calling his books libellous. In 1982 he would still describe the *Tale of the Unextinguished Moon* as a work of "ideological subversion". Neither the prisons nor labour camps in which Gronsky had himself been incarcerated changed his opinions.

It would take much longer for Pilnyak's works to be restored to the readers. All his works were withdrawn from every library and bookshop after his arrest and anyone found with one in their possession risked punishment. An entire generation grew up before his books began to be published again in 1976.

A formal request for information about the confiscated manuscripts was made by our commission. "They have not been preserved."

Boris Pilnyak will never now finish his last novel. His life instead shrank to the full stop of the executioner's bullet.*

---

*The standard form of execution in the 1930s was and indeed today is a single bullet fired at point-blank range into the back of the head.

CHAPTER 8

DENUNCIATION AS A
LITERARY GENRE

"We shall not surrender Pavlik Morozov!" they had warned me at the Lubyanka. They did not intend to betray their helpers, that innumerable army of informants or "secret employees" spread out among the population.

Of course, the denunciation as a literary genre has always existed. But it may be doubted that it ever achieved such extensive development as in the Soviet Union. It was publicly declared the honourable duty of every citizen to report on his family, friends and neighbours and failure to do so was a criminal offence.

Young Pioneer Pavlik Morozov was held up as a Soviet martyr and an example to several generations of schoolchildren. He informed on his father, chairman of one of the new collective farms, for protecting "kulaks". The father was shot and Pavlik himself murdered by his uncle and other villagers.

It was among the writers, however, as might only be expected, that the genre reached its most elaborate and varied forms.

There was, for instance, the public and universal denunciation. Vengeance must be taken on entire classes and estates in society – the gentry, bourgeoisie, the clergy, well-off peasants ("kulaks") and the rotten intelligentsia. Re-education was time-consuming and, probably, a hopeless undertaking. It was better to finish them off straightaway.

In the *Red Gospel* (1919-20), a very popular book in its day, the poet Vasily Knyazev threatened to

> *Meet their challenge with volleys of gunfire,*
> *Send the gentry and rich to the wall!*
> *Send a hail of lead in answer*
> *To each of their treacherous blows...*

and ended, "Long live the Red Terror!" Knyazev called down doom on himself. Falling under the "Red Wheel" of terror, he died in a camp in Kolyma and was tossed in a common grave.

Then there were the reports that all organizations, small or large, were supposed constantly to supply about the behaviour and views of their members. Particular attention was paid to artists, and above all writers, those workers of the "ideological front". Those in charge of the Writers Union such as Stavsky, Pavlenko and Gronsky would play a direct role in sending other writers to their deaths. The writer Alexander Fadeev, for many years a leading official of the Union, was also very active in this way. Some say that he sent his colleagues to their deaths. Others claim he defended and saved his fellow writers, and perhaps he did. Working in the archive at the Lubyanka, however, I came across many documents bearing Fadeev's signature: "I agree to this arrest . . ." Naturally, he was under orders from Stalin and obliged to approve and countersign these attacks on other writers. The regime isolated and destroyed those artists it could not use and did so, apparently, in the name of literature itself.

It was not surprising, then, that in 1956, when arrested and imprisoned writers began to return one after another from the camps, Fadeev chose to commit suicide. In the last letter he wrote he said:

> With the greatest of joy, I am leaving this life, a release from this vile existence where baseness, falsehood and slander are suddenly poured on you.

The regime had a vast army of informers in its service. Some were formally employed to report on others and some were volunteers; some took money and others worked from conviction. As early as 1921 the Cheka had formulated a special instruction concerning the "30 pieces of silver" such an agent should receive:

> Subsidies in the form of money and goods will undoubtedly bind him to us ... he will become the eternal slave of the Cheka, fearing the disclosure of his activities.

The individual was surrounded by a dense network of informers everywhere, even when he landed in prison. A caretaker might inform on a tenant; a hairdresser on a client; a passenger on the chauffeur; and a wife on her husband. Or vice versa, and in any combination. The motives were ideological zeal, envy, greed, vengeance – or even simply to anticipate and avert a similar blow:

"Why are you here?"
"Because I was lazy."
"What?!"
"I told my friend the latest joke and went to bed, thinking, I'll inform on him tomorrow. Next morning they picked me up: he was quicker off the mark ..."
A well-known anecdote.

I have no particular desire to expose and list the many authors who devoted themselves to this poisonous genre. Yet all the chapters in this book are scattered with the gems submitted by informers, sometimes signing their real names, more often using pseudonyms and nicknames. Not a single investigation could dispense with the fruitful activities of these secret agents, and their treacherous shadows loom behind each victim of the repressions.

The following short letter vividly demonstrates how the denunciations worked and involved large groups of writers.

International Bureau
of Revolutionary Literature

2 January 1928

Dear Comrade Averbakh,

I feel obliged to inform you about the following, and ask you to take urgent measures.

The writer Panait Istrati visited the editorial office of *Herald of Foreign Literature* and informed us of a conversation he had with Comrade Sandomirsky. Sandomirsky advised Istrati not to write anything about either the Bolsheviks or the Soviet Union. If Istrati writes on these subjects, praising 99% and criticizing 1%, then, in Sandomirsky's opinion, this will be enough to turn the Bolsheviks into his mortal enemies. He will not only meet with ill-will on the part of the Soviet and French Communist parties but may also perhaps find it difficult to leave the USSR ...

Istrati not only told me about this conversation, but also Comrades Dinamov, Anisimov and Kogan and, I think, several others as well. We tried, as best we could, to calm him down and persuade him that Sandomirsky was only joking. But I doubt that we were successful.

So I am letting you know that we are having quite a lot of difficulty in attracting writers who sympathize with our cause. We shall not be able to fulfil such a task if such things as the above-mentioned conversation continue to happen.

With Communist greetings
Bela Illes*

It does not matter whether Illes was writing to Averbakh as the head of VAPP, the All-Russian Association of Proletarian Writers, or as the literary adviser and close relative of Yagoda, the secret police chief. In either case, the end result was the same. German Sandomirsky was eventually arrested and shot. The above letter is preserved in his Lubyanka file with a note specifically forbidding anyone other than state security employees to become acquainted with its contents.

It is also clear that this was a vicious circle. If a person did not inform and react to this "criminal" behaviour, he might himself be incriminated with concealing the crime.

In 1937, at the height of the Purges, Comrade Konstantin Sedykh, a poet,

*Bela Illes (1895–1974): writer and participant in the 1919 Hungarian revolution, who spent the years 1922–45 in the USSR and then returned to Hungary.

wrote to another poet, Comrade Ivan Molchanov who was in charge of the Writers Union in the Irkutsk Region:

> I feel obliged to inform you of the following.
>
> On the evening of 30 November Innokenty Trukhin, of whom you have already heard, turned up at my flat in the company of someone I did not know but whom he introduced to the poet Anatoly Pestyukhin, who was then visiting me, and to myself as the poet Ryabtsovsky (or Ryabovsky, I don't remember which). They were both drunk.
>
> I was extremely surprised by such a visit since I have never been on close terms with Trukhin. So I was not very welcoming. Trukhin took not the blindest notice. He pulled a bottle of vodka out of his pocket and began to invite me to drink. In the conversation that followed, quite unprovoked by any remark or anyone else, Trukhin launched a vile, counter-revolutionary attack on Comrade Stalin. He said the following: "Do you think you lot matter? If I get going I'll take Stalin himself to pieces!"
>
> I rapidly stopped Trukhin and immediately made him and his friend leave the flat . . .
>
> Trukhin considers himself a Soviet poet. Although these words were spoken when he was drunk, they reveal the features of a hostile person. I think, for instance, that if he was a real Soviet person then he would not even have permitted himself to make such an attack when he was drunk . . .

Perhaps Sedykh was driven simply by the urge for self-preservation. After receiving this letter, however, Comrade Molchanov could not let matters rest either. He immediately forwarded the text to Comrade Buchinsky in the NKVD, appending, for good measure, his own comments on several young writers:

> I also enclose the tale "One Hot Night". The author, P.I. Korob from the Lower Udin airport, sent it to us for our assessment. The entire story is simply stuffed with counter-revolutionary conversations. I have delayed answering the author.
>
> . . . When Anatoly Pestyukhin was on duty, Sadok, a student of the finance-economics institute brought me his story "Ivan Zykov". . . It is a lampoon on Soviet reality, a slander of the collective farms and collective-farm workers . . . There can be no doubt about the ideological harmfulness of this story . . .
>
> Filippovich, a cadet from the military technology college, came to ask advice about his play *The Enemy*. He has a certain gift. However, the play deserves criticism only as a political mistake by its author. By reason of

his ideological and political short-sightedness he has written an anti-Party play. There can be only one verdict: *The Enemy* is a harmful play and not Soviet...

Molchanov later delivered two reports on his activities. The first was to Stavsky in Moscow, the secretary general of the Writers Union:

Only after the February plenum of the Central Committee, and after we had studied the speech and closing remarks of Comrade Stalin was self-criticism set in motion in the Writers Union in Eastern Siberia.... The writers A. Balin, Is. Goldberg, P. Petrov and M. Basov were excluded from the Union because of their links with counter-revolutionary organizations ... They have all been arrested by the NKVD. Alien individuals had contaminated the literary environment: Novgorodov, a young writer, the poet V. Kovalyov, the poet A. Targonsky...

The second report was sent to the Regional Party Committee:

A blunting of vigilance led to the contamination of the regional branch of the Writers Union with enemies of the people. Such inveterate enemies of the people as Basov, Goldberg, Petrov and Balin were in charge of the branch for a long time before they were unmasked.

Immediately after their exposure the board was re-elected. The new board quickly set about liquidating the consequences of these wrecking activities. After the arrests, there remained two members in the Writers Union, I. Molchanov and K. Sedykh.

"Woodpecker"

To the reading public he was Boris Dyakov, a writer of stories and plays and a member of the Writers Union.

Dyakov's autobiographical *Tale of Endurance* was among the first books to appear about the arrests under Stalin. It came out almost at the same time as Solzhenitsyn's *One Day in the Life of Ivan Denisovich* and even competed with it in popularity. Dyakov presented himself as an innocent victim but he only remotely recalls Solzhenitsyn's hero. In the camps he remains a rock-firm Bolshevik and apologist for the Soviet system, who depicts the mass arrests as a regrettable mistake. If one is to believe him, the zeks behind the barbed wire only thought of how to fulfil the plan and serve the Party and government.

Dyakov indeed found himself in the camps. Page after page of his investigation file is filled with the letters he wrote to the NKVD and the Central Committee, describing his own life:

My childhood and early youth took place before the Revolution. I was born into the family of a minor clerk, with all the vices typical of an old intelligentsia family. ... While still under-age I went off to fight in the Red Army. After 1921 I worked in the Soviet trade unions and, in 1929, began to work for Party newspapers. Thus, my character and my views were shaped in the struggle to overcome my own shortcomings and survivals of the past and, most important of all, in the battle against various enemies.

In 1936 he was recruited as an agent by the Sverdlovsk Region NKVD under the pseudonym "Woodpecker". His task was to "expose the counter-revolutionary elements. Soon all these individuals" (names supplied) "were arrested as participants of a Right-Trotskyist organization ..."

He continued to enthusiastically inform and denounce and when he himself was arrested, he asked his former masters to intercede:

I feel it my duty to inform you that for a number of years I have been an agent of the secret police. Moreover, no one forced me to do this work. I did it of my own free will because I have always believed and still believe today that it is my duty to constantly and in any circumstances help the security organs to uncover the enemies of the USSR. ... Some examples.

I helped to unmask the anti-Party opportunist leadership in the Rasskazovsk and Kozlovsk districts in the Central-Black Earth Region ...

I gathered materials for the press, exposing the wrecking activities of a number of veterinary workers who were responsible for the excessive incidence of plague among cattle and pigs ... Viktorov, the head of the veterinary service, was soon arrested and sentenced to be shot. As later became clear, these materials had also been used as part of the accusation.

In 1936 *Stalingradskaya Pravda* carried my sketch attacking the Trotskyist director of the Barricades Factory Budnyak. In 1937 they told me in the Stalingrad NKVD that Budnyak had been shot and the sketch added to the case file ...

I submitted reports to the NKVD about:

– the anti-Soviet agitation carried out by individuals and a group of persons engaged in literature and the arts, and in particular, the libellous works of the local writers G. Smolyakov, I. Vladsky and others (convicted by the NKVD);

– the systematic hostile agitation conducted by G.I. Gorelov, a Finnish citizen and actor with the Stalingrad dramatic theatre, under the cover of mental illness (convicted 1941);

– the hostile discriditation [sic] of the famous Soviet writer Alexey

Tolstoy by F.I. Terentiev at a celebration in the editorial office in 1936.

I must add that I also reported cases of anti-Soviet moods and behaviour on the part of N.A. Pokrovsky, an actor with the Stalingrad dramatic theatre. He displayed a profound distaste for Soviet playwriting, a scornful attitude to Soviet culture and to all our current existence, to the Communists and to those in control of the arts. He was particularly adept at spreading funny stories . . .

The NKVD moved "Woodpecker" from Stalingrad to the Far East and he began to work with a will there as well:

> In autumn 1937 the *Tikhookeanskaya zvezda** printed my sketch "Under the guise of musical comedy" where I uncovered a group of anti-Soviets in the Khabarovsk theatre. They were arrested . . .

Dyakov earnestly comments: "That is all that I can remember at the moment."

When the war began Dyakov managed to avoid being sent to the front. While others fought and died he continued to make his career. He moved to Moscow, took a leading post in the Komsomol and the organization's own publishing house Molodaya Gvardiya. The pinnacle of his career was his appointment as chief editor of feature films at the Ministry of Cinematography.

He fought against "harmful, ideologically weak scenarios" and their authors, and reported the "subversive work of a number of Soviet film-workers". It was at this moment that he stumbled and fell, convicted under the same Article 58. The timing could not have been worse, he explained:

> . . . certain individuals who are imbued with bourgeois aesthetics and who introduced Hollywood morals to script and screen are still installed in certain parts of the Soviet film industry. With the help of Cinema minister I.G. Bolshakov had begun to gradually uncover them. Had it not been for my arrest I would have exposed each and every one . . .
>
> Although I am now in a camp uneasiness does not desert me. There remain persons in certain film organizations who have sabotaged the further success of Soviet cinematography, through their own will, or perhaps that of others, and tried to emasculate the ideological content of our films . . . I gave full details in my statement addressed to the minister of State Security dated 29 May 1950 . . .

In the camps as well he also provided his services:

> In October 1950 at camp No 2 of Ozerlag I committed myself in writing to help state security unmask persons carrying on anti-Soviet agitation.

*(Lit. Pacific Star): daily Party newspaper of the Soviet Far East.

This cooperation is sincerely and honestly provided and gives me the moral satisfaction of knowing that here, in unusual conditions, I am of a certain use in the common cause of fighting the enemies of the USSR.

With increasing frequency, the "Woodpecker" sent complaints to Moscow from Siberia:

All my adult life and all my work should convince you that I deserve your political trust . . .

Do not let my life and my creative abilities be destroyed in vain. I can, I must, I want to still be of great use.

Trust me, and I shall justify that trust in every respect . . .

Save my life!

Soon after Stalin's death Dyakov was one of the first to be released and rehabilitated. Since he had been incomparably better fed and looked after in the camps than the other prisoners, he was able to carry on working. He was made an honorary Veteran of Labour and liked addressing the young.

In 1987 a three-volume autobiography appeared in a large print-run. In one of his last interviews he said:

I cannot tell a lie . . . When I was in the camps, unlike Solzhenitsyn, I met not only scoundrels but people who had not lost their faith in the force of Lenin's truth and in the inevitable victory of social justice . . . Solzhenitsyn depicted everything in a gloomy light.

And if the socialist-realist writer Boris Dyakov could be so confident when glasnost and democracy had already been proclaimed then we may assume that his double, the "Woodpecker", was certainly far from dead and still pursuing his highly successful genre.

"Tell me something," Anatoly Zhigulin asked me one day. "You go to the Lubyanka. What kind of people work there now? The same type who once beat me?"

"I don't actually know very many of them," I replied. "They're military people, after all: order them to pardon, and they'll pardon; order them to beat people and, probably, there'll be those who will beat people. What about our fellow writers? They sit in the Writers Club chattering about all kinds of risky subjects, pretending to be free artists. They'll get you talking and then dash off a denunciation. Of their own free will, moreover! That's even more despicable!"

"You're right," he said, "Unfortunately, you're right. It's a habit they can't shake off!"

A writers gathering and a middle-aged woman, a famous public figure and today a member of the editorial board of *Nash sovremennik*, is on the stage, passionately denouncing the past and supporting perestroika. A letter by her contemporary Yury Dombrovsky has just been published in which he tells how she denounced him as "anti-Soviet" when being cross-questioned herself and thus helped to send him to the Gulag. Dombrovsky died many years ago now. She has not refuted what he wrote nor shown any signs of penitence.

I open a recent issue of *Novy mir* and read a selection of poems by an unjustly neglected poet. They are certainly good but I cannot read them without a sense of unease, knowing from the Lubyanka archives that he betrayed an entire group of young poets who were as gifted and possibly better writers. Among them was Daniil Andreev, son of the Russian writer Leonid Andreev.

There were also some curious moments in our work.

For years a modest photographer worked for one of the writers' organizations, taking pictures of the writers during their gatherings, official meetings or informal events. He had also been supplying the KGB with the necessary photo materials. When perestroika came he decided to seek commissions elsewhere and wrote to us, asking if we wanted to use his archive? There were a great many pictures of writers who had once been arrested there . . .

As well as the telephone calls and threatening letters from the many Stalinists still among us, and from those who had most to fear from such disclosures, there were some less expected reactions. Once I arrived at the Lubyanka to be informed that they had received a letter, addressed to Kryuchkov himself, the KGB chairman, requesting him to stop showing us confidential documents. We had no right to examine them and might distort facts and undermine the reputation of respected figures. Of course, we shall keep working with you, they told me, but we must warn you to be more careful what you decide to publish – these documents are still classified as Highly Confidential.

Later I found out that the author of the letter was a grandson of one of the writers whose manuscripts I was trying to get returned and on whose case file I was working.* He knew about the existence of our commission and lived in Moscow – why had he not simply picked up the phone and told me directly of his concern? After the publication of my article about his illustrious grandfather, indeed, he rang me up with words of thanks and shamefacedly admitted that it was he who had written to Kryuchkov.

What are we to do with our informers? When the secret archives began to open society was deluged with a flood of exposures. The links of politicians, priests, writers and scientists with the secret police were widely discussed. Most often this has been used for settling old scores or gaining political advantange, alas, and not in the cause of truth.

*According to the law, now being more strictly implemented, only relatives are allowed access to such case files and must give their permission for anyone else to look at them.

There have also been cases where certain writers have publicly repented for their past sins as informers and have almost made a virtue out of such revelations. It became even more difficult to separate truth from falsehood, to distinguish humility and pride.

I believe the informers have already been punished. The sin of treachery is punishment in itself, staining their conscience, distorting humanity and corrupting their souls.

CHAPTER 9

MANDELSTAM STREET

THE FILES ON OSIP MANDELSTAM

"Isolate but Preserve"

What street is this?
It's Mandelstam's Street.
What the devil kind of name is that?
No matter which way you say it
It always comes crooked not straight.

Today Mandelstam Street is brightly lit. The only part where, until recently, the light failed was the stretch that passed by way of the Lubyanka. Official sources kept a stubborn silence about Mandelstam's two periods of imprisonment and his final, fatal journey. This was understandable. The poet had passed an irrevocable verdict on Stalin's state. Until 1987 he was still considered a criminal and not officially rehabilitated.

"My case will never be closed," Mandelstam once said. It has been closed, but only now that the state itself is no more. Only now is it possible to illuminate that dark section of Mandelstam Street. After insistent requests the terrible files were at last released from their secret depositories: the two investigation files from 1934 and 1938 in the KGB, the supervisory file at the Procurator General's Office, and Mandelstam's prison file in the Ministry of Internal Affairs.

In the meantime the memoirs of the poet's contemporaries and of his wife Nadezhda achieved a legendary stature. In some cases they concur with the files, in others they contradict them, weaving together to tell the complex and tormented story of his last years. Mandelstam's poetry of the time also throws its own light on events:

> *The dry-ration Russian folk tale! The wooden spoon – Hey-halloo!*
> *Where are you, you three fine lads, from the iron-gated GPU?*

On the night of 16–17 May 1934 OGPU operatives Gerasimov, Veprintsev and Zablovsky carried out the first search and arrest at flat 26, 5 Nashchokin Street in Moscow.

Apart from learning the names of those Chekists, we can now correct certain other details. Nadezhda Mandelstam always referred to the night of 13–14 May. After so many years this was an understandable error. All the official documents, however, say the OGPU arrived on 16 May; and since Mandelstam's photograph was taken and his investigation file opened the following day we have no reason to doubt them. The search warrant was signed by Yakov Agranov (and not Yagoda, as was thought before).

Now it is known exactly what was confiscated during that search: "letters, notes of telephone numbers and addresses, and manuscripts on loose sheets of paper, a total of 48 pages." They are not in the file and a search of the Lubyanka archives produced nothing: evidently these papers were burned. Why did they take so little? The answer is simple. The Chekists knew exactly what they were looking for – one poem and a particularly seditious piece of verse at that. The papers they selected were piled on a chair, the rest were thrown on the floor and unceremoniously trampled underfoot.

That evening Anna Akhmatova had arrived from Leningrad to visit Mandelstam. There was nothing in the flat for the guest to eat so the poet went next door and returned with an egg. They were too busy talking, though, to eat it at once. Another person also dropped by and firmly installed himself. The translator David Brodsky had been specially sent on ahead, believes Nadezhda Mandelstam, to make sure the poet had no chance to destroy any manuscripts before the search began. Even when Mandelstam went out to the neighbours Brodsky clung to him and would not let him out of his sight.

The search went on for hours. Each book was examined, including the spines, and their bindings were cut open. The OGPU men worked their way through every drawer and examined each crack and crevasse. While this was going on, various other things happened. One of the Chekists lectured those present on the dangers of smoking and generously offered them all fruit drops instead. Akhmatova suddenly remembered the egg and persuaded Mandelstam to fortify himself before his journey. As it was getting light Brodsky, who had calmly sat there all this while, left as strangely as he had appeared, this time at a word from the senior Chekist Gerasimov.

Nadezhda packed things into a small suitcase (toiletries, clean shirt collars) and Mandelstam selected seven books to take with him, including a copy of Dante's *Inferno*.

When they led him away it was already light. He embraced Nadezhda and he kissed Akhmatova, who was fated to see one close friend or relative after another leave for prison and the camps:

> *I called down death on my dear ones, and they died one by one.*
> *O grief, these graves I foretold with my words!*

Left alone, the two tired women tried to guess what had prompted the arrest. Shortly before, when Mandelstam was in Leningrad, he had slapped Alexey Tolstoy's face for his boorish behaviour. Tolstoy declared that he would not let the matter rest and went to complain to Gorky. The words supposedly spoken by the father of Soviet literature were soon being repeated: "We'll teach him to strike Russian writers!"

If this incident lay behind the arrest then things were not that bad. No one was sent to prison for a slap. If poetry was to blame, that was worse ...

They let close friends know what had happened and, just in case, took the most valuable manuscripts for safekeeping to trusted acquaintances. A wise precaution, because Gerasimov came back once more that day and again began digging through the papers. He left empty-handed. The manuscript he was looking for was not there. Had the OGPU really heard something about Mandelstam's great act of sedition, his poem about Stalin? If they laid their hands on that then there would be no forgiveness. The poet knew this but when he read the poem to Akhmatova he said: "Today poetry must take a civic stance."

Deprived of the seas, of leaping and soaring

By then Mandelstam had filled in the standard form at the Lubyanka:

PLACE OF WORK OR TYPE OF OCCUPATION: writer
PROFESSION: writer
SOCIAL POSITION: writer

His political past took up only half a line: "I have never been a member of any party."

They were of a different opinion at the OGPU. At the top of the form has been added the note, "Counter-revolutionary writer, Shivarov." The poet's case was in the experienced hands of the Secret Political Department's 4th Section which kept a watch on writers, sniffing out and eliminating the "criminals" in their ranks. And the most professional and hard-bitten of all the literary experts at the Lubyanka, it was believed, was Nikolay Khristoforovich Shivarov. The terror of the writers, he was all too familiar to them as "Khristofor'ych of the Lubyanka". (Ironically the patronymic recalled another policeman in the history of Russian literature, Count Alexander Khristoforovich Benckendorff who kept his eye on Pushkin.)

The file reveals that this Khristofor'ych was born in Bulgaria, and was now 36, a strongly built man at the height of his powers. Mandelstam, still only 43, looked much older than his years, with his balding head and greying beard.

Nadezhda Mandelstam saw the interrogator during a visit to her husband in prison (but forgot his surname):

A large man with importunate, shrill intonations of an almost theatrical manner (the kind favoured at the Maly Theatre), [...] the celebrated Khristofor'ych was a man not lacking in snobbery, who seemed to positively enjoy his job of intimidation and unbalancing the psyche. Everything about his appearance, his glance, and his intonations demonstrated that his charge was a nonentity, a despicable beast, a human outcast [...] He bore himself like the member of a superior race, despising physical weakness and pitiful intelligentsia assumptions. His well-practised manner testified to this and although he did not scare me, during that visit I felt myself shrinking under his gaze ... In my presence he told O.M. that the sense of fear was useful for a poet – "you said so yourself" – it helped the verse to come and O.M. "would receive a full measure of this stimulating sensation" ...

Mandelstam later used fewer words to describe Shivarov:

Everything about that Khristofor'ych is inside out and back to front ...

Mandelstam's appearance at this moment is preserved in the photograph pasted into his file. With folded arms and tightly sealed lips he gazes directly at the camera, and at us, without any fear in his eyes.

Shivarov had his own assessment of Mandelstam's worth. That March he had dealt with another poet Nikolay Klyuev and despatched him to exile in Siberia. He would not waste time on pleasantries now, especially since Mandelstam's guilt could hardly be less in doubt or more terrible.

> *Young admirers of white-toothed rhymes,*
> *Give me of blue sea but an inch, no more than a needle's eye!*

Giving the prisoner no time to recover, Shivarov summoned him for interrogation the next day. It would last all night and into the following morning.

Before he came to the point Shivarov asked two indirect, less important questions, evidently to put Mandelstam off his guard:

Q. Have you been abroad?
A. The first time I was abroad was in 1908, when I spent several months in Paris. The purpose of the visit was educational, and I began to study French poetry. The second time was in 1910 when I studied at the university in Heidelberg, but only for one semester. The third time, in 1911, I was in Berlin and Switzerland for several weeks and made a three-day trip to Italy.*
Q. How long have you been writing?
A. In an amateurish way, since I was a child. My professional experience began in 1909 when my verse was published for the first time, in *Apollon.***
Q. Why do you think we have arrested you?

Mandelstam's reply was non-committal. Shivarov suggested he read out some of the poems that might have been the reason for his arrest. Mandelstam accepted the challenge and read two poems, one after another :

*Other sources suggest that Mandelstam studied at Heidelberg in 1909, was in Berlin in 1910 and in Switzerland and Italy, in 1908 and 1909.
**Mandelstam's first publication was, in fact, in *Apollon*, No 9, 1910.

> *For the resounding valour of millennia to come,*
> *For the high-sounding name of the great human race,*
> *I've cut myself off from honour and joy*
> *At my ancestors' feast, from my cup and my place.*
>
> *The wolfhound century leaps at my throat*
> *But it isn't wolf's blood that flows through my veins,*
> *You'd do better to shove me, like a cap, up the sleeve*
> *Of the hot fur coat of Siberia's steppes . . . **

And then:

> *But the walls are accursedly thin,*
> *There's no place more I can run,*
> *And, like a fool, I must sit*
> *And play on a comb for someone.*

His interrogator asked him to speak more slowly and wrote down the verses as he recited. Mandelstam had not performed for such an audience, such an admirer, before. With reason he once said that poetry was nowhere valued so highly as in Russia: there people were shot for it.

Shivarov was not satisfied, however. These poems were not the reason for Mandelstam's arrest. He opened a file and triumphantly presented a page to the poet: "Did you write this?" Mandelstam acknowledged he was the author. "Recite it to me," said Shivarov.

While the poet recited Shivarov attentively compared the texts.

> *We live without sensing the country beneath us,*
> *At ten paces, our speech has no sound*
> *And when there's the will to half-open our mouths*
> *The Kremlin crag-dweller bars the way –*

"I've got something different here," commented Shivarov, "*All we hear is the Kremlin crag-dweller, The murderer and peasant-slayer*".

"That was the first version."

If the secret police had a copy, one of the poet's acquaintances was working for them. Mandelstam had never trusted this poem to paper although he had recited it more than once and to many people. It remains a mystery who informed on him. Perhaps it is not so important: "If it was not one, then it was another," Mandelstam would later indifferently say.

The writing of such a poem was a terrorist act for Shivarov and the verse itself, an unprecedented, criminal document. He inserted it in the deposition of this interrogation as the decisive incriminating evidence:

*Translated by Bernard Meares.

Q. Do you recognize yourself guilty of composing works of a counter-revolutionary character?

A. I am the author of the following poem of a counter-revolutionary nature:

> *We live without sensing the country beneath us,*
> *At ten paces, our speech has no sound*
> *And when there's the will to half-open our mouths*
> *The Kremlin crag-dweller bars the way.*
> *Fat fingers as oily as maggots,*
> *Words sure as forty-pound weights,*
> *With his leather-clad gleaming calves*
> *And his large laughing cockroach eyes.*
>
> *And around him a rabble of thin-necked bosses,*
> *He toys with the service of such semi-humans.*
> *They whistle, they meow, and they whine:*
> *He alone merely jabs with his finger and barks,*
> *Tossing out decree after decree like horseshoes –*
> *Right in the eye, in the face, the brow or the groin.*
> *Not one shooting but swells his gang's pleasure,*
> *And the broad breast of the Ossetian.**

According to Nadezhda Mandelstam, who recorded the poet's account of the interrogation, Shivarov made a detailed analysis of the poem and pressed him to explain why it had been written. Mandelstam replied that he hated fascism.

"In what do you see fascism?" asked Shivarov. Not receiving any answer, he ceased to press him.

This exchange, naturally, was not included in the deposition.

Khristofor'ych handed the poet some paper. He suggested that Mandelstam write out his counter-revolutionary squib and then sign it. On a cross-hatched page torn from a school notebook he wrote down the 16-line death sentence. Nadezhda Mandelstam recalled:

I was angry that he did not deny everything as a conspirator is supposed to do. But it was quite impossible to imagine O.M. in the role of a conspirator. He was an open-hearted person, incapable of any clever manoeuvres.

Long before, when he was just beginning to write, Mandelstam said that a poet must never, in any circumstances, justify himself. That was "impermissible . . .

*Mandelstam's poem about Stalin was not, as it is sometimes termed, a "satire" but a virulent assault that included slighting personal references (the fingermarks Stalin left on borrowed books, his uncertain paternity – the Ossetian reference). In the Lubyanka version the poet replaced "large laughing cockroach whiskers" at the end of stanza one with "eyes".

Mandelstam's autograph copy of his poem about Stalin, "Appended to the record of O. Mandelstam's interrogation, 25 May 1934" and countersigned by Shivarov. See p 173.

The one thing that cannot be forgiven. Because poetry is the awareness that you are right . . ."

At last the investigators had the proof they had fruitlessly sought in the Mandelstams' room, the poem in the author's own hand. Shivarov added it to the file with satisfaction. More than half a century later we can retrieve it for immortality.

Play on, till the artery bursts

In his cell in the Lubyanka's Inner Prison Mandelstam now felt himself doomed, condemned to death. "We never had any doubt that if they learned of that poem they would kill him," said Nadezhda Mandelstam. The interrogator had convinced the poet of this and conducted the case as if preparing for a future collective trial. The poet and his accomplices, ie those who had heard the poem, were threatened with unavoidable execution. Mandelstam was not only guilty for his own misfortunes but also for those of others.

This psychological torture was enough in itself without the physical mistreatment that, of course, was not recorded in the investigation file. All we know, from Mandelstam's own words, is that he was kept in a two-person cell with a companion who was evidently a stool-pigeon. He tried to scare Mandelstam about the forthcoming trial and to convince him that all his friends and family were already in prison. Mandelstam would respond by asking: "Why are your fingernails clean? Why do you smell of onion after they interrogate you?"

He was worn out by lack of sleep and interrogations that went on for hours at a time. The bright lamp in the cell hurt his eyes and his eyelids became inflamed. He was given salty food to eat and nothing to drink. They put him in the punishment cell and made him wear a straitjacket. In the next cell he heard the weeping voice of his wife and could no longer tell whether this was reality or a hallucination.

The result was an acute traumatic psychosis and an attempt at suicide – Mandelstam slashed the veins on both his wrists. Earlier, those who had already been in prison told him that most of all they felt the lack of a cutting object, and so he concealed a razor blade in the sole of his boot. The jailers seized the blade and bound up his wrists. The investigators had another end in mind for the poet.

Meantime his wife and friends had immediately sought help. Akhmatova managed to see Yenukidze, the business manager of the Council of People's Commissars, and a man close to Stalin. Nadezhda Mandelstam and Pasternak rushed to the *Izvestiya* offices to talk to Bukharin, then chief editor of the newspaper, and he promised to do all in his power: "He hasn't written anything unwise, has he?"

"Nothing special, nothing worse than you know of," replied Nadezhda Mandelstam disingenuously.

Naturally, the poet's patron knew nothing of the Stalin poem or it is unlikely he would have helped. When later it was read aloud to him he took fright and renounced Mandelstam.

They also appealed to other writers but with little effect. Demyan Bedny advised them not to interfere. Seifullina asked some Chekists of her acquaintance to find out what was happening and they gave her the same advice. At best, the writers expressed sympathy; at worst, they took the side of the poet's tormentors.

There were, in fact, many who maliciously rubbed their hands. The strangest rumours began to circulate in Moscow. There were even descriptions of how Mandelstam had behaved during his interrogation. Nadezhda Mandelstam names the source as Pyotr Pavlenko, an orthodox prose-writer and apologist of Stalinism. He knew what was happening at first hand: his friend Khristofor'ych, the investigator on the case, invited him to be present at the interrogation. Hidden either in a cupboard or between the double doors of the office, he heard everything. Mandelstam, he gleefully reported, presented a pathetic figure, chattering nonsense and clutching at his falling trousers . . . Perhaps, this was done on direct instructions, to replace the martyr's halo with a caricature.

Mandelstam himself would subsequently confirm Pavlenko's involvement. He told his friend Emma Gershteyn:

> I was being taken up in the lift somewhere with several other people. I
> fell down and began to jerk uncontrollably. Suddenly above me I heard
> a voice: "Mandelstam, Mandelstam, aren't you ashamed of yourself?"
> It was Pavlenko.

It is amazing that Pavlenko did not even bother to conceal his presence. Perhaps he was sure that Mandelstam would never be set free now, or able to tell others how he had been treated. It might still be possible to doubt this, did not Pavlenko's underhand role unexpectedly find confirmation in the newly uncovered documents from the Lubyanka. But more of that later.

I read the permitted texts
I catch the stumbling speech

On 25 May Mandelstam was again taken to his investigator. This is the date on the last deposition. In fact, it was a summing-up of all the preceding interrogations and no one knows how many there were in reality: Mandelstam said there were a great many. Now Shivarov examined the poet's biography from the very beginning, providing a comparatively objective account of his shifting views.

Q. How were your political views formed and how did they develop?
A. As a youth I was very friendly with the son of Boris Sinani, the famous

176

Socialist Revolutionary.* My first political views were shaped under the influence of Sinani and other members of the SR party who used to visit him. In 1907 I worked as a propagandist for an SR workers' group and organized spontaneous workers' meetings. In 1908 I began to be attracted to anarchism. When I left for Paris that year I intended to make contact with the anarcho-syndicalists there. However, once there I developed a passion for art and my growing literary gift pushed my political enthusiasms into the background. After returning to Petersburg I did not align myself with any revolutionary parties. There began a period of political inactivity which lasted until the October Revolution in 1917.

I took a sharply negative view of the October coup. I regarded the Soviet government as usurpers and this found expression in my poem "Kerensky" published in *Volya naroda*.** A reversion to SR views can be found here: I idealized Kerensky and called him one of Peter's nestlings while labelling Lenin a demagogue.

Approximately one month later I moved sharply in favour of Soviet causes and people and this led to my participation in the work of the People's Commissariat of Enlightenment to create a new type of school.

Late 1918 onwards saw the onset of a political depression provoked by the harsh methods used to establish the dictatorship of the proletariat. By then I had moved to Kiev and, after its seizure by the Whites, to Feodosia [in the Crimea]. There in 1920, after my arrest by the Whites, I was faced by a choice between emigration and Soviet Russia: I chose Soviet Russia. The incentive to flee Feodosia arose, moreover, from my sharp revulsion at White Guard activities there.

After my return to Soviet Russia I began to integrate into Soviet reality, first through literature and then by directly working [for Soviet institutions], as an editor, and as a writer myself. A growing trust in the policies of the Communist Party and the Soviet regime became typical of my political and social outlook.

In 1927 this confidence was shaken by a not very profound but sufficiently passionate sympathy for Trotskyism, and was then restored in 1928.

In 1930 a great depression afflicted my political outlook and my sense of ease in society. The social undercurrent of this depression was the

*The Socialist Revolutionaries were the Bolsheviks' most serious rivals and in 1917 won the largest number of seats in the short-lived Constituent Assembly.
**(Lit. The People's Will): the Right SR daily newspaper, published in Petrograd between April 1917 and February 1918.

liquidation of the kulaks as a class. My perception of that process was expressed in the poem "A Cold Spring", which is attached to the present deposition and was written in summer 1932 after I returned from the Crimea. By then I was beginning to feel trapped in society and this feeling was intensified and sharpened by a number of clashes of a personal and literary character ...

The poem about the terrible famine in the Ukraine and south Russia that the poet himself witnessed was in the file. It was written out by the interrogator but signed by Mandelstam and preserves a variant that differs from the well-known version:

> *The spring is cold. Crimea, shy and hungry,*
> *As under Wrangel, just as guilty,*
> *Bundles on the ground, patches on tatters,*
> *The vapour, just as sour and biting.*
> *The hazy distance, just as handsome,*
> *The trees, their buds beginning to swell,*
> *Stand like strangers, and only pity*
> *The Easter folly of almond blossom.*
> *Nature does not recognize its own features.*
> *And the terrible shades of Ukraine and Kuban –*
> *On the felted land starving peasants*
> *Stand at the gate, but do not touch the latch.*

Shivarov returned to Mandelstam's main crime, his "counter-revolutionary lampoon of the Leader of the Communist Party and the Land of the Soviets." He wanted to identify all who knew this poem. This took some time.

Listing those who had visited the poet, Shivarov forced the names from his charge one by one. In fact, many people had heard this poem but Mandelstam would only confirm those whom the investigator knew of. Khristofor'ych mixed crude threats with more subtle approaches. He named an individual and said he had obtained the testimony directly, implying that the person was already under arrest. To underline how much he knew of Mandelstam's private life, and he was indeed well-informed, he would give nicknames to the poet's acquaintances ("Bigamist", "Outcast" and "Theatre-lover"), thereby linking them, by association, to the informers who also went under pseudonyms at the Lubyanka.

Q. When this lampoon had been written, to whom did you recite it and to whom did you give written copies?
A. I recited it to: (1) my wife; (2) her brother Yevgeny Khazin, a writer of children's books; (3) my brother Alexander; (4) my wife's friend Emma

The text of Mandelstam's poem "The spring is cold...", written out by his interrogator, Shivarov. See p 178.

Gershteyn, who works in the research-workers section at the Central Council of Trade Unions; (5) Boris Kuzin, of the Zoological Museum; (6) the poet Vladimir Narbut; (7) the young poetess Maria Petrovikh; (8) the poetess Anna Akhmatova and (9) her son Lev Gumilyov.*

I did not give written copies to anyone, but Petrovikh took down this lampoon as I read it, promising, it is true, to then destroy her copy.

This lampoon was written in November 1933.

Q. How did the individuals you name react to the recital of this lampoon?

A. Kuzin noted that this was the most full-blooded of all the works I had read to him during 1933.

Khazin noted that the subject had been vulgarized and the individual was wrongly interpreted as the dominant force in the historical process. A. Mandelstam said nothing but shook his head reproachfully.

Gerstein praised the poetic merits of the work. As far as I remember there was no extensive discussion of the subject.

Narbut said to me: "This did not happen," meaning I should tell no one that I had read him this lampoon.

Petrovikh, as I have said, wrote it down from my words and praised its great poetic merits.

Lev Gumilyov approved the piece with an emotional expression like "great" but his judgement blended with that of his mother Anna Akhmatova, in whose presence he heard the poem read.

Q. How did Anna Akhmatova react during the recital of this counter-revolutionary lampoon and how did she judge it?

A. With her customary laconicism and poetic acuity, Anna Akhmatova pointed out the "monumental, rough-hewed, broad-sheet character of the piece". This was a correct assessment. For while an enormous force of social poison, political hatred and even contempt for the person depicted has been concentrated in this foul, counter-revolutionary, libellous lampoon, she recognized its great power and that it possesses the qualities of a propaganda poster of great effective force . . .

At this point Khristofor'ych was clearly getting carried away, and decorating his charge's replies with his own extravagant labels. On the other hand, he had little reason for restraint. "Do they really suppose that when future generations sort through these archives they will believe everything as blindly as our crazed contemporaries?" Nadezhda Mandelstam asked in amazement. Yet Shivarov was not writing for posterity, but his own superiors. And since the poet signed everything he was given without reading it, why should he bother?

*Of those in this list Kuzin was arrested twice, Gumilyov three times and Narbut died in the camps.

Q. Does your counter-revolutionary lampoon "We live . . ." express only your own perceptions or the attitude of a particular social group?

A. My lampoon "We live . . ." is not a document of personal perceptions and attitudes but expresses the perceptions and attitudes of a part of the old intelligentsia which considers itself the custodian and transmitter to the present time of the values of previous cultures. In the political sense this group has acquired from various opposition movements the habit of drawing on historical analogies that distort contemporary reality.

Q. Does this mean that your lampoon is a weapon of counter-revolutionary struggle only for the group you describe or could it be used for the purposes of counter-revolutionary struggle by other social groups?

A. In my lampoon I followed what has become a traditional approach in the old Russian literature of using a simplified presentation of the historical situation and reducing it to a confrontation between "the country and its ruler". Indubitably, this lowered the level of historical understanding of the group I described above and to which I myself belong. Yet it was precisely in this way that the poster-like expressiveness of the lampoon was attained, which makes it a widely applicable weapon of counter-revolutionary struggle which could be used by any social group . . .

The investigation was coming to an end. All they were waiting for now was a decision from above. Then a miracle occurred. The petitioning on the poet's behalf achieved its goal and came to the attention of Stalin. The hero of the counter-revolutionary lampoon issued an unprecedented and compassionate decree.

Shivarov hastily drew up the charge sheet, using the most moderate expressions: "Accused of composing and distributing counter-revolutionary works." Mandelstam signed a statement:

> I consider the investigation of my poems to be correct. Since no other accusations in any other formulation were brought against me, and not being aware of any other offences on my part, I consider the investigation to have been correct.

On 26 May, precisely ten days after his arrest, the Special Board of the OGPU Collegium decreed that the accused should be exiled for three years to the town of Cherdyn in the Urals. In the course of a day Mandelstam was rapidly tried and sentenced and ordered to leave under special convoy no later than 28 May after a visit from his wife:

> An excerpt from the minutes of the Special Board is hereby attached, together with the person of the convicted individual.

During Nadezhda Mandelstam's visit, a suddenly jovial Khristofor'ych informed them why the sentence was so unexpectedly mild: superior authority had been clement and instructed them to "isolate but preserve" Mandelstam. Shivarov now behaved quite differently. He scolded Mandelstam for his bad behaviour and complained of him to his wife. Apparently when Shivarov asked the poet's attitude to the Soviet regime, Mandelstam replied:

> I am prepared to cooperate with all Soviet institutions apart from the Cheka.

Another miracle occurred during the visit. It was suggested that Nadezhda Mandelstam should accompany her husband into exile. This was not compassion, of course. The convicted man was simply in such a condition that he could not be left without supervision and care. She agreed immediately and the Chekists wasted no time in filling out the necessary instructions and orders.

Mandelstam was sent into exile and his file, to the archive. But hardly more than a week passed before he again demanded attention.

A hop. I'm in my right mind

The prison voices continued to haunt Mandelstam. They talked of crime and punishment, and would list the people he had betrayed. He began to believe they had already been shot. The senior guard escorting him, a kindly lad (also called Osip), advised Nadezhda: "Do calm him down! It's only in bourgeois countries they shoot people for poems ..." The poet meanwhile constantly expected vengeance to strike and would name the hour: "Today at six ..." His wife secretly shifted the hands on his pocketwatch.

Mandelstam could not withstand the strain. It finally seemed easier to take his own life than to wait for another to do the job.

To OGPU
from Alexander Emilievich Mandelstam

APPEAL

On 28 May my brother O.E. Mandelstam left for exile after being sentenced by the OGPU to three years in Cherdyn. My brother's wife N.Ya. Mandelstam, who accompanied him into exile, has informed me by telegram from Cherdyn that he is now suffering from psychiatric illness, that he raves and hallucinates and threw himself out of a first-floor window. She says there is no medical treatment available in Cherdyn (the only medical staff are a young non-specialist doctor and a midwife). It has been suggested that he be moved to the Perm psychiatric hospital which may have negative consequences, she reports.

Please have my brother examined and, if psychiatric illness is confirmed, transfer him to a city where he can receive trained medical treatment as an out-patient, somewhere near Moscow, Leningrad or Sverdlovsk.   6 June 1934

This appeal was added to Mandelstam's file. It seems to have alarmed his OGPU supervisors: Stalin had ordered them to "preserve" the poet. Memoranda were sent flying to the Urals instructing the local OGPU to have the convicted man's psychiatric health examined, to aid in his treatment and put him in a hospital.

On 10 June the Special Board reviewed the case and decreed that Mandelstam should only be prevented from living in the Moscow and Leningrad Regions and in a further ten major Soviet cities. He decided to move to Voronezh. Someone had praised the city and it was nearer Moscow.

His friends and family believed that Bukharin's intervention had led to the review: he was among those whom Nadezhda Mandelstam had bombarded with telegrams from Cherdyn. Probably the petitioning of his friends had also helped. In his letter to Stalin Bukharin wrote: "Poets are always right, history is on their side," and added, "Pasternak is also worried…" Stalin realized that the Mandelstam affair was already being widely discussed and any outcome would be linked directly to his name.

It was then that he made his famous telephone call to Pasternak. This became common knowledge because Pasternak saw no reason to conceal it and throughout his life would return to his conversation with Stalin. As more people in literary circles heard about it, however, what happened became distorted and this led to conflicting versions and much gossip. One account, typical of the writing fraternity, is recorded in the investigation file. When the playwright Iosif Prut wrote in support of Mandelstam's rehabilitation in the late 1950s, he gave the poet Kirsanov's version of the telephone call. Stalin's secretary Poskrebyshev rang up Boris Pasternak:

"Comrade Stalin will now speak to you!"

Stalin indeed took the receiver: "The poet Mandelstam has recently been arrested. What can you say about him, comrade Pasternak?"

Boris, evidently, took severe fright and answered: "I don't know him at all well! He was an Acmeist while I support a different literary tendency. So I can't say anything about Mandelstam!"

"Well, I can say that you're a very poor friend, Comrade Pasternak!" said Stalin and replaced the receiver.

Prut not only confused the dates (he claimed the call took place in 1938) but when perestroika had already begun he again reproduced a dialogue that presented Stalin in a positive light. While supporting Mandelstam's rehabilitation this venerable playwright, who proudly described himself as "a member of the USSR Writers Union since the day of its foundation", cast a shadow on Pasternak who, supposedly, betrayed his fellow writer and was little short of responsible for his misfortunes.

What happened was rather different. Nadezhda Mandelstam has recorded what Pasternak himself told her not long after:

> *Stalin.* Mandelstam's case is being reviewed. Everything will be all right. Why didn't you appeal to the writers' organizations or to me? If I was a poet and my poet-friend found himself in trouble I would have gone up the wall to help him.
>
> *Pasternak.* Writers' organizations have not dealt with such matters since 1927 and if I had not been making some efforts you probably would not have known anything about it. (Here Pasternak added something about the word "friend", wishing to clarify his relations with Mandelstam which did not, naturally, fit into the concept of friendship.)
>
> *Stalin.* But he is a great poet, isn't he? A master?
>
> *Pasternak.* Yes, but that's not the point.
>
> *Stalin.* What is the point, then?
>
> Pasternak replied that he would like to meet and have a talk.
>
> *Stalin.* What about?
>
> *Pasternak.* About life and death.
>
> At this Stalin put down the receiver.

Stalin was testing the reaction of various writers and he knew that Pasternak would not lie. The first Congress of Soviet Writers was being prepared in Moscow. Stalin needed a favourable outcome. It was a game of cat and mouse with the poet and with all the intelligentsia: he would show himself as a friend and, at the same time, give them a scare.

"Those rhymes must have made an impression," commented Mandelstam on Stalin's phone call, "if he kicked up such a fuss about reviewing the case."

This was no more than a postponement, however. Stalin never forgave anyone and certainly not a direct attack on himself. At that moment Mandelstam would have been more dangerous dead. There was still time to break him and make him bend to Stalin's will. Unlike many others, Mandelstam had no illusions. He was convinced that vengeance had only been delayed until a more suitable moment.

I must live, though twice I have died

All the ensuing years of exile in Voronezh, Savyolovo and Kalinin were a feverish series of attempts by Mandelstam to come to terms with reality and find himself a niche within the Soviet system. He was no "cloud-dweller". He was afraid of being left behind by history and tried with all his might to keep in touch with his contemporaries and to get on with writers' organizations. But each time he would fail. More and more he became convinced that he was a renegade whom nobody needed. All that remained were a homeless wandering existence, poverty, humiliation and the constant surveillance of the secret police.

In 1937 he wrote to Kornei Chukovsky:

> ... physically crippled, I went back to work. I said those who condemned me were right. I found historic sense in it all ... I hurled myself headlong into my work. For this, they beat me ... I am treated like a dog ... I'm a shadow. I don't exist. I only have the right to die ... It is useless to appeal to the Writers Union. They wash their hands of me. There is only one person in the world to whom one can and must appeal in this case* ... Help me ... I shall not survive if I am again sentenced to exile ...

Mandelstam took the final step, enduring the last humiliation. He wrote not a letter to Stalin but an ode. Having once put the Leader in the stocks for public derision he forced himself to write a poem in his praise. It was an unnecessary act since hundreds of zealous hack-writers could do this much better than he. For a period he lost the sense of his own rightness. Then he would admit, "It was an illness."

He was not alone in this. When Akhmatova's son was arrested she tried to buy his life back from Stalin with poems. Pasternak also succumbed, not from any personal necessity but influenced by the universal derangement and idolatry of Stalin and a desire to be like the rest. In none of these cases did they write real poetry.

> *All night I expect important guests,*
> *Gently rattling the door-chain fetters.*

In spring 1938 the Litfond made a charitable gesture — they offered the Mandelstams a two-month holiday at the Samatikha rest home not far from Moscow. Before he left he managed to see Vladimir Stavsky, the general secretary of the Writers Union.

"I shall struggle in poetry for the creative music!" Mandelstam told him.

Stavsky listened attentively, wished him a good holiday and promised, when he returned, to reach a decision as to what to do about Mandelstam's verse and finding some way for him to make a living. But he knew quite well that Mandelstam would not be coming back: he had already prepared a letter to Yezhov.

*ie Stalin.

USSR Union of Soviet Writers, Board

People's Commissar of Internal Affairs,
Comrade N.I. Yezhov   16 March 1938

Dear Nikolay Ivanovich,
Part of the literary world is very nervously discussing the problem of
Osip Mandelstam.

As everyone knows, Osip Mandelstam was exiled to Voronezh 3-4
years ago for obscene libellous verse and anti-Soviet agitation. Now his
term of exile has ended. At present he and his wife are living outside
Moscow (outside the "compound limit").

In practice, he often visits his friends in Moscow, for the most part
writers. They support him, collect money to help him, and make of him
a figure of suffering, a brilliant and totally unrecognized poet. Valentin
Kataev, I. Prut and other writers have openly defended him, and in
outspoken terms.

In order to defuse the situation O. Mandelstam has been provided
support through the Litfond. But this does not resolve all the problems
linked to O. Mandelstam.

It is not simply, or even primarily, a problem of the author himself, a
writer of obscene, libellous verse about the leadership of the Party and
of all the Soviet people. It is a question of the attitude of a group of notable
Soviet writers to Mandelstam. I am writing to you, Nikolay Ivanovich,
to seek your help.

Recently O. Mandelstam has written a number of poems. However,
they are of no special value according to the collective opinion of
comrades who I requested to look at them (in particular, Comrade
Pavlenko, whose review I herewith attach).

Once again let me request you to help resolve the problem of Osip
Mandelstam.
With Communist greetings
V. Stavsky

To the letter is attached the following "review":

The poems of O. Mandelstam
I have always considered, reading Mandelstam's earlier poems, that he
is not a poet but a versifier, a cold and cerebral compiler of rhymed
compositions. I cannot dispense with such a feeling now as I read his
latest verse. For the most part they are cold and dead and lack what, in

my view, is the most important thing in poetry – they have no spirit, no confidence in their line.

The language is complex, obscure and smells of Pasternak.

One could hardly consider the following lines to be models of clarity:

> *Where is that bound and fettered groan?*
> *Where Prometheus, support and aid of the cliff?*
> *Where the kite, the yellow-eyed pursuit*
> *Of its claws, flying up from under its brows?*

It is hard for me to review these poems. Since I neither like nor understand them, I cannot assess their possible significance or value. The system of images, language and metaphors, the abundance of flutes, aories and so on, all seem something we have already read long ago.

Comparatively good (and better than the rest) are the landscape verse. There are several other good poems: (1) "If our enemies took me . . .", (2) "Not a floury white butterfly . . ." and (3) "A world begins, frightening and great . . ."

There are some good lines in the "Verses about Stalin", a poem filled with strong feeling, which sets it apart from the rest. Overall, though, this poem is worse than its individual stanzas. There is a great deal of clumsy phrasing which is inappropriate to the theme of Stalin.

I do not have the former poems of Mandelstam to hand so as to check how far he has moved beyond them now, but as I read I cannot recall a great difference. Perhaps this should be attributed to me, and my dislike of Mandelstam's verse.

Is this Soviet poetry? Yes, of course. But only in the "Verses about Stalin" do we feel this unreservedly. In the other poems we must guess that they are Soviet. If I was asked, should these poems be published? I would answer, No, they should not.

Pyotr Pavlenko

Again Pavlenko made a fateful appearance in Mandelstam's life. It is unclear why a man who never wrote anything but prose was asked to provide this review. "The writers exceed everyone else in their savagery and degradation," Nadezhda Mandelstam would say, thinking particularly of Pavlenko. She did not know of this review, however, among all the other works of the future Stalin-Prize winning author.

Yet again the documents prove that the Writers Union created by Stalin was not just a means of repressing free speech and stifling creative originality but also acted as a secret informer and a branch of the Lubyanka. In this case it was not simply as a proletarian writer but as general secretary of the Writers Union that Vladimir Stavsky spoke for all the writers in the country. The final and fateful train of events in Mandelstam's life had been set in motion.

Stavsky would die several years later, as a war correspondent during the Great Patriotic War. Pavlenko survived until 1951, honoured and prosperous. Streets were named after him and Boris Pasternak, until the day of his death, was fated, ironically, to live on Pavlenko Street in Peredelkino. (It retains the name to this day.) No one has read the works of Stavsky or Pavlenko for years but they hold an honoured place in the Soviet encyclopedias and scholarly studies.

Mandelstam had predicted this vengeance earlier when he wrote in the Fourth Prose:

> It was all as frightening as a child's nightmare. *In mezzo del cammin del nostra vita* — half-way down the path of my life I was left alone in the dense Soviet wood with robbers who said they were my judges ... I am to blame. There can be no disputing ... My name has been stamped and punched all over me by the ticket-collector ... And still it's not enough for them, it's not enough ... The eyes of Russian writers gaze at me with a canine, imploring tenderness: O die, can't you! Where does it come from, this servile malice, this slavish contempt for my name?

There is a stamp on Stavsky's letter: STATE SECURITY 4TH DEPARTMENT, RECEIVED 13 APRIL 1938. Yezhov held on to the letter for about a month, evidently discussed it with Stalin and then handed the matter on to his subordinates.

The head of the 4th Department's 9th Section Yurevich put together a report that skilfully developed Stavsky's themes:

> After he had completed his term of exile Mandelstam turned up in Moscow and tried to play on public opinion by a demonstrative display of his "impoverished position" and ill health.
>
> Anti-Soviet elements among writers and critics, used Mandelstam for their hostile agitation, making of him a figure of suffering and organizing collections of money for him among writers. Mandelstam himself goes begging around writers' flats.
>
> According to available information, Mandelstam has kept his anti-Soviet views to the present. As a result of his psychological imbalance he is capable of aggressive acts.
>
> I consider it necessary to arrest and isolate Mandelstam.

All the "compromising material" in the writer's biography was listed in this report: son of a merchant of the first guild, former member of the SR party, later aligned with the anarchists ... And the greatest crime of all, "wrote a sharply counter-revolutionary lampoon against Comrade Stalin and distributed it among his acquaintances by reciting aloud," had never been forgotten, although there were now new bosses at the Lubyanka. The hour of retribution had come.

The warrant for Mandelstam's arrest was signed on 28 April 1938 by Frinovsky, the deputy commissar for Internal Affairs.

I enter the coming age, it seems,
And it seems I shall not see it come

The Mandelstams found the rest home very comfortable. For the first time in many years the outcasts enjoyed a long-awaited respite. They had their own room, full board and the attention and care of the staff. It almost seemed too good to be true: "We haven't fallen into a trap, by any chance?" Mandelstam wondered. But he dismissed these doubts.

It was indeed a trap. Twice there were calls from the Writers Union to check how the guests were, and that the local authorities had called and made sure they were still there. They had been put in a rest home so that the secret police could keep a watch on them and easily pick them up . . .

In Moscow the trial of the Right–Trotskyists bloc had come to an end. On 15 March Nikolay Bukharin was shot. The fate of Mandelstam's former patron probably played its part in deciding his fate (Stavsky's denunciation was dated 16 March). May was just beginning. May Day, International Worker's Day, had been celebrated. Shortly before dawn on 3 May they came for Mandelstam.

This time the Chekists (Ilyushkin, Shyshkanov and Shelukhanov) did not waste time. The whole operation took a few minutes. Papers were shoved into a bag, "a manuscript and correspondence in one file; and one book, author O. Mandelstam," and the arrested man was taken out, put in a truck and driven off.

At the Lubyanka they removed the remnants of his personal life: the small suitcase, a pillowcase, wooden walking stick, braces and tie. The form Mandelstam filled in had "Terror" written on it and underlined twice. Evidently that was the line the investigation was supposed to take.

There is one deposition for an interrogation on 17 May. It was a clear case, already investigated once, and all that remained was to observe the formalities. Junior Lieutenant Shilkin was the investigator.

Q. You have been arrested for anti-Soviet activities. Do you acknowledge your guilt?
A. I do not accept my guilt of anti-Soviet activities.
Q. Why were you arrested in 1934?
A. In 1934 I was arrested and convicted of anti-Soviet activities which took the form of the composition (over a number of years) of counter-revolutionary poetry ("Kerensky", "Spring", "Cassandra" and others). I was sentenced to three years exile in Voronezh.
Q. After this exile ended you were forbidden to live in Moscow. Despite

this you came up to Moscow almost legularly.* Tell me who you were coming to visit and with what purpose?

A. When my term of exile ended in summer 1937 I came to Moscow, not knowing that I was forbidden to live there. After this I moved to the village of Savyolovo and in November 1937 went to live in Kalinin. I must admit that I am guilty of repeatedly visiting Moscow although it was forbidden and I had no permission to do so. The aim of these trips was, in essence, to find work through the Writers Union since I could not find myself a job under the conditions in Kalinin. Apart from this I was trying through the Writers Union to gain a critical assessment of my poetic work and [satisfy] my need for creative contact with Soviet writers. On the days I came to Moscow I would stay with Shklovsky (writer) or Osmyorkin (artist) to whom I read my poems. In addition to the above-mentioned individuals, I also read my poetry at Valentin Kataev's flat, to Fadeev and to Pasternak, Markish,** Kirsanov, Surkov, Yevgeny Petrov, Lakhuti† and Yakhontov (actor).

Q. The investigators know that when you were in Moscow you engaged in anti-Soviet activities about which you are now keeping quiet. Give an honest testimony.

A. I was not engaged in any anti-Soviet activities.

Q. Did you make visits to Leningrad?

A. Yes, I did.

Q. Describe the aims of your visits to Leningrad.

A. I went to Leningrad to get help from writers there. Tynyanov, Chukovsky, Zoshchenko and Stenich†† provided such help.

Q. Who gave you material help in Moscow?

A. The Kataev brothers, Shklovsky and Kirsanov.

Q. Tell me about the nature of your meetings with Kibalchich.‡

A. I met Kibalchich purely on business and no more than three times. The first time was in 1924–5 when I visited him at the Leningrad State Publishers to be given translation work. The second time I went to his flat and this was also necessitated by the collection of translating work. The third time was in Leningrad in 1932 when I invited several Leningrad writers, including Kibalchich, to my hotel and read them my "Journey to Armenia". I never met him again after that . . .

*Here and in other places the text as recorded by the investigator displays many errors and peculiarities of orthography and grammar.
**Perets David Markish, Yiddish poet and playwright. Shot after the trial of the Jewish Anti-Fascist Committee in 1952.
†Surkov, Petrov (Kataev) and Lakhuti were all writers.
††V Stenich, translator and critic, was arrested in 1938 and shot.
‡Victor Serge. See chapter 7.

Here the interrogation ended, rather strangely and quite unlike the usual ferocious Lubyanka style. The interrogator suffered a total defeat and did not obtain any of the required confessions. He was not trying particularly hard, it would seem. There was no real investigation and not a single specific accusation was made.

Three prison doctors examined Mandelstam:

> ... he is not suffering from psychiatric illness but is of a psychopathic inclination, prone to obsessive ideas and fantasizing. Although mentally unwell, he is quite responsible for his actions.

Investigator Shilkin did not go to much trouble in drawing up the charge sheet. He made extensive use of Stavsky's letter, occasionally copying it out word for word. A few things he did add himself, however: "Mandelstam remained in close contact with enemies of the people Stenich, Kibalchich (up until the expulsion of the latter from the USSR), and others." The accusation of "terror" was removed as unproven and the poet was charged, as in 1934, under Article 58:10, anti-Soviet agitation.

On 2 August the NKVD Special Board decreed that Mandelstam, "a merchant's son and former SR", be sent to a labour camp for five years. This time the sentence was to "isolate" but not necessarily "preserve": one look at the condemned man was enough to realize he would not survive. A few days later he was transferred to Butyrki prison in Moscow to await transport to Kolyma.

> *The familiar hands of blessed wives*
> *Will gather the light ash*

Osya, my beloved, distant friend,
My darling, I have no words with which to write this letter, a letter that you, perhaps, will never read. I am writing it into the void.

What a joy our childish life together was, Osyushka. Our quarrels, our squabbles, our games and our love ... Do you remember how we dragged our beggars' feasts back to our poor vagabond caravan-homes? Do you remember how good bread tastes when it has taken a miracle to find it and then is shared between two ... Our happy poverty and the poetry ... ?

I bless every day and every hour of our bitter life, my friend, my companion, my sightless guide ...

I never found the time to tell you how I love you.
It's me, Nadya. Where are you?

From his arrest until the winter began, nothing was known about Mandelstam. In mid-December his brother Alexander received his one and only letter, the last words of the poet:

Dear Shura,

I am in Vladivostok, SVITlag,* barrack 11. I was given five years for KRD [Counter-revolutionary Activities] by the Special Board. I left Moscow, Butyrki prison, with a transport on 9 September and we arrived 12 October. My health is very poor. I am emaciated in the extreme, I've become very thin, almost unrecognizable, but send clothes, food and money – though I don't know if there's any point. Try nevertheless. I get terribly cold without any [warm] things.

Dearest Nadenka, I do not know if you are alive, my sweetheart. Shura, write to me at once about Nadya. This is a transit camp. They didn't take me to Kolyma.** I may have to winter here.

I embrace you my dears,

Osya

Nadezhda rushed to help. She sent him food parcels and money. The investigation file contains one more testimony to her fearless battle for her husband's life and freedom — until now it was not known:

Moscow
19 January 1939

Dear Comrade Beria,

In May 1938 the poet O.E. Mandelstam was arrested . . .

This second arrest was totally unexpected. Mandelstam had just finished a book of poetry, and the question of publishing it had been constantly put before the Union of Soviet Writers. We could more likely have expected his complete restoration and return to open literary activity than his arrest.

I cannot understand how the investigation into Mandelstam's counter-revolutionary activities was conducted. As a consequence of his illness over a number of years I did not leave him for a moment and yet I was not brought into the investigation either as an accomplice or at least as a witness.

Let me add that during his first arrest in 1934 Mandelstam suffered a severe psychosis and the investigation and exile, moreover, took place when he was already ill. At the time of his second arrest Mandelstam's condition, physically and mentally, was seriously unstable.

I request you to:

1. Assist in having O.E. Mandelstam's case reviewed and clarify whether there were sufficient grounds for his arrest and exile.

*North-east corrective labour camp system.
**The last ships carrying prisoners to Magadan before the sea became impassable usually left in late October, and anyway Mandelstam would obviously have been unable to work.

2. Verify the mental health of O.E. Mandelstam and clarify whether exile was appropriate in this respect.

3. Finally, check whether someone does not have a personal interest in his exile.

And one more thing: to clarify the moral rather than the legal side of this issue — did the NKVD have sufficient grounds for destroying a poet, a master, when he was actively and loyally writing poetry.

Nadezhda Mandelstam

This characteristically daring letter points to the hand behind the scenes. The use of the word "master" was not fortuitous: perhaps Stalin who had used the term in his conversation with Pasternak would take heed?

But the answer, when it came, was not from Stalin or Beria. On 5 February 1939 a money order was returned to Nadezhda Mandelstam, "Because of the death of the addressee," they informed her at the post office.

That same day there were celebrations to mark the awards received by more than one hundred and fifty writers, the names of whom were published in *Literaturnaya gazeta*. Among them were Stavsky who received the "Badge of Honour" while Pavlenko was awarded the Order of Lenin, the highest prize of all. Only a few remembered Mandelstam and grieved for him. Among the watchdogs of literature only Fadeev shed drunken tears: "What a poet we've destroyed!"

The NKVD examined Nadezhda Mandelstam's complaint and Sergeant Nikitochkin found that the poet did not merit acquittal. This latter decree, confirmed only in 1941, tells us that Mandelstam was "serving his sentence in Kolyma". The same file, however, contains different information. On the back of one of the pages has been added a brief note: "Died, 21 December 1938 in SVITlag (Magadan Region)."

As soon as the money order was returned Nadezhda Mandelstam applied to the Main Camp Administration, to the Gulag in short, with a request that they check this information and give her an official death certificate. Mandelstam's prison file reveals that it took almost 18 months to confirm the details. When she received the certificate it stated that O.E. Mandelstam died aged 47 on 27 December 1938. But the same document indicated that the death had been registered in May 1940.

The state had mislaid a person. Or, having lied itself, had become entangled in its own deceptions.

In 1956, three years after Stalin's death, Nadezhda Mandelstam submitted a new appeal for the review of her husband's case. She received a certificate lifting his conviction which was "issued to citizen Osip Mandelstam"(!), and sent to Cheboksary where his widow was then living. The procurators revealed that her husband had still not been rehabilitated for his earlier offence: the 1934 charges remained in force. She appealed again:

> I request the Procurator's office to also review the 1934 case since I know that Mandelstam was quite innocent and was exiled then for his verse against the Cult of Personality which he incautiously read aloud to several close acquaintances.

The still Stalinist procurators consulted and decided that Mandelstam had been rightly convicted the first time. Nadezhda Mandelstam would not live to see her husband rehabilitated.

> *Am I real, after all,*
> *And will death truly come?*

With the coming of perestroika Mandelstam's verse began to be published everywhere, in books and in newspapers, and his poems were even put to music by popular singers.

The centenary of his birth was approaching and voices were raised demanding his full rehabilitation. The KGB were forced to react and began checking their files. In Perm nothing could be found about his first place of exile. In Voronezh they uncovered a certain Iosif Mandelstam who had been in prison and whose father was also called Emil. The KGB investigation department remained under the illusion that the poet had still been alive in 1956, living with his wife in Cheboksary, and requested material from their colleagues there.

An attempt was also made to find Mandelstam's investigators and the Chekists who searched his flat. Khristofor'ych served in the Organs until 1937 when he was dismissed. By then he was already working for Sverdlovsk NKVD. After this all trace of him disappeared although there were rumours among the writers that he had been shot or, others said, had committed suicide. In 1987 his colleagues preferred to keep the secret: "It has not proved possible to establish or to cross-examine . . ." It was evident that they were not really trying. This did not prevent them adding that in the case of Khristofor'ych, "There were no reports that he had infringed socialist legality . . ."

The KGB investigation department sought out and cross-questioned the handful of elderly witnesses who had known Mandelstam. The writer Kaverin told them:

> He was a proudly independent man . . . I have no doubt that Mandelstam wrote the poem against Stalin. No one could write about Stalin with such expressiveness and force. No one else would ever have dared . . .

However, state security was in no hurry to mend its ways. From 9 am to

5.30 pm, one day, in the presence of two witnesses, investigator Pamfilov read copies of Nadezhda Mandelstam's memoirs published in the West and added the following report:

> The author makes a clearly tendentious attempt to show that in the 1930s the Soviet Union lived through nothing less than a "bloody terror". The "punitive organs then rooted out the intelligentsia and imposed uniformity of thought, keeping everyone in a terrible state of fear . . . until the death of Stalin".
>
> N. Mandelstam does not see any difference during those years between the Soviet regime and fascism . . .
>
> N. Mandelstam libellously asserts that O.E. Mandelstam was not granted rehabilitation because the "plan for exterminating people was passed down from above" and the "struggle with idealism was and will remain the main task of this epoch".

Nevertheless, on 28 October 1987 the Supreme Court finally cleared the poet's name.

> *Yes, I lie in the earth, moving my lips*
> *But what I shall say, every schoolchild will learn*

In Mandelstam's prison and camp file the true date of death can finally be established. There the last photograph is preserved, a worn-out old man with an almost bare skull instead of a face, but held as proudly as before. There we find his right thumb-print and a note on distinguishing features ("a birth mark on the lower third of his left upper arm"). And there is the death certificate drawn up by Dr Kresanov. Mandelstam was taken to the sickbay on 26 December and died the next day at 12.30 pm. Cause of death: heart failure and arteriosclerosis.

When the thumb-print of the deceased was being verified his name was entered as "Mendelstam" ("What the devil kind of name is that? . . .")

The poet's last days can be recreated from scraps of reminiscence provided by rare witnesses who were in the same camp. Some of them only broke silence when they were convinced at last that change was irreversible.

In the transit camp Mandelstam was referred to not by his surname but simply called "Poet", a title his tormentors from the Lubyanka had denied him. He was considered to be half-mad and in December was already a "goner" who did not even get up off the board beds.

"Alive?" the criminals who brought round the food would shout. "Hey, you! lift your head!"

The poet weakly raised his head and received his ration. Each day the dead and the dying were carried past him — there was a typhus epidemic in the camp.

Shortly before the New Year snow storms descended on the Pacific coast. It became much colder and there was a fierce wind. The prisoners from barrack 11 were taken to the wash-house to be deloused. Yury Moiseenko stood next to Mandelstam:

> We undressed, hung up our clothes on a peg and then handed them over for heat treatment. It was as cold inside as out. Everyone was shivering and Osip Emilievich's bones were just knocking together. He was no more than a skeleton, with a wrinkled hide . . . We shouted, "Hurry up! We're frozen stiff!" We waited 40 minutes before they told us to go and get dressed. We went to get our clothes . . .
>
> A sharp smell of sulphur struck our noses. Immediately it became stuffy, the sulphur drilled into our eyes until we cried . . . Osip Emilievich took three or four steps, turned away from the heat-treatment room, raised his head proudly, drew a long breath and collapsed. Someone said, "He's done for," . . . A woman doctor came in with her case. "What are you staring at? Go and get a stretcher."

The end was prosaic and terrible. They fastened a wooden board with his number to one leg, tossed the corpse in a cart together with others, took them out of the compound and threw them into a common grave.

"It's unlikely there'll ever be a street on this Earth named after Mandelstam," said his widow.

Perhaps that's not so important, I thought to myself, as I was writing this chapter. For all of us that street already exists. When the postman brought the latest newspapers, however, I read that a memorial plaque had been unveiled at the very heart of the Latin quarter in Paris on the house where Mandelstam once stayed. A few days later his name echoed back from the other end of Eurasia.

On the outskirts of Vladivostok, it was reported, on the site of the former transit camp Pechorskaya Street had been renamed after Mandelstam.

Just as in his poem:

> But little was straight about him,
> His morals were not lily-white,
> And therefore this street
> Or, rather, this pit
> bears the name of
> that same Mandelstam.

CHAPTER 10

THE ARRESTED WORD

THE FILES ON NIKOLAY KLYUEV AND ANDREY PLATONOV

The "arrested word", for the most part, has already become smoke and ashes and is lost to us forever. Those literary treasures that were eventually found and released from the Lubyanka survived by a miracle.

The most important of these discoveries were some manuscripts linked not only by the stature and talent of their two authors but also by the time of their composition: the very beginning of the 1930s, at the height of the campaign for "total" collectivization, not just of the countryside but of all aspects of life. They are, therefore, of both literary and historical significance, documents of a tragic era.

The Song of the Great Mother

"Come and see us. Our congratulations! There are some poems as well ..."

The name of the poet Nikolay Klyuev, arrested more than half a century earlier, was in one of the first lists I submitted to the Lubyanka, hoping to find manuscripts that had survived in their secret depositories.

In front of me they placed not only the investigation file but a thick folder stuffed with odd sheets and slips of paper, on which the poet, in his large convoluted hand, had added corrections, variants and marginal notes. All were mixed up with letters, notepads, newspaper cuttings, and tiny scraps of paper with surnames and addresses. It was difficult to sort them out and understand what was of value here, or even put the separate pages of the same work back together. Exciting months were spent, deciphering the manuscripts and letters, and comparing what we found with what had already been published. When Klyuev's own voice was at last freed from the pile of yellowed paper, we discovered poetic masterpieces that few had heard or seen before.

> There is a rare and exceptional mood in Klyuev's poetry, the pathos of a discoverer ... What is he? Some exotic bird or the forerunner of a new force, of a popular culture? (Nikolay Gumilyov)

> Klyuev is a great event in my autumnal life ... (Alexander Blok)

> The heart of Klyuev unites East and West, the shepherd's truths with a magical wisdom, and the lamentations of the Earth's four corners ... (Andrey Bely)

Klyuev came from majestic Olonets,* where the Russian way of life and the tongue of the Russian peasant are cradled in a Hellenic importance and simplicity... (Osip Mandelstam)

Klyuev is my teacher. The tender apostle Klyuev bore us in his arms. (Sergey Yesenin)

Thus spoke the different poets of Russia's Silver Age. But to the Iron Age that rapidly followed, he was an obscurantist and reactionary: "a hostile element" (*Literaturnaya gazeta*, 1930), "a medieval mystic" and "father of kulak literature" (*Literary Encyclopedia*, 1931).**

Soviet writers led Klyuev to the gates of the Lubyanka and handed him over. Of course, they had the approval and encouragement of the authorities but it was with exceptional zeal and malice that they began their campaign of harassment and persecution. The poet was first driven from their ranks, excluded from the Writers Union, hounded in the press, and reduced to poverty and hunger. He could only survive by reciting poetry at others' celebrations and banquets and, sometimes, seeking alms in the market or outside the church.

Only a small effort was now required to complete his ruin.

What happened was later described at a literary evening, openly and frankly, by the man chiefly responsible for Klyuev's downfall. Party functionary Ivan Gronsky, chief editor of both *Izvestiya* and *Novy mir* in the 1930s, was speaking in 1959, during the Thaw. Stalin had been denounced yet Gronsky remained sure of his own rectitude and displayed not a hint of penitence.

Gronsky and the young poet Pavel Vasiliev, one of Klyuev's pupils, were married to sisters and shared the same flat. One day Vasiliev told his brother-in-law certain details of Klyuev's unconventional private life.

I rang up Yagoda and requested him to kick Klyuev out of Moscow within 24 hours. "Arrest him?" he asked. "No, simply exile him." After this I informed Iosif Vissarionovich Stalin of my instruction, and he gave his approval...

The arrest was carried out on 2 February 1934 by Nikolay Khristoforovich Shivarov. Three and a half months later, after he had finished with Klyuev, "Khristofor'ych" would tackle another poet, Mandelstam. And in both cases the arrest warrant was signed by Yakov Agranov, deputy head of OGPU.

After the search, Klyuev and his confiscated manuscripts were taken to the

*Klyuev came from the Olonets region in northern Russia, a region that provided many generations of story-tellers and was at the centre of the Russian epic tradition.
**The post-Stalin edition of the *Literary Encyclopedia* would be little less harsh, talking of "Klyuevism" as a stage most others, like Yesenin, had grown out of.

Inner Prison at the Lubyanka. From the moment he filled out the standard form, his interrogator began to re-write his biography. Klyuev wrote: Nationality, Great Russian; Education, literate. Shivarov crossed out both and inserted: Russian, Self-taught. And the prisoner, it seems, was not tamed by words alone. To judge by the photograph, taken at the Lubyanka and preserved in the file, his tragic features clearly show abrasions and scars, traces of "active methods of investigation".

For Shivarov the case was straightforward and prestigious even, since it had been approved by the highest authority. So he tried to wind it up rapidly, within a month. First, the prisoner was read the accusation:

> Since citizen Klyuev has been sufficiently unmasked as actively engaging in anti-Soviet agitation, through dissemination of his counter-revolutionary literary works . . . he shall be charged under Article 58:10 of the Criminal Code.

On 15 February the decisive interrogation took place. It is barely likely that Klyuev would describe his own views as "reactionary" and yet, as a whole, the document has a truthful, authentic ring. Klyuev did not conceal his attitude to the Soviet regime, or disown his compositions, and Shivarov was not forced to make special efforts in editing the prisoner's replies.

> *Q.* What are your views on Soviet reality and your attitude to the policies of the Communist Party and the Soviet authorities?
> *A.* My views on Soviet reality and my attitude to the policies of the Communist Party and the Soviet authorities are determined by my reactionary religious and philosophical outlook.
>
> As a descendant of a family of Old Believers, going back on my mother's side to the Archpriest Avvakum, I was brought up on the early Russian culture of Korsun,* Kiev and Novgorod. I absorbed a love for the old pre-Petrine Russia and became its bard.
>
> The building of socialism in the USSR under the dictatorship of the proletariat finally destroyed my dream of Old Russia. Hence my hostile attitude to the policies of the Communist Party and the Soviet authorities, which were aimed at the socialist reconstruction of the country. I regard the practical measures adopted to implement such policies as a violent attack by the state on the nation, which is bleeding profusely and suffers a burning anguish.
>
> *Q.* How do your views find expression in your literary activities?
> *A.* My views were fully expressed in my work. I can give the following illustrations.

*Early Russian name for the Black Sea city of Kherson, in antiquity the Greek town of Khersones.

My view that the October Revolution plunged the country into an abyss of misfortune and suffering and made it the most unhappy land in all the world, was expressed in the poem "There are demons of cholera, leprosy, plague . . ."

I believe that the policy of industrialization destroys the foundations and beauty of the Russian popular way of life, and is accompanied, moreover, by the sufferings and death of millions of people. This I expressed in my "Song of Gamayun".* The idea was more precisely and specifically expressed in my poem about the White Sea–Baltic canal.**

The collectivization, being carried out by the Communist Party, will completely destroy the foundations and beauty of that Russian popular life of which I was the bard. I regard collectivization with mystic horror, as a devilish delusion.

I expressed my views about collectivization, as a process that is destroying the Russian countryside and is fatal for the Russian nation, in my poem "The Burned Ruins".†

Q. To whom did you recite the works cited here, and to whom did you give the texts to read?

A. I read "The Burned Ruins" mainly to writers and critics, actors and artists. Usually this was at my acquaintances' homes before guests whom they had invited. Thus, I read "The Burned Ruins" at the homes of Sophia Tolstoy,†† the writers Sergey Klychkov, Vsevolod Ivanov and Yelena Tager, the artist Nesterov and in certain other places that I cannot now recall.

In my absence the poet Pavel Vasiliev took away certain unfinished poems from my lodgings. I suppose that "The Song of Gamayun" was among them.

Klyuev evidently considered Vasiliev to blame for his arrest. Without permission Vasiliev had taken poems that formed part of the indictment. Vasiliev also told his brother-in-law Gronsky something that prompted the latter to ring up Yagoda. This not only concerned Klyuev's private life, we may surmise, but also his seditious verse, such as the "Song of Gamayun".

It was because Klyuev's poems confirmed his testimony that they were preserved, as the proof of his anti-Soviet views. The same happened with Mandelstam. Both provided irrefutable evidence for their investigators and so

*Gamayun was a prophetic bird in Russia's folklore and its Christian apocrypha.
**See footnote on p118.
†"The Burned Ruins" (Pogorels'hchina) in Nikolay Klyuev, *Poems,* Translated by John Glad (Ann Arbor: Ardis, 1977).
††Grand-daughter of Lev Tolstoy and last wife of Sergey Yesenin.

condemned themselves. They could not do otherwise, for sincerity is the essence of poetry.

While working in the Lubyanka archives I examined the fate of dozens of writers. People reacted differently when they found themselves in the hands of the OGPU. Some immediately and obediently gave the testimony required, even repenting non-existent sins without particular pressure being exerted. Some broke down at a certain point in their interrogation, unable any longer to withstand the violence. Yet others changed their tactics and, having given the required testimony, then denied it during their trial.

Klyuev and Mandelstam alone remained firm and uncompromising. The most fragile and poetic souls, it might seem, they proved the most steadfast. They could either be destroyed or accepted for what they were. In Klyuev's case there was also a profound religiosity and his faith provided a strong support, a counter to earthly vacillation.

Attached to the deposition of Klyuev's interrogation is a cycle of unpublished poems, "Destruction", of which we were hitherto unaware. At its heart lies "The Song of Gamayun", a terrible prophecy addressed to the future.

The Song of Gamayun

Bitter tidings to us came:
Aral's depths lay in deathly mire,
Rare the storks nests in Ukraine,
The grass of Mozdok ceased to sing
And in Sarov's radiant refuge
Underground the wheels did scrape!

Dark clouds the tidings brought:
Silt and shallow the blue Volga,
In Kerzhenets fell men did fire
Green fortresses of fir and pine,
And rotting, Suzdal's wheatfields gave
Birth to lichen and tree roots tangled.

The cranes are calling to us,
Gathering for their last flight.
Hen chaffinch died moulting
Plagued by aphids' greed,
Only the shaggy bees did wheeze
Their greetings to the mushrooms.

Bitter tidings to us came:
No longer lives our native land

Aral's depths lay in deathly mire
Gritsko fell silent in Ukraine
And the North, that swan of icy chillness,
Flowed out in an endless, homeless wave
Ships and sailors warning:
No longer lives our native land!

Gamayun is the bird of prophecy and one cannot read these lines today without a shudder. How could Klyuev have known that the Aral Sea would silt up and then cease to exist, due to the barbaric construction of numerous drainage canals? Is the "homeless wave" of the North not a reference to the foolhardy government plans to make the Northern rivers flow southwards, into the deserts of Central Asia? Until not long ago the scraping of "underground wheels" near the Sarov* monastery would have remained an enigma for most. Now we all know that the secret city of Arzamas 16, where nuclear weapons were prepared above and below ground, was located there. It was here that Andrey Sakharov lived and worked for almost 20 years.

The other poems by Klyuev, discovered in his Lubyanka dossier, are full of similar prophecies. The "rider from Karabakh" bore "black tidings": from the late 1980s we anxiously followed events in the Armenian enclave of Nagorno-Karabakh. The great Siberian rivers of Irtysh and Yenisey "beat against the ocean, like a beggar at the door" – and was not Russia, the most richly endowed country in the world, now begging for help from other nations? And then Chernobyl...

Then the Star Wormwood fell,
Air and water turned to bile
Human life defiling,
To leave Russia, an unsmiling
Land without bird or fish!

Klyuev's case was the eighteenth to be considered at the meeting of the OGPU collegium on 5 March 1934: Send him to a concentration camp for five years, they decided, then commuting this sentence to exile to the Narym Territory in Siberia, for the same period.

When he reached his place of exile Klyuev wrote to his closest friend, the poet Sergey Klychkov:

I was sent to the stake for my "Burned Ruins", just as my forefather the Archpriest Avvakum was burnt to death in Pustozersk.** Whether I wish

*Founded by the other wordly St Seraphin (1759–1833).
*Medieval north Russian town to which Avvakum was exiled and then, in 1682, burned at the stake.

it or not, my blood links two epochs: that of Tsar Fyodor Alexeevich, lit by the bonfires and flares of self-immolation, and our own youthful and therefore, in many ways, ignorant epoch. I have been exiled to the settlement of Kolpashevo, in the Narym Territory, to certain and painful death ... Four months in prison and then in various transports passed quickly and easily by the leaves of the calendar, but picked my bones clean ... The sky is ragged, slanting rains are carried over thousands of miles of bog, the wind never ceases. This is what they call summer here. Then ferocious winter, with frosts of –50 degrees and I am naked, without a fur hat even, wearing someone else's trousers because mine were stolen in the prison cell. Think, dearest friend, how to help my muse whose prophetic eyes were viciously put out!

Meanwhile that August the first Congress of Soviet Writers was being grandly celebrated in Moscow. Klyuev sent an appeal but it was not discussed. The delegates were far too busy and none of them dared to mention dangerous subjects, or disgraced colleagues, in their speeches. They were saluting the radiant present and the yet more radiant future: for many of them, it would also bring imprisonment and execution.

Sergey Klychkov risked his life and linked the exiled Klyuev with the outside world. Soon he was shot. In letters from Siberia Klyuev mentioned two other names. "How is Osip Emilievich?" he asked of Mandelstam, then also in exile, "I heard that he's supposed to be in Voronezh?" And of Pavel Vasiliev: "Will he really walk past my execution with no more than a drunken smile? ... His guilt towards me is of the blackest..." Within a few years they would also both be dead, Mandelstam in the Vladivostok transit camp and Vasiliev, shot immediately.

Klyuev saw in the New Year of 1935 in Tomsk, to which he had been transferred from the small provincial town of Kolpashevo. This should have eased his position, it was a city and a little nearer to Moscow. Yet he was still in Siberia and an exile without rights. Fundamentally, his situation had not improved. Klyuev continued to share accommodation with strangers and go hungry; on Sundays he went to the market to beg.

It was then that Romain Rolland came to visit Gorky in Moscow. The Soviet press made a great fuss about this event. "How did Jean-Christophe find his stay?" Klyuev asked his correspondents, in an ironic reference to Rolland's novel.* "Did he see St Christopher in the Russian rivers?" The exile did not appeal to the French author although the latter might have tried to help him, being received by Stalin himself in the Kremlin. Evidently, Klyuev had no faith that he would succeed. Neither did he try writing to Gorky: "In any case

---

*Jean-Christophe, a 10-volume roman fleuve (1905-12) by Romain Rolland (1866-1944), who was awarded the Nobel Prize for Literature in 1915.

Kryuchkov* would not let my letter through."

He continued to write poetry, though, noting down individual verses on anything that came to hand – torn-off strips of paper, scraps from paper bags.

Until very recently Klyuev's end remained a mystery. In one account he died from a heart attack at a railway station and his suitcase full of manuscripts disappeared. In another, he died in Tomsk prison. A third version, recounted that it was not just in prison but in the prison wash house that he met his end and Anna Akhmatova would repeat a story, supposedly reported by some priest, which exactly reproduced the death of Mandelstam.

Only when the poet's Lubyanka dossier was unsealed was yet another investigation file found, this time from 1937. It turned up in the Tomsk KGB and its contents dispersed all doubts.

In March 1936 Klyuev's life again hung in the balance. A second arrest and imprisonment followed and the prisoner was so weak and ill that he was kept in the prison hospital not a cell. In July he was released temporarily because the Chekists, evidently, did not want him to die in their hands. This time he left prison a cripple and for many months was not able to leave his bed. In his last letter to his friends he wrote: "If they arrest and mistreat me one more time, I shall not survive. My heart cannot endure any more suffering: remember me then in the graveyard . . ."

When he wrote those words his fate was already decided. The archivists showed me an excerpt from the records of a meeting of Siberian Chekists. There they were directly instructed by Mironov, one of the leading NKVD officials:

> Klyuev must be picked up as a monarcho-fascist, not a Right Trotskyist.
> Connect him through this counter-revolutionary organization with the Union . . .

In summer 1937 a new wave of arrests passed through Siberia. Members of the intelligentsia, priests, former Tsarist army officers and thousands of peasants, barely literate and quite illiterate, were shot for belonging to a mythical organization. The Union for the Salvation of Russia was supposed to be operating under instructions from a counter-revolutionary centre in Paris. Its aims were to organize an uprising against the Soviet regime and restore the monarchy at the same moment as the fascist powers attacked the USSR.

A leading role was allotted to Klyuev. A postgraduate at the Tomsk medical institute called Golov was forced to incriminate him:

> The leader and mastermind of the organization was the poet Klyuev. . .
> He is writing verse and a long poem about the atrocities and tyranny of the Bolsheviks.

*Gorky's personal assistant.

On the night of 5-6 June 1937 the poet was again arrested. In the file remains a note that he was suffering heart trouble at the moment of his arrest and when he reached the prison lost the use of his legs. There was, effectively, no interrogation.

Q. Do you acknowledge your guilt?
A. No, I do not consider myself guilty. I was not a member of any counter-revolutionary organization and had not prepared to overthrow the Soviet system . . .
Q. You have been sufficiently unmasked during the investigation. What can you truthfully say about the organization?

Klyuev refused to implicate others: "I do not wish to give any further testimony . . ."

On 13 October the troika of the West Siberian Territory NKVD decreed that Klyuev be shot. An indecipherable scrawl confirms the execution of this sentence on 23-25 October. Probably so many had to be shot that even the highly efficient Chekists could not finish the job in a day.

Klyuev was no more but his poetry lived on and may hold still more revelations. In Russia he is still poorly known and the fullest edition so far of his works, as so often happened before, was published abroad in the 1960s in Germany. Until his rehabilitation in 1988 he remained a criminal. The little that was published was difficult to obtain and few had read it.

He is not easy for contemporary Russians to read. It is as though a bound chest had been dug up, thrown open and found to contain treasures of which we had only ever heard in fairy tales:

> *These psalteries: from Onega's* depths*
> *A splashing wave around the isle***
> *When the moon's carriage*
> *Bearing pearls and wax*
> *Rides across the glittering shimmer*
> *And the forest languour lies*
> *On spruce and Karelian birch.*
>
> *These parables: on John Kupala's day†*
> *Chimes from Kizhi's many cupolas††*
> *Where in flaming veils*

*The lake of Onega in northwest Russia (from which the Neva flows through St Petersburg into the Gulf of Finland).
**Paleostrov, an island in the lake where, in the late seventeenth century, there was a mass self-immolation of the *raskolniki* or Old Believers at the monastery there.
†Mid-summer's eve, when celebrations blend John the Baptist's birth with the Russian pagan figure of Kupala.
††Island on Lake Onega with many wooden churches decorated with innumerable cupolas.

In dawn-red, fish-grey glories
The angels move their wings.

These mysteries: the southwest wind
With sails did rock to sleep,
In the cell a leather book of hours,
Like owlets in a resin-streaked hollow,
Did feed with honeyed fragrance
From the birch-bark lamp
Beneath the Virgin's image . . .

These are the opening lines of *The Song of the Great Mother*. For half a century those prophetic Russian psalteries, those parables and mysteries, were shut up alive in the walls of the Lubyanka.

Rumours and legends about this work circulated for a long time. Klyuev's contemporaries remember how he read them excerpts, and would write them in his friends' commonplace books. They recalled how, in the terrible conditions of exile, he continued to work on the "Song" after it had been confiscated by the secret police. From Siberia he wrote:

> The fate of *The Song of the Great Mother* pains my heart. It took me over
> six years to compose it. I gleaned the Russian mysteries one by one . . .
> It is an intolerable pity . . .

An almost mystical destiny had been prepared for Klyuev's best work. Both the Soviet secret police and the invading Nazis tried to destroy it. The literary critic Ivanov-Razumnik preserved some fragments of the "Song" in his house in Pushkino (former Tsarskoe Selo). Then Ivanov-Razumnik was exiled and during the war his archive was destroyed. Another part of the poem was safeguarded by Klyuev's acquaintance the writer Nikolay Arkhipov, at the time curator of the Peterhof Palace museum. He put the manuscript in a secret hiding place in the high tiled stove in the main hall. But Arkhipov was arrested and the palace was burnt to the ground by the Germans.

The poem had been lost forever, it seemed. Then, like the magical city of Kitezh in Russian folk legend, rising from beneath the waters of Lake Svetloyar after the Tatars had gone, the manuscript surfaced once more, from the vaults of the KGB archive.

The work is enormous, there are about 4000 lines in the manuscript we found. The date of its composition is indicated as 1930–1 and an alternative title "The Last of Russia", was also given.

The poet's mother Praskovya Dmitrievna served as the model for the heroine of the "Song". A story-teller and ritual mourner herself, a "golden branch of Avvakum", she taught the poet to read and write and confirmed him in the faith

Песнь о великой матери.   1.

—

Эти гусли — глубь Онега,
Плеск волны палеостровской,
В час, как лунная телега
с грузом жемчуга и воска
проезжает зalbo лесной,
и томит леса я нега
Ель с карельскою березой.

                пичуг
Эти ~~пташки~~ — в день купал
звон на кижах многоглавых,
где в горящих покровалах,
в заревых и рябых славах
плещут ангела крыла.

Эти тайны парусами
убаюкивал шеломник,
в келье корельский головник,
как свея рдуле с можжухой,
их кормил душистой вяткой
От берестяной лампадки
перед образом пречистым.

Эти вести — рыбья стая,
что плывет редея, тая,
лосось с Ваги, язь из Водла,
ленцы с Мегры, где суровят мерда,
бок изодран о мотчей драке
за лазурную плотицу,
но прочитать до дна не всякий
может глубокую страницу. —

Кто пречист и слухом золот,
дым и безверьем не расколот,
как береза острым клином,
и кто жеребием единым
связан с родимой вдовицей,
тот — алела на странице,
тот между креста песта лесы,
и танцуемо водимой
по тропинкам междусибробой
красоте заглянет в очи
Светлой девушке с поморья.

of his dissenting forebears. "The Old Belief is a serious, universal and principled movement," the writer Andrey Platonov once commented; "Moreover, we know what has come of progress but there's no telling what might still come of the Old Belief..."

Klyuev dedicated his best works to his mother but here the Great Mother is also Russia, Mother Earth and the Virgin. This not only echoes the works of Russian thinkers like Vladimir Solovyov, Nikolay Fyodorov, Pavel Florensky and Sergey Bulgakov but also the inward "deep" philosophy of the Russian people themselves. This last is a mystery for contemporary Russians not so much through the fault of the KGB as our own lack of understanding, inner freedom and spirituality.

The poem is made up of three parts or, as Klyuev called them, clusters: the youth of the Mother; the childhood of the author-hero, describing how he became the bard and poet of his people; and the end of old Russia. In the last part, historical figures like the Tsar's family, Rasputin and Sergey Yesenin appear, as do the world war and other new misfortunes that are advancing on Russia:

> The carriages startled the calm-eyed elks,
> We opened the chest and raised up the icons,
> And in a grey cloud, live iconostasis,
> Set off, winds whistling, towards Tsar and City.
> The further, the sadder ... roll-ups and curses,
> A pale little company, no fine young lasses,
> Mean little houses rotted with drinking
> For lack of the Russian spirit and smile!
> There stands Petersburg, a cage made of iron,
> Nowhere to weep there or take ease of soul.
> They drove the antlered ones into the barracks –
> Where's the Bird of Joy, the Tsar's bright regalia?
> Attention, men! The corporals are yelling:
> An officer's coming! Now, by the right ...
> Left, right! Left right!
> Ah, what a land! Rich grass-covered motherland!

When he turned to the Soviet era, Klyuev depicted it uncompromisingly as the Apocalypse, the reign of the Antichrist, fating the Russian soul to perdition.

> No finer nation is there
> Than bears in its eyes
> Furrows of thought in water
> Left by swan-game swimming!

No wiser nation is there
Than bears between its brows
The blue-elk winter refuge,
Cedar grove untainted,
Where no path leads the proud
To the word's enchanted tower!

The sounding string
And wings and humankind
All there take their source . . .

Yet the time, wound up, has come
All prophecies came to pass
And between Russian brows
No more the lynxes spring!

The icon's visage is scorched
By the smoke of hell's delusion
And the still depths of Slavic eyes
Are not stirred by the magic elk!
The prophetic swan is speared
For the feast of the raven flock
And with his donkey's tail
The Devil sweeps away the stars!

The poem culminates in the flight of the hero and his "dead friend". The latter resembles Sergey Yesenin: "Flee, flee, my dead friend, from blizzard, black and red!" They fly from the accursed present and beyond the "last pass" meet a banner-bearing procession of Russian saints. They prepare to sail for the invisible City of Kitezh which, according to Klyuev, is not Russia's past but its future.

Lev Trotsky once rightly guessed in Klyuev the "duality of the peasant, that Janus in bast shoes, who with one face looks to the past and with the other, to the future." He thought this condemnation. In fact it was praise, the tribute of "our filthy education" (Klyuev's phrase) to a natural majesty.

The Technical Novel

"Does Platonov interest you?" asked Krayushkin. I had come to the Lubyanka to work on the next investigation file.

I froze. Platonov had never been arrested, so what was the curator of the Lubyanka archives referring to? Seeing my reaction, he gave a knowing grin, opened his safe and took out a thick file. It was bound like a book, with neat printed letters on the cover:

OGPU
SECRET POLITICAL DEPARTMENT
Highly Confidential
UNPUBLISHED WORKS BY ANDREY PLATONOV
(confiscated during a search)
Moscow, 1933

"What do you say to that?" Krayushkin asked.

What could I say? The discovery of these manuscripts was an event. I greatly admired Platonov as a writer... But how had the typescripts ended up at the Lubyanka? Who were they confiscated from, and during what search?

Neither Krayushkin nor the others working in the archive offered any explanation. Either they really did not know or they preferred not to say. One thing was clear, though. The file had only survived by a miracle, for it was not marked "For Permanent Retention". One of the archivists, Vladimir Vinogradov, recalled that many years earlier when they were having one of their regular clear-outs, he pulled this file from a stack of folders set aside for destruction and transferred it to the current section of the archive. Whether professional instinct or genuine understanding prompted his action, Platonov's manuscripts owed their survival to this impulsive act.

Platonov endured various forms of repression. For years they did not publish him, isolating him from his readers and condemning him to poverty. Moreover, as it now turned out, his manuscripts had also been arrested. And if their survival was accidental, their confiscation was quite deliberate. A special dossier was opened on the writer and it contained other documents. The first was drawn up by a familiar hand:

REPORT
on Andrey Platonov,
author of the attached works

Platonov is a manual worker's son and himself a former worker. He studied at a technical college but did not complete the course, and then worked as a consultant engineer for the All-Union Council of the National Economy. Recently he has been working in the Fine Mechanics Trust where he was given an award for designing electrical scales. Platonov lives on the salary from this job. In the past his literary income was quite large but he has hardly been published at all during the last two to three years and is not receiving any royalties. He is not well off.

He avoids the company of professional critics and writers. Maintains unstable and not very close relations with a small group of authors. Nevertheless he is popular among writers and considered a master.

Leonid Leonov and B. Pilnyak enthusiastically rank him as their equal and Vs. Ivanov even declares him the best contemporary prose author.

Of his published works the most well known are: *The Birth of a Master*, his first long tale; *The Sluices of Epiphany*, the basic idea of which is the analogy between Peter's time and the epoch of socialist construction in the USSR; and *For Future Use*, a satire on the organizing of collective farms.

The editors of the journal *Krasnaya nov* were reprimanded for publishing *For Future Use* and only after that, in effect, did Platonov begin to be "given the treatment" and cease being published. Platonov then said: "I don't care what others say. I wrote that story for one person (for Comrade Stalin), he read the tale and in essence has given me his reply. The rest does not interest me."

The works Platonov has written since *For Future Use* speak of the deepening anti-Soviet attitudes of the writer. They are characterized by approaches to the main problems of socialist construction that are essentially satirical and counter-revolutionary.

Platonov has tried to get these works published, in part or in full, arguing that their publication is not only permissible but necessary and in the interests of the Party: ". . . After all, there is no writer who has such an approach to the inmost secrets of souls and objects as I do. A good half of my work helps the Party to see all the mould covering certain things better than the Workers and Peasants Inspectorate."

Platonov reads his works only to his closest friends, A. Novikov and I. Sats,* and does not allow his manuscripts to be passed around.

Appendix: Three satirical works by Platonov:

1 The Technical Novel. The most important chapters are included here.

2 The Juvenile Sea, a Novel.

3 14 Red Cabins.

This report was compiled by an officer of the Secret Political Department's 4th Section, the tireless Nikolay Shivarov. To give him credit, he provides a clear idea of the author's biography and his work. Platonov was undoubtedly a brilliant writer but did not join literary circles. Of course, Shivarov was aided by his "sources", Platonov's own remarks clearly come from such informers' reports. That collective and official informer, the Union of Soviet Writers, also made a modest contribution: it provided the "Declaration" submitted by

---

*The writer A. Novikov was arrested in 1940 and shot. Ilya Sats was secretary to Lunacharsky (until 1929 the People's Commissar for Enlightenment).

Platonov when he applied to join the Union and the questionnaire he then filled in.

Shivarov's report was aimed at unmasking one more enemy of the people among the writers and demonstrating his anti-Soviet, counter-revolutionary nature. It reads very like the dozens of other such reports with which investigation files usually began. At the Lubyanka they started compiling such a dossier when they intended to "isolate" a certain individual. The trap was set, all that was now needed was permission from above to arrest him.

But why did they start taking an interest in Platonov in 1933?

It was a critical period in the writer's life. After the publication of "For Future Use" (1931) the wrath of the "Leader of All Times and Nations" himself descended on Platonov. "At that Kondrov rolled his fist up in a copy of *Pravda* and gave the district chairman a blow on the ear with it." A response to this kind of provocative passage was inevitable. The writer's wife says that Stalin wrote "Bastard!" on the story after he had read it. "Give him a good belting – 'for future use'," other sources say he ordered, in conversation with Fadeev.

> In the month of March, 1930, a certain feeling unfortunate man, tormented by his concern for universal reality, got onto a long-distance train and left the city of Higher Command far behind.

The opening words of "For Future Use" seemed all too likely to describe the writer's imminent fate.

He was still only 33 and at the peak of his creative powers. His best works were written during these years, *Chevengur*, *The Foundation Pit*, *The Juvenile Sea* . . . But the public would not be able to read them until much later. Platonov's manuscripts found their way not to editorial offices but to the Lubyanka where they were attentively studied by literary specialists in uniform.

Platonov appealed to Gorky for help. "No one trusts me now," he wrote to the highest authority in Soviet literature. "I would like you to have faith in me. Being branded a class enemy makes it not only psychologically impossible to live, but practically impossible as well." Gorky did not reply. In May 1933 a now despairing Platonov again implored Gorky: "Can I be a Soviet writer or is that objectively impossible?" No reply.

That autumn, he sent yet another letter: "I am asking you, as the chairman of the Organizing Committee of the USSR Writers [Union], to help me go on writing. For two and a half years they have not published me . . . Please, if you do not consider it necessary to give up on me as a writer, then give your assistance. I need this simply in order to survive physically and carry on working." Again, no reply.

In February 1934 Platonov sent Gorky his short story "Dusty Wind" with a request to help get it published. He adds: "My difficult situation prompts me to appeal directly to you." Gorky tried to edit the story but finally rejected it, because of the irrationality of its contents which "bordered on gloomy raving".

Of the three works bound in the Lubyanka dossier, two were also preserved in the Platonov family archive and were published in Russia not long ago, in the late 1980s. The Lubyanka versions of *The Juvenile Sea* and the *14 Red Cabins*, it is true, do contain new fragments and certain variant readings.

The third manuscript, however, *The Technical Novel*, is a quite unknown work. Neither Platonov specialists nor even the writer's daughter, who did so much to make his works available, had any idea such a novel existed. The typescript was carelessly produced and contains mistakes. A subtitle "Excerpts from the manuscript of an unpublished novel" has been added. Who decided what to reproduce, where the rest of the manuscript is, and whether Platonov ever completed the novel all remain unclear. The finished parts of the text are linked by brief summaries of the missing sections. It is like a building with the scaffolding still in place. The scale, quality and architecture, however, are immediately apparent.

"I am a technical man," Platonov would say.

This is his "technical" novel. It grew out of one of his early short stories, "The Motherland of Electricity". Some pages of the two works are identical and this is quite typical of Platonov: the story-line offers different versions, plots branch off and live an independent existence, images split and multiply and the outcome is indeterminate.

The hero of the earlier work is a young man during the Revolution, who dreams of electricity. All around there is drought, famine and suffering. Yet for the time being, nothing contradicts Lenin's formula: "Communism equals the Soviet system plus the electrification of the entire country". The hero is a child of his time, like Platonov himself. Written in the first person, the original short story is thoroughly autobiographical: at the time the author was enthusiastically building electric power stations and even wrote a booklet on "Electrification".

Platonov was drawn to the Revolution and to technology because he wanted to help the world and save the starving. At the beginning of the novel he writes:

> The student-workers were about to study electricity. At that time rumours of this mysterious force, a lightning-charged object just like the October Revolution itself, were spreading throughout the country... In certain villages, the most remote and forgotten, as it happens, the chairman of the rural Soviet together with the clerks and the blacksmith were already building an electric power station by the village well, using motorcycles abandoned by the fleeing imperialists... When he learned of this, Dushin laughed for joy and told everyone that all of socialism,

perhaps, would start with electricity in a sad, straw-thatched cabin. This was the October revolution transformed from hope into matter . . .

The novel is set in the 1920s at the beginning of socialist construction in Russia. The main hero Simeon Dushin, the first-person narrator, now becomes in some way an unacceptable and hostile figure for the author. Platonov looks back on a fanatical former self, pitiless in his striving towards an ideal. The dream is tested against life and found to diverge increasingly from the truth. The author's identity is now divided between Dushin and Shcheglov, the main characters in the novel, and neither has full possession of the truth, they are all only seeking for it. Each has his own dream and his own truth, but how can they be reconciled?

> Dushin wanted the earth to lie an imperishable tomb in which the living cause of reality would be preserved; he wanted socialist science to be able to open the tomb of the world and ask the innermost recess: What's up? And then the acute ear of exact science, perhaps, would catch the quiet plaintive answer. Dushin secretly feared that the people who came after would generate such an energy of action that they would destroy every last piece of the world's substance and nothing more would ever happen.
>
> Shcheglov also agreed to the inviolability of the earth because his father and mother, four sisters and seven brothers, were lying in their graves and he lived alone and must now make all the shattering forces of incomprehensible distance answer to science. However, when Shcheglov gazed up sullenly from under his brows into the depth of the night or saw people wearing each other out with their bustle, he understood that man is a local, poor phenomenon, that nature is wider, more important than the mind and that the dead had died forever.

Platonov invented very little, life itself guided his pen. He created his heroes by giving them part of his being, as a mother brings her children into the world – once born, they exist independently, following their own destinies. This deeply personal embodiment of the admirable idea of mankind's salvation leads them, in the end, to a painful if natural confrontation and an open clash.

At one time Dushin and Shcheglov worked happily on the same steam engine. Their author had also served on that locomotive, celebrated in a song of the time: "Fly on, our Engine, next stop the Commune!" But now they wander around the cemetery of dead metal where their engine came to rest, without ever reaching its destination. It is then the friends discover that their ways have divided.

> "Mitya!" said Dushin. "We can't go on like this. See what gloom lies all around! Will they really bury us in our graves without a trace? Lenin is still alive, after all! . . . Let's build an electric power station! We shall soon

organize socialism and triumph over the very essence of matter!"

Shcheglov kept silent. He disliked the pride of Dushin who aspired to the absolute technical subjugation of the entire universe. He did not feel within him a precious object, more valuable than all the world and worthy to dominate it. Shcheglov had a modesty in his soul and placed man in the universal sequence of numerous natural accidents. Nor was he ashamed to live on such terms . . . He did not believe that the cosmos became aware of itself through man and was moving rationally towards its own goals . . . So Shcheglov kept silent.

"You don't want to," asked Dushin. "So you're against electricity and communism? You don't believe in them?"

"No, I'm not against them . . . Tell me, how much copper will you need for your wires?"

"OK, I'll tell you: about a million tons for the first section!"

"Farewell!" said Shcheglov. "With such plans you won't even overcome this province's darkness, not to speak of the gloom of eternity, as you say . . . Simeon, take a look," he pointed into the night at the empty ploughed fields. "Look how quiet and dark everything is, beneath our dead locomotive. Unhusked millet is turning over in the people's stomachs and because of hunger there is not even enough strength for the heart to beat normally – the pulse beats less frequently . . . Do you see?"

"Well, go on!"

"So listen: when we have at least 1000 tons of copper, we must first make kopecks out of it, not wires . . ."

"You're a petty, miserable man! You have the tiny mind of a Philistine. Why I was your comrade I cannot understand!"

Someone's solitary cart rumbled over the bridge, and the rising glow of the moon began to light the east. Shcheglov patiently heard out Dushin's words in silence. Then he told him: "If you listened not to your own mind but to all the world which, for some reason, you want to conquer (probably so as to destroy it), if you became a simple, and, perhaps, sad human being . . ."

"You're a shit, Dmitry, and a stupid person – you're no electrician."

"Possibly . . . Don't take offence, that's all. Well, farewell!"

"Forever and ever," announced Dushin and did not offer Shcheglov his hand . . .

The friends parted, each into his own solitude. Shcheglov went to spend the night with strangers. Dushin returned to the former prison where he was sheltering. All the way there he "cursed aloud and laughed at that bastard, his former comrade, stamping out all his cooling attraction for him".

The student Dushin, Platonov's former self, who had once feared that people would destroy all the matter in the universe, now became more and more rigid in unswerving service of his ideal. He was transformed into a typical Soviet engineer, subjugating and squandering nature. The hero's metamorphosis reaches its logical conclusion when he begins dreaming how "to organize humanity" more simply and to lock up the "universal historical truth" so it becomes as accessible and obedient as any other implement.

The creed of the regime and its enthusiasm for the taming of nature and man find full expression in the book Dushin writes. All the serious people in the province gather in the club to hear him read from it:

> A modest thinner Dushin came up to the table. In a quiet voice he began to read out his work about the application of electricity for socialism . . .
>
> Dushin noticed ironic smiles and sometimes glanced into the hall with hatred . . . He realized that he must be indifferent to the smile of the enemy of the proletariat and of electricity, and continued to read his work with the dignity of one who owns the truth . . .
>
> Leaving the technical side, Dushin again returned to the people and advised them to live simply and without extravagance because the basic truths of life had already been discovered: in society, Lenin, and in production, electrical engineering. To put these truths into practice one or two generations must be expended without pity in battle and labour. If pity and tenderness seized us, they would hold back people's emotion and will to work and inevitably they would only organize steam-engine capitalism . . .

When Dushin leaves for the country to implement his ideas and tries to adapt the available means, a motorcycle and a pump, for irrigating the fields he experiences defeat. The water pressure is too low. The regime, however, in the person of the local chairman, is not discouraged: "Even though science gives only a drop, we shall squeeze out a sea with the trunk of the masses," he declaims. As in another of Platonov's novels, the foundation pit of socialism was dug with enthusiasm but proved nothing more than a mass grave.

Lenin who inspired and organized electrification used just the same methods. In a 1920 instruction he wrote:

> Mobilize all the engineers and electrical engineers without exception, and all graduates of physico-mathematical faculties and so on. In no less than 2 (?4) lectures a week they must teach no less than 10 (?50) persons electricity. If they're successful, reward them. If not, prison.

Thousands of gifted self-taught men and women, skilled workers and craftsmen, drove themselves to exhaustion at the bidding of the Party ignoramuses. In

Platonov's novel the Party Committee is headed by Chunyaev "former stoker of the central heating system". Chunyaev wants to establish his own final order not only in the province under his control but throughout the land. Communism is already close at hand, and all that is needed is to stretch electric wires along the disintegrating wattle fencing of the village. Admittedly, he does not quite know what electricity is.

"Like a rainbow, is it?" he asked.

"Lightning," explained Dushin.

"Ah! Lightning," Chunyaev concurred. "So that's it! Well, let's get on with it . . . We've got ourselves in such a fix, my friend, that all we really need now is lightning – heat at one blow! Scientific and magnificent! . . . Let that bastard-electricity do the suffering! It's not alive now, is it?"

"We don't know," replied Dushin. "It's a mystery . . . What if science finally sees, Comrade Chunyaev, that the world is made up only of questions?

A fury of thought appeared on Chunyaev's large, kind face: "Really?! Probably because nothing has worked out properly for all those billions of years. Well, so be it! We shall then make of those questions one resolved problem. That's the kind I am! And so are our masses. We shall find out exactly where man came from: from the apes, or still worse! We shall dig up all the dead, we'll find their boss Adam, set him on his feet and ask: Where did you come from, either God or Marx – tell me, old man! If he speaks the truth, we'll resurrect Eve. If not, we'll re-educate him. That's the kind we are! We live responsible lives. We're a terrifying lot!

The most vivid image in the novel is unexpected and surrealistic, a wise old woman no taller than a small child. Dushin meets her in an open field, where she has lagged behind the church procession praying for deliverance from the drought.

"Stop praying, granny, there's no point. Nature will not hear words or prayers. She only fears work and reason."

"Reason!" announced the old woman with understanding and clarity. "I've been alive so many years that all I am is bones and reason. My flesh has long been used up in work and worry. There's nothing much left to die in me, it's all died away already, bit by bit. Just take a look at me."

The old woman stood in front of Dushin and raised her skirt, having forgotten shame, love and any other unavoidable feeling. Truly, little living matter, suitable for death and rotting in the ground, remained on the old woman. Her bones had ceased growing even in childhood when the sorrow of hunger and labour began breaking down the girl ... The body grown in her mother's milk had also been worn out thereafter in physical labour ... Now Dushin saw a paltry creature with bones, cutting like knives through the brown, scarred skin of its legs. Dushin bent down dubiously and tested that skin – it was already dead and hard as a fingernail and when Dushin, feeling no shame in his misery, further bared the old woman he could not see a hair on her. Between the blades of her bony legs there hung down the shrivelled dark dried remains of her children's native land. No scent or warmth came from the old woman. Dushin studied her like a mineral and his heart immediately grew tired and his reason became embittered. The old woman submissively took the scarf from her head and Dushin saw her bald skull, which had cracked into its constituent bones, was about to fall apart and surrender to irretrievable ashes the sparingly gathered, patient mind, that had come to know the world through toil and misfortunes ...

"Do we only bow down before God? We also fear the wind, icy ground, hail, drought, neighbour, passer-by – and each time we cross ourselves! Do we really pray out of love? We've already nothing left to love with!"

She pulled up her jacket and showed her breast. Two dark dead worms hung there, having eaten into her breast cavity, the remnants of her milk vessels. The skin was sunk between the ribs, but the beating of her heart was not noticeable and her entire chest was so small that only a dry little something could be inside. The old woman had nothing to feel with, and all that remained was to suffer and live in her mind.

Such a breast could already do nothing, neither love, nor hate, but one could lean on it and weep.

Dushin went away, filled with emotion and lamentation ...

Platonov created a new hero for Russian literature, the orphaned nation, deprived of God or Mother Earth or, even worse, of both, perhaps.

Platonov was a writer in advance of his time. In one of his articles he wrote "a great artist demands that his readers conquer or, at least, master him". The writing is so dense that a few pages are often enough at one sitting.

He was a dispassionate comrade for another human being, wishing him liberation from the rule of any illusions, even that of his own omnipotence.

Yet where is freedom? It lies far in the future, beyond mountains of labour, and the new graves of the dead.

The last words of the *Technical Novel* flew over the heads of his contemporaries to us.

Andrey Platonov was never arrested. To various other refined punishments, however, the regime added a final, almost mortal blow. In 1938 his beloved 15 year-old son was arrested and convicted of "terrorism and espionage".

> With the aid of the investigator who was interrogating me, I gave false, fantastic testimony and signed these depositions because he threatened that my parents would be arrested.

This statement came from the investigation file of Platon Platonov. Prison, the camps, tuberculosis and an early death followed . . . Platonov himself would then die of the same disease.

During his last years, following the war, he lived in great deprivation. He occupied a room in the left wing of the Literary Institute, on Tver Boulevard in Moscow, where Soviet writers were trained.* He could be seen through the windows sweeping the courtyard and many took him for the caretaker.

---

*In the 1920s the house where Herzen grew up was used by the non-Communist All-Russian Union of Writers. Several writers, including Mandelstam and Platonov, then lived in the building's left wing. In 1933 it became an evening school for young authors. In 1939 it passed under the control of the Writers Union, becoming the Gorky Literary Institute.

CHAPTER 11

CORRECTING THE ENCYCLOPEDIAS

Depository No 7

One morning Krayushkin rang me up: "I'm going to Butovo today. Do you want to come along? I think you'll find it interesting. It's worth seeing." It was a radiant autumn day. After prolonged and chilly rains the sky had suddenly cleared and the sun was shining.

At the Lubyanka the day before they had shown me files from top secret Depository No 7 for the first time. These had been concealed from outside eyes longer than all the rest. Until the very last moment, the KGB had insisted that nothing of the kind remained.

Depository No 7 contained the orders for shooting prisoners and the statements confirming that the sentences, passed by judicial and extra-judicial bodies, had been carried out. In brief, execution lists. From 1921 onwards these documents were stitched together in thick files and gradually built up into an enormous collection – 400 volumes, page after page of surnames marked with a tick in red pencil, "sentence carried out".

Only after the August putsch in 1991 and the collapse of the Communist regime did these documents surface. The archivist held out file No 182 and opened it where a marker lay: "You were asking for details about Efron's death . . ."

In verse dedicated to her husband, Marina Tsvetaeva had once written: "Your name shall be inscribed on tablets." If she had only known what "tablets", apart from her books, would preserve Sergey Efron's name!

It was autumn 1991. The file recorded what had happened exactly 50 years before. The Germans were approaching Moscow and as the monster of war devoured thousands on thousands of our fellow citizens, a bloody harvest was being reaped in the prisons of Moscow. Our own fascists were hurriedly disposing of the "enemies of the people".

> To Comrade Major Pustynsky, head of the NKVD's Butyrki prison
> Transfer to the NKVD commandant the below-mentioned persons condemned to be shot:
>   1 Efron Sergey Yakovlevich
>   [there followed 135 other names]
>   On the orders of Comrade Kobulov, Deputy People's Commissar of Internal Affairs.
> From Head of NKVD Prison Administration, Major Nikolsky
> 16 October 1941.

Lower down the same page was added the handwritten note:

On 16 October 1941 the under-signed carried out the sentences for the shooting of 136 (one hundred and thirty-six) persons listed in the above.
Head of the NKVD commandant's department, Major...
Head of 17th section of 1st special department, Senior Lieutenant...

The signatures are indecipherable.

Today it is almost impossible to imagine what happened then, on an autumn day perhaps as bright and sunny as this. How they were summoned from their cells, gathered together, counted, hurriedly pushed into lorries marked MEAT or BREAD, and driven out of the prison gates and rapidly along the Moscow streets to the unknown place of execution.

We left the Lubyanka in two cars. In the first, apart from Krayushkin and myself, was a Russian journalist who had been searching for the mass burial sites of Stalin's victims for several years. In the second travelled a film crew from the American ABC TV. On the way I told my companions of the little piece of research I had carried out the previous night after looking at the execution lists. At home I had taken down the Soviet *Literary Encyclopedia* and written out in two columns the dates it gave for the deaths of writers who died during the terror and the true dates preserved in the Lubyanka archives. The falsification was obvious.

Relatives were told of sentences to "Ten years without right of correspondence" and their families sought for them, and waited for them to return when they were already long dead. Even after rehabilitation in the mid-1950s phony dates and causes of death were entered in the certificates then handed out, and to this day these were included in all the encyclopedias and handbooks. Krayushkin commented: "It was done on orders from above, from the Party leadership. Have you noticed how they mainly shifted the dates into the war years?"

"How do the writers intend to commemorate their dead colleagues?" asked the journalist. "They should put up a monument!"

"They should," I responded. "But what kind? They've already met and discussed it. There is a memorial plaque in the Writers Club commemorating the 70 members of the Union who died during the war. It was suggested an identical plaque be put up for those shot earlier. But there would not be enough room: all the walls would be covered, inside and out ... and the café and restaurant are there."

"It's a problem all right!" Krayushkin gave a grim smile. "But the dead know no shame, as they say. What are we to do about the living, though? Our archive isn't a collection of scholarly texts, after all, but a minefield linked by a thousand threads to the present day. Say, you publish the name of some NKVD man, a mass murderer. Nothing wrong in that: he's deserved dishonour. But just imagine his relatives. Suddenly it turns out that their favourite grandfather, a respected decorated figure, was a murderer and torturer. How are his children and grandchildren to accept the truth? It's a delayed-action explosive and quite innocent people suffer when it goes off."

"I remember another case," I recalled. "I came to your archive and they said to me: We're giving the widow of the writer N. his manuscripts. They were preserved by chance in his investigation file. Have a look, perhaps it contains something of literary value. I opened the file – and there was the writer's correspondence with his mistress . . . Immediately I could imagine his elderly, sick wife coming in and, with shaking hands, taking this page and reading it . . . No, I said, don't give her this!"

"But you yourself were demanding that the archives be opened," laughed Krayushkin. "Abolish censorship, you said!"

"Close the archives! Restore censorship – in cases like this. Each individual has a right to privacy."

Suburban dachas were flashing past the car windows. We turned off the main road and ten minutes later came to a halt. This was Butovo. A solid painted fence, and gates with a side-entrance through a booth, from which someone immediately came up to our car. This was still not the Butovo we needed, as it turned out. This was the KGB dacha settlement and the man waiting for us was our escort. We had stopped to pick him up.

A little further, on the other side of the road, was the place we needed. There was another fence, but it was tilting, neglected and falling down. From nowhere appeared the watchman, scruffy and unshaven, in a cheap ill-fitting track-suit. For some reason I do not remember at all how we got past this fence but it was not easy and took more than a minute: we may even have untwisted the wire holding the gate shut, or pushed apart the palings to get inside. The incongruity between what I expected and what we saw, though, was firmly imprinted on my memory. For a tragic place it had a very mundane, run-down appearance.

We were in a large sunlit orchard. Rows of low apple trees, their spreading branches heavy with ripe rosy-cheeked fruit, stretched into the distance. As we walked further across the uneven, grass-covered earth the Americans filmed and the journalist explained:

> Under our feet lie the remains of the tens of thousands who were shot here. At the height of the arrests in the late 1930s they were brought to Butovo from the different Moscow prisons in closed lorries. The execution squads worked in a terrible hurry, day and night, the shots drowned out by the deafening noise of the running engines. People were lined up above a previously-dug trench and shot . . . They filled in the pit, levelled off the earth and prepared another trench.

I talked to the local people and searched for witnesses. They do not want to talk or remember and they're afraid to this day. But I did learn something. They said that there was a little building over there where the execution squad relaxed and kept its weapons. They were all done for. Even though the executioners were given spirit to drink they did not last for long. Some went mad, they say, and there were some suicides. They were regularly replaced with new men . . .

We came to a halt in the middle of the orchard. The Americans, at first smiling and noisy, fell silent and their faces became overcast. Every now and again the orchard seemed to sigh itself, as the branches swayed in gusts of wind and the fading leaves rustled.

"Butovo is one of the most terrible places in our country," said the journalist. "But how many other sites there are like it! And there are no monuments or eternal flames there . . ."

We were about to leave. The journalist plucked an apple from a tree and offered it to his American colleague.

"Here, take it as a souvenir."

The American reached out, and then said, "No. Thank you, but no."

Embarrassed the journalist placed the apple on the ground. I glanced at Krayushkin. His face had turned to stone. He quietly muttered something to himself.

"What's that?" I asked.

"Unfortunate country . . ."

Lev Tolstoy at the Lubyanka

"I cannot remain silent!" Tolstoy proclaimed in 1908 when the tsarist government sentenced terrorist revolutionaries to death:

> And this is happening, moreover, in Russia where ordinary people consider any criminal deserves their compassion and, until very recently, where there was no legal death penalty. How proudly I told Europeans this, I remember, and now one execution follows another . . .

In the 1880s, Tolstoy recalled, there had only been one executioner for the whole of the Russian empire. Now the number of hangmen was rising, day by day. Counter-revolution was using terror in response to the terror of the revolution – peasant raids on landowners, and assassination attempts against official figures.

"We cannot go on like this," Tolstoy declared. "Or, at least, I cannot and will not do so." The authorities should either stop the killings or, he demanded, execute him just as they were hanging "those embittered and frivolous people who began this violent struggle". He drew the following conclusion for the authorities:

By participating in these frightful crimes you are not only failing to heal
the disease but intensifying it and driving it deeper within.

Tolstoy's article had a wide resonance throughout the world, and was translated and reprinted everywhere. The tsarist authorities made no reply to his
thunderous denunciation. The revolutionaries whose lives the writer was
defending, however, did not remain silent. The same year, Vladimir Ulyanov
(Lenin) published "Lev Tolstoy as the Mirror of the Russian Revolution" where
he described him as "a landowner playing the Holy Fool", a "laughable" prophet
who had "discovered new recipes for the salvation of mankind", a utopian and
reactionary. Tolstoy's teachings, in Lenin's view, "were deprived of the slightest
practical meaning, and of any theoretical justification".

Tolstoy's humanism and appeals for clemency, and his defence of every individual's inalienable right to life did not suit the future leader of the proletarian
revolution. Within 10 years Lenin's views had the upper hand and had Tolstoy
still been alive then he would not have escaped the avenging sword of the Cheka.

Tolstoy, nevertheless, still managed posthumously to visit the Lubyanka. His
daughter Alexandra was arrested, as were almost all his pupils and the Tolstoyans
who lived by his teachings. And, I was to discover, even his own words were
arrested and imprisoned by the Soviet secret police.

In January 1991 the local KGB in Cheboksary, capital of the distant Chuvash
republic on the Volga, were looking through the old archive file on a certain
Pochuev. Like thousands of others, of course, the charges against him were fabricated. At the end of the file was pasted a card sleeve from which the unsuspecting
KGB man drew a worn, grey envelope. Inside was a thin typed sheet of paper and
– he could hardly believe his eyes – at the top of the page, "14 December 1909,
Yasnaya Polyana" and at the bottom a dashing signature, "Lev Tolstoy"!

His superiors in Moscow were rapidly informed and the file was hastily sent
on to them: the Lubyanka wanted to check for itself. With unconcealed triumph,
Krayushkin showed me the file. Several days later, after the signature and corrections added to the typewritten letter had been checked and compared, we were
sure that this was really Tolstoy's work.

Pochuev was one of the revolutionaries he had been defending in his article.
Exiled to the Urals city of Orenburg for his part in the 1905 Revolution, Pochuev
began working as a school teacher. From there he wrote, asking Tolstoy the
eternal question which so many asked the famous writer: How should he live and
what was the purpose of life?

Tolstoy gave the following answer:

Nikolay Alexandrovich, I cannot tell you anything that I have not already
said in my books, some of which I hereby send you.

224

For the most part your situation is covered by the sections 28 Aug. and July, 27 June in the "Day by Day" books. If someone sets himself moral self-improvement as the main aim of his life (not service of others but moral self-improvement of which service of others is always a consequence) then, I believe, no external circumstances can prevent him from reaching his goal. That is my answer to your question. As far as improving your material position is concerned, I would advise you to write the most truthful description of your life you can, if that is not too hard to do. The story of what a young man of the people, who has freed himself from superstition, must endure could be very instructive for many others. I know editors who would happily print such a story in their publications, supposing naturally that it is well-written, and they would pay well for it.

Lev Tolstoy

Tolstoy compiled his "Day by Day" books* from aphorisms and parables drawn from thinkers of various times and nations, and from his own works. This would be a constant companion, in Tolstoy's conception, for anyone who was seeking the meaning of life. The underlying themes were Christian faith, repentance and moral self-improvement as a release from the evil reigning in the world and within the individual.

The subsequent fate of Nikolay Pochuev indicates that, like so many others, he did not heed Tolstoy's advice. Returning from exile to his native Chuvashia, he became leader of a Social Democrat group which made a famous appeal to Lenin. After the October Revolution Pochuev was in the avant-garde of socialist construction and the first to enter the collective farm. His portrait, as a famous revolutionary, hung in the Chuvash republic's museum. Until 1937.

An NKVD troika sentenced him to 10 years in the camps and he never returned.

Among other papers, Tolstoy's letter was arrested with Pochuev. It was evidently of no interest to the secret police and no mention is made of it in the investigation file. There it rested until the present day.

What else may we still find in the secret archives of the Lubyanka? I asked myself that question many times, as I sat there reading the letters of Vladimir Korolenko and Fyodor Chaliapine, and the interrogations of Nikolay Berdyaev and of Konstantin Tsiolkovsky, the "father" of Soviet space exploration.

We shall have to rewrite our history and the contents of the KGB archive will force us to correct our encyclopedias time and again.

---

*Tolstoy's *Readings* (Selected, Collected and Allocated Day by Day), were first published in 1905. Here he offered his correspondent a selection of his own aphorisms, and quotations from Carlyle, Pushkin, Robertson, the Bible and Confucius.

CHAPTER 12

STORMY PETREL IN A CAGE
THE FILES ON MAXIM GORKY

Mask and Reality

Maxim Gorky lived and died, honoured and feted by the Soviet authorities. They never arrested or imprisoned him. Knowing, however, that the Lubyanka did not neglect a single major writer, let alone such a world-famous figure as Gorky, I requested any files on him in the KGB's archive. It was a shot in the dark but I was sure that the fine net cast by the Soviet secret police would certainly catch such a big fish as Maxim Gorky:

> Dear Vladimir Ilych,
>   I shall not work with Zaks and do not want to talk to him. I am too old to allow others to mock me . . . And as a whole I see it's time for me to step down . . .

It took a great deal of searching, in libraries and archives, before I could appreciate the significance of this unknown letter from Gorky to Lenin in 1920. In the process, I made an extraordinary discovery: Gorky was a writer without a biography.

In countless publications the same carefully selected facts, recited as a kind of hagiography, were repeated time and again. The four-volume "chronicle" of Gorky's *Life and Work* contained numerous gaps and inconsistencies. There were references to letters which had never been published in the Soviet Union and those that were, had been severely cut. The same was true of articles, even photographs, and of the often barely accessible archive materials.

At school we had all learned by heart Gorky's "Song of the Stormy Petrel", flying between the storm clouds and the sea, a prophet of the Revolution's victory who cried, "Let the storm rage yet more fiercely!" We read *The Mother*, the first classic of socialist realism, highly praised by Lenin (and found it boring). Of course, we knew his play *The Lower Depths*. There seemed to be two Gorkys. One was a set of stereotypes, drummed into our heads, a portrait with moustaches, which hung in every school and library, usually beside the portraits of Lenin and Lev Tolstoy. This was an icon we could not criticize. The other Gorky was indubitably a gifted writer although he was read less and less. My generation flaunted a preference for his contemporary Bunin.

Some years later I would unexpectedly be forced to confront Gorky again. My friend the artist Shumilin had died and since he had no family I was left with the melancholy task of tidying up his studio. I had already packed up all his paintings and called a taxi when I happened to glance into the mezzanine. Two large round objects lay there, wrapped up in paper.

I unrolled one and stepped back with a start. A cement copy of Lenin's death mask. The other was lighter, it was a plaster cast of Gorky's face in death. I hastily shoved them in a bag and took them with me. Afterwards I tried ringing the Gorky museum and the Lenin museum but they already had copies. These enigmatic and frightening masks lie to this day in my store.

According to the official version, Lenin and Gorky were great friends. The documents I found at the Lubyanka presented their friendship in a rather different light.

They first met in 1905, two rebels from the Volga, and took a liking to one another. To begin with Gorky, the better-known and better-off, patronized Lenin* whose party was only just establishing itself. If Gorky, as often happened, strayed from the party line, Lenin firmly criticized him but this did not spoil their relations. For the time being these seemed little more than theories and visions and Gorky would parry Lenin's reproaches and attacks with a smile: "I know I'm a bad Marxist. And, anyway, all of us artists are a little crazy..."

When the October Revolution took place, however, deeds replaced words. Horrified by what happened thereafter, Gorky, writing in the *Novaya zhizn* newspaper,** made public his rejection of the Bolshevik takeover which he saw as the tragedy and ruin of Russia. The newspaper was closed down in summer 1918 on Lenin's orders and Gorky's critical articles, soon re-published abroad as a single volume entitled *Untimely Thoughts*, were banned. (Later generations in the Soviet Union would not be taught anything about this Gorky.)

At the time, however, Lenin remained calm:

No, Gorky will not abandon us. This is all temporary, uncharacteristic. He will certainly come back to us, you'll see...

And Lenin was proved right. Soon Gorky announced, in a letter to his first wife, Yekaterina Peshkova:

I intend working with the Bolsheviks as a free agent. I am fed up with the senseless academic opposition of *Novaya zhizn*...

Maxim Peshkov, then working for Felix Dzerzhinsky, confided to Lenin:

Papa is beginning to reform and move leftwards. Yesterday he even got into a serious argument with our SRs who, after 10 minutes, shamefully fled.

*Among several *noms de guerre* the revolutionary Vladimir Ilych Ulyanov (1870–1924) often used the pseudonym Nikolay Lenin. Alexey Maximovich Peshkov (1868–1936) became widely known in the 1890s, writing under the name of Maxim Gorky.
** (Lit. New Life): a daily Left Menshevik newspaper, published in Petrograd from April 1917 until July 1918.

When Fanny Kaplan attempted to assassinate Lenin on 30 August 1918, Gorky visited the wounded leader in the Kremlin and once again felt himself a Bolshevik. Later he would acknowledge:

> I did not understand what October [ie the 1917 October Revolution] meant until the attempted assassination of Vladimir Ilych. It was a very friendly meeting but, naturally, the sharp all-seeing little eyes of dear Ilych regarded my "deluded" person with evident regret . . . His attitude towards me was that of a strict teacher, a kind and concerned friend.

Friendship was restored and took a highly practical form. Gorky organized the World Literature publishing house, set up the all-Russian Commission for Improving Living Conditions of Scholars and Scientists, and directed the Expert Commission which had established a special depository for nationalized works of art and other precious objects. Thanks to these three organizations not only valuable cultural artefacts but many scholars, writers, artists and musicians survived. Living in Petrograd, surrounded by the hunger and desolation of the Civil War, Gorky abandoned his own work and set about saving the intelligentsia: finding them groats and dried fish, obtaining firewood, keeping their apartments and protecting them from arrest.

Without Lenin's support it would have been impossible to carry on these titanic labours. The two frequently met on Gorky's visits to Moscow. In mid-1919, however, a new cooling in relations occurred. Seeing that respect for culture and the Revolution were less and less compatible, and that his own efforts were making no difference, Gorky despaired.

Lenin again set about correcting his friend. He wrote:

> You are clearly losing your nerve . . . You go so far as to conclude that the Revolution cannot be made without the intelligentsia. This is simply an unhealthy overreaction! . . . You are not engaged in politics . . . but in a special form of activity where you are surrounded by the embittered bourgeois intelligentsia . . . It's understandable that you have made your-self unwell: you find life not only hard, you write, but "extremely unpleasant". I'll say! . . . I do not want to pester you with advice but I cannot help saying: you must radically change your situation and surroundings, your work and your place of residence, or else life may become irreversibly objectionable.

With ever greater insistence, Lenin advised Gorky to leave the country – advice that not only disappointed and irritated the writer but led him to suspect that the Leader simply wanted to rid himself of a persistent defender of the new regime's opponents.

Lenin would not let him rest:

My dear Alexey Maximovich,

... Overall the arrests of these Kadet (and sub-Kadet) types were necessary and correct.

When I read your frank opinion on the subject, I particularly remember a phrase of yours that stuck in my memory during our conversations (in London, in Capri and later): "We artists are crazy people."

That's just it! You pronounce extraordinarily wrathful words, and for what reason? Because a few dozen (or even perhaps a hundred) little Kadet and sub-Kadet gentlemen are in prison to *prevent plots* ... What suffering, just imagine! What injustice! ...

The workers and peasants are strengthening their intellectual forces in the struggle to overthrow the bourgeoisie and its hirelings, those petty intelligentsia and capitalist lackeys who imagine themselves the brains of the nation. They are, in fact, not its brains but its excrement ...

By early 1920 their relations were approaching breaking point. Gorky tried as hard as he might to maintain his role but he could not help dropping certain remarks. During Lenin's 50th birthday celebrations he compared the Soviet Leader to Peter the Great and, ranking him higher, nevertheless commented:

And suddenly we see a figure which fills me, though not a timid man, with horror. There is something frightening about the sight of this great man, who pulls the levers of history on our planet as he wishes ...

At the demonstration to mark the opening of the Second Congress of the Communist International, Lenin and Gorky still walked side by side. Behind the scenes Lenin acted otherwise. Commenting on Gorky's articles for the *Kommunisticheskii internatsional** he wrote:

There is *nothing* communist and a great deal that is anti-communist in these articles. Henceforth *such* articles must, under no circumstances, be printed in the journal.

In September 1920 a new crisis developed and it was then that the unknown letter to Lenin I discovered in the Lubyanka archives was written.

The adviser on cultural affairs to the Council of People's Commissars (the Soviet government), a certain Zaks, was obstructing the work of the new World Literature publishing house set up by Gorky and the publisher Grzhebin. Further changes were required, Zaks suggested, in the contract they had concluded with the People's Commissariat of Enlightenment.

The first draft of the letter, a laconic ultimatum, is dated 15 September 1920.

*(Lit. Communist International): the journal of the Comintern.

Dear Vladimir Ilych,
I shall not work with Zaks and do not want to talk to him. I am too old to allow others to mock me ... I see it's time for me to step down...

In a passage in the second undated and unfinished draft Gorky hinted at the malign influence of Zinoviev, then Petrograd Party leader and third in the unspoken Bolshevik hierarchy after Lenin and Trotsky. Zinoviev had been particularly insistent that *Novaya zhizn* be closed down and even once dared to have Gorky's flat searched, threatening his close friends and relatives with arrest.

Now thanks to the envy or whims of Comrade Zaks (whose only merit, so far as I know, is to be Zinoviev's brother-in-law) all my work is going to wrack and ruin... I am firmly decided. I have been patient long enough. It is better to die of hunger than permit all...

Gorky wrote the third and, evidently, final version of this letter the next day, 16 September 1920:

Dear Vladimir Ilych,
The proposed alterations to the agreement reached on 10 January with myself and Grzhebin totally annul that contract. It would have been better not to keep tormenting me for three weeks but simply say "the contract is annulled".

I have, in fact, been led by the nose not just for three weeks but over several months during which I have carried out an enormous task: 300 of Russia's best scholars and scientists have become involved in the wide popularization of learning and scientific knowledge – dozens of books have been commissioned, submitted and printed abroad, etc, etc.

Now all my work is going to wrack and ruin. So be it.

However, I have rendered some service to my country and the Revolution and am of too advanced an age to allow people to continue mocking me and treat my work with such negligence and stupidity.

I shall not work or discuss with Zaks and his kind. I also decline to continue working in the organizations established through my efforts: World Literature, the Grzhebin publishers,* the Expert Commission, the all-Russian Commission for Improving Living Conditions of Scholars and Scientists, and all other institutions where I have worked up until now.

I cannot behave otherwise. I am tired of this senseless muddle,
Best wishes,
A. Peshkov

*Private publishing house in Petrograd (1918–23), with branches in Moscow and Berlin.

АШ.-б.-　　　　　　　　　　　　　　　Копия

ВЛАДИМИР ИЛЬИЧ,

Пред"явленные мне поправки к договору 10-го Января со мной
и Гржебиным - уничтожают этот договор. Было бы лучше не вы̆тя
гивать из меня жилы в течение трех недель,а просто сразу сказать
"договор уничтожается".

В сущности меня водили за нос даже не три недели,а несколько
месяцев, в продолжение коих мною всетаки была сделана орромная
работа:привлечено к делу широкой популяризации научных знаний
около 300 человек лучших ученых России,заказаны,написаны и сдань
в печать заграницей десятки книг и т.д.

Теперь вся моя работа идет праком.Пусть так.

Но я имею пред родиной и революцией некоторые заслуги и доста
точностар для того,чтоб позволить и дальше издеваться надф мною,
относясь к моей работе так небрежно и глупо.-

Ни работать,ни разговаривать с Заксом и подобными ему я не
стану.И вообще я отказываюсь работать как в учреждениях создан
ных моим трудом - во "Всемирной Литературе",издательстве Гржеби
на, в "Экспертной Комиссии" в"Комиссии по улучшению быта ученых"
так и во всех других учреждениях, где работал до сего дня.

Иначе поступить я не могу.Я устал от безтолковщины.-

　　　　　　　　　Всего добраго. /подпись/ (А. Пешков)

16.IX-20г.

　　　　　　Верно:　　

The secret police transcript of Gorky's letter to Lenin, 16 September 1920. See p230.

231

　　　　　　ВЛАДИМИР ИЛЬИЧ,

　　Пред"явленные мне поправки к договору 10-го Января со мной и
Гржебиным - уничтожают этот договор.Было бы лучше не вытягивать из
меня жилы в течение трех недель,а просто сразу сказать "договор
уничтожается".

　　В сущности меня водили за нос даже не три недели,а несколько ме
сяцев в продолжении коих мною всетаки была сделана огромная работа:
"привлечено к делу широкой популяризации научных знаний около
300 чел. лучших ученых,России, заказаны,написаны и сданы в печать
заграницей десятки книг и т.д.

　　Теперь в угоду зависти или капризам т. Закс, за которым я знаю,
пока, одно достоинство: он шурин Зиновьева.- Теперь вся моя работа
идет прахом.Пусть так.

　　Но - я уж достаточно стар,я имею пред родиной и революцией солид
ныя заслуги,ценимыя иначе,а не степенью родства или свойства с
начальством и достаточно стар для того,чтоб позволить и дальше
издеваться надо мною,относясь к моей работе так небрежно и глупо.
Ни разговаривать,ни работать с Заксом и подобными ему я не стану.
Да и вообще я отказываюсь работать как в учреждениях,созданных
моим трудом - во "Всемирной Литературе",издательстве Гржебина, в
"Экспертной комиссии" в "Комиссии по улучшению быта ученых" так и
во всех других учреждениях,где работал до сего дня.- Я знаю,чем
это грозит мне,но мое решение твердо.Довольно я терпел.Лучше издох
нуть с голода, чем позволять все то,что до

　　　　　　　　　Верно: *М.Авантинский*

*Примечание: Согласно показаний Гуже-
бина - оригинал этот написан собстве-
норучно М. Горьким и адресован т. Ленину.*

　　　　　　　　　　　　　　　　М.Авантинский

21/III 22г.

Incomplete draft of Gorky's letter to Lenin, September 1920. See p 230.

Evidently the letter was sent and reached its addressee, for on 22 September Zaks was reprimanded and instructed by the Central Committee to immediately release six million roubles for the publishing house and requested "not to complicate or obstruct in any way the work of Comrade Gorky in Petrograd or abroad". The matter did not end there. Soon Gorky was complaining again to Lenin about Zaks and the affair dragged on for a year until Lenin ordered that Zaks be given a "super-scolding".... "Otherwise there will be a super-scandal: Gorky will leave and we shall be in the wrong ..."

In the same Lubyanka file lay another letter from Gorky to Lenin:

Dear Vladimir Ilych,

The Communist Vorobyov, an old Party member and a person with a long revolutionary past, has been arrested. Bukharin, Trilisser, Stasova and others all know him.

He was arrested because *Chernov's boots** were found in his flat.

Those who have set eyes on these boots, however, say that they are women's lace-up boots and belong to a certain Ida who, as could be established by an expert investigation, is indisputably a woman.

Supposing that this unpleasant business can give you little satisfaction, you will perhaps prevent its further development ...
A. Peshkov

Копия

А.М.-6.-

ВЛАДИМИР ИЛЬИЧ,

Арестован коммунист ВОРОБЬЕВ,старый партиец,человек с большим революционным прошлым.Его знают Бухарин,Трилиссер,Стасова и т.д..

Арестован он потому,что у него найдены сапоги ЧЕРНОВА.-

Но по словам людей зрячих эти сапоги суть - женския ботинки, принадлежащия некой Иде,несомненной женщине,что можно установить экспертизой.-

Полагая,что этот скверный анекдот не может быть приятен Вам,Вы, может быть прекратите дальнейшее развитие его...

/подпись/ (А.Пешков)

В е р н о: М/Авантунский

Another version of this letter (dated 24 September 1920) was taken from the Central Party Archive and only published in 1991. Even then, however, the story of the boots was ommitted and replaced with an eloquent string of omission marks ...

*Victor Chernov was a prominent Right SR, minister in the Provisional Government and speaker of the short-lived Constitutional Assembly in 1918. Before emigrating, he lived illegally for some time in Soviet Russia.

In this case, Gorky had his way. Lenin showed the letter to Dzerzhinsky who established that Vorobyov had sheltered SRs but only "through kindheartedness, not from any political sympathy". The case was handed over to the Party to resolve and Vorobyov died in 1938 – a year few of the old guard survived.

These typed copies of Gorky's letters in the Lubyanka file bear the code "A.M. 6" in the top left hand corner of each page. What this means the present employees of the Lubyanka would not explain. At the end of each text against the typed entry "checked" has been added a hand-written signature, "M. Slavatinsky". The unfinished second draft of the letter about Zaks bears the additional comment: "According to Grzhebin's testimony this passage was written out by Gorky himself and addressed to Comrade Lenin," and, again, the signature "M. Slavatinsky, 21 March 1922".

The surname was familiar. Reading the investigation files of other writers, such as the poet Alexey Ganin, shot in 1925, I had already come across the head of the OGPU Secret Political Section's 7th department. He was a merciless killer. Gorky was also among his charges, it seems, and Slavatinsky had taken testimony from the writer's friends and acquaintances. Moreover, he had done so in 1922 when Lenin and Dzerzhinsky were both alive and, evidently, had given their approval.

Lenin and Gorky met for the last time on 20 October 1920 at Yekaterina Peshkova's flat in Moscow. This is a famous event. It has been described countless times and was dramatized in Yutkevich's film *Man with a Rifle* (1938), with the "Appassionata" playing in the background. Yet it was not so much a meeting of close friends as a parting, during which Lenin insistently prompted Gorky to emigrate:

> Listening to your stories, one even starts to fear that he will not manage to write them all down. You're doing nothing to look after your health, moreover, and it has completely gone to pieces. Push off abroad, to Italy or Davos . . .
> If you won't go, then we'll have to send you . . .

This last phrase stuck firmly in Gorky's memory and long afterwards he would still return to it. Only two years were to pass before expulsion became a way of dealing with dissent, and dozens of members of the intelligentsia would find themselves abroad. Gorky did not know that then. Yet when someone truly needed to leave the country the government made no haste to let him go.

In the summer of 1921 the poet Alexander Blok was dangerously ill. Gorky bombarded Lenin and Lunarcharsky, The People's Commissar for Enlightenment, with telegrams: "Blok is suffering from scurvy and nervous exhaustion. Let him go to Finland for treatment. Here he will certainly perish!"

While they were debating whether to grant the poet an exit visa he died.

Eighteen days later on 25 August another poet, Nikolay Gumilyov, was shot as a member of a White Guard conspiracy though there was no evidence of his involvement. Gorky's intercession did not succeed in this case either.

With the deaths of Blok and Gumilyov in August 1921 began the martyrology of writers who fell victim to the new Soviet regime. The two poets meant nothing to Lenin and their names do not appear in his papers. For Gorky the individual had intrinsic value: for Lenin people were no more than raw material with which to feed the bonfires of world revolution. Gorky acknowledged this 10 years later, when he took a more sober view of past events:

> For Lenin contemporary reality was only material for building the future...

On 8 October 1921 Gorky wrote the Soviet leader a farewell letter before leaving for Europe. His last concern was for the three organizations in which he had invested so much energy and effort. Without him, however, they either rapidly ceased to function, like the World Literature publishers which closed in 1924, or became largely inactive.

Lunarcharsky remembered Lenin commenting on Gorky's departure:

> He has delicate nerves... He is an artist, after all. It's better if he leaves, gets some treatment and rest, and takes another look at all this from far off. Meantime we shall sweep our street and then we shall say: "Things are tidier here now, we can even invite our artist..."

Lunarcharsky added:

> And so Alexey Maximovich, hounded by his illness and the necessity of saving his life, which we all so valued,... was separated from us by distance. But this did not break our ties. A thread through which blood flowed, a vessel leading to the heart of Alexey Maximovich, remained...

One of those threads, as we can now see, was woven in the Cheka. It would never let the writer go. Towards the end of his life it became a mighty cable and at the other end would be a different Leader, Stalin.

The Gorky Specialists of the Cheka

Events stranded the writer between the intelligentsia and the authorities, between Russia and the West, and it was impossible to hold this position long. Torn between a desire to maintain his independence and a fear of being left behind by the locomotive of the Revolution, Gorky wavered constantly.

In summer 1922 leaders of the SR party were put on trial in Moscow. Learning of this in Heringsdorf, the small coastal town in northern Germany where he was then staying, Gorky wrote to Anatole France to raise public concern in Europe.

The letter was then published in the emigre Menshevik newspaper *Sotsialis-ticheskii vestnik:**

3 July [1922]

Esteemed Anatole France,
The trial of the Socialist Revolutionaries is taking the form of a cynical and public preparation for the murder of those who have sincerely served the cause of freeing the Russian people. I most earnestly request you to appeal once again to the Soviet authorities indicating that this crime is impermissible. Perhaps your weighty opinion will save the valuable lives of these socialists. I enclose a letter I have sent to one of the Soviet leaders.
Very best wishes,
Maxim Gorky

Gorky sent France a copy of his appeal to Rykov, the head of the Soviet government. Copies of both letters are preserved in the Lubyanka file.

1 July [1922]

Dear Alexey Ivanovich,
If the trial of the Socialist Revolutionaries ends in murder, it will be a premeditated and foul murder.
I request you to communicate my opinion to L.D. Trotsky and others. I hope that it does not surprise you since throughout the Revolution I have pointed out a thousand times to the Soviet authorities that it is senseless and criminal to destroy the intelligentsia in our illiterate and uneducated country.
I am now convinced that if the SRs are killed that crime will evoke a moral blockade of Russia on the part of socialist Europe.
Maxim Gorky

His appeal to Anatole France indeed had a wide resonance and alarmed the Kremlin. Lenin called Gorky's letter "vile" and Trotsky instructed that *Pravda* should "produce a *mild* article about the writer Gorky whom nobody in politics takes seriously. To be published in foreign languages". *Pravda* soon lashed out at Gorky in a strongly-worded attack entitled "Almost in the Lowest Depths": "By his political statements abroad Gorky is harming our Revolution. He is doing it great harm . . ."
Probably these appeals nevertheless influenced the treatment of the SRs. For although the Presidium of the Central Executive Committee confirmed the death

*(Lit. Socialist Herald): a Menshevik weekly set up in Berlin, which published between 1921 and 1963, noted for the accuracy of its reporting on the Soviet Union.

sentences passed by the Revolutionary Tribunal, it halted their implementation in return for a complete cessation of activities on the part of the SRs.

The publication of Gorky's book *On the Russian Peasantry* aroused even greater indignation among the "visionaries" of the Kremlin (as Wells had called Lenin). At this point an article entitled "Maxim Gorky Abroad" was added to the Lubyanka dossier. It is difficult to establish its origin since neither author nor date of composition are indicated: it may have been a survey compiled at the Lubyanka itself, a report by one of its many foreign agents, or a note prepared for publication.

> After his departure abroad Gorky was besieged by a great number of emigre newspapers trying to find out his attitude to the Russian Revolution and the Russian people.
>
> In summer 1922 Gorky published several articles in foreign newspapers that caused a sensation among the public in Europe and aroused condemnation in our press.
>
> In these articles, now issued as a separate brochure by I.P. Ladyzhnikov publishers under the title *On the Russian Peasantry*, Gorky pronounces a very unfavourable judgement on the Russian people and, in this connection, on the socialist revolution it has created. The overall conclusion... is of the "tragic nature of the Russian Revolution among semi-savage people" and the tragic nature of Bolshevism which was in *concept* a movement of urban and industrial culture, electrification, precise and complex organization and industrialization but in *execution* turned out to be an uprising of peasant spontaneity, cruel, savage, anarchic and destructive. Hence the conclusion: "With others of his kind, Lenin, an amoral person who regards the sufferings of the people with aristocratic indifference, a theoretician and dreamer with no acquaintance with real life, carried out a planetary experiment, and it has failed."
>
> Nevertheless, Gorky is inclined to consider all the sufferings brought on the Russian people by Bolshevism to be beneficial since they have strengthened and purified the popular spirit and will.
>
> Public opinion in Europe, naturally that which is anti-Soviet in mood, has made good use of Gorky's reputation among the masses.
>
> Recently Gorky, hitherto striking an apolitical pose and presenting himself as primarily a defender of Russian culture, has drawn closer to socialist anti-Bolshevik groups (Abramovich, Martov, Dan, Chernov, Slonim and Shreider).* On their initiative Z.I. Grzhebin publishers has begun to produce an historical journal, *Chronicle of the Revolution*,

*Menshevik and SR leaders.

which presents itself as a non-Party socialist publication and tries to give a dispassionate assessment of the revolutionary events of the past century. Gorky is participating very closely in the journal . . .

It is difficult to believe that the Menshevik and SR circles with which Gorky has become closely involved abroad, and which are so hostile to us, will be able to maintain a dispassionately historical tone in their journal.

Press reports about Gorky were thoroughly analyzed at the Lubyanka, publications in emigre newspapers were typed out, and translations were made from a variety of languages. Reading these pages, compiled by the tireless Gorky specialists of the Cheka, we can trace the twists and turns in his behaviour and see that inconsistency which was then discussed all over the world and which all interpreted to suit their own views.

One emigre paper accused Gorky of defaming the Russian people, another announced the decision of the Soviet government to arrest the writer if he crossed the Russian frontier. In autumn 1922 they all united to attack him when, following what seemed a total break with the regime, he suddenly announced his loyalty to Soviet Russia. The only policy with which he could not agree was its treatment of the intelligentsia. The Russian people as a whole did not require defending, in his view, but needed to be closely guided and controlled, something the Bolsheviks had proved very capable of doing.

Among other themes, Gorky raised the issue of anti-Semitism and the role of Jews in the Revolution (concerns of his that were either ignored later, or played down). In a discussion with the correspondent of the American newspaper *Forward* Gorky declared:

I believe that the appointment of Jews to the most dangerous and leading positions can often be explained as a provocation. Since many followers of the Black Hundreds have found their way into the Cheka these reactionaries have tried to ensure that Jews occupy the most dangerous and unpleasant posts.

Not only Gorky but all those who came in contact with him were brought under surveillance.

When he was in Heringsdorf the French writer and editor of *Les écrits nouveaux*, André Germain, came to visit him. An entranced Germain shared his impressions with Maria Bagration, another acquaintance of the Gorky household, who lived in Tbilisi, Georgia. The letter, intercepted and translated into Russian by the Georgian Cheka, was sent on to Moscow where it passed across Comrade Slavatinsky's desk.

If the portrait given by this unsuspecting informer is naïve, it is more truthful than the icon of the *Bolshevik Herald* subsequently offered by Soviet propaganda:

> Without asking my name, I was received with a simplicity and nobility that links the author of the "tramps" with the kings of Homer's shepherds. Without the slightest formality, I found myself in the presence of a carelessly dressed man, whose great height overwhelmed me, with a peasant face of powerful and severe features, beneath which one could guess at a fascinating and varied life, but one already drawing to its close . . .
>
> Gorky was above Bolshevism, neither accepting nor fighting against it. This is what those in authority cannot forgive him, and what disappoints the supporters of socialism when they can understand him. Saving art and learning, aiding the spiritual development of Russia – he was always attracted to such work. The Bolshevik bosses understood this (one may hate them but one cannot now dispute their severe majesty). They allowed him to direct artistic and scholarly commissions, to speak about the pure beauty of works of art in front of enraptured audiences of workers and soldiers . . . They demonstrated a certain flirtatious toleration of his free activities, like the Maenads carrying Orpheus' lyre in their midst, like our bloody forefathers of 1793 summoning the shades of the great departed to their feasts, like the tyrant Dionysius taking pride in Plato's company. With a heroic pride, Gorky refused to oblige them . . .
>
> [. . .]
>
> He deeply respects France, England and Italy. . . Suddenly the following strange phrase fell from his lips: "The Latin and English races must exercise a controlling influence in the world as more aristocratic than others . . ."

Vast numbers of Gorky's letters and, in particular, letters to Gorky were collected by the Lubyanka and, if published, would make a book in themselves. Here I am citing only unpublished materials or those fragments that were removed before publication. Gorky's letter to Yekaterina Peshkova from Marienbad on 3 March 1924 is typical of the latter. The following passages were always cut in the published versions:

> It is time, I think, to stop talking about my being under someone's influence. People should remember that I am 55 and have a very considerable experience of my own . . .
>
> . . . If I had really been susceptible to influence then long ago I would have submitted to Vladimir Ilych who was superb at influencing others and today I would be dining on diamonds, running around with ballerinas, and riding about town in the best automobiles . . .

This was written, we may note, only six weeks after the death of Lenin.

Gorky was then trying to find his place again in an unrecognizably changed world, a new era and a new Russia to which he came from the nineteenth century, the world of Tolstoy and Chekhov. He was not alone in this dilemma. Many felt uprooted and were searching for some source of stability and certainty. They turned to a living classic for an answer.

Several years earlier the young writer Sergey Alinov sent Gorky a short story and wrote asking him to give his opinion. In August 1924 Alinov wrote again. The metamorphosis was striking. Not only did Alinov send three books (including one full-length novel) instead of a modest manuscript. His tone was now quite different:

> My Dear Alexey Maximovich,
>
> . . . You advised me to "search for the truth" and when I asked where it might be found, you said: "The truth lies beyond the bounds of political views and programmes," but where exactly was unknown.
>
> [. . .]
>
> Dear oh dear, Alexey Maximovich! Russian writers have long sought the truth but they did not find it and probably this was because, like you, they also did not know what this truth was and where exactly it lay . . .
>
> The strangest things are happening in Russia, Alexey Maximovich, people are somehow thinking in a quite new way and if in the West people are less mobile than objects and if the free circulation of objects is enormous in the West and people there to this day are, to use an expression of Trotsky's, firmly anchored in their own social settings, then at home, in Russia, Alexey Maximovich, objects are less mobile than people . . .
>
> I attach myself not to all humanity but to that group of people who are now living around me and who need me now (if you wish, there is no other way to reach "humanity"); instead of "eternity" I concentrate my efforts on that section of time in which my contemporaries are now living, struggling, suffering and experiencing joy; instead of "justice" I attach myself to a political programme; instead of an unknown "truth", to a certain half-truth . . .

Alinov's views must have aroused the approval of the Lubyanka's Gorky specialists. Slavatinsky added a note: "This letter was written by the Communist Alinov to the writer Maxim Gorky."

A letter sent not even to Gorky but to his son Maxim Peshkov evoked a very different reaction. Although Mikhail Nikolaev, then employed by the Mezhdunarodnaya kniga (International Book) organization, had written a purely personal, teasing note to a friend, it was closely read by OGPU and added to the file. Slavatinsky sensed something here and after instructing that copies be added to the files on Gorky and on Kryuchkov (Gorky's secretary) he suggested, "We must have something on Nikolaev. Pay serious attention to him."

The OGPU was particularly interested in Gorky's work and views, and his attitudes towards the enemies of the Soviet regime. All such phrases and sentences were marked and noted. In a letter from Gorky to the writer Bogdanovich on 4 August 1925 the following phrase was underlined:

> A former well-born Russian will tell you how he earned money in Paris
> by publicly having intercourse with a ram. If only you knew what foul,
> rotten creatures these Russian emigres are ... And how ill-tempered!
> Well, the devil take them, they'll all be dead soon ...

Gorky's dossier was already a vast enterprise involving the labours of numerous Chekists. The letters are covered with notes: "To the 7th department", "For Comrade Agranov", "For Comrade Slavatinsky: to be filed", "For Comrade Gendin: Gorky file" and "Checked against the original, V. Sheshken". One signature after another decorates their pages.

On a Long Lead

The second period covered by the file extends from 1926 to 1928. Lenin had died and Stalin was taking control. The blunt Dzerzhinsky was also dead and had been effectively replaced by the devious Yagoda: Menzhinsky, the official new head of OGPU (the renamed Cheka), was ill for much of the time. The OGPU was evolving into a vast secret police organization that operated not only in the Soviet Union but also abroad.

Now there were two who did most of the work on Gorky's file. One, unidentified, signed himself "K.S." The other we have already encountered, Nikolay Khristoforovich Shivarov. In the 1930s he would beat a confession from Klyuev and intimidate Mandelstam, and it was he who opened the file on Platonov and many others. For the time being, however, he was still evidently learning his trade.

The writer lived at his villa in Sorrento, with its view of Vesuvius, a world-famous figure surrounded by family, friends and guests. He worked incessantly, compiling his epic *Life of Klim Samgin*, writing articles and memoirs, and keeping up a very wide correspondence. Nothing, it might seem, could have been better. His health, it is true, had "gone to pieces", to use Lenin's expression, but that was already history and evidently irreversible. As for nostalgia, Gorky declared he did not know of such an affliction.

Within the loving and devoted household all used touching nicknames: Gorky was Duka, his daughter-in-law Nadya was Timosha, his new wife and assistant Maria Budberg was Titka and his secretary, Pyotr Petrovich Kryuchkov, was Pepe Kryu ... His son Maxim and tiny granddaughters Marfa and Darya were with him. Then there were others who were almost members of the family: the artist Ivan Rakitsky, "Nightingale", as indolent as he was gifted, had once flown into their house, while still in Petrograd, and never left; and bustling Lipa, the medical sister Olimpiada Chertkova, was another voluntary helper... Yekaterina Peshkova, no longer Gorky's wife but still a faithful friend, spent long periods with them. The French army officer Zinovy Peshkov* would pay visits. Yakov Sverdlov's brother, he had earlier been adopted by Gorky...

Soon Gorky would be 60. It was time to decide where he stood. He was, in one sense, an emigre, if an involuntary one. When he once learned that Krupskaya, Lenin's widow, had drawn up a list of books to be withdrawn from libraries which contained the Bible, the Koran, Dante and Schopenhauer, he resolved to renounce his Soviet citizenship and even began to draw up a declaration to that effect. But then he set it aside.

He was criticized by both camps. Mayakovsky announced that Gorky was a corpse and of no further use to literature. The White Guards in Paris took particular delight in condemning him, and his essay about Lenin was described as the greatest crime in the history of Russian literature.

An unknown letter preserved in the Lubyanka archive to his young friend the writer Vsevolod Ivanov in the Soviet Union gives a good idea of his views at the time.

8 September 1927

...I was very surprised when you wrote: "It is painfully difficult to understand and accept that the Russian peasant is no Christian, no humble servant of God, but a visionary bandit." I did not expect that you could have imagined such a thing, or consider acceptable the literary idealization of the peasantry by the Narodniks.** I was never thus afflicted although the Narodniks tried hard to bring me up to hold just such views. Moreover, I am congenitally incapable of understanding how the masses, a nation or a class can be idealized. I am a bad Marxist and am not inclined to shift responsibility for life from the individual to the masses, the collective, a Party or some group.

Moreover, I know there is more life in a peppercorn than in a handful of poppy seed. It would be dishonest and laughable, I believe, if I thought otherwise. I shall not deny, naturally, that the peasant is a bandit, predator and anarchist but he is not fated, I think, to remain so for long

---

*Zinovy Peshkov fought in the French army during the First World War. When France was liberated in 1944 he returned as a general and would be sent as De Gaulle's representative to South Africa and China. Died in 1966.
**The "populist" radicals of the later nineteenth century who were the intellectual and political predecessors of the Socialist Revolutionaries.

now. He was a robber and anarchist because, of old, he had no belief in the stability of his social existence and this lack of faith also accounts for his "dreaminess". Personally I would not have wished him such a faith since these are not the times when one should believe blindly. The human world has reached an era that audaciously shakes and undermines any and every faith and certainty, while so-called inorganic matter gives malign evidence of its own instability.

The drama of emotions concealed in your words, seems more or less intelligible to me. When I imagine all the ignorant and chaotic vastness of the Russo-Chinese, Indian and any other rural areas, and see in front of it the very small, quite crazy Russian revolutionary – even if he has found Archimedes' lever – then such a balance of forces arouses a certain anxiety in me for the fate of the Russian revolutionary, and for you in particular.

You are profoundly right when you say: "What we have to understand and experience exceeds the knowledge, understanding and even the emotions of our fathers." That's very true. It greatly exceeds them . . .

Evidently, you do not lead an easy life. I very much advise you to visit Italy. "Loafing about" here is pleasant and amusing. You will rest, think, and take a look at yourself. It's time that you wrote something big.

I hear nothing about Babel. I would be disappointed if again he does not visit me. I greatly value Babel and rate him highly.

Only yesterday I got back on my feet and was able to write again. A few days ago I first felt how near that unpleasant thing they call "death" is to a person. I am full of camphor which they injected me with five times, camphor and some other liquid as well. I feel revolting . . .
My very best wishes,
A. Peshkov

This is not at all the Gorky we knew and it is understandable why the letter was kept under lock and key until now. In another unpublished letter to Vsevolod Ivanov from early 1928 Gorky announced his firm intention of returning to Russia. The letter opens, however, with anger against the Russian emigration:

Dear friend,
. . . The real reason why your namesake [Vyacheslav Ivanov]* refused to publish his verse in *Krasnaya nov* was of course the fear that he would compromise himself in front of "right-minded people". If he had "broken his fast" by cooperating with your journal, the emigres would have bitten off his fingers, ears and nose. And something else as well.

*Poet, critic and scholar, Vyacheslav Ivanov (1866–1949) was the host of the famous "Tower" literary salon in pre-Revolutionary Petersburg and principal theorist of Symbolism. Permitted to leave Russia in 1924 he settled in Italy, converting to Catholicism two years later.

They are going quite off their heads here: Sergey Bulgakov has written a book about the *Unflinching Conception.* Yevlogy together with Struve* has thought up a new religion which adds the Holy Wisdom to the Trinity, and so on. Their God-building activities do not prevent them from a virulent hatred of one another.

Yes, I shall come in May and, it seems, we shall not meet: why the devil must you go to Tashkent? And why have you sent me volume 2, without first sending volume 1? I very much like reading you, send it.

This jubilee begins to make me feel famous, like Mary Pickford, and I am already afraid that they will suggest marrying me off to Serafimovich.** Listen, there is a colony near Kharkov for "socially dangerous" children that has been in existence now for six years. I am its honorary president. The organization, its conditions and its life are extraordinarily interesting. I correspond with the children and for each of my letters I receive 22 from them, the same number as the chiefs heading the various work detachments there. It's terribly intriguing.

Is there someone in *Krasnaya nov* who might go there and describe the colony? It's worth it.

But there's no need to mention my name.

Best wishes,

Yours, A. Peshkov

In the first letter to Ivanov Gorky rejected the Russian peasant. Here he rejects the Russian intelligentsia which he had defended, at one time, from the new barbarians and to which he considered he himself belonged. Now it was Soviet methods of upbringing that interested him. His vanity was flattered by the attention of delinquent children, as though he did not understand that this was a performance staged specially for him, and one of those threads by which he was being attracted and entangled.

The Lubyanka archive on Gorky offers a very mixed selection of documents. Quite possibly, not only intercepted and copied correspondence was included here but also items provided by OGPU agents and some taken from the writer's own archive which was removed from his house immediately after his death. Witnesses testify that part of Gorky's archive, an entire suitcase-full, was taken from Sorrento to London by his last wife Maria Budberg. There are grounds for believing that this suitcase eventually also found its way to the Lubyanka.

*Reference to Yevlogy, Bishop of Russian Church Abroad, and Pyotr Struve, leading members of the emigration in France.
**Alexander Serafimovich (1863–1949), author of the classic revolutionary novel *Iron Flood* (1924), had contributed to the *Znanie* almanach founded by Gorky in 1903 and wrote in a similar style.

After so many years it is difficult to establish the truth with any certainty. The Gorky materials passed through many hands and were partially dispersed. With some frustration the KGB archivists told me that the Party archive had constantly "robbed" them (Gorky, for some reason, came under the Party's jurisdiction) and at various times other items were passed on to different state depositories. That which remains at the Lubyanka, however, is invaluable.

Among those who wrote to Gorky and with whom he corresponded were people of every background, occupation and ethnicity, from the famous to the quite unknown. His correspondence testifies to the enormous work he carried out with young writers. His efforts here were phenomenal and unrivalled – no one did as much as Gorky: he was "mid-wife" to an entire generation of Soviet writers, among whom were indisputable masters like Babel, Olesha and Paustovsky. Yet the greatest discovery here is not his correspondence with other writers but the letters he received from ordinary people in the Soviet Union who simply wanted to open his eyes to what was going on there.

Dear Alexey Maximovich,
The cruelty and bloodthirsty nature of the Bolsheviks can be seen from the numerous executions that are now taking place here, even for petty political and other crimes like embezzlement. It has been shown by the numerous murders of our best people who are wholeheartedly devoted to the interests of ordinary people; it has been shown by the bestial vengeance exacted on the children of the tsar . . .

Do you really feel no indignation at the cruelty of the ruling party? Do you not feel obliged, exercising your authority and influence, to show that party quite how loathsome and vile it is to adopt such a casual disregard for human life? Are you not obliged to expose the hypocrisy of its outrage and protests when other governments apply incomparably weaker punishments and repressive measures to members of the Communist Party who have resorted to violent methods for seizing power? At one time, our best people – L. Tolstoy, V. Solovyov, V. Korolenko – raised their voices against such vileness on the part of the tsarist government. Scholars and scientists also protested and discussed the matter from various points of view. And now? We all remain silent as if our mouths were full of water. There is no protest or condemnation, as if all this was correct. As for praising the Soviet authorities, any number of willing participants can be found: neither do scholars and scientists feel any inhibition here. This is very sad because it demonstrates the appalling moral decline of our intelligentsia . . .

Most probably the reason lies in a lack of courage, as one becomes convinced wherever one looks. When a regime like the present is in power, all fear freely and sincerely to express their opinions about a political issue or action taken by the government. People are afraid to speak, afraid to write in private letters and only whisper to one another, glancing about them as they do so...

If you do not know this, then you do not know Russia today. If you do know but are not raising your voice then you are committing a serious sin. Of course, Alexey Maximovich, you respected and highly regarded L. Tolstoy, Chekhov and Korolenko.* How do you think they would have regarded the Soviet regime and its ruling party? Undoubtedly, they would have condemned it most severely. They would not have remained silent.

A.K.

This letter, like many others, was understandably anonymous and bore no return address. Amazingly, Gorky either did not appreciate this or kept up the pretence that he did not understand, firmly shutting his eyes and blocking his ears.

He even wrote angry rebuttals in the Soviet press of his critically-minded correspondents: "To Anonymous and Pseudonymous Correspondents", "To the Mechanical Citizens of the USSR", and "Once More about the Mechanical Citizens". Having always proclaimed that love for his fellow human beings was his only faith, Gorky proved impervious to the piercing cries of the suffering, humiliated and oppressed people of his native land. All letters sent abroad, especially to such a person as himself, were strictly censored and led to the surveillance of their authors. Even anonymity and pseudonyms were not always enough to protect them. Perhaps Gorky simply did not understand that?

Evidently not, otherwise he would not have written to Kryuchkov his secretary:

> *Rul*** suspects that I pass letters from "mechanical citizens" on to the GPU. They have no shame, the scoundrels.

Yet there is much proof in the file that the stormy petrel had now become a decoy, used to attract and trap dissenters.

For instance, on a letter sent to Gorky from Moscow by one Andrian Kuzmin, Shivarov added, "Original has been photographed, and [the copy] kept by Comrade Medvedev. He has been instructed to keep a watch on Kuzmin":

---

*A well-known writer and publicist, Vladimir Korolenko (1853–1921) spoke out most famously during the notorious anti-Semitic Beilis case of 1910. A striking series of critical letters to Lunarcharsky, written during the Civil War just before his own death, went entirely unanswered.
**(Lit. Rudder): an emigre newspaper published in Berlin, 1920–31. Initially a Kadet publication, it was edited by Vladimir Nabokov Sr.

Citizen Maxim Gorky,

A few words about your article marking the tenth anniversary of the October Revolution and your reply of 23 December to "Anonymous and Pseudonymous Correspondents".

Let me warn you: the author of these lines is 52 and has never (before or now) belonged to any party or privileged group. Consequently, there is no specially hostile attitude to either the past or the present [in what he writes]. This is a practical view of life, as it really is ... Your article (both the one and the other) aroused a great deal of rumour and gossip which could roughly be summarized as follows: Gorky is having it both ways. On the one hand, he seems to give his approval to all that has happened since 1917 and, on the other hand, it is as if he does not ... It is, of course, fine to praise things that you have not yourself experienced. Once I read a somewhat poetic description of a cavalry attack during a battle and thought to myself: entertaining and attractive, but what a good thing the author himself did not take part ...

You live far away. In good time, you declined the pleasure of becoming a blind and mute object of an experiment that was conducted against your wish and that of almost all the population of your country ...

And, in general, taking a sober view, without malice or blindness, is it possible to sympathize with something that is being done against the will of almost all those who surround you? One can be indignant about any cruelty but one must not fail to mention that this experiment has reduced the country to a kind of "cannibalism". As far as your historical analogies with Peter the Great's time are concerned, you are stretching the point, in my view. We should not seek a moment comparable to that we are now experiencing in the time of Peter and his reforms but, if you will, in the reign of Emperor Paul I.

After that extravagant and embittered man came to power he tried, until he was himself removed, to forcibly transform the Russian into a Prussian, making him run the gauntlet and striking him with the flat of the sword ... In Petersburg, in the Hermitage, there is a picture by Professor Sharleman called "Parade in St Petersburg"... Peasants, dressed up as Prussians, stand motionless in the frost, in pigtails and wigs, wearing no more than their dress uniform. People put up with this for six years.

We are now also approaching the time when all are beginning to be fed up with the "playing at socialism" of Paul's heirs. And there are signs that the heirs themselves are sobering up, prompted by a sense of self-preservation. All are therefore amazed by your article – for 10 years he was silent and suddenly he begins to sing the praises . . . of something which even its creators are beginning to regard differently, and which has clearly led to a dead end.

You chose a bad moment to speak out but, incidentally, writers always were bad politicians.

The announcement in the Soviet press that Gorky was coming back to Russia prompted many of the letters preserved here. One of them began:

You will see for yourself what the USSR is like at the present moment. Don't go, like a VIP, for this purpose to the Volkhov hydro-electric dam or to the rebuilt factories and plants, as foreign delegations do. They only see the external, calm side of our culture, only observing what they are shown . . . Do the opposite. Forget that you are a well-known writer. Do not travel anywhere with official guides, as if you were under arrest, but . . . go wherever your heart leads, as the nation's observer, as you did in your youth. . . Without a doubt, you will soon see new divisions in the nation and among them new tendencies, new movements in thought. These new developments . . . penetrate everywhere under the tireless administrative influence of the authorities and as a consequence of a material dependence of the masses on the central authorities that is unheard-of and unprecedented in capitalist states.

At the head of this movement are a small handful of people, Lenin's associates . . .

The country was preparing to meet Gorky's return by celebrating his sixtieth birthday and remarks about the forthcoming jubilee peppered the newspapers. One of those who wrote to Gorky enclosed a cutting from the Moscow evening paper *Vechernaya Moskva*, so that the writer would appreciate how the regime was enforcing universal love for the proletarian writer:

Gorky Jubilee in Higher Education
The Main Administration for Vocational Training yesterday sent a special letter. . . to the boards of all higher education institutions and other educational bodies under its control. Between 26 March and 1 April celebrations should be held in all educational institutions with lectures about the life and work of Gorky, accompanied by literary and musical performances. By Gorky's sixtieth birthday (29 March) exhibitions devoted to his work should be organized.

The accompanying letter was anonymous:

248

29 March 1928

Dear Sir,

As a Russian scholar who has been working, now, for 25 years in higher education, I consider myself obliged, despite instructions, to avoid taking any part in the official celebrations of your jubilee. Holding your brilliant literary talent in high esteem, I consider such celebrations to be equally offensive to you, our greatest living Russian writer, and to us, as scholars and representatives of the Russian intelligentsia which always attributed serious value to similar celebrations only if they were a free expression of public sympathy and emotion.

But I am writing to you at this time not so much to give you some idea of how spectacles of this kind are organized in Soviet Russia. With a heavy heart, I want to tell you of the incomprehension that disturbs and provokes involuntary indignation among a great many Russian people, who have long been accustomed to take pride in you as one of the praiseworthy Russian writers whose names are linked with the best Russian masters of the written word. I refer to your articles in the Soviet press. There you consistently speak out with (you must forgive me) an extraordinary degree of flippancy against the very same people, against those remaining representatives of the Russian intelligentsia who have not yet been finished off by the Soviet regime. In so doing you conceal behind your great name the outrageous falsehood of contemporary Russian life. From your fine distance, enjoying complete freedom and independence (if under the protection of the fascist government and blessed sky of Italy), inhabiting a superb villa with no limits on your living space, you repeat, after the official lying press of Soviet Russia, what those who have lived through the last 10 years in Russia itself know to be falsehoods – untruths that cannot be justified by any, even the highest, goals and ideals. You do so, moreover, before the eyes of the entire civilized world (infected as its ruling circles may be by bourgeois falsehood).

. . . I know that you will throw this letter into the waste basket with a contemptuous smile as one more anonymous, pitiful and feeble outpouring of an enemy of the proletariat etc. Yes, you are a free writer and in your letters to the Soviet press, using that monopoly, you can say whatever you wish in defence of the Soviet authorities, you can harass us without any fear of reprisal. You cannot hear anything from us in reply: our hands our bound and the Soviet gag is forced into our mouths. But knowing this, do you suppose that you are acting as a champion of the free word?

. . . Even were we backward people who do not understand the majesty of the cosmic tasks and noble slogans of the social revolution

249

(though that is not the case at all), does it not seem to you that opponents should be treated honestly? One does not strike someone whose hands are bound. I do not wish to believe, as so many are saying, that you are knowingly writing falsehoods or that you have sold out to the Soviet authorities. If I thought that, of course, I would not have written to you. Yet I cannot fathom out why you take on yourself the right to judge so hastily that which you do not know, have not seen and are not yourself experiencing.

From the depths of Russia, the voice of a rural truth-seeker carried all the way to Sorrento. If not highly educated, conscience prompted the author to write to Gorky:

We peasants, living far from the centre of Mother Russia, having heard of your coming back, will be joyful to see you return. We hope that your visit will correct our blunders and the mistakes of our rulers, since there are great many of them somehow – embezzlement, petty tyranny, that even goes so far as counter-revolution and this is because, we peasants believe, the labour law was not implemented openly.

There is a great deal more to tell you. We have so many rulers locally – our petty bosses, like the rural soviets – and they just behave like royalty, almost never carrying out the laws we have and, in particular, the Land Code . . . And if someone is a communist, ie, a Party member, then you cannot get anywhere near him and his word is law . . . Yet if I was bold enough to say he was wrong then, first, you risk being called an unfriendly element and, second, you will be told that it is being done for reason of Party discipline. They pass you on, higher and higher, for instance, to the district and then even the province supports him but what he's doing is plain counter-revolution . . .

Therefore we are asking you, our guest, to take this into account. Everything written here is true. Such an important cause is being badly carried out and it's bad when Communists spoil and mess things up under pretext of communism. And the court somehow does not follow the existing law properly. They are not afraid of the law but of each other . . . So we are asking you to help our leaders to implement a simple, strict law so that each of us in the village will know it [. . .] So he will not fear he will be harassed and we need this quickly
Respectfully yours
Ivan Bol —
peasant

Private guests who came to visit Gorky from the Soviet Union also told him a great deal. They likewise were added to the GPU lists. When looking through the investigation files of other writers, for instance, I came across a report by agent "Sayanov":

> Great attention should be paid to those whom Gorky has invited to visit him abroad in Sorrento. It is very likely that here also a certain number of enemies have wormed their way in, deceiving an honest and open-hearted old man.
>
> I know of one such "visitor", invited to Italy by Gorky, from the words of P.P. Kryuchkov: Zubakin B.M., an unsuccessful poet and, it seems, historian of religion ...

Once someone brought our commission an entire packet of the carefully preserved verse of this excellent poet. I spoke about Zubakin on television, showed his portrait, read some of his poems and, as always in such cases, numerous letters followed. Many remembered him and his tragic death, during exile in the North. Perhaps this denunciation by "Sayanov" contributed to his arrest ...

. It is unlikely that Gorky had any idea of the extent of this control and surveillance. He felt suspicion, occasionally expressed indignation, but he held different views: these solitary voices were drowned out by others – his visitors, his family, his secretary and the Soviet press – constantly asserting that his place was in his native land, it was there he was needed most of all. And indeed, where were most of his readers? Where was he most published? Recently he had received a considerable sum from the Soviet government, for books already published and for those still only being prepared for the press.

With the same determination that Lenin had once shown in pushing Gorky into emigration, Stalin now tried to draw him back. His unwillingness to return was discussed everywhere and cast doubt on the country's leadership: Gorky applauded the regime but preferred to go on living in fascist Italy. Stalin wanted to place Gorky in charge of literature and bring it under control, establishing a hierarchy there like that already operating within the Party. "Just look up in the skies," well-wishers told Gorky, "even the birds fly north every spring ..."

A Stifling Embrace

In 1928, after an absence of almost seven years, Gorky was again in Russia where, in Lunacharsky's words, "the triumphant proletariat ecstatically seized him in its gigantic embrace".

His first trips were triumphal tours of Soviet achievements. He would spend the summer in the USSR and then return, each autumn, to Sorrento. Stalin himself found Gorky a home in Moscow, an art nouveau town house, not far from the Kremlin, built off the central Boulevard ring at the turn of the century for the millionaire Ryabushinsky. Immediately it became a meeting-place for the Soviet leaders and the country's artists and writers. Gorky was also allocated two enormous dachas with their own security guards, in the Crimea and at Gorki outside Moscow.

Triumphant fanfares greeted the writer's return. What was going on at a different level can be established by examining another layer of evidence in the Lubyanka archive, the investigation files of Yagoda, Gorky's secretary Kryuchkov and the critic Leopold Averbakh who were arrested in 1937 as enemies of the people and members of a counter-revolutionary conspiracy.

The OGPU immediately began to manipulate Gorky and placed him under secret surveillance. He was also personally supervised by Yagoda. On Gorky's very first trip back to Russia Yagoda, who originally came from the same city, Nizhny Novgorod, paid him a visit. They were even relations of a kind: Yagoda's wife Ida was Sverdlov's niece and her uncle, Zinovy, had been adopted by Gorky (taking his real surname Peshkov).

To begin with, we may suppose, Yagoda kept a careful and respectful distance from the writer. Gradually, however, with each succeeding visit, he became more and more familiar. He was under direct instructions from Stalin to win the writer back to the Soviet Union. Yagoda also began to recruit his own personal agents in the Gorky household. Undoubtedly the next link in this chain was Pyotr Kryuchkov.

Gorky's secretary was a short, snub-nosed, balding blond, who wore pince-nez; stocky and well-fed, he did not have a striking appearance. Those who met him remarked on his unusually hairy hands and the ring set with a large alexandrite which he wore all the time. The stone had a history of its own. It had been brought to Gorky from the Urals and he had it set in a ring and gave it to his second wife, Maria Andreeva. Then the alexandrite moved from her hand to that of Pepe Kryu, who for a time was also her secretary.

Kryuchkov began working for Gorky in 1918. Gradually he took control of the writer's public, literary and publishing contacts and finally became not only his secretary but a kind of double who often stood in for Gorky and spoke on his behalf. To give him credit, this intelligent methodical man was a great help to the writer and became quite indispensable to him in his work and daily life.

We do not know if Kryuchkov had ties with the OGPU (from 1934 known as the NKVD) before he became acquainted with Yagoda but thereafter his double role is beyond doubt. In prison he told how Yagoda, until he himself was arrested, constantly visited Kryuchkov's flat, and that they also often met at Gorky's house. "We became friendly," said Kryuchkov.

Q. Did you meet Yagoda at the NKVD building?

A. About five to six times a year I visited Yagoda in his office.

Q. On what business did you go to see him?

A. I often visited him in connection with my trips to Italy, to see Gorky. And sometimes about money.

Q. What money?

A. In 1932, for instance, Yagoda on his own initiative gave me $4000 to buy a car for Gorky abroad. In 1933 Yagoda offered me $2000 (although I did not request them), justifying the offer by saying that we did not have enough money to wind up the villa in Sorrento. I took the money without signing a receipt...

This extraordinary confession means that Gorky was being financed by the OGPU when he was still living in Italy. Gorky could not help but know of the Lubyanka's generous presents and this adds another, extremely prosaic aspect to his acquaintance with Yagoda. Furthermore, as Kryuchkov's testimony revealed, money was supplied not just to Gorky but to other members of his family:

Kryuchkov. Several times I received hard currency from Yagoda for M.I. Budberg, also without receipt. In 1936 Yagoda handed me and Gorky's daughter-in-law, N.A. Peshkova, 400 pounds sterling, again for Budberg (they had asked for 300). Finally in September 1936* N.A. Peshkova told me that she had received a large sum in dollars through Yagoda's personal secretary Bulanov. Peshkova commented, with embarrassment: "Why did they foist such a large sum on me?"

Interrogator. What explanation is there for Yagoda's generosity?

Kryuchkov. It was, of course, quite intentional. These bribes to people close to Gorky were a part of the strategy he had been following, especially since the beginning of 1931 – for his own purposes he wanted to monopolize control of the Gorky household...

Kryuchkov described this insistent attention in some detail. It reached the point where Gorky, after several of Yagoda's lengthy and detailed stories, exclaimed in exasperation: "Why does he tell me things I should know nothing about?" Yagoda even confided to Gorky how the OGPU had organized the kidnapping of the White General Kutepov** – perhaps he was secretly hoping that Gorky would make him the hero of one of his works?

During his interrogation, Kryuchkov mentioned two women as being particularly close to Gorky.

*In other words, after Gorky had died.
**Alexander Kutepov, leader of an anti-Bolshevik organization in France, disappeared after being seized in broad daylight in Paris on 26 January 1930.

Maria Budberg, alias Zakrevskaya, alias Benckendorff, was known as Titka or Moura in the Gorky household. She was an enchanting and daring woman who had several notable lovers: the intelligence agent Bruce Lockhart, H.G. Wells and, of course, Gorky, whose unofficial third and last wife she became. In *The Iron Woman* Nina Berberova tried to solve the mystery of Budberg's life, and gave up, defeated. It is thought that she was a double agent, working for both the British and the Soviet Union, but no proof, if it still exists, has been unearthed to confirm or dispute this.

There is one indirect piece of evidence, apart from the money that changed hands, suggesting that Budberg had links with the OGPU. Kryuchkov's investigation file opens with a list of eight people whom he "compromised". Moura, marked down as a "participant in an anti-Soviet Rightist organization", was the only one not to be arrested and shot. In 1938 when Yagoda and the others were on trial she was, it is true, already far away in London. Yet it would have presented little difficulty for the NKVD to track her down there.

The second woman mentioned by Kryuchkov was Nadya Peshkova, Timosha, Gorky's daughter-in-law and the mother of his grand-daughters. Yagoda attempted an even deeper penetration into the Gorky household through Timosha. In this case, however, he was evidently motivated not just by calculation but a genuine passion. All noted the beauty and exceptional femininity of Nadya Peshkova – she was, commented Romain Rolland, "young, very beautiful, merry, simple and delightful" – her gifts as an artist, and her talent in running the household.

There is no evidence that she had an affair with Yagoda, only countless stories of the importunate and immodest attentions of the ubiquitous Genrikh which embarrassed the object of his affection. So against her will or willingly, she also came, like all members of the household, under the influence of Yagoda and could on occasion help him, at least with some information.

Many of the numerous cooks, chauffeurs, librarians, gardeners and cleaners at Gorky's Moscow house and his two dachas could also have been recruited and used for intelligence purposes. They were not necessarily agents of the Lubyanka, however. Many helped the secret police quite sincerely and voluntarily, as loyal Soviet citizens or acting, as they thought, in Gorky's best interests.

There were also certain Chekists who often visited the writer, like Simeon Firin and Matvey Pogrebinsky. Gorky was very stirred by the idea of Communist re-education and these two men were in charge of the use of forced labour to re-educate the misguided masses: Firin headed the White Sea canal camps and was deputy head of the Gulag, while Pogrebinsky was in charge of special communes for ordinary criminals.

So Gorky was surrounded by a tight cordon of the Lubyanka's servants on his visits to Russia and, especially, after he returned for good in 1933. Even his daily supplies were entrusted to the same NKVD department that looked after the wants of Stalin and the Politburo and Gorky's house was linked by a direct telephone line to Yagoda's office.

Cut off from the outside world, from real life, Gorky made no effort to break free, accepting the tributes and privileges he was offered without protest.

The NKVD also had a large number of informers among the writers. I came across reports by at least four such "secret associates", their identity concealed behind pseudonyms, who all used to visit Gorky and regularly passed on what they heard and saw. The writer's wider literary contacts were, to a great extent, imposed and not freely chosen.

Yagoda, during his interrogation, told how he

> introduced a group of writers to Gorky – Averbakh, Kirshon and Afinogenov – and Firin and Pogrebinsky were sometimes with them. These were my people whom I gave money to sing my praises, not only at Gorky's house but among the intelligentsia as a whole. They cultivated the idea that I was a major statesman, an important figure and a humane man. I organized their intimacy with Gorky for my own purposes.

Kryuchkov gave similar evidence:

> These people formed Yagoda's special network around Gorky. Apart from everything else, their role was to elevate Yagoda in Gorky's eyes, advertising his role in re-education through labour, ie, in a field that particularly interested Gorky. For his part, Yagoda tried with all his might to raise the importance of this network, and have it put in charge of literary organizations.

Leopold Averbakh provided this account during his interrogation:

> I and a number of my comrades often visited Gorky and were firmly linked to him. In practice we were drawing him into our group struggle. Yagoda used to mock us: we were not doing enough to involve Gorky, did not know how to use our ties with him, and were being unnecessarily fastidious. The basic theme of his thoughts, again quite typical of his approach, boiled down to the following: in a struggle all methods are permissible, you should abandon your romantic moralizing and inhibition, you members of the rotten intelligentsia, and make use of Gorky as a force . . .

To begin with Gorky had not liked Averbakh. A loud, pushing and self-assured demagogue, he was more capable of intrigue than original writing.

Stocky and forceful, with a round shaven head like a billiard ball, and a confident trained voice, he resembled the hero of the new era, the Komsomol activist, pioneer and leader. He could hardly boast about his books so instead he constantly hinted at his closeness to the Party elite: his mother was Yakov Sverdlov's sister, his wife the daughter of Bonch-Bruevich, a close Lenin associate, and his own sister Ida was Yagoda's legal wife. The all-pervasive web of Sverdlov family connections also provided a link through his uncle, Zinovy Peshkov, with Gorky. In a sense, even they were related, if very distantly.

As the leader of the Russian Association of Proletarian Writers, RAPP, Averbakh laid a claim to control all literature. As a relation of Yagoda he had access to devious means to get his way. At times he would prove stronger even than Gorky. When the latter tried to defend Zamyatin, Bulgakov and Pilnyak from the persecution of RAPP, arguing that they were not obstructing the course of history by their activities, Gorky's words went unheeded: his article in their defence was not published. Averbakh and his kind were then in control of editorial policy.

Yagoda did everything to ensure that Gorky appreciated his brother-in-law. When Gorky was living in Moscow the two dropped by together almost every weekend. Averbakh even stayed in Sorrento for several months and there he was able to gain the trust of Gorky. In 1937, in his statement to Yezhov, now Commissar of Internal Affairs, the arrested Averbakh said:

> I particularly tried to hurry Gorky's move from Sorrento and when I went to Italy Yagoda, for reason of his own plans, asked me to use every means to convince Gorky that he should leave Italy for good.

Averbakh returned from Sorrento "happy and proud". Gorky had already packed his cases for his next trip to the Soviet Union and Averbakh had succeeded in a request of his own: Gorky had allied himself with RAPP. He hurried to report to the Central Committee that Gorky considered that RAPP was carrying out the Party line in literature.

Averbakh had miscalculated, however. The Party had its own plans for dealing with literature. A few months later in April 1932, quite out of the blue, the Central Committee decree on the "perestroika" or "reorganization of literary-artistic organizations" was announced. RAPP, which only yesterday had been termed the Central Committee "cell" in literature by the Soviet press, and Stalin's "big stick" by emigre newspapers, was dissolved. An Organization Committee, headed by Gorky, was set up to put an end to group and factional fighting in literature and unite all in a single Union of Soviet Writers. Averbakh had no wish to lose his privileged position and, following his Bolshevik instincts, launched into battle. This only did him more harm and attracted the anger of the Boss himself. Stalin summoned all these squabblesome writers into his presence and gave Averbakh a public dressing-down after which our bully, naturally, conceded the fight.

That year saw the next great celebration in Gorky's honour. His 40 years as a writer were marked with indecent pomp and ceremony. Stalin ordered that Gorky's name be scattered throughout the country: in Moscow the Literary Institute, the central park and the city's main street were all named after him; the same was true of many other towns and cities; and both Nizhny Novgorod and the surrounding region, hundreds of factories, collective farms and schools now bore his name. The drama theatre in Leningrad and even the Art Theatre in Moscow added his name to their titles.

"But, Comrade Stalin, the Moscow Art Theatre is really more associated with Chekhov," the literary functionary Ivan Gronsky timidly tried to object.

"That doesn't matter. Gorky is a vain man," replied Stalin. "We must bind him with cables to the Party."

Gorky accepted the present and made no objections. He did not need to fear the critics: it was already forbidden to criticize him. In this way, a cult of Gorky in literature was created in the image and likeness of that already established for Stalin.

On 26 October 1932 a famous gathering took place at Gorky's town house in Moscow that would determine literary polices for years to come, until Gorbachev's perestroika in fact. The different participants have left their own, usually tendentious, interpretations of the event. On the whole these served their interests and only repeat what it was permissible to say at the time.

Now materials hitherto hidden in secret archives permit us to reach a more objective assessment of what happened that evening.

Tables covered with white cloths filled the dining room. The curtains were drawn and the chandelier glittered.

The room was full and the place of honour was occupied by the Kremlin leaders – Stalin, Molotov, Voroshilov and Kaganovich... But here they were simple and accessible, joking, eating and drinking with evident pleasure. Around them sat about fifty writers who were rather more restrained in their behaviour. Akhmatova, Mandelstam, Pasternak, Platonov, Bulgakov, Babel, Bely, Klyuev and Pilnyak were not present. Instead there were a great many other gifted but trusted writers, and yet more literary functionaries and activists.

Today many of the speeches delivered then seem of little interest and, moreover, do not have any great relevance to literature. To begin with it was decided how to organize the country's literary affairs – who should be in charge and how things should be run – and the members of RAPP and the Organization Committee made their peace. Another problem presented more difficulties. The assembled writers needed to know not only how to live but how to write.

The wise Stalin proposed the most progressive theory, Socialist Realism.

To be fair, he was not the only author of the single correct doctrine. Gorky himself had done a great deal in this direction. At an earlier gathering of writers he suggested:

> Should we not unite realism and romanticism in a third form that would be able to depict the heroic present in brighter tones and speak of it in a more elevated and dignified manner?

In turn, he identified the origin of this idea as Lenin. Speaking of Lenin's "rare ability to look at the present from the future", he spoke of the elevated vantage point this permitted. Together these should be the foundations of that "Socialist Realism of which we are beginning to talk".

Now Stalin took up the idea: life must be depicted as it should be, not as it is. We must live in the present but look at it from the future! Probably no one has ever understood what exactly Socialist Realism is. Ivan Gronsky, who attended the evening in Gorky's house, attempted on another occasion to provide an answer: "Socialist Realism is Rembrandt, Rubens and Repin* put at the service of the working class."

But let us return to the gathering that autumn in Gorky's house. As the evening passed the writers relaxed. Fadeev urged Sholokhov to sing. The writer Malyshkin pushed his way forward to clink glasses with Stalin. "Let us all drink the health of Comrade Stalin!" shouted the poet Vladimir Lugovskoi.

At this moment the novelist Nikiforov jumped up. He was sitting opposite Stalin, who had refilled Nikiforov's glass several times, and this encouraged the writer to declare:

> I'm fed up with this! We have drunk Stalin's health one million one hundred and forty-seven thousand times. He is probably fed up with it himself...

There was a deathly hush. Then Stalin got up, stretched out his hand and shook Nikiforov's fingertips:

> Thank you, Nikiforov, thank you. I am indeed fed up with it.

The room hummed like a hive.

It was then that Stalin called writers the "engineers of the human soul", adding that the production of souls was more important than that of tanks. The People's Commissar for War, Voroshilov, was about to object but he was firmly put in his place. After this the proud writers went home.

*A noted Russian artist, Ilya Repin (1844–1930) was accused in his time of producing "leading articles" on canvas. The change of borders after the 1917 October Revolution left his country estate in Finland and he, wisely, decided to remain there.

The first Congress of Soviet Writers two years later only made public what had been minutely worked out and decided in Stalin's study and then in Gorky's dining room. A few years would pass and every fourth participant of that evening was in prison and many were shot (including, of course, the naïvely incautious Nikiforov).

When Averbakh and Kryuchkov found themselves in prison they described in great detail what went on behind the scenes in the literary world. In their testimony the head of the NKVD Yagoda rises before us, in different guises, directing events while remaining out of sight himself.

Yagoda did everything, Kryuchkov said, to ensure that Averbakh was appointed general secretary of the new Union of Writers, under the chairmanship of Gorky. He attempted to gain the latter's agreement, even supplying him with specially slanted OGPU briefings. In 1933, to the same end, Yagoda instructed Averbakh to write a letter to Stalin. Kryuchkov added:

> Yagoda's agents became particularly active in 1934 when the congress was due to take place. As a result Gorky, in a letter to Stalin, again nominated Averbakh to a leading position in the Union. Yagoda was very interested in this and asked me repeatedly whether Stalin had made any response.

We knew nothing before of these efforts on Gorky's behalf, of his letters to the Kremlin in support of Averbakh. The trail leads from the Lubyanka to Stalin's archive, which to this day is closed to investigation: there lie the answers to many of the mysteries not only of our history but of Soviet literature.

Under interrogation, Averbakh wrote an entire treatise about the personality and underhand schemes of Genrikh Yagoda. Only yesterday he had exploited his family ties with the head of the NKVD and displayed a servile respect for him. Now he tried in every way to clear his own reputation by smearing that of his brother-in-law:

> Now I see Yagoda in a different light . . . Now I understand that his attitude to Gorky was not at all one of love for the old man or long attachment, or a natural attraction to the enormous inner enrichment that contact with Gorky gave. He needed this contact to replace his own lack of communication with the Soviet public, to substitute for his lack of roots in the working class and the Party.
>
> I was always rather surprised and unpleasantly shocked by the concern with which Yagoda asked whether his name had come up in conversation with Gorky . . . I thought this was because of his friendship with Timosha. Now it is clear to me that it concealed a simple fear that Gorky, a wise connoisseur of his fellow human beings, would

understand and see through his mean little soul and sense his inner decay and corruption...

Yagoda did not understand literary issues. Evidently that was not the task he set himself. He read very little and only knew of a number of names and works from hearsay. All Yagoda's literary acquaintances (apart, of course, from Gorky) he got to know through me... In conversation with Gorky we would say that Yagoda was not a politician but an administrator, an organizer, who honestly implemented the Party line...

...Yagoda always talked of his people with revolting cynicism. It was amazing the pleasure he took in anything that spoke badly of someone... Only one thing was sacred, a successful intrigue...

It became clear to me that a definite political game lay behind Yagoda and Gorky's relations. He was constantly afraid what the Party leadership thought of him... He needed Gorky as a weapon in his game, hoping for his support and, if he was exposed, for his protection. He calculated that recollection of his lengthy acquaintance with Gorky would be seen as testimony of his long service as a revolutionary... Most important of all, Yagoda tried to ensure that he met other members of the Politburo at Gorky's house so that the latter would influence their assessment of him...

Kryuchkov also emphasized this particular concern of the Lubyanka boss in his testimony:

Yagoda's other line of action in Gorky's household was his attempt to constantly keep in touch with what the members of the Politburo were saying when they visited Gorky...

As a rule, he himself was not invited to these meetings. Those who informed Yagoda were myself and Timosha. Usually, as soon as the Politburo members had left Gorky Yagoda would either come to visit, that same day, or ring me up and ask: "Did they come? They've left now? What did they talk about?... Did they say anything about us? What exactly?" etc. Usually I told him what I found out from either attending these conversations or from Gorky.

When I visited Stalin, on Gorky's instructions, Yagoda would ask what we talked about and I would tell him. In particular, this was the case in 1931–3 when I visited Stalin, bringing letters from Gorky abroad. Yagoda asked me about the contents of these letters...

Yet more unknown letters that lie in Stalin's personal archive...

A letter from Gorky to Averbakh was formerly kept in the latter's investigation file. Subsequently it was transferred to the Central Committee archive but there remains a reference in the file to its existence and a brief resume of its contents. As a result of Yagoda and Averbakh's activities, Gorky had written from Sorrento, indicating which writers should be published, what general trend literature should follow and what kind of heroes it should promote.

Gorky no longer protested, as under Lenin, against the methods being used. On the contrary, as Averbakh testified during his interrogation,

> Gorky placed an incredibly high value on the work of the NKVD with criminals and spoke of it with tender rapture, with tears of joy. He felt a warm, somehow simply personal gratitude to those who performed this work. I think it played an enormous role in his attitude to Yagoda that this work was linked to his name . . .

It has been suggested that Gorky was opposed to violence. He would have obstructed the Great Purge of 1937, and so Stalin had him removed. Today we can state categorically that this is either an invention or a delusion. Gorky, the second most important figure in the country, made no protest against the law of 7 August 1932 under which children of only 12 were made liable to the same punishments as adults, including the death penalty, even for simple theft. He did not notice the arrests of Klyuev or Mandelstam. In 1929 he visited Solovki and expressed his admiration for the first Soviet concentration camp.

Visiting the construction of the White Sea Canal, Gorky embraced Yagoda and was moved to tears: "You rough fellows do not realize what great work you are doing!" Gorky was to edit perhaps the most deceitful book in history, the collective work of several dozen Soviet writers who in the *White Sea Canal* ecstatically applauded and justified slave labour.

It was Gorky who supplied the authorities with a terrible slogan during collectivization in their struggle with the "kulaks": "If an enemy does not surrender, he must be exterminated" (*Pravda*, 15 November 1930). "I pant with fury as I read the reports of those scoundrels' trial," he wrote, at the very same time, about the fabricated and shameful show trial of the "Industrial Party", representatives of the older pre-revolutionary engineers and technicians. In March 1931 he agreed that the Mensheviks, among them some of his former friends, should be put on trial. Calling them criminals and wreckers, he added that not all of them had been caught and that the rest must also be tracked down and arrested.

"How magnificently Stalin is operating!" he exclaimed in a letter to Khalatov, the head of the State Publishers. A year later he would already be referring to the head of the Party as the Boss (perhaps it was Gorky who confirmed the application of this title to Stalin in the Soviet vocabulary?)

After Kirov was killed and supposed spies and saboteurs were being shot, without investigation or trial, after conviction by the troikas, Gorky would declare:

> The enemy must be exterminated ruthlessly and without pity, paying no
> attention to the gasps and groans of the professional humanists! (*Pravda*,
> 2 January 1935)

Gorky became not only a victim of Stalin and the NKVD but also one of their
weapons in the country's spiritual enslavement. Only moral and civic
degeneration lay ahead and these undoubtedly were part of the illness that
hastened his death.

Death Approaches

In May 1934 Gorky suffered a terrible blow. After an illness lasting only a few
days, his son Maxim died.

Few believed his death to be natural. Young and healthy, an energetic and
sporting man, Maxim was an avid air pilot. He was planning to make polar expeditions and had already visited the Arctic. He was, it is true, a drinker but this is
nothing unusual in Russia. Then suddenly he died from an ordinary cold.

Members of the household have left contradictory accounts. "Daddy is poorly.
He caught a cold at the airfield and is lying down and coughing," wrote Gorky
to his grand-daughters. Timosha recollected that Maxim "caught a chill while
out fishing". "After a drinking bout," Kryuchkov later confessed, "I led Max out
into the garden and left him asleep there on the bench . . ."

The authorities qualified Maxim's death as deliberate murder – but only in
1938 when Yagoda and Kryuchkov were among the accused in the last great show
trial, that of the Right–Trotskyist bloc. By then Gorky himself had died and his
death was linked to that of Maxim: the murder of his passionately beloved son
was a blow aimed at the father, deliberately weakening Gorky's health, inflicting
a severe pyschological shock that made him indifferent to public activities and
speeded up his death. The "Right–Trotskyist bloc" had to remove Gorky, the
NKVD now agreed, because he would have obstructed the coup they were
planning against the Party leadership.

Supposedly it was Yagoda who decided to murder Gorky's son, Maxim
Peshkov. He organized a conspiracy involving Kryuchkov and a number of
doctors – the Gorky family physician Levin, and Professor Pletnyov and Dr A.I.
Vinogradov of the NKVD medical section. A most detailed account of the plot
was given in Kryuchkov's file. "What was your personal interest in all this?" asked
his interrogator. Kryuchkov replied:

> I was interested in the removal of Maxim as Gorky's heir. Yagoda was well
> aware of this and exploited my ambition. . . . Over the years I enjoyed
> Gorky's full confidence and was master in his home, in all his literary and
> publishing affairs, and could dispose of his funds without any supervision.

The idea came to me that if I removed Maxim Peshkov I would be left in sole possession of a considerable literary legacy, which provided a vast income. Yagoda's suggestion coincided with my personal ambitions and I accepted it without lengthy hesitation.

In conversation Yagoda hinted that he was aware that I had been misappropriating Gorky's wealth . . .

In Kryuchkov's deposition the proposal appeared as follows:

Yagoda. We must remove Gorky.
Kryuchkov. But how?
Yagoda. You know how much Alexey Maximovich loves his son. If Max goes this will have such a shattering effect on Gorky that he will become a harmless old man.
Kryuchkov. Are you suggesting that I kill Max?
Yagoda. It is in your interests. . . . Dr Vinogradov says that alcohol has a bad effect on Max and this will be enough to ruin his health and speed up the end. Think about it . . . Dr Vinogradov will worry about the rest. He is Max's doctor and knows him well.

Kryuchkov went to work. He got Max very drunk and left him in a draught. But this did not yet endanger his life. "You should leave him out drunk in the snow," proposed Yagoda. The first effort of this kind was made in March, but only resulted in a light cold. Yagoda pressed Kryuchkov to hurry. Another unsuccessful attempt was made in late April. In early May, however, "after a drinking bout," Kryuchkov admits in his deposition, "I led Max out into the garden and left him asleep there on the bench . . ."

Maxim developed a temperature and headache and took to his bed. "The subsequent treatment by Dr Levin, and later by Dr Vinogradov, was in effect a murder . . ." Levin had diagnosed a light influenza. Then Vinogradov appeared:

He brought with him all the necessary medicines from the NKVD medical unit and, ignoring the objections of [the family nurse] Chertkova, gave Max something to drink from his first-aid set, although Chertkova asserted that the same medicine was already in the Gorky family's medicine chest. As a result Max's condition worsened, he became totally weak and could not leave his bed.

Peshkov's wife and Gorky himself began to insist that other doctors be consulted. Levin and Vinogradov objected strenuously, saying that there was nothing dangerous about his illness and that they expected a sharp improvement in his condition. A struggle developed around the sick man's bed between Chertkova and Vinogradov. Vinogradov tried to give him the medicine he had brought and Chertkova again demanded that these medicines be taken from the family's medicine chest. I do not know if she suspected something but she insisted very energetically on her right to personally administer medicines ... At least, I remember Vinogradov's remark as she left the room one time, "Is there no way of getting rid of that old woman?"

Despite all Vinogradov's effort ... Max's condition began to improve markedly. I remember that when I informed Yagoda, he said: "Blunderers. They've doctored so many others and they can't cope with a trifle like that." As I found out later, Yagoda then spoke to Vinogradov. The latter told me that we must find a way to make Max drink some champagne. "Genrikh Georgievich told me", Vinogradov said, "that you know everything and must help me. I am calculating that the patient will develop stomach pains as a result and this will provide an easy pretext for giving him a laxative. That will finish him off."

I did as he said. A few hours later Max began to complain of stomach pains. Vinogradov immediately gave the patient a laxative. As he left the room, Vinogradov told me: "Well, now we may consider our job done. This is a very risky business, even a non-specialist can see that to give someone a laxative when they're running such a high temperature would kill them. See you don't say a word!"

After this Max's condition declined rapidly. He fell unconscious, and became delirious. At 11 am Maxim Peshkov died ...

All this reads like a detective novel, and a bad one at that.

Before the trial began the Gorky family doctor, A.I. Vinogradov, died in unclear circumstances in the hands of the NKVD. The investigation into his role was closed. Vinogradov perhaps carried the truth about Maxim's death to his grave. Now that we have Kryuchkov's file in front of us we can begin to unravel the mystery of Maxim Peshkov's death. These were not the only suspicious deaths in this case: the head of the Kremlin medical administration, Khodorovsky, also under investigation, died at the same time from causes unknown. There seem to be rather too many coincidences here.

Christian Rakovsky, a famous Bolshevik revolutionary convicted during the same trial, uttered some prophetic words in prison (they were passed on by one of the NKVD men also being interrogated then):

I shall write a statement that describes all the court intrigues of the Soviet methods of investigation... Let at least those who read such declarations know the truth... I may well die soon, I may already be a corpse – but remember my words... Some day the corpses will rise and speak.

On 8 March 1938 the October Hall of the House of Unions was filled to over-flowing. They were not there to celebrate International Women's Day, however, but to condemn a "band of murderers and traitors".

Among the 21 accused were people famous throughout the country: Bukharin, Rykov, Rakovsky and Yagoda. Foreign observers who were present claim that Stalin, the main producer of this spectacle, followed the performance, seated in a special booth in the gallery. At a certain moment, the light shifted and all could clearly see his silhouette.

Vyshinsky was sitting in the procurator's seat. Behind him sat his assistant Lev Sheinin,* investigator for specially important cases and, at the same time, a writer of the new Stalin type.

It was the morning hearing. Yagoda was being cross-questioned and he looked quite different from when he had been in power: his hair had turned whiter, he was thinner, bent and gloomy. The murders he had organized were listed – Kirov, Kuibyshev, Gorky – and he confirmed his guilt. But at the mention of Maxim Peshkov's name he snapped: "I did not put ... Maxim Peshkov to death."

Vyshinsky read out Yagoda's deposition during his interrogation.

Vyshinsky. Did you give this testimony, accused Yagoda?
Yagoda. I gave such evidence, but it is not true.
Vyshinsky. Why did you make such a deposition if it is not true?
Yagoda. I do not know.
[...]
Vyshinsky. Why did you lie during the investigation?
Yagoda. I have told you. Permit me not to answer that question.

Yagoda pronounced this last phrase with such fury that, an American observer notes, the whole audience gasped. The judge Ulrich intervened but Yagoda turned to him and said menacingly (his retort was not subsequently included in the official report):

You can put pressure on me, but do not go too far. I shall say everything that I want to say... but do not go too far...

Everyone was shaken. If Stalin was present even he might have wondered whether his whole plan was about to be wrecked.

When the hearing resumed that evening Yagoda already looked a completely broken man. His voice could barely be heard.

First his secretary Bulanov described the special poisons laboratory that his chief had created and personally supervised. Yagoda was, Bulanov said, "excep-

* Author of detective and adventure stories, Lev Romanovich Sheinin (1906–67) worked in the Procurator's Office from 1923 to 1950 and assisted at the Nuremburg Tribunals.

tionally" interested in poisons. The son of a chemist, Yagoda had been familiar with chemistry from his childhood and worked before the revolution as a chemist himself. The Soviet secret police made wide use of poisons abroad and at home.

> *Vyshinsky*. Accused Bulanov, and was the killing of Maxim Peshkov also Yagoda's work?
> *Bulanov*. Of course.
> *Vyshinsky*. Accused Yagoda, what do you say to that?
> *Yagoda*. I admit my part in the illness of Peshkov. I request the court to hear this whole question *in camera* ...

Then Yagoda pulled out a piece of paper and slowly began to read out his confession, stumbling over the words as if he was seeing the text for the first time. When he reached the "medical killings" he again only acknowledged his "part in causing Max's illness" and repeated his request to give his explanations *in camera*. Vyshinsky asked the question two more times, with the same result. Almost losing his patience, he yelled at Yagoda: "Do you acknowledge your guilt or not?"

"Permit me not to answer that question," replied Yagoda.

That day Yagoda would not accept responsibility for the murder of Maxim Peshkov and when, at the close of the hearing, Vyshinsky listed those whom Yagoda had murdered, and the latter agreed to each one (Kirov, Kuibyshev, Gorky and now Menzhinsky as well), Maxim Peshkov's name was not mentioned.

During the closed hearing Yagoda "fully confessed to organizing the killing of Comrade Maxim Peshkov, admitting that he had pursued private aims in doing so". Triumphantly, in his final summing-up, Vyshinsky revealed how this murder had been committed and added that Yagoda had explained that he had not wanted to speak in public since "his motives for committing the crime were exclusively personal ..."

"Yagoda was in love with Peshkov's wife," concluded the American ambassador in Moscow Joseph Davies, "and everyone knew it." This is indeed the most human version and, probably, the most likely. Yagoda had no other reason for killing Maxim Peshkov.

His pursuit of Nadezhda Peshkova, of Timosha, began while her husband was still alive and became insistent and importunate after Maxim's death. Krandievskaya, the wife of Alexey Tolstoy, recalls a striking scene at the Gorky dacha:

> A short, balding man in military uniform came up the steps onto the verandah from the garden. His dacha was not far away and he would come almost every morning to drink coffee for half an hour, leaving his car behind the building. He was in love with Timosha and wanted her

to return his affection. "You still do not know me, I can do anything," he would tell the distraught Timosha, who complained of his attentions . . .

Four years after Maxim Peshkov died, when the trial ended almost all the members of the "Right–Trotskyist" bloc were shot immediately.

Two hours after Max's death the Party and government leaders came to visit Gorky and express their condolences. "It's over," he replied and changed the subject.

Just before he died Maxim Peshkov dreamed that he saw an aeroplane. Waking up, he drew it on a cigarette packet and explained how it was built. Exactly a year later, in May 1935 the newspapers announced that the enormous airplane *Maxim Gorky*, with its crew and dozens of shock workers on board, had crashed.

During the last two years of Gorky's life he was a broken man and an obedient instrument of the authorities. In his public statements he would habitually praise Stalin but they were no longer as close as they had formerly been, and a certain distance and coolness was detectable in their relations. The cause is not clear. Perhaps Gorky tried to intercede for the disgraced Kamenev, finally pushing the Leader's patience too far. Perhaps he had failed to write a major and epoch-shaping work about Stalin and had not praised him as he had Lenin, though hints were dropped more than once and materials for the Leader's biography were thrust upon him. There had even been announcements in the press: Gorky is about to publish . . . But he could not find the strength and did not carry out this public commission.

Everything indicates that the Leader no longer bothered how he treated the writer. Gorky decided to visit Italy but was not allowed to leave. The cage had shut.

Suddenly *Pravda* published a lampoon by the Party hack Zaslavsky criticizing the old man for his liberalism, for suggesting that Dostoevsky's *Devils* be published again. Despite outward success and fame, Gorky's life more and more resembled house arrest. In his memoirs the writer Shkapa recalls overhearing a despairing monologue. Gorky was mumbling to himself:

> I'm so very tired. It's as if they'd put up a fence around me and I can't step over. I'm surrounded, trapped. No way forward or back! I'm not used to this . . .

Extraordinary things began to happen in the writer's house. They even tampered with the newspapers. On several occasions a single copy of a paper was printed specially for Gorky, with the necessary cuts and alterations (the Gorky museum possesses one such issue). This was justified as concern for the old man's peace of mind. His constant depression, however, brought his end nearer more rapidly than old age or illness.

Reading what he wrote at the time, you occasionally wonder if he was entirely in his right mind. For instance, shortly before he died, he decided that one hundred writers should be mobilized, "given one hundred themes, and then they will rewrite the world's books anew, sometimes combining two or three in one." The aim? ". . . so that the world proletariat can read them and learn from them how to make world revolution." In this way, Gorky explained:

> all world literature and history, the history of the church and philosophy must be gradually rewritten: Gibbon and Goldoni, Bishop Irenaeus and Corneille, Professor Anfilonov and Julian the Apostate, Hesiod and Ivan Volnov, Lucretius and Zola, *Gilgamesh* and *Haïawatha,* Swift and Plutarch. The entire series must end with oral legends about Lenin.

Meanwhile the NKVD maintained an unsleeping surveillance over Gorky's household and its guests. The secret police promoted and openly financed those whom it found useful. During his interrogation, Averbakh admitted that he constantly used the free services of the NKVD's supplies department and that other members of Gorky's circle were similarly provided for without any great effort at concealment. Averbakh named the writer Kirshon, the artist Pavel Korin who taught Timosha (Yagoda had a studio specially built for him), the writers Afinogenov and Fadeev who received flats in an NKVD apartment block, while Kryuchkov was "in this sense, quite at home in the NKVD."

The special role played by Gorky's secretary is described in the numerous reports that flooded the Lubyanka after his arrest. The contributions of agent "Altaisky", to this day marked "Highly Confidential", are in a sense the memoirs of an informer and pass on the stories of those close to Gorky. For instance, he heard the following from the writer Alexander Tikhonov:

> Kryuchkov was capable of anything . . . His task was to take full control in Gorky's home and he tried to achieve this by all means available. In particular, he managed to keep Gorky's old friends at a distance. He would spread rumours [about them], call off visits by other writers and simply not allow some to come at all. I was the only remaining old friend and he tried to keep me away by any means.
>
> To achieve this Kryuchkov and Yagoda had to keep Timosha under their control. The affair between Yagoda and Timosha saved Kryuchkov from the threat of an unacceptable outsider coming into the house. I doubt that she loves him. . . Yagoda and Kryuchkov created such an atmosphere that it was frightening to talk to Timosha: if you were not careful, you would be arrested. It was good for her that all this happened (ie, the arrest of Yagoda and Kryuchkov) because she would not have got out of this mess by herself.

There was something very suspect about the whole situation. Just take the way Kryuchkov lived. He spent Gorky's money on himself as he wished. Yagoda and Kryuchkov were close friends. They went to the baths together... And this business arrangement was the foundation for their "extravagant lifestyle". I never visited Yagoda's dacha but I have heard many times how he boasted of his "2000 orchids and roses..." Kryuchkov took an active part and they suited each other very well. Together they organized drinking parties and orgies.

Gorky spent his last spring in the Crimea, at his dacha in Tesseli. André Malraux visited him there. In Isaac Babel's investigation file and his own testimony the Lubyanka archives reveal new details of this meeting:

Babel. Malraux came to the USSR to see Gorky about the World Association of Revolutionary Writers. He was accompanied by Koltsov and Kryuchkov. At Alexey Maximovich's request, I also went but was no more than a decorative figure during the visit.

I clearly remember that when Malraux asked Gorky, Was Soviet literature now experiencing a period of decline, he answered in the affirmative. Gorky was then very concerned about the open polemic being waged against the Formalists* in *Pravda* and the articles about Shostakovich with which he was not in agreement. During the last months of his life in the Crimea Gorky made a distressing impression... From the very first day of my visit I sensed the atmosphere of loneliness that Yagoda and Kryuchkov had created around him, by trying to isolate him from all that was more or less fresh or interesting. Gorky's mood seemed very low... He frequently said that he was being prevented in every way from returning to Moscow and to the work he loved. Not to mention the orgies with dubious women that Yagoda and Kryuchkov organized there, under cover of night, when Gorky had gone up to sleep. Kryuchkov gave all Gorky's relations with the outer world an odious, insincere and bureaucratic tone that was quite uncharacteristic of Alexey Maximovich... Kryuchkov deliberately selected Gorky's visitors so that he did not see anyone apart from the Chekists of Yagoda's circle and the charlatan inventors.** These artificial conditions began to weigh ever more heavily on Gorky and were responsible for the melancholy and lonely state in which we found him at Tesseli not long before his death –
Interrogator. Get back to your own testimony!

*When not a vague term of abuse, this refers to a trend in literary interpretation represented by Shklovsky and Tynyanov.
**An allusion to, among others, the doctors of the Institute of Experimental Medicine who claimed they would soon be able to "cure" old age and other diseases. See footnote on p271.

No less than seven versions of Gorky's death have been suggested. Yet somehow none of them manages to capture the truth.

According to the official Stalinist version Gorky's death was a villainous murder. It formed part of the vast plot organized by the Right-Trotskyist bloc and directed by Bukharin, Rykov, Yagoda and, from afar, Leon Trotsky. Their aim was to overthrow Stalin and seize power. As the loyal friend of the Leader, Gorky was an obstacle in their way and must be removed. The bard of Kazakhstan Djambul Djabaev, sang:

> *You loved Stalin, the genius of this world,*
> *You would have lived among us many years yet*
> *Had not the serpent sting of Yagoda*
> *Had not the poison of the murderers*
> *Come to you in the doctors' white coats*

In fact, Stalin needed to set a new wave of arrests and shootings in motion and Yagoda unfortunately knew far too much about the Leader. Stalin himself defined the guilt of Yagoda when, in his telegram to the Politburo on 25 September 1936, he announced that the "OGPU was four years late" in beginning the Great Terror. There was a weakness in the plans for the trial, however. Only one victim, Kirov, was available for so many evil-doers. So the recent deaths of Kuibyshev, Menzhinsky, Gorky and his son were very convenient: they were all proclaimed victims.

Turning back to Kryuchkov's file we find Yagoda instructing him to "destroy Gorky's health". Kryuchkov hesitates and experiences torments of conscience but Yagoda threatens him and says that he will otherwise unmask him as the murderer of Maxim Peshkov and the embezzler of the family's wealth.

> *Yagoda*. When they arrest you no one will believe your words. You are not a stupid man, and you can see that my people will be conducting the investigation. Gorky's already old and will die soon anyway...
>
> After his death you will be almost the richest man in the USSR. Commentaries to his letters alone are priceless...
>
> Stop whining and get on with it... Since his son's death he has no strength left.
>
> Let in more draughts and fresh air. He only has one lung, and even that isn't working properly.

Kryuchkov again went to work.

> I did everything I could to make Alexey Maximovich catch cold and weaken his organism: I "forgot" to close the windows when he went to sleep, I distracted him with work on the fourth volume of *Klim Samgin* knowing that it was extremely harmful for him to become too tired. In

the Crimea . . . I organized nights out in the open by a bonfire. Naturally, the smoke from the fire . . . and the sharp contrast in temperature also had a negative effect on his health. As a result of the above criminal actions on my part, Alexey Maximovich often felt a chill when still in the Crimea and began to complain of his general condition . . .

Yagoda pressed him to hurry. In spring 1936 he rang from Moscow: "Persuade Gorky to come back to Moscow and find the opportunity on the way to carry out your mission."

Gorky would not be persuaded. Then Timosha rang up and told him not to hurry back: the little girls had influenza. Kryuchkov informed Yagoda but he brushed aside the problem: "Tell Alexey Maximovich that the children are quite healthy."

Finally they left. On the way Gorky felt unwell and on 30 May at his dacha outside Moscow he fell seriously ill. This, at least, is what Kryuchkov said under interrogation.

Gorky's doctor Levin was the next target of his testimony. For several days, according to Kryuchkov, he concealed the correct diagnosis and only when Alexey Maximovich himself insisted on 2 June that he had lobar pneumonia was the doctor forced to agree with him. Even then Levin delayed taking the vital decisions. The doctor instructed Kryuchkov to hinder the administration of the necessary medicines; he insisted that Professor Pletnyov be called in to treat the patient and he obstructed the visit of Dr Speransky* who was trusted by the household. In Kryuchkov's version the end came as follows:

> At the consultation held shortly before Gorky's death Professor Pletnyov suggested that he be injected with a saline solution. The professor knew perfectly well, I should add, that this had an extremely enfeebling effect on Gorky's organism, yet he nevertheless suggested it. This injection finally wrecked Gorky's health and a second injection of digitalis, on the advice of that same Pletnyov, destroyed his heart function and this led to the death of Alexey Maximovich . . .

We shall never learn the truth about Gorky's death, the literary specialists lamented. Yet there was a document that monitored precisely the course of the writer's last illness up until death itself . . . A photocopy of the medical record of Maxim Gorky, retrieved from the bottomless depths of the Lubyanka archive, lies before me.

Comparing this authentic chronicle with the official version preserved in

*A charismatic and unscrupulous man, Alexey Speransky regularly expounded the extravagant theories of the Institute of Experimental Medicine at Gorky's house in front of the Kremlin leaders and the writer's other guests.

Kryuchkov's testimony we immediately come across major discrepancies. The correct diagnosis was made in good time. The best doctors gathered and consulted more than once and took the most decisive measures to save the writer's already hopelessly worn-out and illness-shattered organism. What kind of investigation did the NKVD conduct into Gorky's death if they did not examine this record? Evidently they did take a look. Then they hid the doctors' notes as thoroughly as they could and kept them concealed in their depositories until the present day.

Leonid Levin, the doctor treating Gorky, notes:

> 28 May. Yesterday Gorky returned from the Crimea to Moscow. He had a difficult journey, did not sleep and finds its hard to breathe...
>
> 1 June. Influenza and bronchial pneumonia...
>
> 2 June... Patient did not sleep this night. Consulted Professor Lurie and Doctor Ginzburg... Sharp changes in both lungs linked to old tubercular developments...
>
> 4 June. Consulted Professor Pletnyov. Same diagnosis. Patient in very serious condition...
>
> 5 June. Consulted Dr Lang. Same diagnosis and therapy...
>
> Night of 7 June passed relatively calmly. Gorky slept at intervals, there were no drastic falls in heart function during the night. No new affected areas in the lungs. Patient rather more lively than before. Same therapy... [signed] Konchalovsky, Lang, Levin.
>
> 8 June. Overall condition remains serious. At 5 pm the patient's condition worsened...

Gorky's condition was acute and the situation seemed so hopeless that day that the doctors decided nothing more could be done. His close friends and relatives all came to say their farewells: Yekaterina Peshkova, Timosha, Maria Budberg, Chertkova and Rakitsky. The scene around the bed of the dying man has been reconstructed from their memoirs.

Gorky opened his eyes and said: "I am already far away, it is very hard for me to return..." After a pause, he added: "All my life I have thought how I might improve this moment..."

Kryuchkov entered the room and announced that Stalin was on his way (evidently he had rung and warned Stalin about Gorky's condition). "Let them come, if they can get here in time," said Gorky.

Chertkova went to consult Dr Levin. She remembered how she had restored Gorky to life once before in Sorrento by giving him a massive injection of camphor.

"If his condition is hopeless all the same, allow me to inject him with 20 ccs."

"As you wish," a resigned Dr Levin replied.

The camphor indeed brought the patient back to life and when Stalin entered, with Molotov and Voroshilov, they were amazed by Gorky's buoyancy. They had expected to find him at death's door.

Stalin started to take control: "Why are there so many people here. Who's in charge?"

"I am," replied Kryuchkov.

"Who's that sitting beside Alexey Maximovich, dressed in black. A nun, is she?" said Stalin, pointing at Budberg. "All she lacks is a candle in her hands."

Kryuchkov explained.

"And who's she?" Stalin pointed at Chertkova who was wearing a white coat. Kryuchkov told him.

"Get all of them out of here apart from that woman, the one in white, who is looking after him."

In the dining room Stalin saw Yagoda.

"And what's that creature hanging around here for? Get rid of him! You will answer for everything with your life," Stalin warned Kryuchkov. "Why is there such a funereal mood here? A healthy person might die in such an atmosphere!"

Gorky began to talk about literature but Stalin halted him: "We'll talk business when you are better," and asked whether there was any wine in the house.

They drank to Gorky's recovery. On their way out they embraced the writer. Later Gorky regretted this act: "It was wrong of me to kiss them. I have a cold and might infect them . . ."

Gorky lived for another 10 days after this. Two times during that period Stalin came to visit him. On the first occasion the patient was not well and the doctors did not allow them to meet. The second time they spoke for 10 minutes, for some reason discussing the French peasantry.

During his last days, when Gorky periodically regained consciousness he tried to clutch hold of life, and pronounced a few intermittent phrases. They showed him a newspaper with the draft of the new Constitution: "We are engaged in trifles and now the very stones in our country are singing . . ."

Once he woke up during the night and said to Chertkova: "Do you know, I was just arguing with God. How we argued! Shall I tell you?"

9 June. Patient passed a bad night, waking often. Oxygen, camphor . . . This morning he was rather confused, now his mind is clearer. In bad condition. [Signed] Lang, Pletnyov, Konchalovsky, Levin.
13 June. No change for the better, despite the enormous quantities of subcutaneous and intramuscular injections of heart medicine. At times his pulse sinks as low as 90 and then quickly increases again. He is clear-headed. About 1 pm he expressed a desire to see his grand-daughters, which was permitted . . .

On 17 June Gorky's condition rapidly worsened.

About 9 am he was unconscious. His raised arm falls back inert, he does not react to anything and does not speak . . . A torpid condition. Large quantities of caffeine, camphor and oxygen . . . drank three quarters of a cup of milk.

After a comparatively good night suddenly began, at 6.30 am, to spit up blood . . . Simultaneously experienced considerable respiratory difficulties, increased cyanosis and intermittent consciousness. At 8.30 he briefly fainted. Many emphysemic wheezing noises in the lungs . . .

The last night had come. Outside a storm raged and hail pelted down. All Gorky's family and friends were there. The doctors who had been living nearby all these days sat about the round table downstairs and consulted although every-thing was already clear. The patient was kept alive with oxygen and consumed 300 packets during the night: they were passed hand by hand, in a constant conveyer from the truck, up the stairs to the dying man's bedroom.

18 June. A very bad night. Very excited, continual delirium, will not drink and often refuses oxygen . . .

11 am In a deep comatose condition. Delirium has almost ceased . . .

Does not react to injections. Loud tracheal inspiration.

Pulse rapidly began to disappear. Cannot be felt. No expiration (mirror test). Death occurred with paralysis of heart and respiration . . .

On the reverse side of the final page in the medical history is listed the clinical diagnosis:

1. . . . TB of the lungs, cavities, bronchoecstasia, emphysema of the lungs, pneumosclerosis, pleural union;

2. Arteriosclerosis of the aorta and coronary vessels of the heart, cardiosclerosis;

3. Cardiac insufficiency;

4. Bronchial pneumonia;

5. Lung failure ?;

6. Infectious nephrosia.

There followed the signatures of four doctors: Lang, Konchalovsky, Pletnyov and Levin.

During the trial both Levin and Pletnyov announced that they were the murderers of Maxim Gorky. Only now have the documents that explain their behaviour become available. Among them is an appeal to the leaders of the country from Vladimir prison by a 69-year-old professor who was considered Russia's best heart doctor. Pletnyov wrote:

All the charges made against me were a falsification. My "confession" was forced out of me by violence and deception . . . When I did not give way the investigator literally said: "If the leadership suppose you to be guilty then even if you were 100% innocent, you would all be guilty. . ."

Appalling bad language was used against me, and the threat of the death penalty. I was dragged by my collar, choked and tortured with sleeplessness: over a period of five weeks I slept for only 2–3 of every 24 hours. They threatened to tear out my throat and with it my confession; they threatened to beat me with rubber truncheons... All of which reduced me to a paralysis of half my body. . . I am numbed by the cold-blooded lying of those pygmies and worms who are carrying on their subversive work. Show that truth is as possible to establish in the Union [USSR] as in other civilized countries . . . May the truth shine forth! . . .

Today the doctors who treated Gorky have been rehabilitated. Not long ago a special medical investigation concluded that the diagnosis and treatment were correct and that death came naturally. All that was lacking was the medical history of Gorky's last illness.

There is one more little-known document of Maxim Gorky's last days. This is not the false concoction of the Lubyanka depositions nor the dry if truthful record of his last illness but the notes that the writer himself tried to keep before his death. Tucking them into the last book he had read, Tarle's biography of Napoleon,* he recorded his failing mind's flashes of lucidity:

Objects become heavier: books, pencils, the glass and everything seems smaller than it was.

. . .The night has no end and I cannot read.

. . .They forgot to give me a knife to sharpen the pencil.

Slept almost two hours. It is getting light.

It seems I'm better . . .

A very complicated sensation.

Two processes are linked together:

a sluggishness of the nervous system – as if the nerve cells were being extinguished and ash covers all, all thoughts turn grey,

and at the same time the stormy onset of a desire to speak, which turns into delirium, I can tell that I am not speaking coherently although some phrases are still comprehensible.

They say pneumonia. I can tell, I will not survive.

I cannot read or sleep.

Gorky dictated his last note:

End of the novel, end of the hero, end of the author.

*Also one of Stalin's favourite books.

Life after Death

In his will Gorky asked to be buried beside his son in Moscow's Novodevichy cemetery. When Yekaterina Peshkova learned that the government intended to cremate Gorky instead and place him in the Kremlin Wall, she rang up Stalin: if it was really not possible to carry out the deceased's last wish, then at least the family should be given a handful of ash to bury in his son's grave. It was up to the government to decide, Stalin said. Yagoda passed on their decision. The government had not considered it possible to meet this request...

Something similar happened to Gorky's archive. On the very day that the sculptor Merkurov was taking his death mask, and the writer's brain was being transported in a bucket to the Brain Institute, the members of the commission to deal with Gorky's literary heritage and correspondence were announced. In practice the archive came into the possession of the NKVD.

There is a story that the secret police discovered carefully hidden notes in Gorky's house and that Yagoda, after he had read them, indignantly exclaimed (in the words of a Russian folk saying):

> No matter how well you feed a wolf, he always yearns to be back in the forest!

Whether this really happened I do not know. After Kryuchkov was arrested, however, he told his interrogator that when he informed Yagoda what the writer's archive contained the latter showed a great interest. In particular, he persisently enquired whether there was anything there about the "comrades", ie, members of the Politburo. Timosha had supposedly told him in 1935 that Gorky kept such notes... "Don't worry," Yagoda reassured Kryuchkov. "As long as I'm alive you will live in style."

The head of the NKVD showed no restraint in his dealings with the dead man's family. Bulanov, his secretary, kept a check on the income of Gorky's heirs, their current accounts and how they spent their money. In 1937 when he had been demoted to People's Commissar for Communications, Yagoda continued to interfere and advised Timosha to withdraw Gorky's house and dachas from NKVD control and then she would be complete mistress of them all.

Certainly the archive was of special interest to the secret police. Time and again the tireless informers told them to search through its contents. "Sayanov", for instance, reported:

> There should be letters in Gorky's archive (which, as I hear, has now been sealed by the NKVD) that are of enormous political value. These are not only letters unmasking enemies of the people which, evidently, the NKVD has already removed, but correspondence with those who have yet to be exposed. It would be a great mistake, in my view, not to

study all these materials. It should be borne in mind that enemies tried any means to work their way into Gorky's house... Undoubtedly, not all the ties of this household have yet been liquidated. A certain number of people are still gathering around Kryuchkov, who is now in charge of the Gorky Museum.

Attention should be paid to certain editorial boards that were formerly linked to Gorky, especially *Our Achievements*. I do not know if Vigilyansky and other members of this journal have been arrested yet; I think they are under arrest since they are very suspicious politically...

The slaughter of all of Gorky's entourage was thus being stealthily and steadily prepared. When Kryuchkov was arrested an NKVD informer confidentially told Captain Zhurbenko that Kryuchkov had concealed part of the archive and that "there might be something there".

Zhurbenko. What, for instance? Attacks on the Writers Union?
Informer. Not just that.
Zhurbenko. Things against the Party leadership?
Informer. Against certain of its members ...

Gorky's house was thoroughly searched, and more than once. When Kryuchkov was arrested they even cut potatoes open in a search for precious stones. "Is that all you've managed to find?" asked Yelisaveta Kryuchkova, sarcastically. The informer "Altaisky" described this scene to Captain Zhurbenko and helpfully added, "Timosha has already been interrogated ..."

Meanwhile Zhurbenko was also gathering material on Kryuchkov's wife in preparation for her arrest. A very close friend of hers, a writer and also an informer, known as "Zorin", gave a most detailed report after each of their meetings. Once, in despair, Kryuchkov's wife told him:

I am standing on the brink of the abyss and can trust no one. I only have you and my son Petka. If I did not have you and Petka I would shoot myself...

A few days later she was arrested as an accomplice of Yagoda. At her trial she would deny any political ties with him and claim that he had tried to make her his mistress. She was shot the same day.

As they faced inevitable death, many looked back over their past life. Even Yagoda, imprisoned at the Lubyanka, began to reveal a more human face. He could not eat or sleep, it is said, but only ran back and forth across his cell. Suddenly he exclaimed: "God exists!"

"What's happened?" asked his NKVD guard.

"It's very simple," explained Yagoda. "I deserved nothing but gratitude from

Stalin for my loyal service. I had earned the severest punishment from God, however, since I broke his commandments a thousand times. Now look where I am – and decide for yourself whether God exists . . ."

At the end of Gorky's play *Somov and Others* GPU agents arrest almost all the characters. Those surrounding Gorky suffered a similar fate. Whether they were Party members, Chekists, informers or merely writers they were almost all arrested, shot or driven to commit suicide.

The women were more fortunate. Lipa Chertkova almost outlived Stalin. Yekaterina Peshkova survived to witness Khrushchev's Thaw. Timosha lived to see Brezhnev's rule. And the Iron Woman, Maria Budberg, outlived them all.

CHAPTER 13

THE END OF THE UNION

It was early morning and I was hurrying past the quiet dachas to catch the local train into Moscow. On the corner of the street, next to their workshop, some mechanics I knew were working on a car.

"Well, your Gorbachev's had it now!" one of them said, almost cheerfully.

"What's that?" I stopped.

"You mean you haven't heard? Perestroika's over! There are new people in the Kremlin now – Yanaev, Yazov, Kryuchkov and Pugo . . ." He counted them off, bending the fingers to his palm, one by one, and then held up his clenched fist suggestively.

I turned around and went back home. I wanted to hear for myself. Why had he said "your" Gorbachev? Because he had given us writers freedom of speech? Meanwhile, life for everyone had only become harder, less predictable.

I had known this might happen. In June I dropped into the Writers Club for some reason. Usually empty during the summer, it was now swarming with people.

"What's going on?" I asked.

"Where have you been?" they replied. "The military-patriotic committee is sitting. They're commemorating the fiftieth anniversary of the beginning of the Great Patriotic War."

I glanced into the Large Hall. There were a great many uniforms there and on the stage army marshals led by the Minister of Defence, Yazov himself, were sitting in the presidium among the secretaries of the Writers Union. The first secretary of the Union, and chairman of our commission, Vladimir Karpov, was speaking:

> Why do you allow yourselves to take orders from a man in a suit?
> We suffered incalculable losses in 1941 because our army was then
> commanded by a civilian, by Stalin. Today, 50 years later, the situation
> is the same. The Fatherland is in Danger!

The applause were thunderous. The army had found moral support among the writers.

Actually, I did not notice any major writers sitting there. Sergey Mikhalkov, who headed the Russian Federation's branch of the Union, was indeed in the presidium but as these subversive sentiments were applauded he made a rapid exit. Having survived under every regime, beginning with Stalin, he knew better than to become too closely involved in appeals to overthrow the ruling authorities. Soon the sadly notorious "Word to the Nation" would appear, signed by the writer-ideologists of the "red and brown", Communist-chauvinist alliance.

So now it had happened.

At home I turned on radio and television and on both could be heard the announcements of the self-appointed junta: a state of emergency had been declared, Gorbachev was seriously ill, and the new State Committee for the State of Emergency was taking over the running of the country.

When I reached Moscow the tanks and personnel carriers were rolling down the streets. I was supposed to read the proofs of my latest article for the *Ogonyok* magazine, in which I had a regular column.

"The magazine's unlikely to come out now," the editors told me. "We're printing leaflets instead." The "Appeal to the Nation" by Russian President Boris Yeltsin was being photocopied there. I grabbed a packet of leaflets and set off for the White House. On the barricades and at the spontaneous meeting in progress there I saw many familiar writers' faces.

The next evening, the decisive night of 20–21 August, a thin drizzle was falling and it was very chilly. Bonfires were burning. I used my journalist's pass to get through two cordons but then was stopped: I had no gas mask and they were expecting the assault to come any moment now. Spetsnaz were already moving towards the Russian parliament building. Then they halted. We heard rumours that two tanks were burning on the nearby Garden Ring. Suddenly all the lights in buildings around us went off. Minutes, hours passed. Someone even claimed to have seen Mstislav Rostropovich by one of the bonfires . . .

It was already getting light when an announcement was made: the State Committee's forces were withdrawing and quitting Moscow.

There followed the euphoria of victory. Thousands gathered in front of the parliament building. All Moscow seemed to be out, marching along the streets. They reached the citadel of the old regime, the Central Committee building on the Old Square. Then they moved on to the Lubyanka, and there were appeals to the crowd to storm the KGB headquarters.

"Whatever can he be making of all this?" I asked, nodding at Felix Dzerzhinsky's statue.

"Tomorrow he won't be here," a voice in the crowd replied.

I thought this was a joke. The next morning I learned that during the night the statue had indeed been pulled down.

The Shattered Mirror

Swept up by the current of events, and now seeing the Lubyanka through the eyes of those who had risen against the putsch, I could not help wondering, all the same, what was happening to the archives – to the precious manuscripts and documents inside the building?

A battle was going on inside KGB headquarters as well, it turned out. While Kryuchkov and his supporters were carrying out the putsch, others were doing whatever they could to prevent it. Some drew up lists for arrests and even executions but others not only refused to implement them but even informed the Yeltsin team who was about to be arrested. Some gave orders for the White House to be seized; others refused to obey.

Contradictory and alarming reports surfaced in the newspapers and all kinds of rumours circulated. The secret police were burning their documents, they were loading them into lorries and transporting them elsewhere. The archivists, according to other sources, were fighting off threats on two fronts: they ignored instructions from their superiors to destroy documents and were barricading the entrances into the archive in case the infuriated mob broke in. Naturally, they were not very talkative about this themselves. But from their meagre accounts I learnt that all the archive depositories, with the exception of certain files identifying their agents, had remained where they were, untouched, in the building's numerous departments and sections.

The secret police had lost their omnipotent master. The activities of the Communist Party were halted. The old system was rapidly collapsing. That New Year's Eve we said farewell both to Gorbachev and to the USSR, the state we had lived in all our lives!

Trying to adapt to the rapidly changing situation the KGB changed its name several times. After Yeltsin's decree declassifying the Party and other archives, the doors of the restricted depositories began slowly to open.

Society proved unprepared. Among the discoveries and revelations that flooded the press there were many frivolous, unverified sensations, as well as provocations and forgeries. People were not accustomed, after all those years, to the truth and did not know what to do with it. I remember various reactions to my different publications.

"You're merely boosting anti-Semitism," said a very educated Jewish woman of my acquaintance. "Babel, you tell us, betrayed his friends during his interrogation and handed them over to the secret police. That's what the Jews are like, they'll be saying now!"

"It was a mistake to paint such a moving picture of that Russophobe Babel," commented a famous writer who had been in the Gulag himself. "He was a dark horse, a cynic. A thoroughly Soviet character, who hung around the secret police, was friendly with executioners, worked for the Cheka and was welcome in Yezhov's house. Until, that is, they came for him . . . He deserved what happened."

Then my article about Pavel Florensky appeared.

Many in patriotic and church circles consider your article in *Ogonyok* to be a Zionist provocation. The Orthodox church is about to canonize Florensky. . . But you say he gave in during his interrogation and agreed that he was a fascist . . . In that case what ever kind of saint is he?

Intransigent Bolsheviks accused me of being anti-Soviet for undermining the KGB, the sword and shield of the Revolution.

"Do you know? They're saying that you're a KGB captain," confided a tipsy friend one evening. "They don't allow ordinary people to look in their archives . . ."

"And what did you say?"

He guffawed. "I told them you were a KGB colonel!"

"You think too highly of me," I replied. "I'm only a lieutenant."

I was nonplussed, nevertheless, when it was suggested that our Commission should save and preserve the works of the imprisoned poet Osenev.

This was the literary pseudonym of the former chairman of the USSR Supreme Soviet, Anatoly Lukyanov. Friend and traitor of Gorbachev, he had joined the putsch and was now in the Matrosskaya Tishina prison. When I set eyes on his verse, however, in some cheap newspaper I was relieved to find that there was no poet Osenev – only a scribbler no more successful in literature than in politics.

Uproar in the Rostov House

The old town-house on Vorovsky St survived Napoleon's occupation of Moscow. But now events there were making it shudder with concern. The chauvinist writers had set an effigy of the poet Yevtushenko on fire in the courtyard:

> Down with the usurpers!
> Zionism shall not triumph!
> Russia for the Russians!

Their cries alarmed the crows and passers by and the figure of Tolstoy, seated in the centre of the courtyard, seemed more bowed and engrossed in silent thought than usual.

What happened in the Rostov house was a distorted reflection of events in the country at large. To begin with, an emergency gathering of the Writers Union secretariat supported the putsch. A day later, when it became clear that the coup was not succeeding, other democratic literary secretaries met, under the leadership of that indefatigable tribune of the people Yevgeny Yevtushenko. Grabbing a briefcase filled with compromising documents, their former colleagues fled. This was not the end of the scandal, however.

On the ruins of the USSR Writers Union arose the Commonwealth of Writers

Unions. While our democrats argued and debated how to reorganize the literary community Yevtushenko, disdainful of such bureaucratic occupations, left for a prolonged visit to the USA. In his place he installed Timur Pulatov, an Uzbek who wrote in Russian. The latter quickly organized another palace coup in the Rostov house and, proposing an Islamic-Orthodox alliance to confront the Catholics and Zionists, moved over to the side of the now resigned but embittered chauvinists, mainly from the Russian Federation branch of the old Union. The result was the International Community of Writers Unions, a body that had as little right to its pretensions as its leader.

The pillage of the Rostov house began. Rooms, money, archives, telephones, typewriters and secretaries were fought over. Doors were broken down and new locks added. Letters were intercepted and opened, documents stolen. Papers, journals and books belonging to previous inhabitants were thrown out into the courtyard by the new masters. In this way an invaluable collection, built up over many years, of literature in the other languages of the Soviet nations was destroyed.

A hitherto modest typist marched vengefully down the corridors like a Valkyrie, yelling, "Let us purge ourselves of the Jews!" Nina and Nadya, old friends who for years had sat side by side in the office (one dealt with incoming post, the other with outgoing mail), now found themselves in different camps and stopped talking to each other...

Our Commission did not go unscathed by Pulatov's pogrom. We had to fight for the room where we worked and kept our archive, and for the very right to exist. Eventually an unstable and hostile compromise was reached and the amicable-sounding Commonwealth and Community divided the Rostov house between them.

Thus died the Union of Soviet Writers. Created 60 years earlier, to triumphant fanfares, it was in outward appearance, a vigorous, powerful and energetic body – in fact, swaddled by ideology, it was bound hand and foot by censorship and its guardians in the NKVD and the Central Committee. This was a fittingly shameful and farcical end to a tragic and false existence.

A Homeless Craftsman

In 1919 Alexander Blok was arrested by the Cheka. He was only kept in prison one night, in the same cell as a great many other very different people. Everyone was there, from the monarchists and Kadets, to the Mensheviks and SRs. Until morning they argued passionately about the future of Russia. Blok alone remained silent. Finally, tiring of their polemics, they turned to him: "What do you think, Alexander Alexandrovich?"

"What you're saying is all very interesting and entertaining," he replied, "But where will the artist, with his homeless craft, go to in your future?"

The Revolution, which, incidentally, Blok himself had invoked and welcomed, triumphed. Artists who wanted to serve their own vocation, not the Revolution, found themselves out of favour and superfluous.

Under the Soviet regime writers suffered from an infinite variety of repressive measures. These went beyond execution and imprisonment, internal exile and expulsion abroad, to cripple the life and work of many others. Marina Tsvetaeva was driven to commit suicide. Others were harassed and not published for years on end. Many were forced to "step on the throat of their own song" and drown the promise of their first works in feeble praise of the regime. They killed their talent in order to live.

> *Of love one whispers or sings.*
> *One cries or grits one's teeth in pain.*
> *In honour of the slain one stays silent*
> *Or talks at the top of one's voice.*

These lines come from a letter by a woman who was in the camps of Kolyma. Somehow it seems they were not written on a flimsy page from an envelope, but engraved in stone.

March 1993, Moscow

POSTSCRIPT

In early 1994 preparations got under way to celebrate the centenary of Isaac Babel's birth. A fresh examination of the Lubyanka archives uncovered new documents and information.

For instance, Babel had not been held at the Lubyanka during the first month of interrogation as I had then been led to believe. After completing the formalities there he was immediately put in another automobile and taken away, to be "prepared" at a still more inaccessible place. This was the notorious Sukhanovka, the NKVD's main torture centre, located outside Moscow in the secluded former St Catherine nunnery. It was there also that Nikolay Yezhov was held and tortured by the new master of the Lubyanka, Lavrenty Beria.

Another search was made for the 24 folders of manuscripts confiscated from Babel. Now it might be possible to find out where junior Lieutenant Kutyrev took those seven sealed parcels, and on whose orders. Searches had already been made several times before – in 1955, 1956, 1964 and in 1988 – but without any success. In early 1994 a new and thorough check was made: if the manuscripts themselves could still not be found, then perhaps some reference to them might be uncovered in the archives of the Federal Counter-Intelligence Service (successor to the KGB).

The manuscripts were nowhere in the archive. No record that they had been transferred to other organizations was unearthed in the correspondence files of the NKVD. An attempt to track down Kutyrev established that he had died not long before, in June 1993. At the same time, no record of the destruction of the manuscripts was found either.

Little hope now remains that they have survived, although even today we cannot confidently say that the secret archives of the Lubyanka have been fully investigated and opened. And there still remain the vast Party and Presidential archives with their own secret and inaccessible caches.

For years a soot-stained chimney released a stream of smoke over the Lubyanka and for decades sprinkled Moscow with the ash of incinerated manuscripts. How many books were consumed by that chimney, never to be read by another person!

THE LITERARY–POLITICAL CONTEXT

For a few months after the Bolsheviks seized power in October 1917, periodicals and publishers continued to operate much as before. The dispersal of the Constituent Assembly, however, the breakdown of the Bolshevik coalition with the Left Socialist Revolutionaries, and the onset of the Civil War in summer 1918 led to the closure or banning of all remaining non-Bolshevik publications. The following two and a half years of bitter hostilities reduced the country to ruin, and its inhabitants to hunger and starvation. Only a few favoured projects like Gorky's World Literature series managed still to appear, providing some writers with work and food. Yet amid this chaos and destruction, an apocalyptic expectation that a revolutionary "world conflagration" was imminent fired the enthusiasts of the new Proletarian Culture in the Proletkult movement.

In 1921 the now-named Communist Party confirmed its monopoly over the political system, and even prohibited the formation of factions within its ranks. The next year it organized its first great show trial, putting the leaders of the Socialist Revolutionary Party in the dock. This severity accompanied the temporary relaxation of the New Economic Policy which, until the late 1920s, permitted a successful but peculiar and unstable form of mixed economy to come into being. Private entrepreneurs reemerged and cooperative ventures were set up. Several pre-revolutionary publishers resumed work, and at the time more than a hundred literary cooperatives were in operation. A variety of groupings could therefore compete openly for readers (and privately for official support). Several of them – LEF, RAPP and the critics of Pereval – claimed to be Marxist and vied to be considered the true voice of progressive or revolutionary literature. LEF (Left Front in Art) insisted that the revolutionary content of the new art demanded a revolutionary form. The theorists of RAPP (Russian association of Proletarian Writers) preferred realist art and psychologically-motivated characters; so did the group, which formed around the *Krasnaya nov* journal, and called itself Pereval (Mountain Pass) because it hoped to blaze a trail out of present difficulties into a new flowering of Soviet literature. Yet not one of these groups could claim the unequivocal support of the classics of Marxism in their disputes or, more importantly, that of the Party leaders. There was then no hard or recognizable official line on literature. A loose association of writers such as the Serapion Brotherhood, who first gathered in 1921, and insisted on the individual freedom of the creative act, demanding that art again be independent of political or social commitment, were also not only tolerated but actively published. Indeed, the majority of the old and new talented authors were Fellow-Travellers, those who were not members of the Party or proletarian in any sense but, in some general way guardedly sympathetic, or at the least not overtly hostile to the new Soviet regime.

Many writers had already emigrated. Others remained within the country. Yet at the beginning of the 1920s, the distinction between acceptably "Soviet" writers and the rest was not yet hard and fast. With the exodus, principally to Europe, of between one and two million former subjects of the Russian Empire after the Revolution there were now well-known writers, a great many readers and a wide variety of Russian-language periodicals and publishing houses abroad. It was far from clear how long the new regime in Russia would last. Some outside the country saw it evolving back towards a capitalist more liberal society. Therefore, one reason why Pilnyak, among others, also published outside the USSR in the 1920s was simply to avoid having his works pirated abroad. (The Soviet Union would not sign the copyright convention until 1973.)

The other reason, though, was the restraint of censorship, formally organized in 1922.

This was neatly demonstrated by the publishing history of Zamyatin's anti-utopian novel *We*: written in 1920, its eventual appearance abroad in a Russian version in 1927 was one of the pretexts used for ending this "liberal" period of guidance rather than control. Until then, the Party was busy restoring a devastated economy and preoccupied with its own internecine struggles; and, anyway, it had no clear idea what to do with literature. Lenin's artistic tastes were conservative, and he disapproved of the Proletkult claims to artistic monopoly; Trotsky, politically the most radical and interventionist leader, was culturally speaking more independent and did not support control of the arts; and in the 1920s Stalin posed as a moderate, in alliance with the artistically liberal Bukharin. In 1925 the party even announced that it was "in favour of free competition between the various groupings and currents" in literature.

Nevertheless, the Soviet government had already secured the "commanding heights" in that field as well, by establishing new publishing houses and, especially, new "thick" journals (the traditional Russian vehicle for serious new literature). The monthlies *Krasnaya nov* (1921) and *Novy mir* (1925) were under the control, respectively, of the Old Bolshevik Alexander Voronsky and Vyacheslav Polonsky, both Marxist critics, who were independent but reliable editors. However, even during this most liberal period, there were certain writers, "internal emigres" like Mandelstam and Klyuev who found it difficult to be published at all. Soon the Fellow-Travellers also had to decide how far they would let the Locomotive of Revolution carry them, and then discover what happened if they decided to leave the train earlier.

In 1936, a decade later, 108 newspapers and 162 periodicals were still being published in Russian outside the Soviet Union. By then, however, the institutional and personal ties of the 1920s, between the West and the emigration, on the one hand, and the USSR on the other, had almost all been severed and only a few licensed literary ambassadors, like Ehrenburg could still move back and forth. Voronsky had been chosen and appointed as a chief editor of *Krasnaya nov* in 1921 by Lenin himself; his dismissal in 1927 signalled the wider change.

In 1928, as part of the forced industrialization of the first Five Year Plan, the remaining private businesses (including publishing and printing) were abolished. Henceforward, all enterprises belonged to the state, or retained a diminishing vestige of independence as cooperative property. Ultimately state control over the appointments to such organizations, and the Party's reservation of key literary posts to its nomenklatura, would render censorship an almost superfluous additional restraint. But first independent individuals had to be replaced by those tamed by and trained within the system.

The original "Great Leap Forward" of 1928–33 was in many ways a return to the spirit and methods of the Civil War. It began with its show trial of the "bourgeois" engineers, then of the supposed leaders of banned political parties (real and mythical). "People from the past" like the priest Florensky were arrested and exiled, and sent to work on vast industrial projects like Magnitogorsk or the White Sea Canal. The culmination was the appalling suffering of the Ukrainian and North Caucasian famines of 1932–3. Yet although the "enemy" this time was almost entirely unarmed, the various campaigns of the first Five Year Plan generated genuine enthusiasm in many of the younger generation (coupled to realistic hopes of rapid advancement). The elimination of mass illiteracy, for instance, though partly illusory, promised almost to double the number of readers. The supporters of RAPP, the Russian Association of Proletarian Writers, an organization increasingly difficult to distinguish in its membership from the Party and the Komsomol, dominated the literary scene with evident official encouragement. Led by the indefatigable critic Leopold Averbakh, its members felt sure they were destined to control and meet the needs of the newly literate masses. Therefore, the abrupt

288

and unexpected abolition of all literary groupings in 1932 and the creation of a single Union of Soviet Writers at first seemed to the embattled opponents and victims of RAPP to offer an escape from increasingly vicious attacks.

Two years later there were definite indications that the worst was past. At the Seventeenth Party Congress in January 1934, called to celebrate "victory" in the first Five Year Plan, all the leading former opposition figures within the Party (except for Trotsky) were present once again and delivered penitent speeches. The first congress of the new Writers Union that August likewise brought the various factions and tendencies back together, apparently reconciled under Gorky's chairmanship. The new doctrine of Socialist Realism, it seemed might still leave some latitude of expression and if not, perhaps one could remain tactfully silent until things changed?

It subsequently became clear that neither literary gifts nor proletarian zeal would be sufficient or desired under the new system. Just as the repenting former opposition leaders within the Party were thereafter systematically arrested, exiled or executed, so the writers were tamed or silenced, and replaced by those whose conformity was in no doubt. Many then imprisoned or shot were, like Mikhail Koltsov or Vladimir Kirshon, of indisputable loyalty to the Party and to Stalin. However, in literature, as elsewhere, Stalin did not want allies but unquestioning subordinates. Meanwhile, the Writers Union set about incorporating its members into the new Soviet elite. For the select few – in 1934 it had about 1500 members, as against the 4000-strong membership of RAPP – the Writers Union offered comprehensive provision of flats and dachas, rest-homes, sanatoria and medical care, and special access to goods, travel and publication. Privately these privileges might be mocked by sceptics like Babel, but not refused. Bulgakov satirized the "planning" of the new MASSOLIT with its "small" queue of a hundred or more writers lining up for "full-value creative vacations from two weeks (short story, novella) to one year (novel, trilogy)" in Leningrad "(Winter Palace)" and resorts like Yalta. Bulgakov had, thanks to Stalin, reached accommodation with the new theatrical establishment. Other writers had to fall back on past connections and friendships and were lucky if they could survive by finding work in their field, such as translation, editing or writing for children. The very different fates of several members of the Serapion Brotherhood (Fedin, Ivanov, Kaverin, Tikhonov and Zoshchenko), which had effectively disbanded in 1929, is eloquent illustration of the rifts that followed.

For these who lived to see the German invasion in 1941 (the great majority of the writers who perished under Stalin did so in the late 1930s), a certain wartime relaxation permitted long-silenced voices, such as those of Akhmatova and Pasternak, briefly to be heard again. In the stultifying last years of Stalin's rule, ideological control was reimposed on literature with the expulsion of Akhmatova and Zoshchenko from the Writers Union in 1946, and a final, devastating attack on Platonov as a writer. The last writers to die at Stalin's hand were those linked to the wartime Jewish Anti-Facist Committee, tried and executed in the summer of 1952.

Even before Khrushchev's "Secret Speech" in 1956 denouncing Stalin, surviving political prisoners began to be released from the Gulag, and in the late 1950s almost all the authors here discussed were rehabilitated, or formally declared innocent of the charge of various forms of counter-revolution.

Under Stalin no one had been safe from the threat of imprisonment and execution (not Molotov's wife, not Kaganovich's brother). The new elite wanted the security to enjoy its privileges, and so was in no hurry to acknowledge all the claims of those it had displaced. Stalin was demoted, but not totally rejected, his corpse being removed in 1961 from Lenin's mausoleum and reburied next to it. Such reluctance also applied in literature. The full artistic rehabilitation of Lenin's and Stallin's writer-victims was drawn out over decades and not completed in most cases until perestroika. The treatment meted out to Pasternak in 1958 clarified what had changed and what remained the same.

A year after his great post-war novel was rejected for publication in 1956 by *Novy mir*, the Italian publisher Giangiacomo Feltrinelli issued *Il dottore Zhivago* in translation. In 1958, three days after accepting it, Pasternak was bullied into rejecting the Nobel Prize for Literature. The Soviet authorities, however, made an attempt to placate public opinion inside and outside the USSR, publishing a long letter from the editorial board of *Novy mir* to Pasternak, justifying their act of self-censorship. Such explanations, accompanied by threats, sanctions, privileges and pressures, now replaced the universal terror of the Stalin years. Khrushchev's personal approval in 1962 for the publication of Solzhenitsyn's *One Day in the Life of Ivan Denisovich* was a striking instance of the manipulation of Literature for political purposes. A variety of safety valves evolved to keep the dissatisfaction of writers and the reading public within manageable limits.

State control of publishing and censorship remained in force. The crime of literary dissidence (the unsanctioned writing, distributing and possession of literature) was down-graded from "counter-revolution" to the non-capital offence of "anti-Soviet agitation propaganda". This was the charge against the writers Sinyavsky and Daniel, publicly tried and sentenced in 1966 for publishing their works abroad. At the same time, and in tiny quantities, old and new forbidden works and authors began to appear – whether in the "pre-Gutenburg" form of samizdat, smuggled copies from abroad, or tiny state-published print-runs intended for officials (naturally, including the Writers Union) and a few lucky members of the wider public.

When the Communist authorities decided to release this flood of words in 1986 there were major novels, poetry and plays by twentieth-century Russian writers that either had not been widely available in the USSR or had simply not been published at all for up to 70 years (not to mention certain ideologically unsound "reprehensible" works by, for example, Gogol). The circulation of the "thick" Soviet journals would swell to up to a million copies each before the flow finally subsided.

Today the private archives, preserved abroad and within the country, have become accessible. But the full story of the Soviet regime's manipulation of literature and writers cannot be told until the closed state depositories and archives, where arrest and execution lists, scenarios for future show trials, and other documents may still be preserved, have been opened.

In 1991 there were alarming and well substantiated reports that hundreds of pages of the Akhmatova dossier had been burnt by the KGB during the August putsch. From the very start, however, the secret police photographed many of the documents it held. Later it turned to microfiche. There are strong grounds for believing that copies were frequently made and have been retained elsewhere.

After the memoirist Lev Razgon saw what little remained in his file and in those on four other members of his family, all arrested in the 1930s, he commented wistfully: the truth has been concealed as carefully as Kashchey the Deathless hid his life. Prince Ivan almost failed to defeat the villainous sorcerer of Russian folk tale when the egg containing the needle, in which Kashchey's life finally reposed, threatened to drop into the deep sea.

JOHN CROWFOOT
Moscow, August 1995

290

BIOGRAPHICAL NOTES OF PRINCIPAL FIGURES

Afinogenov, Alexander Nikolaevich (1904–41): Playwright whose early plays (1926–9), were staged at the Proletkult Theatre, where he served as its literary manager and then as its director. A leader of RAPP in the early 1930s, his later plays, including *An Eccentric* (1929), *Fear* (1931), *Mashenka* (1940) and *On the Eve* (1941), concerned the role of the intelligentsia during "socialist construction".

Akhmatova, Anna Andreevna (pseud. Anna Arkadievna Gorenko) (1889–1966): Poet. Akhmatova was acknowledged before the Revolution as a leading member of the Acmeist school to which her husband of 1910–18, Nikolay Gumilyov, also belonged. Refusing to emigrate, she endured an enforced silence from 1923 to 1941 when none of her work was published. It was then that she composed her masterpiece, *Requiem* (1935–40), recording the experiences that swept her third husband, art critic Nikolay Punin, and son, Lev Gumilyov, among tens of thousands of others into the camps. Again banned from publication from 1946 onwards, a gradual rehabilitation of her work (and return of her son from the camps) began after 1956, but the complete versions of *Requiem* and her other major work, *Poem without a Hero* (begun in 1940), could only be published in Russia in the late 1980s. Lydia Chukovskaya's record of her conversation is being published in English in three volumes as *The Akhmatova Journals* (Vol 1 1938–41, Vol 2 1952–62, Vol 3 1963–6).

Andreev, Vadim Leonidovich (1902–76): Poet, essayist and novelist, and son of the writer Leonid Andreev (1871–1919). After the Revolution, he stayed in Finland with his father, then lived in Switzerland and France. He took Soviet citizenship in 1946.

Andreev, Daniil Leonidovich (1906–59): Poet, and son of Leonid Andreev. Author of a mystical work, *The Rose of the Universe*, which he wrote during his 10 years solitary confinement in Vladimir prison.

Arkhangelsky, Alexander Grigorievich (1890–1938): Satirical writer, and a regular contributor to the satirical review *Crocodile*. Author of humorous parodies of poets and writers.

Arosev, Alexander Yakovlevich (1890–1938): Writer, and member of the revolutionary movement from 1905. During the October Revolution he commanded troops in the Moscow region. In 1920, he presided over a revolutionary tribunal in the Ukraine before becoming the USSR's plenipotentiary in Lithuania and then in Czechoslovakia. From 1934, he presided over the Association for Overseas Cultural Relations. He perished during the purges. His prose was devoted to the Revolution and the Civil War.

Astafiev, Viktor Petrovich (1924–): Novelist and short story writer. Born in the Krasnoyarsk region, where he now lives, he volunteered for the front in 1942, sustaining a war wound in Poland two years later. His work classes him amongst the "village prose" school of writers. Author of the novels *The King-Fish* (1972–5) and *The Sad Detective* (1985), the novellas *The Shepherd and the Shepherdess* (1971) and *The Last Bow* (1976–88), and the short story cycle *Blazes* (1985).

Averbakh, Leopold Leopoldovich (1903–37): Literary critic who made his way to a controlling position in Soviet literature through the Komsomol, the proletarian literary movement associated with RAPP (Russian Association of Proletarian Writers) of which he was a leader, and marital ties that connected him to Sverdlov and Yagoda. His supremacy between 1928 and 1932 was overturned by the creation of the Writers Union. Shot 14 August 1937.

Babel, Isaac Emanuilovich (1890–1940): Celebrated short-story writer of Jewish origin, born in Odessa. A meticulous craftsman whose small output includes the exotic *Odessa Tales* (1927) and the vividly brutal short story sequence *Red Cavalry* (1926), drawing on his Civil War experiences. He also adapted his tales for the stage (*Sunset*, 1928; *Maria*, 1935). Always regarded with suspicion by the authorities, although held in high esteem by fellow writers, he largely fell silent in the 1930s. Arrested in May 1939 he was shot on 27 January 1940. Rehabilitated 1954.

Bagritsky, Eduard (pseud. Eduard Georgievich Dzyubin) (1897–1934): A revolutionary romantic, Bagritsky fought with a Bolshevik guerrilla group during the Civil War. In 1925 he moved to Moscow, became associated with the Pereval group and in 1926 produced perhaps the best revolutionary poem of the 1920s, the "Lay of Opanas". This tells of a peasant who fights on the wrong side during the Civil War and dies for it, but the hero is the Bolshevik commander. In 1930 he joined RAPP and hymned the first Five Year Plan in his collections *Victors* and *The Last Night* (both 1932). Died of a respiratory ailment.

Bedny, Demyan "the Poor" (pseud. Yefim Alexandrovich Pridvorov) (1883–1945): The court poet of the new Soviet rulers. Having joined the Bolshevik Party in 1912, he was one of the regime's most effective propagandists, especially during the Civil War. He lived in the Kremlin itself until 1936 when he suffered a period of disgrace for a comic opera libretto mocking the *Warrior Heroes* of Russia's past.

Bely, Andrey (pseud. Boris Nikolaevich Bugaev) (1880–1934): Major Symbolist poet, novelist and critic, and (after the Revolution) writer of important memoirs on literary and intellectual life in the first years of the century. A great figure in Russian intellectual life, he considered art a theurgy and never lost faith in his country's mystical renaissance. His novels, notably *Silver Dove* (1909), *Kotik Lataev* (1922) and his masterpiece *Petersburg* (1913, revised 1922) were a new departure in Russian prose and their experimental manner together with Bely's other experiments with form, were influential in the early Soviet period, especially on Futurist aesthetics and Formalist studies.

Beria, Lavrenty Pavlovich (1899–1953): Head of the Soviet secret police from 1938 to his execution on the orders of Khrushchev and others in December 1953. Originally from Georgia, he began his career in the Cheka there, until Stalin moved him to Moscow, where he later replaced Yezhov.

Blok, Alexander Alexandrovich (1880–1921): Leading poet of Russian Symbolism – also a playwright and essayist – who exerted a massive influence on Russian twentieth-century poetry. His first collection, *Verses on a Beautiful Lady* (1904) was partly inspired by Valdimir Solovyov's vision of Holy Sophia, the World Soul. In later verse Blok bitterly mocked his own romantic delusions, but in his great poem about the Revolution, *The Twelve* (1918), he reverted to his visionary manner. He welcomed the Revolution, and worked for a number of Soviet literary institutions, but in 1919 he was briefly arrested in connection with the "Left SR's conspiracy". He died broken and disillusioned.

Bondarev, Yury Vasilievich (1924–): Author of several novels in the 1950s and 1960s about the war experience of his generation, notably *Hot Snow* (1969). Since perestroika he has been a leading figure in conservative nationalist writers circles.

Bonch-Bruevich, Vladimir Dmitrevich (1873–1955): Politician, historian and writer. Active in the revolutionary movement from the 1880s. Administrative officer of the Council of the

People's Commissars (1917–20), he was later the founder of the State Literary Museum in Moscow, and its first curator (1933–9).

Bukharin, Nikolay Ivanovich (1888–1938): Leading Bolshevik, the "darling of the Party", editor of *Pravda* 1919–29, and member of Politburo from 1924 to 1929. A Left Communist during the Civil War, Bukharin and other members of the Right "Opposition" opposed Stalin over collectivization of agriculture and were defeated in 1929. Allowed back as editor of *Izvestiya* (1934–7) he was arrested in February 1937, tried the next year at the last great show trial ("Trotskyist–Rightist bloc") and shot in March 1938. Rehabilitated 1988.

Bukovsky, Vladimir: Noted dissident who took part in the impromptu poetry readings in late 1950s around the new Mayakovsky statue, became involved in human rights movement, was imprisoned and exchanged in late 1970s for Chilean Communist Leader Luis Corvalan.

Bulgakov, Mikhail Afanasievich (1891–1940): Novelist, short story writer and playwright. Son of a professor at the Kiev Theological Academy, he graduated as a doctor from Kiev University in 1916. Between 1925 and 1926 he published three collections of fantastic and satirical stories including *Diaboliad*, and completed the novella *The Heart of a Dog*, which was to remain unpublished in the Soviet Union until 1987. In the same year serialization of the Civil War novel, *The White Guard*, was stopped following an outcry from Party-line critics, but the work took on a new life under the title *The Days of the Turbins* when it was staged at the Moscow Art Theatre in 1930; however, it remained controversial and was banned for years at a time. By 1930, Bulgakov had become so frustrated by the suppression of his prose and the banning of his plays that he wrote to Stalin and begged to be allowed to emigrate. Stalin telephoned him personally and offered to arrange a job for him at the Moscow Art Theatre instead. There Bulgakov wrote a number of plays concerning the relationship between the artist and the state, including *The Cabal of Hypocrites* (1936, banned after seven performances) and *Pushkin* (1940, rejected). He took his revenge on the theatrical world in the satirical novel *Black Snow* (1936–7). In the last two years of his life he completed his prose masterpiece, *The Master and Margarita* (1928–40). However, it was not published in Russia until 1967 (in a censored edition), and only in full in 1973.

Bulgakov, Sergey Nikolaevich (Father Sergy) (1871–1944): Religious philosopher and theologian, who was originally drawn to socialism but became a priest in 1918. He was expelled from Soviet Russia in 1922. He later became a professor in Paris at the Orthodox Theological Institute.

Bunin, Ivan Alexeevich (1870–1953): Writer of short stories and novellas, whose often lyrical celebrations of the Russian countryside had established his reputation by the turn of the century. His most important works are the novellas *The Village* (1909–10) and *Dry Valley* (1911), his fictionalized autobiography, *The Life of Arseniev* (1952), and from among his many stories "The Antonov Apples" (1900) and "The Gentleman from San Francisco" (1915). He was deeply opposed to the Revolution and left Russia for France in 1920. He was awarded the Nobel Prize for Literature in 1933. His account of Russia in revolution, *Accursed Days*, was finally published there in 1988.

Chernov, Viktor Mikhailovoich (1873–1952): Founder and theoretician of The Russian Socialist Revolutionary party. After the February Revolution, he was minister for Agriculture in the Provisional Government from May to September 1917. Opposed to the Bolshevik coup of October 1917, he was elected President of the Constituent Assembly which was immediately disbanded by the Bolsheviks. He then took up arms against the new state. In 1920, he emigrated to Germany, and later to France and the United States.

Chayanov, Alexander Vasilievich (1888–1937): Agronomist and proponent of cooperatives, Chayanov was also a writer and essayist, author among other tales of *My Brother Alexey's Travels in the Land of Peasant Utopia* (1920). Denounced publicly by Stalin in 1929 he was arrested in 1930 and sentenced in 1932 to five years in the camps as a member of the "Peasant Party". Shot October 1937; rehabilitated 1989.

Chukovsky, Korney Ivanovich (pseud. Nikolay Vasilievich Korneichukov) (1883–1969): Writer, children's poet, scholar and translator. He headed the Anglo-American department of the World Literature publishing house set up by Gorky in 1918. An eminent man of letters, he became one of Russia's best-loved children's authors.

Daniel, Yuly (pseud. Nikolay Arzhak) (1925–1989): Prose writer, poet and translator. His trial in 1966, with Andrey Sinyavsky, for having published his works abroad under a pseudonym (including the story "This Is Moscow Calling"), marked a return to the repression of literature in the USSR after the "Thaw" and was widely reported in the West. Sentenced to five years in the camps.

Dombrovsky, Yury Osipovich (1909–78): Novelist. First arrested, and exiled to Alma-Ata in the Central Asian republic of Kazakhstan in 1932. He was subsequently arrested four more times and in all spent 15 years in prisons and the camps and exile. He wrote and published a number of novels including *Derzhavin* (1939), *The Monkey Comes Back to Collect Its Skull* (1959) and *The Keeper of Antiquities* (1964). Shortly before he died, his masterpiece, *The Faculty of Useless Knowledge* (1978), was published in Russian in Paris; it was first published in Russia in 1989.

Ehrenburg, Ilya Grigoryevich (1891–1967): Journalist, novelist, translator and memoirist of prolific output. His first novellas were modernist and hostile to the Bolshevik regime, but in later decades he became its fervent propagandist. While *Izvestiya*'s Paris correspondent, he celebrated the Five Year Plans and the Republican resistance to Franco in Spain. The defeat of France in 1940 inspired *The Fall of Paris* (1941) and won him a Stalin prize. A member of the Jewish Anti-Fascist Committee, with the writer Vasily Grossman he edited *The Black Book* of crimes committed by the Nazis against Soviet Jews. After Stalin's death, he played an important part in the "liberal" movement, first with his novel *The Thaw* (1954), which involved him in heated polemics with several Soviet writers, and then with his memoirs, *People, Years, Life* (1960–5). Despite censorship cuts, these gave a franker account of the fate of the intelligentsia under Stalin than had hitherto appeared in print.

Eisenstein, Sergey Mikhailovich (1898–1948): Film director, teacher and theorist. After his highly successful pro-Bolshevik films of the 1920s, such as *Strike!* (1925) and *Battleship Potyomkin* (1926), he was unable to complete *Bezhin Meadow* (1935–7), based on the story of Pavlik Morozov. Again in favour with the new patriotism of *Alexander Nevsky* (1938), his ambivalent treatment of *Ivan the Terrible* (1943–6), especially in the suppressed second part of the film, aroused the displeasure of both Stalin and his critics.

Emin, Gevork (pseud. Karen Moradien) (1919–): Armenian poet.

Erdmann, Nikolay Robertovich (1902–70): Playwright. Best known for two satirical comedies of the early Soviet period, *The Mandate* (1925) and *The Suicide* (1928). Meyerhold staged the first, but both were banned in 1932 when the latter was in rehearsal. Only after Stalin's death was *The Mandate* again performed (1956).

Eydemann, Robert Petrovich (1895-1937): Socialist Revolutionary, writer and soldier. He commanded one of the Red Army's divisions during the Civil War.

Fadeev (pseud. Bulyga), *Alexander Alexandrovich* (1901-56): Novelist and administrator. A Communist from 1918, he fought in the Red Army during the Civil War and, as a delegate to the Tenth Party Congress, took part in the suppression of the Kronstadt rebellion and was severely wounded. His books include *The Rout* (1927) and *The Young Guard* (1945), both of which were held up in the Stalin years as models of Socialist Realism – though Stalin made him revise *The Young Guard* (1951). He was a RAPP leader (1926-32), a member of the Central Committee (1939-56) and Secretary General of the Writers Union (1946-53), and then its president until 1954. He shot himself in 1956.

Fedin, Konstantin Alexandrovich (1892-1977): Novelist and short story writer. Member of the Serapion Brotherhood, leading Fellow-Traveller and, later, veteran Soviet novelist. He received the Stalin prize on two occasions for the historical novels *First Joys* (1945) and *An Extraordinary Summer* (1947-8). In 1959 he succeeded Surkov as First Secretary of the Writers Union and held the post until 1971. He was Pasternak's next-door neighbour at Peredelkino, and while initially a supporter became a latterday critic.

Florensky, Pavel Alexandrovich (1882-1937): Theologian and savant. Originally a mathematician, he was appointed a lecturer in philosophy at the Moscow Theological Academy in 1908, and ordained a priest in 1911. *The Pillar and the Foundation of Truth* (1914) was a landmark in the renaissance of Russian religious thinking. After the Revolution he followed his scientific career, anticipating the development of cybernetics. Arrested and released after several months of detention and exile in 1928, he was re-arrested in 1933 and sent to the Gulag. He was shot at Solovki islands camp in December 1937. Although some of his work was published by the Tartu structuralists in the 1960s and '70s, a great part of his work remains unpublished.

Frunze, Mikhail Vasilievich (1885-1925): Military leader. From 1905 he took part in the revolutionary movement. Organizer of Bolshevik forces in Belorussia in 1917, he was appointed Military Commissar for the Moscow region in January 1918. He became Commander in Chief of the armies on the southern front in September 1920 and directed operations against Wrangel's White Army. Deputy Commissar for War in March 1924, then Chief of Staff and Commander of the Military Academy in Moscow (which was later named after him), he was thereafter President of the Military Council and Commissar of Military and Naval affairs. He died in 1925 in mysterious circumstances during a routine medical operation.

Galanskov, Yury Timofeevich (1939-72): Poet. He was expelled after two terms at Moscow University for dissident activity. In 1961 he was involved in *Phoenix* No 1, which contained some of his dissident work, and in 1966 he edited *Phoenix* No 2, which contained Sinyavsky's famous essay "What is Socialist Realism?". He was arrested in 1967 and sentenced to seven years hard labour. He died in a prison hospital.

Gorky, Maxim (pseud. Alexey Maximovich Peshkov) (1868-1936): Novelist, playwright and poet. He first became famous as a short-story writer in the 1890s. He wrote the play *The Lower Depths* in 1902, participated in the 1905 Revolution and joined the Bolsheviks, and then from

1906 to 1913 lived abroad, mainly in Capri. He wrote the pioneering work of Socialist Realism, his novel *The Mother* (1906) during a fund-raising trip for the Bolsheviks to the USA. He strongly supported the 1917 February Revolution, and founded the newspaper *Novaya zhizn*. Unsuccessful in his attempts to protect the intelligentsia, he eventually left Soviet Russia in 1921, but was wooed back permanently in 1933. In his last years he became an apologist for Stalin's regime and aided the imposition of Socialist Realism as the literary orthodoxy. Died at Gorki outside Moscow, 1936.

Guber, Boris Andreevich (1903–37): Writer. His stories were largely devoted to life in the countryside, after the Revolution and at the time of collectivization. A member of Pereval and one of the 56 signatories of that group's manifesto, which advocated "organic realism" as opposed to the "wingless descriptions of everyday life" of official fiction or the "dry rationalism" of the Futurists and Constructivists. Like many of his fellow signatories who did not disown the group in the early 1930s, he died in the purges.

Gumilyov, Nikolay Stepanovich (1886–1921): Poet, translator and co-founder of the Acmeist school (1912–13). After his marriage to Anna Akhmatova and before the First World War he travelled to Abyssinia. He was the author of several collections of poetry including *Pearls* (1910), *The Quiver* (1916), *The Pyre* (1918) and *Pillar of Fire* (1921). His poetry and tales are marked by a virile romanticism and a love of adventure and exoticism; they are also influenced by his travels, his distinguished military service and his monarchist beliefs. After the Revolution he produced translations for Gorky's World Literature publishing house and taught poetry in the House of Arts. Shot in August 1921, after confessing his involvement in a rather confused anti-Bolshevik conspiracy.

Gershteyn, Emma Grigorievna (1903–): Literary historian and critic, specialist on Lermontov, close friend of Anna Akhmatova and author of memoirs on Mandelstam published in Russian in Paris (1986).

Herzen, Alexander Ivanovich (1812–70): Philosopher, literary critic and writer. Exiled from Russia in 1847 for revolutionary activities, he published an anti-Tsarist review in London, *The Polar Star* and a political journal, *The Bell*. His best-known work is his monumental autobiography, *My Past and Thoughts* (1852–68). His work, and his ideas on the individual, society and history, were enormously influential on his contemporaries, particularly Dostoevsky and Tolstoy.

Ilf, Ilya (pseud. Ilya Arnoldovich Fainzelberg) (1897–1937): Satirical writer, born in Odessa. Journalist and author of humorous feuilletons for the periodical press during his youth, he became famous for the satirical novels *The Twelve Chairs* (1928) and *The Golden Calf* (1931) written in collaboration with Yevgeny Petrov. The hero of both these novels, a crafty, cynical chancer named Ostap Bender, was a hugely popular character in Soviet fiction, who gave Ilf and his co-writer the chance to satirize the NEP period and the first Five Year Plan. Ilf died of tuberculosis.

Ivanov, Vsevolod Vyacheslavovich (1895–1963): Russian novelist, short-story writer and playwright. In the 1920s, he was a member of the Serapion Brotherhood. His books include a trilogy of short novels *The Partisans* (1921), *Armoured Train No 14–69* (1922) and *Coloured Winds* (1922), of which *Armoured Train* was successfully staged by Stanislavsky in 1927. His early writings contain stylistically inventive and vivid descriptions of his unusual and often dangerous experiences in Siberia and the Far East. Later, he conformed to Socialist Realism.

Israti, Panait (1884–1935): Rumanian writer, who lived in France until 1930 when he returned to his native land. Rolland supported him, calling him the "Balkan Gorky" until, after his visit to the USSR in 1927, he co-authored with Souvarine and Victor Serge *Vers l'autre flamme* (1929), a denunciation of Stalin's regime.

Kaganovich, Lazar Moisevich (1893–1991): A Bolshevik from 1911, he joined the Central Committee in 1924. First Secretary of the Ukrainian party (1925–8), Party Chief in Moscow (1930–5), he was one of Stalin's closest comrades in arms, and a member of the Politburo (1930–57). In 1957, he was excluded from the Politburo and pensioned off for being part of the group led by Molotov (dubbed the "anti-Party group") which sought to overthrow Khrushchev.

Kalinin, Mikhail Ivanovich (1875–1946): Bolshevik politician. A revolutionary worker activist from 1898, and Bolshevik from 1903. When Sverdlov died, Kalinin succeeded him as the titular Soviet head of state, chairman of the Central Executive Committee (later, Presidium of Supreme Soviet). From the late 1930s until 1946 his Estonian wife was held in the camps.

Kamenev, Lev (pseud. Rosenfeld) *Lev Borisovich* (1883–1937): Close collaborator of Lenin and member of the Politburo (1919–26). First an ally and then later opponent of Stalin, he was one of the principal defendants at the first Moscow show trial ("Trotskyist–Zinovievite Centre") in August 1936. Condemned to death and shot immediately; rehabilitated 1988.

Karpov, Vladimir Vasilievich: First Secretary of the USSR Writers Union under Gorbachev; now retired and living at his dacha outside Moscow.

Kataev, Ivan Ivanovich (1902–39): Writer and essayist. He joined the Red Army in 1919, studied Economics at Moscow University and became a member of the Communist Party. A member of Pereval, he wrote a number of novels about peasant life avoiding the stereotypes of Socialist Realism, but in 1930 his novel *Milk* was criticized for idealizing the kulaks (the wealthy peasant class). Died 2 May 1939, a victim of the purges.

Kataev, Valentin Petrovich (1897–1986): Short-story writer, novelist and dramatist. He began as a humorous writer, before moving into a Socialist Realist phase beginning with *Time Forward!* (1932), a substantial novel on the building of a metallurgical plant in Magnitogorsk. This was followed by others devoted to the the Great Patriotic War and the October Revolution, including *Son of the Regiment* (1945), which won the 1946 Stalin prize. After Khrushchev's thaw, he published a series of innovative autobiographical novels: *The Holy Well* (1966), *The Grass of Oblivion* (1967) and *My Diamond Crown* (1966). He was a personal friend of Mayakovsky and an admirer of Bunin's work.

Kaverin (pseud. Zilber), *Veniamin Alexandrovich* (1902–89): Novelist and short-story writer, who was a member of the Serapion Brotherhood. After publishing a number of experimental, fantastic novellas, collected in *Masters and Journeymen* (1923), he moved towards philosophical discussion in *Artist Unknown* (1931), before adopting a more realistic style and conventional approach. His novel *Two Captains* (1938–44) was for decades one of the most popular books among Soviet youth. In the post-Stalin years he played an important part in trying to obtain greater freedom of expression for writers.

Kazin, Vasily Vasilievich (1898–1981): Minor Soviet poet, who sang the virtues of work and socialist values, particularly in his *White Sea Poem* (1936–62), which celebrates the construction of the White Sea canal and its reformative effect on the "criminals" (Gulag prisoners) who built it.

Khlebnikov, Velimir (pseud. Viktor) *Vladimirovich* (1885–1922): Futurist poet noted for his linguistic experimentation. He contributed to the anthologies *A Trap for Judges* (1910, 1912) and *A Slap in the Face of Public Taste* (1912). A poet's poet, admired by his contemporaries including Mandelstam, most of his works were never published in his life time. He died of malnutrition.

Khodasevich, Vladislav Felitsyanovich (1886–1939): Poet, critic and literary historian, associated with the Symbolists. He published his first poems in 1908 but only won general recognition with the publication of *The Way of the Grain* (1920) and *The Heavy Lyre* (1922). He emigrated in 1922, lived in Paris and became a brilliant literary critic and expert on Pushkin. He was greatly admired by writers as different as Nabokov and Gorky.

Kirov (pseud. Kostrikov), *Sergey Mikhailovich* (1886–1934): The murder of Kirov, then first secretary of the Party organization in Leningrad, in December 1934 heralded the onset of the Great Purge within the Party itself. A Bolshevik since 1904, he was installed in Leningrad in 1926 by Stalin to replace Zinoviev. However, his increasing popularity, reaching a peak at the Seventeenth Party Congress in January 1934, alarmed Stalin who was almost certainly responsible for staging his assassination.

Kirsanov, Simeon Isaakovich (1906–72): Poet, friend and disciple of Mayakovsky, with whom he toured the Soviet Union. Born and educated in Odessa, he moved to Moscow in 1925. His poems from the 1920s are full of stylistic invention, word play and fantastic elements. At the beginning of the 1930s, he switched over to Socialist Realism, publishing the narrative poem *The Five Year Plan* (1932). He was awarded the State Prize in 1951.

Kirshon, Vladimir Mikhailovich (1902–38): Playwright, and one of the directors of RAPP, formed in 1925 and disbanded by Stalin in 1932. His best-known play is *Bread* (1930) about the impact of the first Five Year Plan on the Russian countryside. Condemned on a charge of Trotskyism and shot, 28 July 1938.

Klyuev, Nikolay Alexandrovich (1887–1937): One of the "peasant" poets, close to Yesenin and Klychkov. Born into a family of Old Believers, he celebrated a mystical, rural and patriarchal Russia, and hated the city and western civilization. His folkloric and metaphysical poetry was criticized as reactionary from an ideological and an aesthetic point of view. In 1934, he was exiled to Siberia. Re-arrested in Tomsk in 1936, he was shot in 1937. Republished 1977, but not rehabilitated until 1988.

Klychkov (pseud. Leshenkov), *Sergey Antonovich* (1889–1937): Peasant poet and novelist, close to Yesenin and Klyuev. He rejected Soviet reality and mechanized civilization. Arrested in 1937, he perished in the purges.

Kochkurov, see Vesyoly, Artyom

Koltsov, Mikhail Yefimovich (1898–1940): Writer and journalist. Member of the Party from 1918, editor of *Pravda* from 1922. Special envoy during the Spanish Civil War, he wrote

Spanish Journal, based on his experiences. Although faithful to Stalin, he was a victim of the purges.

Korolenko, Vladimir Galaktionovich (1853–1921): Prose writer and publicist of half-Polish origin, born in Ukraine. Best known for his Siberian tales (he spent between 1879 and 1896 in exile and in prison), his humorous account of a peasant in America, *Without a Language* (1895), and his posthumously published autobiography, *The History of My Contemporary* (1922). Prominently involved in public causes before the Revolution, such as the anti-Semitic Beilis case in 1912–13, his most popular work was the March 1917 pamphlet "Fall of the Tsarist Regime". He regarded Bolshevism as demagogy and wrote a series of eloquent letters (all unanswered) to Rakovsky and Lunacharsky denouncing the excesses of the Civil War period and the Cheka.

Kosarev, Alexander Vasilievich (1903–39): Politician. Secretary General of the Central Committee of the Komsomol from 1928. Arrested and shot during the purges.

Krayushkin, Anatoly Afanasievich (1945–): Colonel in the KGB Archives Department; today lieutenant-general in the Federal Security Service for the Registry and Preservation of Archival Repositories. Publicly dismissed for "incompetence" in September 1995.

Kuibyshev, Valerian Vladimirovich (1888–1935): Bolshevik politician. Member of the Party from 1904, he was in charge of the Supreme Council of the National Economy in the 1920s and later of Gosplan, joining the Politburo in 1927. Died reportedly from a heart attack.

Leonov, Leonid Maximovich (1899–1993): Leading novelist and playwright. After his first two novels, *The Badgers* (1924) and *The Thief* (1927), he was led, like many Fellow-Travellers, from general sympathy to active support of the Soviet regime during the first Five Year Plan. His *Road to the Ocean* (1935) was the first major novel to appear after the official adoption of Socialist Realism. Several plays followed. In 1953, *The Russian Forest,* his long oblique novel on the Stalin period, appeared. President of the All-Russian Union of Soviet Writers in 1929 and a Member of the Academy of Sciences from 1972, he was awarded the Stalin Prize in 1943, the Lenin Prize in 1957, and the State Prize in 1977.

Lunacharsky, Anatoly Vasilievich (1875–1933): First People's Commissar of Enlightenment (ie the arts and education) under the Bolsheviks. He joined the Bolshevik faction in 1903 and wrote criticism and plays. A generally liberal figure, he was removed from his post by Stalin in 1929.

Mandelstam (née Khazina), *Nadezhda Yakovlevna* (1899–1980): Wife of the poet Osip Mandelstam. Born in Saratov, brought up and educated in Kiev, she travelled widely before the Revolution, reading and speaking several languages, including English. Exiled from Moscow between 1934 and 1964, she devoted herself, after her husband was sent to the Gulag in 1938, to preserving his work and to achieving his rehabilitation. Her memoirs, *Hope Against Hope* and *Hope Abandoned,* where she graphically describes the literary world of the period from the 1920s to the 1950s, were, like much of her husband's work, not published in Russia until the 1980s.

Mandelstam, Osip Emilevich (1891–1938): Poet and essayist of Jewish origin, born in Warsaw. A member of Gumilyov's Poets' Guild, his first Acmeist collection of poems, *Stone* (1913), won him immediate recognition. It was followed by *Tristia* (1922) and *Poems* (1928), several remarkable works of prose, including the autobiographical *The Noise of Time* (1925), "The Egyptian Stamp" (1927), and "Fourth Prose" (1928–30), "Journey to Armenia"

(1931–2) and "Conversation about Dante" (1933). On his return from Armenia in October 1930, he completed two unpublished collections of poems known as the "Moscow Notebooks" (1930–4). Arrested in 1934 for reciting a satirical poem about Stalin to a small group of friends, he was exiled to Voronezh where he wrote the poems contained in the three "Voronezh Notebooks" (1935–7). After a brief return to Moscow he was again arrested on 1 May 1938 and sent to the Gulag, where he died in a transit camp near Vladivostok that winter.

Markish, Perets Davidovich (1895–1952): Yiddish-language writer, one of the great figures of the Soviet Jewish intelligentsia. Between 1921 and 1926 he lived variously in Warsaw, Berlin, Paris and London. He returned to the USSR in 1926. Author of poems, plays and a biography of Mikhoels, he was shot in 1952, following the trial of the Jewish Anti-Fascist Committee of which he was a member.

Mayakovsky, Valdimir Vladimirovich (1893–1930): Poet and leading Russian Futurist. Born in Georgia, he became involved with the Bolsheviks as a young teenager in Moscow and then with Futurist artists and writers. His reputation rests largely on his four wartime narrative poems, *The Cloud in Trousers* (1915), *The Backbone Flute* (1915), *War and the World* (1916) and *Man* (1917). After the Revolution he wrote many propaganda pieces, including *Mysteria-Bouffe* (1918), *1,500,0000* (1921) and *Vladimir Ilyich Lenin* (1924), but his growing scepticism was expressed in the satirical plays *The Bedbug* (1928) and *The Bathhouse* (1930) directed by Meyerhold. Concern with the new regime and personal difficulties led to his suicide in 1930. After his death he became the object of a veritable cult organized by the authorities, and Stalin proclaimed that he "was and remains the best and most talented poet of our Soviet epoch", adding that "indifference to his memory is a crime".

Menzhinsky, Vyacheslav Rudolfovich (1874–1934): Politician. Vice-president of OGPU (1923–6), he succeeded Felix Dzerjinsky as head of the secret police, of which he was nominally director until his death. As a result of Menjinsky's poor health, it was in fact Yagoda who really administered the political police.

Meyerhold, Vsevolod Emilevich (1874–1940): Leading theatre director. Trained as an actor by Nemirovich-Danchenko, he served as director of the Imperial opera and drama theatres in Petersburg before the Revolution. He supported the new regime in 1917 and organized popular spectacles on a grand scale. During the 1920s he embodied the revolutionary theatre, affirming his "Constructivism", the pre-eminence of the mise-en-scène over the text (with which he took great liberties), and his conception of bio-mechanical acting. Officially disowned in the late 1920s, his theatre was liquidated by decree in early 1938. Meyerhold was arrested in 1939 after a defiant public refusal to accept the doctrine of Socialist Realism in art; a week later his wife, the actress Zinaida Raikh, was found dead in their flat from stab wounds, her eyes gouged out. Shot February 1940.

Mikhoels, Salomon Mikhailovich (1890–1948): Celebrated Yiddish actor and founder, producer and director of the State Jewish Theatre in Moscow. A leading member of the Jewish Anti-Fascist Committee during the Great Patriotic War, he was assassinated on Stalin's orders on 13 January 1948 during the official anti-Semitic campaign that also closed his theatre. Mikhail Vovsi, his brother, was one of the doctors accused in 1952 of trying to assassinate Soviet leaders by medical malpractice in the famous "Doctors' Plot".

Mikoyan, Anastas Ivanovich (1895–1978): Bolshevik politician, who came to prominence under Stalin, entering the Politburo in 1935. Supported Khrushchev within the Party in the de-Stalinization of the late 1950s. Forced into retirement in 1965.

Molotov (pseud. Scriabin), *Vyacheslav Mikhailovich* (1890–1986): Bolshevik politician and close Stalin supporter. A member of the Politburo from 1926, he replaced Rykov as head of government in 1930 and was appointed Foreign Minister in time to sign the 1939 Nazi-Soviet non-Aggression Treaty with Von Ribbentrop. In 1957 he was involved in the unsuccessful attempt to overthrow Khrushchev (the "anti-Party group").

Narbut, Vladimir Ivanovich (1888–1944): Minor Acmeist poet before the Revolution, who in 1918 joined the Bolsheviks. Working as an editor and publisher, he set up the state-owned Land and Factory publishing house. Expelled from the party in 1928, he was later arrested, dying in unknown circumstances Posthumously rehabilitated.

Nemirovich-Danchenko, Vladimir Ivanovich (1858–1943): Co-founder with Konstantin Stanislavsky, of the Moscow Art Theatre, where he produced Chekhov's major plays and the early works of Gorky.

Okudzhava, Bulat Shavlovich (1924–): Poet and novelist. Son of Communist parents, both shot by Stalin, he volunteered for the front in 1942. He became very popular as a poet in the late 1950s when he began to perform publicly, accompanying himself on the guitar. Author of short stories including "Farewell, Schoolboy" (1961) and of several novels, the most recent of which, *The Abandoned Theatre*, won the 1994 Russian Booker Prize.

Olesha, Yury Karlovich (1899–1960): Short-story writer, novelist and occasional poet, translator, film-script writer and playwright. Born into a Polish Catholic family, who moved to Odessa in 1902, he rejected his background and joined the Red Army in 1919. Author of *Three Fat Men* (1928), the novel *Envy* (1927), which he later adapted for the stage, and the posthumous notebooks, *Not a Day without a Line* (1965).

Ordjonikidze, Grigory Konstantinovich (1886–1937): Bolshevik politician. From Georgia, like Stalin, he was imprisoned and exiled before the October Revolution. Responsible with Kirov for imposing the new Bolshevik regime in the Caucasus, he then moved to the economy, being in charge of the People's Commissariat of Heavy Industry when he died. It was given out that he died of a heart attack, but the circumstances of his death remain mysterious.

Osorgin (pseud. Ilyin), *Mikhail Andreevich* (1878–1942): Journalist and writer. Briefly imprisoned for his part in the 1905 Revolution, he spent the following ten years abroad as correspondent for several Russian periodicals. Elected president of the Moscow Writers Union and of the All-Russian Union of Journalists, he was expelled from Soviet Russia in 1922 and eventually settled in Paris.

Ovcharenko, Yakov Petrovich (see Pribludny, Ivan).

Pasternak, Boris Leonidovich (1890–60): Poet and prose writer. Born in Moscow, he studied music, then philosophy, before devoting himself to literature. His third book, a celebration of the hopeful revolutionary summer of 1917, *My Sister, Life* (1922), brought him wide attention. Initially linked to the experimentalism of Mayakovsky and the Futurists, he turned to inward lyrical poems, while writing distinctive prose and longer verse. In the 1930s he increasingly took refuge in translation and again, after a brief respite during the war, in the 1940s when he produced his celebrated versions of Shakespeare. In 1957, *Doctor Zhivago*, a novel he had been writing since the war was rejected for publication in the USSR but appeared in Italian translation. He was awarded the Nobel Prize for Literature in 1958, but a virulent official campaign of denunciation forced him to renounce the award. Expelled from the Writers Union (but not from his dacha in Peredelkino), Pasternak died on 30 May 1960. *Doctor Zhivago* was finally published in Russia in 1988.

Paustovsky, Konstantin Georgievich (1892–1968): Prose writer. Best known for his six-volume autobiography, *The Story of My Life* (1945–63). As editor of *Literary Moscow* (1956) and *Pages from Tarusa* (1961), he tried to introduce new writers and again publish those who were suppressed under Stalin.

Pavlenko, Pyotr Andreevich (1899–1951): Soviet essayist and novelist. After serving as a political commissar in the Red Army during the Civil War, he was secretary of the Soviet Commercial Mission in Turkey (1924–7). His novellas include *Red Wings over the East* (1937), an imaginary account of the conquest of Japan. As a war correspondent, he covered the Soviet occupation of Western Ukraine in 1939, the war with Finland and, after 1941, that against the invading Germans. In 1938 he co-authored the screenplay for Eisenstein's patriotic film *Alexander Nevsky* (1938), and, after the war, the screenplay for the celebrated propaganda film, *The Fall of Berlin*. He won the State Prize three times.

Pilnyak (pseud. Vogau), *Boris Andreevich* (1894–1937): Soviet novelist. His novel, *The Hungry Year* (1921), was the first significant literary attempt to write about the Revolution and established Pilnyak as the dominant figure in Soviet Literature. Between 1922 and 1932 he travelled widely, especially to the Far East and the USA (where he spent five months in 1931). Publicly attacked in 1929 for publishing abroad, the writer had already incurred official displeasure during the scandal of "The Tale of the Unextinguished Moon" (1927): this transparent hint that Stalin forced the Red Army leader Frunze to have an unnecessary medical operation that then killed him was immediately suppressed in 1926 when it appeared. He continued to write and publish in the 1930s. Arrested and shot 1937.

Platonov (surname changed from Klimentov), *Andrey Platonovich* (1899–1951): Short-story writer and novelist. The son of a railway-worker, he fought in the Red Army during the Civil War, and then became an electrical electrical engineer and land-reclamation specialist, returning to work in his native Voronezh region. From 1918 he published articles, verse and essays, passing from the optimistic vision of *Electrification* (1921), through a science-fiction trilogy to the stories that began to appear, from 1926 on, in Moscow journals like *Krasnaya nov* and *Molodya gvardiya*. After the initial success of the collection, *The Sluices of Epiphany* (1927), subsequent tales, such as "Doubting Makar" (1929), were strongly criticized. His major writings of the early 1930s, the second part of his novel *Chevengur* and *The Foundation Pit* (1930), remained unpublished in Russia until the late 1980s. In the latter work, written in Platonov's inimitable and untranslatable prose, workers realize that they are digging not the foundation pit of the new utopia, but a mass grave. Attacked again in the post-war clamp-down, Platonov died of consumption caught from his son who had returned from the camps.

Pravdukhin, Valerian Pavlovich (1892–1939): Essayist and novelist; husband of Lidiya Seifullina. Perished in the purges.

Pribludny, Dmitry (pseud. Yakov Petrovich Ovcharenko) (1905–37): Poet. A street child who was a Red Army volunteer in the Civil War. He came to Moscow in 1921, where he was close to Yesenin. Shot 1937.

Prishvin, Mikhail Mikhailovich (1873–1954): Prose writer who described the nature and animals of the Russian North. Independent of all literary groupings in the 1920s, he retained his individual voice throughout the Stalin period.

Radek (pseud. Sobelsohn) *Karl Bernardovich* (1885–1939): Bolshevik politician and journalist. He took part in the 1905 and October Revolutions and was then a member of the Central Committee and of the Comintern's executive committee (1920–4). Expelled from the party as a Trotskyist in 1927, he rapidly came to terms with Stalin. In 1937 he was sentenced to ten years imprisonment at the second Moscow show trial ("Anti-Soviet–Trotskyist Bloc"). Died in prison.

Rakovsky, Christian (1873–1941): Communist politician of Bulgarian origin. Headed Soviet government of the Ukraine (1918–23), was a founder of the Comintern, then Ambassador to London and Paris (1923–7). Expelled from the Party as a Trotskyist in 1927, he was exiled and did not reconcile with Stalin until 1934. Re-admitted to the party in 1935, he was again expelled shortly afterwards. Condemned to 25 years at the third Moscow show trial ("Trotskyist–Rightist Bloc") in 1938, and shot, with Dr Pletnyov, Olga Okudzhava and 154 others at Oryol Prison, October 1941.

Remizov, Alexey Mikhailovich (1877–1957): Short-story writer, novelist and memoirist. Imprisoned and exiled for eight years (1896–1904) before the Revolution, he emigrated in 1921, settling first in Berlin, then in Paris. His numerous publications range from the novel *The Pond* (1908) to the autobiographical *A Flute for Mice* (1953). Virtually unknown in the USSR until the 1973 collection of his works.

Rykov, Alexey Ivanovich (1881–1938): Bolshevik politician. A member of the Politburo from 1922, he succeeded Lenin's as head of government (1924) but was removed from that post in 1930 after the moderate "Right opposition" that he led with Tomsky and Bukharin was defeated. He was a leading defendant at the last Moscow show trial ("Trotskyist–Rightist Bloc") in 1938, and was shot immediately thereafter. Rehabilitated in 1988.

Seifullina, Lidiya Nikolaevna (1889–1954): Writer and playwright. A school teacher by profession, she enjoyed great success in the 1920s with her stories and especially with her play *Virineya* (1924). Thereafter she was more active as a journalist and educator.

Shklovsky, Viktor Borisovich (1893–1984): Literary scholar, essayist and novelist. A student of philology at Petrograd University, he founded the Society for the Study of Poetic Language (OPOYAZ) in 1916 which developed later into the Formalist movement. In his *Theory of Prose* (1925) he affirmed the autonomy of poetic language and advocated the structural analysis of texts. Linked to the Serapion Brotherhood and the Futurist poets of LEF, he publicly dissociated himself from the Formalist movement in 1930 with an article in *Literaturnaya gazeta*, but after Stalin's death returned to his views of the 1930s.

Sholokov, Mikhail Alexandrovich (1905–84): Soviet novelist. His experiences as a teenager in the Don Military District formed the subject of the many short stories he wrote in the 1920s, and his greatest work, *The Quiet Don* (1928–40). Two further novels, *Virgin Soil Upturned* (1932–60) and *They Fought for Their Country* (1949–69), were of markedly inferior quality and displayed this immensely popular author's increasingly orthodox views. When Sholokov, by then the grand old man of Soviet literature (and Party member since 1932), was awarded the 1965 Nobel Prize for Literature, this fuelled as yet unproved claims that he was not the author of *The Quiet Don*.

Shostakovich, Dmitry Dmitrievich (1906–75): Pre-eminent and prolific Soviet composer. He was influenced in his youth by Bartok, Hindemith, Milhaud and the dodecaphonists. In 1934 Stalin walked out of the premier of his opera *Lady Macbeth of Mtsensk*, which was then attacked in a *Pravda* article entitled "Nonsense instead of Music". He and other leading composers were again condemned in a Party decree in 1948 for "Formalism". Zhdanov is said to have picked out tunes on the piano to illustrate the kind of music the Party required them to compose. He was awarded the Lenin Prize in 1957.

Sinyavsky, Andrey Donatovich (1925–): Literary scholar and prose writer. A well-established scholar by the time of his arrest for publishing abroad under the pseudonym of Abram Terts. These fictional works included *The Trial Begins* (1960) – which appeared at about the same time as his seminal essay "What Is Socialist Realism?" (1959) – and *The Makepeace Experiment* (1963). Sentenced in 1965 with his co-defendant Yuly Daniel to seven years in the camps, he was released in 1971 and allowed to emigrate to France in 1973. Established in Paris, he compiled and published his prison journal, *A Voice from the Chorus*, and the controversial *Strolls with Pushkin* (both 1973) among other works.

Sobolev, Leonid Sergeevich (1898–1971): Novelist. His main interest was in the navy and in seafaring men. He served in the Soviet Navy (1918–31) and was naval correspondent for *Pravda* during the Great Patriotic War. From 1934 onward he was in control of the Russian Federation branch of the new Union of Soviet Writers.

Sokolnikov, Grigory Yakovlevich (1888–1939): Bolshevik politician. He directed the nationalization of the banking system after the Revolution and was People's Commissar for Finance (1922–6). As an Oppositionist he was sent as ambassador to London (1929–34). Condemned to 10 years imprisonment at the second Moscow show trial ("Trotskyist–Anti-Soviet Bloc") in 1937. Died in prison.

Solovyov, Vladimir Sergeevich (1853–1900): Russian religious thinker and poet. He profoundly influenced both the Orthodox revival of thinkers like Florensky, Father Sergy (Bulgakov) and Berdyaev, and the Symbolists (Merezhkovsky, Blok and Vyacheslav Ivanov). A mystic and a liberal in politics, he distanced himself from the Slavophiles by placing his religious hopes not in Orthodox Russia but in a merging of the major churches.

Souvarine, Boris (1895–1984): Politician and French publicist of Russian origin. A member of the executive committee of the Comintern (1919–24), and of the French Communist Party's central committee, he was expelled from both for his Oppositionist views. Thereafter a critical commentator on Soviet and Communist affairs, and author of *Stalin: A Historical View of Bolshevism* (1935).

Stanislavsky, Konstantin Sergeevich (1863–1938): Actor and theatre producer. Founded the Moscow Art Theatre in 1898, with Vladimir Nemirovich-Danchenko, where he established his "Method" described in *An Actor Prepares* (1936). Two of his gifted disciples, Meyerhold and Vakhtangov, subsequently set up as actor-directors in their own right. By the late 1930s the Moscow Art Theatre represented accepted orthodoxy on the Soviet stage and, as such, both it and its chief director were satirized by Bulgakov in his "theatre novel", *Black Snow*.

Stavsky (pseud. Kirpichnikov), *Vladimir Petrovich* (1900–43): Writer and journalist. As a party official in the Kuban, he took part in forced grain requisitions during the Civil War. As secretary of RAPP, he was one of the organizers of the first Soviet Writers Congress (1934) and in 1936, after Gorky's death, was appointed Secretary General of the Writers Union, taking an active part in the purging of other writers. Editor of *Novy mir* (1937–41), he became a war correspondent and was killed at the front.

Stenich (pseud. Smetanich), *Valentin Osipovich* (1889–1938): Party functionary, literary critic and translator. He headed the Central Committee's department of Agitation and Propaganda from 1930 until he himself fell a victim of the purges.

Struve, Pyotr Berngardovich (1870–1944): Philosopher and politician. Like Sergey Bulgakov and Berdyaev, a youthful Marxist, he evolved towards liberalism and in 1905 became a leader of the new Constitutional Democratic Party, the Kadets. After the Bolsheviks seized power, he was a member of Wrangel's White government. Emigrated to France, 1920.

Suleimeinov, Olias Omarovich (1936–): Kazakh poet, who writes in Russian, but draws on the Kazakh oral tradition and poetical writings.

Sverdlov, Yakov Mikhailovich (1885–1919): Bolshevik politician. Exiled with Stalin to Turukhansk, near the Arctic circle, in 1913, he returned to Petrograd after the February 1917 Revolution. First Soviet head of state. Died of typhus during the Civil War.

Svyatopolk-Mirsky, Prince Dmitry Petrovich (1890–1939): Literary historian and critic. Educated at St Petersburg University, he served in the White Army during the Civil War, after which he emigrated with his family to London, where he taught Russian Literature at the School of Slavonic Studies (1922–32). During this period he published his *History of Russian Literature in English* and a study of Pushkin (both 1926). He was an enthusiast of the Eurasian theory, according to which, Russia, situated simultaneously in Asia and Europe, was destined to forge a new civilization and to play a special role in the world. In 1931 he joined the British Communist Party and, in 1932, with the support of Gorky, he returned to the USSR. In 1935, he was arrested following the furore surrounding an article criticizing Fadeev. Arrested again in 1937, he died in the camps.

Tarle, Yevgeny Viktorovich (1875–1955): Historian, member of the Academy of Sciences from 1927, specialist in French history and Franco-Russian relations, and author of essays on the French Revolution and the Napoleonic era.

Tikhonov, Nikolay Simeonovich (1896–1979): Poet, writer and literary bureaucrat. He served in the Red Army during the Civil War. In the 1920s he was noted for the romantic flavour and themes of his ballads. He was influenced by Gumilyov and Khlebnikov, but later adapted to the demands of Socialist Realism. Like Pasternak, a translator of poetry from the Georgian, he served as a secretary of the Writers Union (1944–6), and from 1950 he was Chairman of the Soviet Peace Committee.

Tolstoy, Alexey Nikolaevich (1883–1945): Novelist. Son of a provincial noble. Already popular before the Revolution for his novels and plays about the Volga gentry, he served in the White Army during the Civil War, and emigrated to Paris in 1918. In 1923, on his return to Russia as "a repentant expatriate", he had already begun his trilogy of the Revolution, *The Road to Calvary* (1921–40) and after a brief flirtation with science fiction themes he turned towards large-scale historical works, of which the most famous was *Peter the First* (1929, 1934, 1944). Immensely popular, the circulation of his books rivalling Sholokov's, the "Red Count", as he was nicknamed by other writers, represented the reconciliation of the old Russia with the new and thus found favour with the Soviet regime. A deputy of the Supreme Soviet, member of the Academy of Sciences (1939), entrusted with diplomatic missions to Europe, he lived like a grandee, and after Gorky's death became Russia's grand old man of letters.

Tsvetaeva, Marina Ivanovna (1892–1941): Russian poet and prose writer. She published her first acclaimed collection at 16. She married Sergey Efron in 1912 and published her first mature book of poems, *Mileposts*, in 1916. In 1917 Efron joined the White Army and Tsvetaeva did not see him again until she joined him in emigration five years later. She wrote many of her greatest works in Paris including the poems in *After Russia* (1929), engaged in an intense three-way correspondence with Rilke and Pasternak (1926), and published poems, essays and articles regularly in emigre publications. In 1937, her daughter Ariadna returned to the USSR. In the same year, her husband was implicated as a Soviet secret agent and forced to flee France for Moscow. Tsvetaeva followed him there in 1939 with her teenage son, Mur. Shortly after her return her husband and daughter were arrested. When war broke out Tsvetaeva was evacuated to the town of Yelabuga on the river Kama; there, in August 1941, she hanged herself. Efron was finally shot in 1941, Mur was last heard of in 1944 and Ariadna was released in 1955.

Tukhachevsky, Mikhail Nikolaevich (1893–1937): Soviet military leader. A career officer in the Imperial Army during the First World War, he rallied to the Revolution and was given the command of the First Red Army. In 1920 he suppressed the Tambov peasant uprising and in 1921 the Kronstadt sailors' rebellion. Commander in Chief of the army from 1928, then Deputy Commissar for Defence (1931) and Marshal (1935), he was the Red Army's principal strategist. In 1937, he and many other military leaders were secretly tried and shot.

Tynyanov, Yury Nikolaevich (1896–1943): Writer, critic, literary theoretician and historian of nineteenth-century Russian literature. He taught at the Institute of Art History in Leningrad (1921–30), where he was one of the leading figures of Russian Formalism. He developed his theoretical ideas in *Problems of Poetic Language* (1924) and applied them in *Archaists and Innovators* (1929) in discussions of Pushkin, Tyutchev and others (including Lenin). He also wrote two biographical novels about Russian writers in the time of Nicholas I, and began a third, never completed, about Pushkin. His popular story "Second Lieutenant Khizhe" (1930) was filmed in 1934. As an editor in the Sovetsky pisatel publishing house (1931–43) he created and directed the Poet's Library, which to this day publishes the standard editions of Russian poets.

Utyosov, Leonid Osipovich (1892–1968): Highly popular actor and jazz singer of the 1930s, especially remembered for the film musical *The Merry Ones* (1938).

Vesyoly, Artyom (pseud. Nikolay Kochkurov) (1899–1939): Writer and playwright. A working-class Bolshevik before the Revolution, he served in the Red Army throughout the Civil War. These experiences formed the subject of his plays and his main novel, *Russia Drenched in Blood*. Arrested 1937 and shot.

Volkov, Oleg Vasilievich (1900–): Writer, translator and memoirist. He was a prisoner of the Gulag for 30 years.

Voronsky, Alexander Konstantinovich (1884–1937): Marxist essayist, literary critic and theorist. Member of the Bolshevik party from 1904, with Lenin's blessing he was appointed editor in chief (1921–7) of the first "thick" Soviet review, *Krasnaya nov*, around which he assembled a number of important writers, including many Fellow-Travellers. Between 1925 and 1928 he was part of the Trotskyist Left Opposition and declared himself against the ideological hegemony of the proletariat in literature and the arts; as a supporter of Fellow-Travellers he was sharply criticized by other Marxist literary groups. He was also involved in publishing and acted as mentor to the Pereval group of writers. In 1927, the year he was dismissed from *Krasnaya nov*, he published his memoirs of clandestine revolutionary work, *In Search of the Water of Life and the Water of Death*. Shot 1937.

Voroshilov, Kliment Yefremovich (1881–1969): Bolshevik and close Stalin supporter. People's Commissar for Defence (1934–40), he supervised the purges in the Red Army. Also the Politburo member in charge of the arts. Took part in the unsuccessful (the "Anti-Party Group") attempt to overthrow Khrushchev in 1957.

Vyshinsky, Andrey Yanuarevich (1883–1954): Jurist and Bolshevik politician. He became Stalin's chief prosecutor despite being a Menshevik until 1920. In 1933 he was appointed Deputy Public Prosecutor and then in 1935 Procurator General of the USSR. As such he laid the theoretical foundations for the judicial procedures used in the purges and was the chief state prosecutor during the Moscow show trials. In 1940 he moved to the Ministry of Foreign Affairs, replacing Molotov as its head in 1949. Died in New York while representing the Soviet Union at the UN.

Wrangel, Baron Pyotr Nikolaevich (1878–1928): Russian general whose evacuation from the Crimea in 1920, as the last commander of the White forces in southern Russia, marked the end of the Civil War.

Yagoda, Genrikh Grigorievich (1891–1930): Head of the NKVD. Deputy to Derzhinsky and then Menzhinsky at the OGPU, he was in charge of the security service from 1930. In 1934, when it was integrated into the People's Commissariat for Internal Affairs, or NKVD, he was appointed Commissar, and thus directed the early phase of the Great Purge. Dismissed by Stalin in 1936 for his failure to "unmask the Trotskyist–Zinovievite Bloc", he was replaced by Yezhov. A year later he was arrested and in 1938 shot after the last Moscow show trial ("Trotskyist–Rightist Bloc").

Yakir, Iona Immanuelevich (1896–1937): General. Civil War hero of the Red Army who was in charge of the Kiev Military District (1921–30) and then a member of the USSR Military Council. Arrested and executed, with Tukhachevsky and others, in 1937 as part of Stalin's purge of the army leadership.

Yenukidze, Avel Sofronovich (1877–1937): Georgian Bolshevik and close comrade in arms of Stalin, with whom he fell out in 1935. Shot 1937.

Yevlogy, Metropolitan (1868–1946): Before the 1917 Revolution, Archbishop of Volyn and Zhitomir. In 1922 in emigration he was elevated to the dignity of Metropolitan and appointed administrator of the Russian Orthodox Church in western Europe. Lived in Paris.

Yesenin, Sergey Alexandrovich (1895–1925): Popular "peasant" poet. A protege of Klyuev, he at first accepted the Revolution but then became progressively disillusioned and turned to drink. Briefly married to Isadora Duncan, with whom he travelled to Western Europe and America, his last wife was the grand-daughter of Lev Tolstoy. His suicide in 1925 was further reason for the Communist authorities to discourage promotion of his work.

Yevtushenko, Yevgeny Alexandrovich (1933–): Poet. He trained to be a writer at the Gorky Institute (1951–4) in Moscow. A star performer with Voznesensky, Okudzhava and Akhmadulina at the football stadium poetry readings of the late 1950s, he challenged the legacy of Stalinism in the poems "Babi Yar" (1961) and "Stalin's Heirs" (1962). He was appointed to the presidium of the Writers Union in 1967. In 1993 he published a novel about the failed August 1991 coup, *Don't Die Before Your Death*.

Yezhov, Nikolay Ivanovich (1895-40): Head of the NKVD at the height of the Great Purge. Stalin moved him to state security from the key personnel department of the Central Committee. This period, September 1937-December 1938, is known in Russia as the "Yezhovschina". In 1940 his job done, he was arrested and shot; replaced by Beria.

Zabolotsky, Nikolay Alexeevich (1903-58): Poet. Author of philosophical poems, influenced by Khlebnikov's pantheism, he was at one time a member of the Leningrad-based avantgarde absurdist group, the Oberiuty. His major works, in addition to tales for children, are *Columns* (1929), which provoked howls of rage from Party-line critics (especially "A Celebration of Agriculture") and *Second Book of Verse* (1937), but this too was severely criticized. He was arrested in 1938 and remained in the camps until 1946. After his return, he worked mainly on a series of unsurpassed translations of the Georgian classics. Forbidden to live in Moscow or Leningrad, he settled in Tarusa, where he died of a heart attack.

Zamyatin, Yevgeny Ivanovich (1884-1937): Short-story writer, novelist, critic and dramatist. He became a Bolshevik while a student in Petersburg and was exiled briefly in 1905 before graduating as a naval engineer in 1908. During the First World War he supervised the construction of ice-breakers in England, and added satires on bourgeois conformity ("The Islanders", 1918) to his other literary works. His earliest writings were in the classical Russian satirical tradition of Gogol. As a former Bolshevik he welcomed the Revolution, but from the beginning spoke out against its excesses. In the post-revolutionary period, he was a leading figure in the revival of literature, editing journals, working for publishing houses, teaching, and acting as mentor to the Serapion Brotherhood. His writing of this period, in stories like "Mamaï" (1921) and "The Cave" (1922) is modernist, experimental, and superbly crafted. In 1924 he published his dystopic masterpiece *We* (a work that would influence Aldous Huxley and George Orwell) in an English translation in New York. By 1929, when an unauthorized Russian edition of the novel appeared in an emigre magazine, the mounting campaign against him culminated in a concerted attack for publishing ideologically unsound works abroad. He lost his various posts and his works were banned in the USSR. In 1931, with Gorky's aid and Stalin's authorization, he succeeded in emigrating. He settled in Paris where he died of a heart attack.

Zarudin, Nikolay Nikolaevich (1899-1937): Poet, short-story writer and novelist. From 1924 to 1932, he was president of the literary group, Pereval. He died in the purges.

Zaslavsky, David Iosifovich (1880-1965): Journalist noted for his vituperative feuilletons, generally published in *Pravda*. He was originally a Menshevik and was violently attacked by Lenin in 1917 for his articles in the Menshevik press. In 1919 he "recanted" and declared his allegiance, to the Bolsheviks. In 1929 he wrote a scurrilous attack on Osip Mandelstam, provoking a strong reply by a group of leading writers, including Pasternak.

Zhdanov, Andrey Alexandrovich (1896-1948): Close Stalin associate and a Politburo member from 1939. He implemented the tough ideological line of the postwar years, both in promoting Communist militancy abroad (the founding of the Cominform, 1947) and in a savage campaign intended to terrorize the intelligentsia at home – this found expression in the series of Party decrees (known as the "Zhdanov decrees") condemning alleged deviations in literature, the cinema, philosophy and music. In each case scapegoats were chosen and made examples of (Akhmatova and Zoshchenko in literature, Eisenstein in the cinema, Shostakovich in Music, etc). This period, 1944-53, is known as the "Zhdanovschina", as the earlier terror was known as the "Yezhovschina".

Zinoviev (pseud. Radomylsky), *Grigory Yevseevich* (1883–1936): Bolshevik politician, close to Lenin. Politburo member until 1927, he was also master of Petrograd and president of the Comintern's executive committee until then. At first Stalin's ally in the 1920s, then his adversary, he was arrested in 1935 and sentenced to ten years imprisonment before being condemned to death at a Moscow show trial ("Trotskyist–Zinovievite Bloc") and shot, 1936. Rehabilitated 1988.

Zoshchenko, Mikhail Mikhailovich (1895–1958): Satirical writer and member of the Serapion Brotherhood. Volunteered as a student to fight in the Imperial army, was wounded and invalided out. Admired for his mordant and witty satires of Soviet life, in the 1920s he was the most popular living writer after Gorky. Following the first Soviet Writers Congress of 1934, Zoshchenko came under increasing pressure to conform to the dictates of Socialist Realism. In 1946, after the temporary relaxation of censorship during the Second World War, he was condemned by Zhdanov for his "vulgar parody" of Soviet life and, together with Akhmatova, expelled from the Writers Union. Although gradually rehabilitated after Stalin's death, to the end of his life he scraped a living from translating.

Index

312

Peshkov, Zinovy, 242, 252, 256
Peshkova, Maria Andreeva, 252
Peshkova, Nadezhda A. (Timosha), 241,
253, 254, 260, 262, 263, 266–7, 268,
271, 272, 276, 278
Peshkova, Yekaterina, 74, 107, 227, 234,
239, 242, 272, 276, 278
Pestyukhin, Anatoly, 161
Peter and Paul Fortress, Petersburg, 124
Peterhof Palace Museum, 206
Petersburg University, 127
Peter the Great, 229
Petrov, P., 41, 162
Petrov (Kataev), Yevgeny, 190
Petrovnik, Maria, 180
Pilnyak (Pilnyak-Vogau), Boris, vii, 12, 13,
24, 28, 29, 31, 211, 256, 257; arrest,
145–6; "Che-Che-O", 150; confessions,
forced, 147–8, 149–52, 153–4, 155; death
date, falsification of, 157; *Doubles, The*,
147; execution, 157; and Fellow-
Travellers, 140; and foreign writers,
151–2, 155; harassment, 139–41, 142,
143; interrogation, 147, 149–55; and
Istrati, Panait, 152–3; as a Japanese agent,
146–7, 155; *Mahogany*, 140, 141, 144,
150; 1930s circle, 151; rehabilitation,
144, 157; Revolution, views on, 140; and
Serge (Kibalchich), Victor, 152–3; *Tale of
the Unextinguished Moon*, 140, 144, 149,
157; trial, 156; and Trotskyists, 143,
144–5, 146, 150; and Union of Writers,
148, 150–51; and Vesoly (Kochkurov, N.
I.), Artyom, 154; Yezhov, letter to, 146–7
Pirogovskaya Street, 84
Pirozhkov, 18
Pirozhkova, Antonina Nikolaevna (Isaac
Babel's wife), 22–3, 63, 70–1
Platonov, Andrey Platonovich, 150, 151,
208, 209, 219n, 241, 257; *Birth of a
Master, The*, 211; *Chevengur*, 212; "Dusty
Wind", 212; "Electrification", 213; *The
Sluices of Epiphany*, 211; *For Future Use*,
211, 212; *Foundation Pit*, The, 212; *14
Red Cabins*, 211, 213; *Juvenile Sea, The*,
211, 212, 213; Lubyanka file, 209–10;
"Motherland of Electricity, The", 213;
Shivarov's report on, 210–11; *Technical
Novel, The*, 211, 213–16, 217–18
Platonov, Platon Andreevich, 219
Pletnyov, Professor, 262, 271, 272, 273,
274–5
Pochuev, Nikolay Alexandrovich, 224

Pogrebinsky, Matvey, 254, 255
Pokrovsky, N. A., 164
Polikarpov, K., 123
Politburo, 5n, 9, 15, 60, 73, 149n, 255, 260,
270
Political Red Cross, 74, 107
Polonsky, 149
Polyansky, 107
Poskrebyshev, 183
Postnikov, 63, 66
POUM (Spanish Trotskyist Party), 145
Pravda, 68, 143, 212, 236, 261, 262, 267,
269
Pravdukhin, Valerian Pavlovich, 31
Pribludny, Ivan (Ovcharenko,Yakov), 12, 13
Priestley, J.B., 39
Primakov, 46
Prishvin, Mikhail, 36, 142
Procurator General's Office, 9, 12–15, 17,
20, 63, 66–7, 71, 168, 194
Procurator's Office. *See* Procurator General's
Office
Provisional Government, 233n
Prut, Iosif, 183–4, 186
Pulatov, Timur, 10, 283
Pushkino (formerly Tsarkoe Selo), 206
Pushkin Street, 14
Pustynsky, 220
Putna, 46
Pyatakov, G., 32, 41

Rabochaya gazeta (Workers Newspaper),
102–3
Radek, Karl Bernardovich, 29, 37, 41, 58,
143, 144–5, 149–50
Radzivilovsky, 112, 115
Raginsky, 55
Rakitsky, Ivan ("Nightingale"), 242, 272
Rakovsky, Christian, 37, 57–8, 264–5
RAPP (Russian Association of Proletarian
Writers), 256, 257
Raytman, Yuly, 36
Rayzman, David Abramovich (NKVD
officer), 49, 146, 147, 155, 156
Red Army, 163
Red Cossack corps, 46
Red Cross, World War I medal, 104, 105
REF (Revolutionary Front of Art), 141
Registration and Archive Section, Security
Ministry, 99
Regional Party Committee, 162
Remizov, Alexey Mikhailovich, 36
Repin, Ilya, 258n

Revolutionary Tribunal, 236
Right–Trotskyists, 204, 262, 270
Rodos, Boris (NKVD investigator), 27, 60, 63, 71
Rogozhin (OGPU officer), 113
Rolland, Romain, 203, 203n
Rostov House, Moscow, 282–3
Rozengolts, 57
rue Villa-Chauvelet, 36
Rul, 246
Rusakov, 153
Russell, Bertrand, 39
Russia Insurance Company (Lubyanka building), 18
Russian Association of Proletarian Writers (RAPP), 256, 257
Russian Revolution, 32–3, 58, 60, 102–3, 106, 139, 140, 144, 147–8, 152, 177, 200, 213
Russian State Library (formerly Lenin library), 84
Ryabtsovsky (or Ryabovsky), 161
Rykov, Alexey Ivanovich, 57, 73, 149, 150, 236, 256, 270

Sadok,"Ivan Zykov", 161
Sakharov, Andrey , 107, 202
Salvemini, 39
Samatikha rest home, 185
Sandomirsky, German, 160
Sarov monastery, 202
Sats, Ilya, 211
Savyolovo, 184–5, 190
"Sayanov" (agent), 251, 276–7
Scherbinovskaya, Olga, 144
Schmidt, Pyotr, 46, 55, 104
Schwartzmann, Lev, 24, 26, 27, 49, 60, 71
Scientific Research Institute laboratory, Solovki, 119
Scythians, 147
Sebastopol, 104
Second Congress of the Communist International, 229
Secret Political Department, 4th Section, 170, 211
Security Administration, 2nd department, 49
Security Ministry, Registration and Archive Section, 99
Sedov, Lev, 44
Sedykh, Konstantin, 160-61, 162
Seifullina, Lidiya Nikolaevna, 28, 29, 31, 67, 71, 176

Selvinsky, Ilya, 131–2
Serafimovich, Alexander, 244
Serapion Brotherhood, 147–8. *See also* "Literary–Political Context".
Serebryakov, L.P., 32
Serge, Victor (Kibalchich), 145, 152–3, 190, 191; *Memoirs of a Revolutionary*, 152
Sergienko, 63
Sergiev Possad, 102, 106
Sergiev State Museum, 103
Serikov (NKVD officer), 46, 47, 48, 49, 50, 51, 60; evidence, manipulation of, 50
Shaposhnikova, Maria, 23
Sharangovich, 57
Shcherbakov, 39, 40
Sheinin, Lev Romanovich, 265, 265n
Shelukhanov, 189
Shentalinsky, Vitaly Alexandrovich, vii, x, 5–21, 125, 135, 282; *Green Religion, The*, 5; at Kolyma, 126, 135; in the Lubyanka archives, 95–6
Sheshken, V., 241
Shilkin, 189–91
Shilovskaya, Yelena. *See* Bulgakova, Yelena Sergeevna
Shivarov, Nikolay Khristoforovich (Khristofor'ych), 170–74, 176, 178–81, 194, 198, 199, 241, 246; Platonov, Andrey, report on, 210–11, 212
Shkapa, 267
Shklovsky, Viktor Borisovich, 41, 53, 190, 269n
Sholokov, Mikail Alexandrovich, 36, 258
Shostakovich, Dmitry Dmitrievich 36, 41, 48, 269
Shumilin, 226–7
Shupeiko, 109, 110–11, 112, 113, 114, 115
Shyshkanov, 189
Sinani, Boris, 176–7
Sinyavsky, Andrey Donatovich, 2
Skovorodino, 117
Skvortsov-Stepanov, 149
Slavatinsky, M., 234, 238, 240–41
Slavkin, 72
Smolyakov, G., 163
Sobolev, Leonid Sergeevich, 36, 53
Socialist Realism, viii–ix, 15, 33, 35n, 151n, 226, 258
Socialist Revolutionaries, 177, 188, 191, 227, 233–4, 235–8, 242n
Sokolnikov, Grigory Yakovlevich, 58
Solntseva, 36
Solovki, viii, 18, 106, 116, 117–19, 121, 261

USSR Children's Film Studios (State Publishing House), 23
USSR in Construction (*SSSR v stroike*), 42, 44, 56, 67, 69
USSR Writers Union. *See* Writers Union
Ustinov, Valentin, 5
Utyosov, Leonid Osipovich, 34, 44, 56

Vaillant-Couturier, 37, 68
Vakhtangov Theatre, 36, 52, 92
Valuisky, Alexander, 17, 20
VAPP (All-Russian Association of Proletarian Writers), 160
Vasiliev, Georgy, *Chapaev* (film), 51
Vasiliev, Pavel, 198, 200, 203
Vechernaya Moskva, 248
Veprintsev, 145, 168
Verchenko, Yury, 9, 10–11
Vesyoly, Artyom (Kochkurov, N.I.), 12, 13, 153, 154, 157
Viktorov, 163
Vigilyansky, 277
Vinogradov, A. I., 262, 263–4
Vinogradov, Vladimir, 210
Virta, Nikolay, *Earth*, 52
Vladivostok, 196
Vladsky, I., 163
Volya naroda, 177
Volkov, Oleg, 10
Vorkuta, 122
Vorobyov, 233–4
Voronezh, 183, 184–5, 189, 194
Voronsky, Alexander Konstantinovich, 12, 13, 28–30, 31, 32, 35, 67, 68, 143, 148, 149, 150–51, 153
Voronsky group, 28, 31, 33. *See also* Pereval
Voroshilov, Klim Yefremovich, 48–9, 69, 257, 258, 273
Vorovsky Street (Ministry of Literature), 9, 11, 15
Vyshinsky, 156, 265–6

War Communism, 147, 148
We are from Kronstadt (film), 51
White Guards, 115, 141, 177, 235, 242
Woolf, Virginia, 39
"Word to the Nation", 279–80
Workers and Peasants Inspectorate, 93, 211
World Association of Revolutionary Writers, 269
World Literature publishing house, 228, 229, 230, 235
Wrangel, Baron, 76

Wreckers' Trial, 114
Writers Club, 7, 165, 221, 279; Moscow branch, 5
Writers Congress (1934), 39, 48, 151, 184, 203, 259
Writers Union, 5–6, 32, 34, 45, 69, 141, 143, 148, 150, 153, 155, 158, 198, 256, 277; All-Union commission for literary heritage, 8–18, 133–4, 166, 282, 283; Commonwealth of Writers Unions, 282–3; Congress of Soviet Writers (1934), 39, 48, 151, 184, 203, 259; Eastern Siberia, 162; formation of, 151; as informer, 144, 211–12; Irkutsk Region, 161; and Mandelstam, 185, 186–8, 189, 190, 192; Moscow branch, letter from Okunev, 136; Party Committee, 7, 8; Russian Federation branch, 10, 279, 283

Yagoda, Genrikh Grigorievich, 26, 84, 89, 91, 104, 160, 169, 198, 200, 241, 268–9, 270–71, 273, 277–8; in Averbakh's testimony, 255; demotion to People's Commissar for Communications, 276; and Gorky, 252–3, 254–6, 259–61; interrogation, 255; and Peshkov, Maxim, murder of, 262–4, 265–6; poisons laboratory, 265–6; and Timosha (Nadezhda Peshkova), 254, 266–7
Yagoda, Ida, 252, 253
Yakhontov (actor), 190
Yakir, Iona Immanuelevich, 68
Yakovlev, Alexander Nikolaevich, 9, 11, 12–13, 15
Yazov, Dmitry, 279
Yeltsin, Boris, 281; "Appeal to the Nation", 280
Yenukidze, Avel Sofronovich, 175
Yesenin, Sergey Alexandrovich, 28, 48, 139, 147n, 208; on Klyuev, 198, 200n
Yevdokimov, E.G., 32,
"Yevgeniev" (informer), 120
Yevlakh, Azerbaijan, 104
Yevlogy, Metropolitan, 244
Yevtushenko, Yevgeny Alexandrovich, 282–3
Yezhov, Nikolay Ivanovich (Iron Commissar), 42–3, 44, 49, 58–60, 69, 70, 146, 154, 155, 185–6, 188, 256, 281
Yezhova, Yevgenia Solomonovna (Gladun; Gladun-Khayutina; Gladun-Yezhova; Khayutina-Yezhova), 42, 43–4, 48–9, 55, 56, 58–9, 62, 69, 70

Yonekawa, Professor, 146–7
Young Pioneers, 103, 158
Yurevich (NKVD officer), 188
Yutkevich, Sergey, *Man with a Rifle*, 234

Zablovsky (OGPU officer), 168
Zabolotsky, Nikolay Alexeevich, 36
Zakrevskaya, Maria. *See* Budberg, Maria I.
Zaks, 229–30, 233
Zamyatin, Yevgeny Ivanovich, 139, 142,
   256; emigration, 140; harassment, 140;
   Serapion Brotherhood, mentor of, 148;
   We, 140
Zarudin, Nikolay Nikolaevich, 145; and
   Trotskyists, 148, 151
Zaryanov, 156
Zaslavsky, David Iosifovich, 267

Zavgorodny, 32
Zhdan, 156
Zhdanov, Andrey Alexandrovich, 45
Zhigulin, Anatoly, 10, 11, 12, 136, 165
Zhilin, 104
Zhukov, 7–8
Zhurbenko, 145, 147, 277
Zinoviev, Grigory Yevseevich, 41, 58, 230
Znanie, 244n
Zoological Museum, 180
Zorin, S.S., 29
"Zorin" (informer), 277
Zoschenko, Mikhail Mikhailovich, 139, 190
Zubakin, B. M., 251
Zvenigorod, 32
Zuika (Red Cossack cavalry officer), 46